Recipe Annual

2 0 0 4 E D I T I O N

JAMES CARRIER; FOOD STYLING: KAREN SHINTO

Tamale Tarts (page 117)

By the Editors of Sunset Magazine
and Sunset Books

Sunset Publishing Corporation ■ **Menlo Park, California**

SUNSET BOOKS

VP, General Manager
Richard A. Smeby

VP, Editorial Director
Bob Doyle

Production Director
Lory Day

Director of Operations
Rosann Sutherland

Retail Sales Development Manager
Linda Barker

Executive Editor
Bridget Biscotti Bradley

Art Director
Vasken Guiragossian

STAFF FOR THIS BOOK
Senior Editor
Sally W. Smith

Managing Editor
Zipporah W. Collins

Associate Editor
Marilyn Mansfield

Page Production
Linda Bouchard,
Joan Olson

Indexer
Irene Elmer

Prepress Coordinator
Eligio Hernandez

SUNSET PUBLISHING CORPORATION

Senior Vice President
Kevin Lynch

VP, Administration and Manufacturing
Lorinda Reichert

VP, Marketing Director
Beth Whiteley

VP, Consumer Marketing Director
Christina Olsen

VP, General Manager
Mark Okean

VP, Editor-in-Chief, Sunset Magazine
Katie Tamony

Executive Editor
Carol Hoffman

Creative Director
Paul Donald

Managing Editor
Alan J. Phinney

Art Director
James H. McCann

Style Editor
Yvonne Stender

Senior Editor, Food & Entertaining
Sara Schneider

Associate Art Directors
Dennis W. Leong
Keith Whitney

JAMES CARRIER; FOOD STYLING: KAREN SHINTO

Egg and Vegetable Wrap (see page 16)

Now in its 17th edition, this *Recipe Annual* collects the recipes and food articles from the past year's issues of *Sunset Magazine*.

As in previous years, our writers have combed the West for wonderful recipes, drawing on the wealth of Pacific Rim cultures that enrich Western cuisine. We explore Chinese won ton in February, throw a Russian appetizer party in April, grill with Japanese flair in July, and tour Indian markets and recipes in October.

Straight-up American food also comes into the spotlight: hearty new soups suitable for a party in January, dark chocolate confections in February, Alaskan wild salmon in March, fresh hot doughnuts in May, hamburgers with bacon in July, and bake-fried chicken in September. November, of course, brings Thanksgiving menus—this time scaled for guest lists ranging from 14 to 2, to suit everyone's needs.

Our year's treasury of great food awaits you. Enjoy!

Cover: Chocoate-banana cream tartlets (page 34). Cover design: Vasken Guiragossian. Photographer: James Carrier. Food styling: Karen Shinto.

Back cover photographer: James Carrier (3).

First printing November 2003
Copyright © 2003 Sunset Publishing Corporation, Menlo Park, CA 94025. First edition. All rights reserved, including the right of reproduction in whole or in part in any form.

ISBN 0-376-02715-0 (hardcover)
ISBN 0-376-02716-9(softcover)
ISSN 0896-2170
Printed in the United States

Material in this book originally appeared in the 2003 issues of *Sunset Magazine*. All of the recipes were developed and tested in the *Sunset* test kitchens. If you have comments or suggestions, please let us hear from you. Write us at Sunset Books, Cookbook Editorial, 80 Willow Road, Menlo Park, CA 94025.

Contents

A Letter from Sunset

DEAR READER,

This year had a spirit of regrouping about it. Many businesses began to recover from lean times. And many families who struggled through economic setbacks or suffered blows from the violent turn in current events took time to rearrange their lives around core values. They stopped to consider what's most important to them, what they want to spend their time doing. There's an echo of Ma Joad, at the end of John Steinbeck's classic *Grapes of Wrath,* in the air: "People is goin' on—changin' a little, maybe, but goin' right on."

Sunset has been "goin' on" for more than 105 years now. As I look back over all the food stories we wrote in 2003, in compiling them for this annual collection, I realize that we did a little regrouping too. You told us that you're cooking more than ever now, both for your families and for groups of friends. It seems that people need to come together over food, especially homemade. That puts the joy back into living—makes the "goin' on" fun.

The subjects we offered in these times are telling: they're a happy story about what foods bring comfort to, and inspire, cooks in the West. Classics like slow-braised beef stew with mushrooms (page 19), spaghetti with meatballs and porcini sauce (page 178), and soufflés (page 66) figured prominently. We revisited desserts in the classic mode this year. Our chocolate story in February (page 32) involved all-time favorite fudgy brownies, chocolate-banana cream tartlets, and a very decadent molten chocolate-caramel torte; and our celebration of layer cakes in June (page 126) brought you a traditional buttercream frosting—no pulling back on the butter—plus a load of variations on popular flavors.

But classics are only part of the story. Many of you have told us you find comfort in

The food-writing team, left to right: Sara Schneider (senior editor, food and entertaining), Kate Washington (associate food editor), Charity Ferreira (food writer), and Linda Lau Anusasananan (recipe editor).

THOMAS J. STORY

The food-support team, left to right: Dennis W. Leong (associate art director), Laura Berner (recipe retester), Sara Luce Jamison (style coordinator), Bernadette Hart (test kitchen manager, editorial services), Sarah Epstein (recipe retester), Leslie Smith (recipe retester), Bunnie Russell (recipe retester), Keith Whitney (associate art director), and Dorothy Decker (recipe retester). Retesters not pictured: Angela Brassinga, Marlene Kawahata, and Linda Tebben.

lightening up, in finding a healthy balance in your diet, so in January we brought you a collection of dishes and tips from spa chefs around the West, each of whom has a distinctive approach to creating flavorful, low-fat dishes (page 12).

The traditional foods you want are based on a huge variety of cuisines, because you readers are from a myriad of places. That gave us leave this year to develop a Chinese won ton–making party (page 26), where guests pitch in to wrap turkey-shrimp won ton for soup and dumplings for potstickers. In April, we threw a Russian appetizer party (page 70), involving a combination of homemade dishes—salmon turnovers, beet salad, wild mushroom "caviar"—and staples purchased from one of the many Russian delis in cities on the West Coast. (Don't forget the infused vodkas; you can make them or buy them.) Even our special barbecue section in July rambled around the globe, with beef brisket from Chile (page 146) and robata-yaki from Japan (page 150), always bringing the techniques back home to fit them into your busy lives.

I think of our recipes as food you can—and want to—live with. From simple summer pastas (page 160) to the best holiday turkey (page 216) or standing rib roast (page 246) you've ever made, *Sunset* cooking fits into the limited time most of us have in our lives and offers a realistic nutritional balance—not a roller coaster of deprivations and splurges.

So, in a sense, we've gotten back to basics this year too. But "basic" cooking in the West is fresh and varied—nothing short of exciting. It has been a pleasure to cook with you.

Sara Schneider

Sara Schneider
Senior Editor, Food and Entertaining

TO USE OUR NUTRITIONAL INFORMATION

The most current data from the USDA is used for our recipes: calorie count; fat calories; grams of protein, total and saturated fat, carbohydrates, and fiber; and milligrams of sodium and cholesterol.

This analysis is usually given for a single serving, based on the largest number of servings listed. Or it's for a specific amount, such as per tablespoon (for sauces); or by unit, as per cookie.

Optional ingredients are not included, nor are those for which no specific amount is stated (salt added to taste, for example). If an ingredient is listed with an alternative, calculations are based on the first choice listed. Likewise, if a range is given for the amount of an ingredient (such as ½ to 1 cup milk), values are figured on the first, lower amount.

Recipes using broth are calculated on the sodium content of salt-free broth, homemade or canned. If you use canned salted chicken broth, the sodium content will be higher.

Smoked salmon chowder is one of a quartet of zesty soups that can feed a casual crowd (see page 8).

January

Spicy sausage gives
this hearty, brothy soup
an Italian flavor.

A souped-up party

Offer a quartet of soups for casual winter entertaining

By Linda Lau Anusasananan • Photographs by James Carrier • Food styling by Susan Devaty

Soup spells comfort—in my dictionary, anyway—and that's exactly what many people yearn for after the overindulgent holiday season. A mug or bowl of steaming broth can soothe frayed nerves and recharge party conversation to get the new year off to a happy start. Best of all, a selection of soups is a simple way to entertain casually. Our flavorful soups range from thin to thick, and all make enough to feed a crowd—they can even be made in advance. Make one soup for 8 to 12 guests, or serve all four for a big group. Have partygoers ladle soup into mugs or small bowls, and offer condiments so they can tailor each soup to their liking. Provide a selection of breads, an easy stand-up salad—vegetable crudités with a dip—and cookies, and the meal is complete. Whether you're ringing in the new year, watching the Super Bowl, or just beating the January chill, it's a perfect way to gather with friends.

Italian Sausage and Pasta Soup

PREP AND COOK TIME: About 35 minutes

NOTES: You can prepare soup through step 2 up to 1 day ahead, but do not bring mixture to a boil; instead, cool, cover, and chill. To reheat, lift off and discard fat; bring soup to a boil.

MAKES: About 5½ quarts; 10 to 12 servings

- 2 pounds **hot** or mild **Italian sausages**
- 3 **carrots** (12 oz. total), peeled and chopped
- 1 **onion** (12 oz.), peeled and chopped
- 4 cloves **garlic,** peeled and chopped
- 3 quarts fat-skimmed **chicken broth**
- 2 cans (14½ oz. each) **diced tomatoes**
- 2 cans (15 oz. each) **cannellini** (white) **beans,** rinsed and drained
- 1 tablespoon **dried basil**
- 2 cups **dried large shell-shaped pasta**
- 4 quarts **spinach** leaves (about 12 oz.), rinsed

  Salt and **pepper**

  About 1 cup **grated parmesan cheese**

1. Squeeze sausages from casings into an 8- to 10-quart pan over high heat and stir often, breaking them apart with a spoon, until browned and crumbly, 8 to 10 minutes. Spoon out and discard all but 1 tablespoon fat from pan.

2. Add carrots, onion, and garlic; stir often until onion is limp, 5 to 7 minutes. Add broth, tomatoes (including juice), beans, and basil and bring to a boil.

3. Add pasta, reduce heat, and simmer, covered, stirring occasionally, until pasta is just tender to bite, about 10 minutes. Skim and discard fat. Stir in spinach and cook just until it is wilted, about 30 seconds. Add salt and pepper to taste. Serve soup from the pan, or pour into a tureen. Offer parmesan cheese to add to taste.

Per serving: 397 cal., 41% (162 cal.) from fat; 29 g protein; 18 g fat (6.6 g sat.); 29 g carbo (5.6 g fiber); 947 mg sodium; 49 mg chol.

Soup buffet

Italian Sausage and Pasta Soup

Lemon Grass Chicken Soup

Mexican Beef and Hominy Soup

Leek and Fennel Chowder with Smoked Salmon

Stand-up Salad with Blue Cheese Dressing

Herb focaccia sticks, crusty breads, breadsticks, and/or rolls

Butter or extra-virgin olive oil

Pinot Gris, Sauvignon Blanc, Zinfandel, or Chianti

Cookies of your choice

Lemon Grass Chicken Soup

PREP AND COOK TIME: About 40 minutes

NOTES: You can prepare through step 4 up to 1 day ahead; cool, cover, and chill. Return to a simmer, then continue.

MAKES: 5 to 6 quarts; 10 to 12 servings

- 3 quarts fat-skimmed **chicken broth**
- 2 stalks **fresh lemon grass** (each 12 to 18 in. long), or 6 thin strips lemon peel (each ½ in. by 3 in.; yellow part only)
- 12 thin (quarter-size) slices **fresh ginger**
- 6 or 7 **fresh jalapeño chilies** (3 to 3½ oz. total)
- 1¼ pounds **cabbage**
- 8 ounces **mushrooms**
- 2 **carrots** (8 oz. total)
- 2 pounds **boned, skinned chicken breast halves**
- 4 cloves **garlic,** peeled and chopped
- 1 can (14½ oz.) **diced tomatoes**

  About ½ cup **lemon juice**

  About 2 tablespoons **Asian fish sauce** (*nam pla* or *nuoc mam*) or soy sauce

- ⅓ cup thinly sliced **green onions**
- 5 cups **hot cooked rice**
- 2 **lemons** (5 oz. each), cut into wedges
- 1½ cups chopped **fresh cilantro**

1. In an 8- to 10-quart pan, bring broth to a boil over high heat. Meanwhile,

The aromas of lemon grass, ginger, and chilies infuse this Thai-inspired chicken soup.

1 teaspoon **ground cumin**

3 quarts fat-skimmed **beef broth**

1 can (14½ oz.) **diced tomatoes**

2 pounds **banana squash**

2 stalks **celery** (4 oz. total)

1 can (4 oz.) **diced green chilies**

2 cans (15 oz. each) **golden** or white **hominy**, drained and rinsed, or 4 cups frozen corn kernels

Salt and **pepper**

About 1 cup **sour cream**

About 1 cup chopped **fresh cilantro**

1. In a covered 8- to 10-quart pan over high heat, bring beef, onion, garlic, and ½ cup water to a boil. Reduce heat to medium and simmer for 15 minutes, stirring occasionally. Uncover and cook over high heat, stirring often, until juices have evaporated and meat is browned, 10 to 20 minutes.

2. Add chili powder (use larger amount for spicier flavor) and cumin; stir until fragrant, about 30 seconds, then add broth and tomatoes, including juice. Cover and bring to a boil, then reduce heat and simmer until meat is almost tender to bite, about 1 hour.

3. Meanwhile, slice peel off squash and cut flesh into ¾-inch cubes. Rinse celery and slice diagonally ¼ inch thick.

4. Add squash, celery, and green chilies; cover and return to a boil over high heat. Reduce heat and simmer, covered, until squash and beef are tender when pierced, about 15 minutes longer. Stir in hominy and return to a boil. Skim and discard fat. Add salt and pepper to taste.

5. Serve soup from pan, or pour into a

pull off and discard coarse outer layers from lemon grass and trim off and discard stem ends; rinse lemon grass. Cut each stalk into about 3-inch lengths. With the flat side of a knife, lightly crush lemon grass and ginger. Rinse chilies and cut one or two in half lengthwise (use two if you'd like it spicy); stem remaining chilies (seed, if desired, for less heat), finely chop, and reserve. Add lemon grass, ginger, and halved chilies to boiling broth. Reduce heat and simmer, covered, for 20 to 30 minutes.

2. Meanwhile, rinse cabbage and cut into shreds about ¼ inch wide and 2 to 3 inches long. Rinse mushrooms, trim off and discard stem ends and discolored parts, and slice lengthwise ¼ inch thick. Peel carrots and slice ¼ inch thick. Rinse chicken and cut into ¼-inch-thick slices 1½ to 2 inches long.

3. With a slotted spoon, remove and discard lemon grass, ginger, and chilies from broth.

4. Add cabbage, mushrooms, carrots, and garlic to broth; cover and bring to a boil over high heat. Reduce heat and simmer until carrots are tender when pierced, 8 to 10 minutes.

5. Add chicken and tomatoes (includ-

ing juice). Cover and cook over high heat until chicken is no longer pink in the center (cut to test), 2 to 4 minutes. Add lemon juice and fish sauce to taste. Serve soup from the pan, or pour into a tureen. Sprinkle with green onions.

6. Place rice, lemon wedges, cilantro, and chopped chilies in separate bowls and offer with soup to add to taste.

Per serving: 254 cal., 6% (16 cal.) from fat; 30 g protein; 1.8 g fat (0.4 g sat.); 30 g carbo (3.8 g fiber); 300 mg sodium; 44 mg chol.

Mexican Beef and Hominy Soup

PREP AND COOK TIME: About 1¾ hours

NOTES: You can prepare soup through step 4 (except do not return soup to boil after adding hominy and do not skim fat) up to 1 day ahead; cool, cover, and chill. To finish, lift off and discard solid fat. Reheat to serve.

MAKES: 5 to 6 quarts; 10 to 12 servings

2 pounds **fat-trimmed boned beef chuck** or stew meat, rinsed and cut into ¾-inch chunks

1 **onion** (8 oz.), peeled and chopped

2 cloves **garlic**, peeled and minced

1 or 2 tablespoons **chili powder**

Earthy beef and hominy soup has a Mexican flair.

A creamy, comforting bowl of chowder gets a fresh twist from fennel and smoked salmon.

tureen. Put sour cream and cilantro in bowls and offer to add to taste.

Per serving: 246 cal., 37% (90 cal.) from fat; 22 g protein; 10 g fat (4.7 g sat.); 15 g carbo (3 g fiber); 396 mg sodium; 58 mg chol.

Leek and Fennel Chowder with Smoked Salmon

PREP AND COOK TIME: About 45 minutes

NOTES: Use either soft, cold-smoked salmon (also called lox or Nova-style) or firmer, hot-smoked salmon (also called kippered), or offer both for an interesting mix. If preparing chowder through step 7 up to 1 day ahead, cool, cover, and chill; chill salmon, chives, and fennel sprigs separately. Reheat chowder, covered, over medium to medium-high heat, stirring often.

MAKES: About 4¾ quarts; 8 to 10 servings

- 3 pounds **leeks**
- 2 heads **fennel** (each 3 in. at widest dimension; 2½ to 3 lb. total)
- ¾ cup thinly sliced **chives**
- 2 tablespoons **butter**
- 5 cups fat-skimmed **chicken broth**
- 1 **dried bay leaf**
- 3 pounds **thin-skinned potatoes**
- 1 pound **thin-sliced smoked salmon** (see notes)
- 5 cups **milk**
- ½ cup **all-purpose flour**
  About ½ teaspoon **salt**
  About ⅛ teaspoon **pepper**

1. Trim and discard root ends and coarse tops from leeks. Cut leeks in half lengthwise and rinse under running water, flipping layers to flush out grit; drain, then thinly slice crosswise.

2. Rinse fennel. Trim off and discard root ends and stalks; reserve 2 or 3 sprigs of feathery green tops for garnish, and finely chop enough of the remaining feathery leaves to make 3 tablespoons (discard any remaining greens). In a bowl, mix chopped greens with chives; cover and chill. Chop fennel heads.

3. In a 6- to 8-quart pan over medium heat, melt butter. Add leeks and chopped fennel heads, cover, and stir occasionally until vegetables are very limp, 10 to 12 minutes.

4. Add broth and bay leaf to pan. Bring to a boil over high heat. Scrub potatoes and cut into ½- to ¾-inch cubes.

5. Add potatoes to broth mixture and return to a simmer; reduce heat, cover, and simmer, stirring occasionally, until potatoes are tender when pierced, 15 to 20 minutes.

Stand-up Salad with Blue Cheese Dressing

PREP TIME: About 10 minutes, plus 30 minutes to chill lettuce

NOTES: If making dressing up to 1 week ahead, cover and chill. (You can substitute 1½ cups purchased dressing if desired.) To crisp romaine, trim root ends off lettuce, separate leaves, rinse, and drain well. Wrap in towels, slip into a plastic bag, and chill at least 30 minutes or up to 3 days. Up to 4 hours ahead, arrange vegetables in a bowl; cover with a damp towel, invert a plastic bag over vegetables, and chill.

MAKES: 8 to 10 servings

- 1 cup **reduced-fat sour cream**
- 1 cup **crumbled blue cheese** (about 4 oz.)
- 2 teaspoons **lemon juice**
- 1 teaspoon **Worcestershire**
- 1 clove **garlic,** peeled and pressed or minced
- ⅛ teaspoon **coarse-ground pepper**
- 1 pound **romaine hearts,** rinsed and crisped (see notes)
- 4 ounces **radishes** or cherry tomatoes, rinsed

1. In a small bowl, mix sour cream, blue cheese, lemon juice, Worcestershire, garlic, and pepper.

2. Stand romaine leaves, tips facing up, snugly in a bowl that is one-half to three-fourths the height of the romaine spears. Trim and discard most of the leaves from radishes, leaving one or two small ones attached. Scatter radishes or cherry tomatoes around lettuce.

3. Serve vegetables and dressing together, so guests can dip lettuce leaves and radishes or cherry tomatoes.

Per serving: 112 cal., 66% (74 cal.) from fat; 6 g protein; 8.2 g fat (4.7 g sat.); 4.4 g carbo (1.2 g fiber); 228 mg sodium; 21 mg chol.

6. Cut salmon into strips 2 to 3 inches long and ½ inch wide; put in a bowl.

7. In a separate bowl, whisk milk, flour, ½ teaspoon salt, and ⅛ teaspoon pepper until smooth. Add to potato-broth mixture and stir over high heat until boiling, about 5 minutes. Add more salt and pepper to taste.

8. Serve soup from pan, or pour into a tureen. Garnish with reserved fennel sprigs. Offer with smoked salmon and chive mixture to add to taste.

Per serving: 357 cal., 28% (99 cal.) from fat; 27 g protein; 11 g fat (5.5 g sat.); 40 g carbo (8.6 g fiber); 1,499 mg sodium; 42 mg chol. ◆

Cook smart, eat well

Spa chefs' secrets for light, tantalizing meals

By Linda Lau Anusasananan • Photographs by James Carrier • Food styling by Karen Shinto

Halibut Steamed
with Ginger,
Orange, and Lime

Postholiday diet resolutions number about the same as the adult population. Of course, what constitutes a healthy diet is a matter of debate. What *isn't* debatable is that if the food doesn't taste good, the diet won't stick. "For healthy food to be embraced, not just tolerated, it must have vibrant flavors and textures that are pleasing and familiar—as well as maintain a low-fat nutritional profile," says executive chef Jim Gallivan of Red Mountain Spa in Utah. We went to Gallivan and other talented spa chefs to find out what techniques they use to create terrific-tasting light dishes.

In the first place, we found that while fat is still getting a lot of attention, it's not always as the enemy. Health experts vary on how much they recommend; the generally advised limit is 20 to 30 percent of your day's total calories. Many of the chefs we talked to achieve that through balance—some dishes over that range, some under. But most agree that fat is necessary, even good—especially the omega-3 fatty acids present in salmon and other cold-water fish and the monounsaturated fats found in olive oil and avocados.

Questions of food science aside, most spa chefs share one philosophy: variety, balance, and moderation are the keys to eating well. Their cooking is based on healthy, fiber-dense foods, such as whole grains, and antioxidant-rich vegetables and fruits. To that they add moderate portions of heart-healthy proteins like those in fish, nuts, and legumes.

To make your resolutions a pleasure this year, we collected specific cooking tips and delicious dishes that incorporate them.

Grilled Portabellas with Couscous

> "Remember there are no bad foods, just bad portion sizes and frequency of consumption."
> —*Cary Neff, Miraval*

Halibut Steamed with Ginger, Orange, and Lime

 LIGHT COOKING TIP **Cook fish in citrus-flavored steam, then concentrate the liquid for a sauce; the** citrus juice in the base, as well as zest added at the end, excites the palate and brings out other flavors. Also combine fresh and dry versions of an ingredient—fresh and ground ginger, for instance—to intensify the flavor.

PREP AND COOK TIME: About 30 minutes

NOTES: This lively steamed fish comes from chef Gallivan at Red Mountain Spa in Ivins, Utah.

MAKES: 4 servings

3 cups **orange juice**

⅓ cup **lime juice**

1 tablespoon **ground ginger**

4 pieces (4 oz. each) **boned, skinned halibut fillet**

1 tablespoon **cornstarch**

2 teaspoons minced **fresh ginger**

Salt

Cayenne

Asian chili oil (optional)

Thin shreds **lime** peel (green part only)

1. In the bottom of an 11- to 12-inch-wide steamer or in a deep 5- to 6-quart pan, combine orange juice, lime juice, and ground ginger. Set a nonstick or oiled rack at least 1 inch above surface of juice (elevate, if necessary, on the rim of a cheesecake pan or three clean, empty 2- to 3-in.-tall cans with both ends removed). Cover pan and bring juice to a boil over high heat.

2. Rinse fish. Set pieces slightly apart on rack over boiling juice; cover pan and reduce heat to medium. Steam until fish is barely opaque but still moist-looking in center of thickest part (cut to test), 8 to 10 minutes. Lift out rack. With a wide spatula, lift fish from rack and set on a warm plate; cover to keep warm. Increase heat to high and boil pan juices, uncovered, until reduced to about 1½ cups, 10 to 12 minutes.

3. In a small bowl, mix cornstarch with 3 tablespoons water. Add mixture, along with fresh ginger, to reduced pan juices; stir until boiling. Add salt and cayenne to taste.

4. Divide sauce evenly among four dinner plates. Lay a piece of fish in sauce on each plate. Garnish each portion with a few drops of chili oil and shreds of lime peel.

Per serving: 226 cal., 11% (25 cal.) from fat; 25 g protein; 2.8 g fat (0.4 g sat.); 24 g carbo (0.4 g fiber); 67 mg sodium; 36 mg chol.

Grilled Portabellas with Couscous

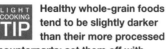 **LIGHT COOKING TIP** Healthy whole-grain foods tend to be slightly darker than their more processed counterparts; set them off with vivid color to increase appeal.

PREP AND COOK TIME: About 30 minutes

NOTES: Executive chef Michel Stroot at the Golden Door in Escondido, California, fills grilled portabella mushrooms with whole-wheat couscous and rings them with bright red and yellow bell pepper sauces (you can use just one color if you like). He tops them with grilled asparagus; green onions work well in the winter.

MAKES: 4 servings

> "Eat smaller, more frequent meals."
> —Dr. Neil Treister,
> Salus Heart and Wellness

- 4 **portabella mushroom caps** (4 to 5 in. wide, 4 to 6 oz. each)
- 8 **green onions**
- 2 tablespoons **olive oil**
- 2 teaspoons **lemon juice**
- 4 teaspoons **balsamic vinegar**
- ¼ teaspoon fresh-ground **pepper**
- ¾ cup **vegetable stock** (recipe on page 18, or used canned broth)
- ½ cup **whole-wheat couscous**
- 2 tablespoons minced **parsley** or fresh basil leaves
  About 1 cup **pepper coulis** (recipe on page 18)
  Salt

1. Trim off and discard any stems from mushroom caps; gently rinse caps and drain well. Rinse green onions; trim off and discard ends. In a small bowl, mix olive oil and lemon juice.

2. Brush smooth sides of mushroom caps and the green onions with oil mixture. Lay mushrooms, smooth side down, and green onions on a grill over hot coals or high heat on a gas grill (you can hold your hand at grill level only 2 to 3 seconds); close lid if using a gas barbecue. Turn onions as needed until lightly browned on all sides, 2 to 3 minutes total. With tongs, transfer to a plate. Cook mushrooms without turning until they are limp and begin to release their juices, 3 to 5 minutes. With a wide spatula, transfer, smooth side down, to a 9- by 13-inch baking pan.

3. Drizzle mushrooms evenly with vinegar and sprinkle with pepper. Add ¼ cup vegetable stock to pan. Cover and bake in a 300° regular or convection oven until hot, 5 to 10 minutes.

4. Meanwhile, in a 1- to 2-quart pan over high heat, bring remaining ½ cup stock to a boil. Stir in couscous. Cover and remove from heat. Let stand until liquid is absorbed, about 5 minutes. Fluff couscous with a fork. If it seems too dry, stir in 3 to 5 tablespoons liquid from mushroom caps. Stir in parsley.

5. Set mushrooms, smooth side down, on plates. Top equally with couscous. Spoon pepper coulis equally around mushrooms and garnish with green onions. Add salt to taste.

Per serving: 220 cal., 35% (76 cal.) from fat; 7.1 g protein; 8.4 g fat (1.1 g sat.); 31 g carbo (4.5 g fiber); 20 mg sodium; 0 mg chol.

Spinach Risotto with Roquefort

 LIGHT COOKING TIP Give a dish pungent flavor without a lot of fat by adding a little bit of rich, high-quality cheese.

PREP AND COOK TIME: About 40 minutes

NOTES: Cary Neff, executive chef at Miraval Life in Balance Resort and Spa near Tucson, describes a healthful style of cooking in his new book, *Conscious Cuisine* (Sourcebooks, Naperville, IL, 2002; $35). This green risotto is adapted from one of his recipes. Serve it with grilled salmon or chicken breasts or increase the portion size and make it an entrée.

MAKES: About 3½ cups; 6 side-dish servings

- ½ cup chopped **onion**
- 1 teaspoon minced **garlic**
- ¼ teaspoon **olive oil**
- 1 cup **arborio** or other short- or medium-grain white **rice**
- 3 to 4 cups hot **spinach broth** (recipe follows)
- 1 tablespoon **Roquefort** or other blue **cheese**
  Sea or kosher **salt**
  Fresh-ground **pepper**
  Finely shredded **lemon** peel (optional)

1. In a 2- to 3-quart nonstick pan over medium-high heat, mix onion, garlic, and olive oil. Add rice and stir until onion is barely limp, 2 to 3 minutes.

2. Stir in 1 cup spinach broth and bring to a simmer, then reduce heat to maintain simmer and stir until liquid is absorbed, 2 to 3 minutes. Add 2 more cups broth, ½ cup at a time, stirring after each addition until liquid is absorbed and rice is tender but still has a slight bite, 20 to 25 minutes total. If rice isn't quite done, add more broth and stir until risotto is creamy.

3. Crumble cheese into risotto and stir until blended. Season with salt and pepper to taste. Garnish with lemon peel.

Per side-dish serving: 139 cal., 9% (12 cal.) from fat; 3.4 g protein; 1.3 g fat (0.3 g sat.); 28 g carbo (2.8 g fiber); 177 mg sodium; 1.3 mg chol.

SPINACH BROTH. In a 2- to 3-quart pan over medium-high heat, stir 1 cup chopped **onion** and 1 teaspoon minced **garlic** in ¼ teaspoon **extra-virgin olive oil** until onion is barely limp, 2 to 3 minutes. Add 3 cups packed rinsed **spinach leaves** and stir just until wilted, about 1 minute. Add 4 cups **vegetable stock** (recipe on page 18, or use canned broth). Purée mixture, one half at a time, in a blender (hold top down with a towel). Return to pan and bring to a simmer. Add about ½ teaspoon **sea** or kosher **salt** and ¼ teaspoon **pepper**. Makes about 4½ cups.

Mango and Jicama Salad with Habanero Vinaigrette

LIGHT COOKING TIP Start with ingredients that are naturally low in fat, and spice them up with low-fat seasonings (chilies have a lot of power in this department).

PREP TIME: About 40 minutes

NOTES: Executive chef Marc Lippman at Las Ventanas al Paraíso in Los Cabos, Mexico, created this stylish salad. If mangoes aren't available, substitute peeled fresh pineapple. Cut the fruit and jicama into same-size slices and stack them.

MAKES: 4 servings

- 2 **firm-ripe mangoes** (1¼ lb. each)
- 1 **jicama** (about 1½ lb.)
  Habanero vinaigrette (recipe follows)
- 1 cup **fresh cilantro,** Italian parsley, and/or mint **leaves,** rinsed and crisped
- 1 teaspoon **extra-virgin olive oil**
  Salt and **pepper**

Spinach Risotto
with Roquefort

Mango and
Jicama Salad
with Habanero
Vinaigrette

Mixed Beans
with Hoisin
Vinaigrette

Egg and
Vegetable
Wrap

1. With a small, sharp knife, peel mangoes. One at a time, set fruit on one narrow edge on a board and cut ⅛-inch-thick slices off each side down to the pit. Save remaining fruit around pits for another use.

2. Cut peel off jicama and discard. Lay jicama on board, flattest side down, and cut into ⅛-inch-thick ovals. Trim slices, if necessary, to match size of mango slices, about 2 by 4 inches.

3. Pour habanero vinaigrette into a rimmed plate. Dip a jicama slice in dressing, turning to coat and letting excess drain back into plate; set jicama on a separate plate. Lay a mango slice on top (if slices aren't perfect, fit pieces together to cover). Repeat to stack a total of four jicama and four mango slices. Coat remaining jicama slices and layer with mango slices to make three more servings.

4. Drizzle remaining dressing equally over stacks. In a small bowl, mix cilantro with olive oil and salt and pepper to taste. Mound equally on stacks.

Per serving: 186 cal., 25% (47 cal.) from fat; 2.2 g protein; 5.2 g fat (0.8 g sat.); 37 g carbo (9 g fiber); 10 mg sodium; 0 mg chol.

HABANERO VINAIGRETTE. Rinse 1 **fresh habanero chili** (about ¼ oz.). Wearing rubber gloves, stem, seed, devein, and finely mince chili; you should have about 1½ tablespoons. In a small bowl, mix 2 teaspoons of the minced chili, ⅓ cup fresh **orange** juice, 2 tablespoons fresh **lime** juice, and 1 tablespoon **extra-virgin olive oil**. With a small, sharp knife, cut ends off 2 **limes** (3 oz. each); cut off peel, including white pith. Holding limes over bowl of dressing, cut between membranes and fruit to release segments and drop them into bowl. Mix gently and add **salt** and more chili to taste, if desired.

Mixed Beans with Hoisin Vinaigrette

 LIGHT COOKING TIP Combine several legumes—a low-fat source of protein—for layers of flavor.

PREP AND COOK TIME: About 15 minutes

NOTES: Executive chef Reed Groban of Willow Stream Spa at the Fairmont Scottsdale Princess in Arizona uses hoisin sauce to add zest to beans. The sauce is available in most well-stocked supermarkets.

MAKES: About 4 cups; 6 servings

---

6 ounces **green beans**

1 **red bell pepper** (about 6 oz.)

1 tablespoon **Asian** (toasted) **sesame oil**

1 tablespoon chopped **garlic**

1 cup cooked **dried garbanzos** or canned garbanzos (rinsed and drained)

1 cup cooked **dried small white beans** or canned beans (rinsed and drained)

⅓ cup thinly sliced **green onions**

Hoisin vinaigrette (recipe follows)

1 tablespoon chopped **fresh cilantro**

1. Rinse green beans and trim off stem ends; cut beans into about 3-inch lengths. Rinse, stem, and seed bell pepper; cut lengthwise into thin slivers about 3 inches long.

2. Set a 10- to 12-inch frying pan over medium-high heat. When pan is hot, add green beans and 3 tablespoons water; cover and cook until beans are bright green, 3 to 4 minutes. Add 1 teaspoon sesame oil, bell pepper, and garlic; stir until pepper begins to soften, about 2 minutes. Add garbanzos, white beans, green onions, and hoisin vinaigrette. Stir until garbanzos and white beans are hot, about 2 minutes. Stir in remaining 2 teaspoons sesame oil. Pour into a serving bowl and sprinkle with cilantro.

Per serving: 137 cal., 21% (29 cal.) from fat; 6.2 g protein; 3.2 g fat (0.4 g sat.); 22 g carbo (3.9 g fiber); 86 mg sodium; 0 mg chol.

HOISIN VINAIGRETTE. In a blender or food processor, whirl ⅓ cup **rice vinegar**, 1½ tablespoons **hoisin sauce**, 1½ tablespoons **water**, and 2 teaspoons chopped **fresh ginger** until smooth. Makes about ½ cup.

Egg and Vegetable Wrap

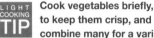 **LIGHT COOKING TIP** Cook vegetables briefly, to keep them crisp, and combine many for a variety of flavors and textures. Use refrigerated egg substitute or all egg whites instead of whole eggs to cut saturated fat in scrambles.

PREP AND COOK TIME: About 40 minutes

NOTES: This colorful wrap from executive chef Guido Ulmann at the Hilton Hawaiian Village Beach Resort & Spa in Honolulu makes a great

---

brunch, lunch, or light supper entrée. He uses red or green tortillas, but any kind of the same size will do.

MAKES: 4 servings

8 ounces **firm tofu**

2 **Roma tomatoes** (6 oz. total)

1 tablespoon **olive oil**

1 cup thinly slivered **zucchini** (¼ in. by 3 in.)

1 cup thinly slivered **red bell pepper** (¼ in. by 3 in.)

1 cup thinly sliced **green onions**

1 cup thinly sliced **spinach** leaves

1 tablespoon thinly sliced **fresh basil** leaves

1½ cups **pasteurized egg product** (such as Egg Beaters) or egg whites

Salt and **pepper**

4 **flour tortillas** (10 in. wide; see notes)

2 cups **mixed baby salad greens** (about 2 oz.), rinsed and crisped

½ to 1 cup **marinara sauce**, purchased or homemade, heated

1. Rinse tofu and cut into ½-inch cubes; drain well and gently pat dry.

2. Rinse and core tomatoes; halve lengthwise, then slice lengthwise.

3. Set a 10- to 12-inch nonstick frying pan over high heat. When hot, add oil, zucchini, and bell pepper; stir often for 1 minute. Add tofu and tomatoes and stir until hot, 1 to 2 minutes. Add green onions, spinach, and basil; stir until wilted, about 1 minute. Add egg product and stir just until softly set, about 1 minute. Remove from heat and add salt and pepper to taste.

4. Meanwhile, wrap tortillas in plastic wrap and heat in a microwave oven on full power (100%) just until steaming, 30 to 45 seconds. Spoon a fourth of the vegetable-egg mixture along one side of each tortilla, about 1 inch from front and to within 1 inch of side edges. Fold front edge over filling, then roll up tightly like a burrito. Cut each wrap in half diagonally or into fourths and set on a dinner plate. Garnish with salad greens and hot marinara sauce, or offer sauce to add to taste.

Per serving: 391 cal., 32% (126 cal.) from fat; 25 g protein; 14 g fat (1.9 g sat.); 45 g carbo (4.5 g fiber); 639 mg sodium; 0 mg chol.

Grilled Salmon Salad with Raspberry Vinaigrette

LIGHT COOKING TIP Combine ingredients known to promote health, with an emphasis on freshness, bright colors, and multiple textures. Choose fats with full flavor; you only need a little.

PREP AND COOK TIME: About 1 hour

NOTES: Tom Dowling, executive chef at Rancho Bernardo Inn, created this salad for Salus Heart and Wellness, located on the same grounds in Rancho Bernardo, California. Fresh or frozen shelled cooked soybeans (edamame) can be found in most supermarkets. If unshelled, you'll need about 1 cup soybeans in pods.

MAKES: 4 servings

- ¼ cup **walnut halves** (1 oz.)
- 12 **asparagus spears** (8 to 10 oz. total) or broccoli florets (1 in. wide and 3 in. long)
- 4 pieces (4 oz. each) **boned salmon fillet**

  Spice rub (recipe follows)
- 3 heads (8 oz. each) **Belgian endive**
- 2 cups **mixed baby salad greens,** rinsed and crisped
- 1 dozen **cherry tomatoes** (1 in. wide; 8 oz. total), rinsed, stemmed, and halved
- ½ cup chopped **red onion**

  Raspberry vinaigrette (recipe follows)
- 1 cup **raspberries,** rinsed
- ½ cup **shelled cooked fresh** or thawed frozen **soybeans** (see notes)
- 4 **pumpernickel rolls**

1. Bake nuts in a 9-inch pie or cake pan in a 350° regular or convection oven until golden beneath skins, shaking pan once, 7 to 9 minutes.

2. Meanwhile, in a 10- to 12-inch frying pan over high heat, bring about 1 inch water to a boil. Rinse asparagus and snap off tough stem ends. Add asparagus or broccoli to pan and boil, uncovered, until bright green and barely tender when pierced, 2 to 3 minutes. Drain; rinse with cold water until cold.

3. Rinse salmon and pat dry. Coat flesh sides equally with all the spice rub. Lay fish, coated side down, on a grill over hot coals or high heat on a

gas grill (you can hold your hand at grill level only 2 to 3 seconds); close lid on gas grill. Cook fish, turning once, until opaque but still moist-looking in center of thickest part (cut to test), 7 to 9 minutes total. Transfer to a plate.

4. Rinse Belgian endive; trim off and discard discolored ends. Set aside 12 leaves; cut remaining leaves crosswise into ¼-inch-wide slices and place in a bowl. Add salad greens, tomatoes, onion, and ¼ cup raspberry vinaigrette; mix gently.

5. Arrange asparagus and whole endive leaves equally around edges of plates. Mound salad mixture equally in center of plates; top with warm salmon. Sprinkle servings equally with walnuts, raspberries, and soybeans. Drizzle remaining vinaigrette over the top. Serve with pumpernickel rolls.

Per serving: 571 cal., 44% (252 cal.) from fat; 36 g protein; 28 g fat (4.4 g sat.); 48 g carbo (13 g fiber); 518 mg sodium; 67 mg chol.

SPICE RUB. In a blender, whirl 1 tablespoon *each* **coriander seeds** and **fennel seeds** and 1½ teaspoons *each* **dried thyme** and **black peppercorns** until finely ground. Makes about 3 tablespoons.

RASPBERRY VINAIGRETTE. In a small bowl, whisk together 3 tablespoons **raspberry vinegar,** 2 tablespoons **extra-virgin olive oil,** 1 tablespoon **walnut oil** (optional), and 1½ teaspoons **Dijon mustard.** Add **salt** and **pepper** to taste. Makes about ½ cup.

Chicken with Fig Sauce

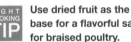

LIGHT COOKING TIP Use dried fruit as the base for a flavorful sauce for braised poultry.

PREP AND COOK TIME: 40 minutes

NOTES: John C. Klock, M.D., of Holistica Hawaii Preventative Medicine Center teaches clients how to cook healthfully with dishes like this chicken.

MAKES: 4 servings

- 6 **dried Black Mission figs**
- 1 cup fat-skimmed **chicken broth**
- 1 teaspoon **ground coriander**
- 1 teaspoon **dry mustard**
- 4 **boned, skinned chicken breast halves** (4 to 6 oz. each)
- 1 tablespoon **olive oil**
- 1 **onion** (about 8 oz.), peeled and chopped

Grilled Salmon Salad with Raspberry Vinaigrette

- 1 tablespoon **all-purpose flour**
- ⅓ cup **dry sherry**
- ¼ cup **balsamic vinegar**

  Thinly sliced **fresh chives**

  Salt and **pepper**

1. Cut figs into quarters and place in a small bowl; cover with hot water and soak until soft, about 15 minutes. Lift figs from liquid and place in a blender or food processor. Add ⅓ cup of the soaking liquid (discard remainder) and the broth, coriander, and dry mustard; whirl until smooth.

2. Rinse chicken and pat dry. Set a 10- to 12-inch nonstick frying pan over high heat. When hot, add 1½ teaspoons olive oil and tilt pan to coat bottom. Add chicken in a single layer and cook, turning once, until browned on both sides, 4 to 6 minutes total. Transfer to a plate.

3. Reduce heat to medium-high. Add remaining 1½ teaspoons oil and onion; stir often until onion is limp and beginning to brown, 2 to 3 minutes. Add flour and stir to coat onion. Add fig mixture and stir until boiling.

4. Return chicken to pan. Cover and simmer over low heat until chicken is no longer pink in center of thickest part (cut to test), 5 to 7 minutes.

5. With tongs, transfer chicken to plates. Stir sherry into sauce. If desired for a smoother sauce, pour through a fine strainer into a bowl. Spoon sauce equally over chicken, then drizzle each portion with 1 tablespoon vinegar. Sprinkle with chives and add salt and pepper to taste.

Per serving: 255 cal., 18% (47 cal.) from fat; 30 g protein; 5.2 g fat (0.9 g sat.); 17 g carbo (2.2 g fiber); 98 mg sodium; 66 mg chol.

> **"A little dark chocolate, fresh fruit, and red wine is a great way to end a meal."**
>
> —*Dr. Neil Treister, Salus Heart and Wellness*

Spa staples: stock, sauce & dressing

Vegetable Stock

PREP AND COOK TIME: About 2½ hours

NOTES: A fresh vegetable broth or stock is a staple for most spa kitchens. This all-purpose version comes from executive chef Neff at Miraval Life in Balance Resort and Spa. Cool, cover, and chill it up to 1 week or freeze up to 6 months.

MAKES: 2 quarts

- 1 **leek** (about 12 oz.)
- 3 **onions** (1½ lb. total), chopped
- 3 **carrots** (12 oz. total), scrubbed and chopped
- 2 stalks **celery** (4 oz. total), chopped
- 8 ounces **mushrooms,** quartered
- 2 **Roma tomatoes** (6 oz. total), rinsed and quartered
- 1 head **fennel** (about 1 lb.; optional), stalks trimmed, and chopped
- 1½ teaspoons **dried parsley**
- 1½ teaspoons **dried thyme**
- 1½ teaspoons **dried oregano**
- 1 tablespoon **black peppercorns**

1. Trim and discard root end from leek; split leek in half lengthwise and rinse well under running water, flipping layers to release grit. Coarsely chop leek and place in an 8- to 10-quart pan. Add onions, carrots, celery, mushrooms, tomatoes, fennel, parsley, thyme, oregano, peppercorns, and enough water to cover vegetables (about 2 qt.). Bring to a boil over high heat, then reduce heat and simmer, uncovered, for 2 hours, adding water as needed to keep vegetables barely covered.

2. Line a colander with a layer of cheesecloth (or use a large, fine wire strainer); set over a large bowl. Pour stock mixture into colander and drain vegetables well; discard vegetables. You should have about 8 cups stock. If you have less, thin with water; if more, boil, uncovered, until reduced to that amount.

Per ½ cup: 18 cal., 6% (1 cal.) from fat; 0.6 g protein; 0.1 g fat (0 g sat.); 4 g carbo (0.9 g fiber); 10 mg sodium; 0 mg chol.

Pepper Coulis

PREP AND COOK TIME: About 25 minutes

NOTES: Executive chef Stroot at the Golden Door uses red and yellow pepper coulis side by side in plate presentations to add color, moisture, texture, and flavor. If you're in a hurry, instead of roasting fresh peppers, you can use 1¼ cups rinsed, drained canned roasted peppers. You can make the coulis ahead of time; cover and chill up to 3 days or freeze up to 6 months.

MAKES: ¾ to 1 cup

Rinse 1 **red** or yellow **bell pepper** (about 10 oz.); pat dry. Set pepper in a 9-inch pie or cake pan and broil 3 to 4 inches from heat, turning as needed, until charred on all sides, about 15 minutes total. Let cool. With a small, sharp knife, remove and discard skin, stem, and seeds. Coarsely chop pepper and place in a blender or food processor. Add 1 tablespoon water and 1 teaspoon **olive oil;** whirl until smooth. Add **salt** and **cayenne** to taste. If coulis is thicker than desired, thin with 1 to 2 more tablespoons water.

Per ¼ cup: 26 cal., 42% (11 cal.) from fat; 0.5 g protein; 1.2 g fat (0.2 g sat.); 3.7 g carbo (0.9 g fiber); 1.2 mg sodium; 0 mg chol.

Charred-Tomato Vinaigrette

PREP AND COOK TIME: About 45 minutes

NOTES: Instructor-chef John Vollertsen of the Vista Clara Ranch Resort & Spa in Galisteo, New Mexico, created this mildly sweet and tangy dressing to add a bit of zip to greens. You can make it up to 3 days ahead; cover and chill.

MAKES: About 1 cup

- 4 **Roma tomatoes** (12 oz. total)
- 2 tablespoons **extra-virgin olive oil**
- ½ teaspoon **granulated sugar**
  About ¼ teaspoon **salt**
- 2 tablespoons **balsamic vinegar**
- 2 tablespoons **red wine vinegar**
- 1 teaspoon firmly packed **brown sugar**
- 4 **fresh basil** leaves (each 2 in. long), rinsed, or ½ teaspoon dried basil
  Pepper

1. Rinse and core tomatoes; cut in half lengthwise. Set halves, cut side up, in a 9-inch cake pan. Brush cut sides with a total of 2 teaspoons oil. Sprinkle evenly with granulated sugar and ¼ teaspoon salt. Bake in a 400° regular or convection oven until tomatoes are browned, 35 to 45 minutes. Let cool.

2. In a blender, whirl tomatoes, balsamic vinegar, red wine vinegar, remaining 4 teaspoons olive oil, brown sugar, and basil until smooth. Add salt and pepper to taste.

Per tablespoon: 22 cal., 73% (16 cal.) from fat; 0.2 g protein; 1.8 g fat (0.3 g sat.); 1.5 g carbo (0.3 g fiber); 38 mg sodium; 0 mg chol. ◆

Time for tea

There's a tea renaissance brewing, introducing Westerners to the depth and diversity of hand-picked teas. Celadon Fine Teas, a new store in Albany, California, is on the leading edge, capturing the spirit but recasting the form of the classic Asian tea shop. The central feature is a bar shaped like the covered tea cup called a *gaiwan*. The staff explains the rituals of a tea ceremony and the differences between basic families of teas. Visitors can buy bulk teas and tea supplies, or attend lectures by world experts. 1111 Solano Ave., Albany; (510) 524-1696. For more tea news: www.teasociety.org

—Peter O. Whiteley

Tea through the day…

TIME	A.M.	Midday	P.M.
SIP THIS	Red tea *(also called black tea in Europe)*	Green tea or oolong tea	White tea or a red tea such as Pu-Erh
FEEL THIS	A brain kick-start. Red tea has a higher concentration of caffeine than other teas (though it's about a fifth of what you get in coffee).	Peace of mind. Green teas have less caffeine, while oolong teas are very aromatic. A gentle break from the stress of the workday.	At one with the universe. White teas have very low caffeine and are a soothing drink for the evening. Pu-Erh is extolled for reducing cholesterol and aiding digestion.

Oven-browning gives crockpot short ribs extra succulence.

Slow food

New electric cookers make the most of beef stew

By Jerry Anne Di Vecchio

Photographs by James Carrier • Food styling by Basil Friedman

Even a food writer has to eat crow now and then. Take me and electric slow-cookers, for instance: When they were introduced several decades ago, my scoffing knew no limits. Recently, however, crockpots have in some important ways been reinvented. They're generally wider, so foods that used to be smashed by their own weight aren't. I gave cookers another chance and discovered some delicious possibilities. If you take two more steps—transfer the tender but rather dull-looking meat to a hot oven, then boil the juices it has cooked in—the meat browns quickly, and the sauce concentrates and takes on complex flavor. Reunite the parts, and the final dish exhibits all the benefits of traditional slow-braising but has taken much less attention overall.

Slow-braised Beef Stew with Mushrooms

PREP AND COOK TIME: 5½ to 6½ hours slow-cooked, 3 hours baked

NOTES: Don't confuse beef short ribs with back ribs cut from the beef loin. If you don't have a slow-cooker, put meat in a 2-inch-deep, 4- to 5-quart baking pan (about 9 by 13 in.); heat liquids and flavorings (step 2), pour over meat, and seal with foil. Bake in a 350° oven until meat is very tender when pierced, 2½ to 3 hours. After 1 hour, check liquid and add water up to original level. Reseal pan with foil and return to oven; after 30 more minutes, check and adjust liquid level again. When meat is tender, continue with step 3; leave meat in pan, draining off liquid, or

transfer to a casserole. You can make this dish up to 2 days ahead; let cool, then cover and chill. Bake, covered, in a 350° oven until meat is hot, 20 to 25 minutes. Serve stew with hot cooked rice or mashed potatoes.

MAKES: 6 to 8 servings

4 pounds **boned, fat-trimmed beef short ribs** or chuck

1 **orange** (2½ in. wide), rinsed

1 **onion** (about 8 oz.), peeled and finely chopped

About 1 cup fat-skimmed **beef** or chicken **broth**

1 cup **dry red wine**

½ cup **port** or cream sherry

¼ cup **balsamic vinegar**

2 tablespoons **soy sauce**

1 teaspoon **dried thyme** or 2 teaspoons fresh thyme leaves

3 or 4 very thin slices (quarter size) peeled **fresh ginger**

½ teaspoon **Chinese five spice**

1 pound **mushrooms** (1- to 1½-in.-wide caps)

2 tablespoons **butter** or olive oil

2 tablespoons **cornstarch**

Salt and **pepper**

¼ cup chopped **fresh chives** or green onions

1. Rinse meat; cut into 3- to 4-inch lengths (for chuck, about 1 in. thick and 1½ in. wide) and place in a 5- to 6-quart slow-cooker.

2. With a vegetable peeler, pare orange part of peel from orange and sliver it; save orange for other uses. In a 1½- to 2-quart pan, combine peel, onion, 1 cup broth, wine, port, vinegar, soy sauce, thyme, ginger, and five spice. Bring to a boil over high heat. Pour liquid over meat. Turn slow-cooker to high, cover, and cook until meat is very tender when pierced, 5 to 6 hours.

3. Rinse and drain mushrooms; trim off and discard stem ends. Cut mushrooms in half lengthwise and place in a 10- to 12-inch frying pan; add butter.

4. Skim off and discard fat from liquid in slow-cooker. Ladle 1 cup liquid into pan with mushrooms. Stir mushrooms often over high heat until liquid has evaporated and mushrooms are lightly browned, 13 to 17 minutes.

5. With a slotted spoon, lift meat from juices in slow-cooker and lay in a single layer in a shallow casserole (about 9 by 13 in.). Pour mushrooms over meat. Bake in a 375° regular or convection oven until meat is sizzling and browned, 12 to 15 minutes.

6. Meanwhile, measure remaining liquid from slow-cooker. If less than 2 cups, add beef broth to make 2 cups, pour into a 2- to 3-quart pan, and bring to a boil over high heat; if there is more, pour into pan and boil, stirring occasionally, until reduced to 2 cups, 8 to 12 minutes. In a small bowl, mix cornstarch with ¼ cup water. Pour into boiling liquid and stir until thickened, about 30 seconds. Pour evenly over meat and mix gently to blend with liquid in casserole, adding salt and pepper to taste. Sprinkle with chives.

Per serving: 468 cal., 50% (234 cal.) from fat; 46 g protein; 26 g fat (12 g sat.); 10 g carbo (1.2 g fiber); 450 mg sodium; 142 mg chol. ◆

Cold snap

Put dinner on the table fast with a well-stocked freezer

By Linda Lau Anusasananan
Photograph by James Carrier

It's dinnertime and everyone is starving. Open the refrigerator, and it's almost bare. Does this scene sound familiar? All is not lost if you have a stash of emergency rations. Check out your supermarket's freezer section and stock up on building blocks for a meal. Bags of trimmed vegetables and shrimp keep frozen for months, ready to use for impromptu and easily varied meals. For this fast and satisfying menu, we add spices, canned tomatoes, and shelf-stable couscous to give convenient ingredients a Moroccan flair. Experiment with your own favorite combinations to produce quick, hearty, and healthy dinners that belie their icy origins.

Shrimp and Vegetable Tagine with Couscous

PREP AND COOK TIME: 30 minutes

NOTES: A vegetable mixture with corn works well in this dish; it may be labeled Mexican or Southwest-style. To thaw shrimp, place in a colander and run cool water over them just until thawed, about 5 minutes; drain well.

MAKES: 6 servings

- 2 cups **vegetable broth**
- 2 teaspoons **olive oil**
- 1 package (10 to 12 oz.; 1²⁄₃ to 1³⁄₄ cups) **couscous**
- 2 cloves **garlic,** peeled and minced
- 1 tablespoon **chili powder**
- 1 teaspoon **ground coriander**
- ¹⁄₂ teaspoon **ground cumin**
- ¹⁄₄ teaspoon **hot chili flakes**
- 1 can (14 oz.) **diced tomatoes**
- 1 package (14 to 16 oz.) **frozen mixed vegetables** (see notes above and sidebar at right)

- 1 package (12 oz.) **frozen uncooked peeled, deveined shrimp** (51 to 60 per lb.), thawed (see notes)

- **Salt**

- ¹⁄₄ cup chopped **parsley,** fresh cilantro, or mint leaves

1. In a 2- to 3-quart pan over high heat, bring broth and 1 teaspoon olive oil to a boil. Stir in couscous, cover pan, and remove from heat. Let stand until broth is absorbed and couscous is tender to bite, about 5 minutes.

2. Meanwhile, in a 5- to 6-quart pan over medium-high heat, stir garlic in remaining teaspoon oil until it just begins to brown, 1 to 2 minutes. Add chili powder, coriander, cumin, and chili flakes; stir until fragrant, about 30 seconds. Add tomatoes (including juices) and bring to a boil over high heat. Stir in frozen vegetables and cook, stirring often, for 3 minutes.

▲ **Menu suggestion**
To accompany this quick, delicious Moroccan dinner of shrimp and vegetable tagine with couscous, offer purchased hummus with pocket-bread triangles and sliced cucumbers for dipping, plus a Sauvignon Blanc or sparkling water to sip. A plate of dates, dried apricots, pistachios, and cashews and cups of hot mint tea are an easy, gracious finishing touch.

Add thawed shrimp and cook, stirring often, until shrimp are opaque but still moist-looking in center of thickest part (cut to test) and vegetables are hot, 4 to 5 minutes. Add salt to taste.

3. With a fork, fluff the couscous; spoon equal portions of it into wide, shallow bowls. Spoon shrimp and vegetable mixture, including juices, evenly over couscous and sprinkle with parsley.

Per serving: 325 cal., 10% (32 cal.) from fat; 21 g protein; 3.6 g fat (0.5 g sat.); 52 g carbo (5.1 g fiber); 266 mg sodium; 86 mg chol. ◆

When to choose frozen

Vegetables with a dense, firm texture hold up best when frozen. Good choices include artichoke hearts, asparagus, cooked dried beans, broc- coli, carrots, cauliflower, corn, green beans, pearl onions, peas, soybeans, sugar snap peas, water chestnuts, and winter squash.

Frozen vegetables with a high water content tend to collapse and turn mushy when thawed unless cooked before freezing. Avoid such choices as bell peppers, cel- ery, mushrooms, chopped onions, and tomatoes. Leafy greens, such as spinach, can be good if liquid is squeezed out before use.

New Year's resolutions

I've made my share of New Year's resolutions through the years, but none quite as delicious (or easy to keep) as the ones about wine. Here are mine for 2003.

1. Try more different kinds. There are more than 5,000 grape varieties in the world, but many of us drink the same one, or ones, week after week (the equivalent of eating chicken every night). Here are some I plan to try more of this year: **Albariño** from Spain; **Pinot Gris** from Oregon; **Riesling** from Alsace, Austria, and Australia; southern French reds like **Gigondas; Barbera** and **Dolcetto** from Italy; and **Syrahs** from all over the American West.

2. Set aside a "wine discovery" budget: $20 a week. With that, I'll buy wines I don't know, and hopefully by the end of the year, I'll have made all kinds of delicious new discoveries.

3. Create a permanent wine space in my refrigerator. After a long day at work or when a friend drops over unexpectedly, I want to be able to open that door and know there's a good white waiting inside. The first bottle I'm going to put there: **J Pinot Gris** (about $18). Pinot Gris is as "hot" as a variety gets right now, and this is one of the best in California. Its exotic aroma is all about peaches, apples, and rain-fresh country air, its flavor evocative of peaches and apricot purée.

4. Order the least expensive bottle in a restaurant. This takes courage, but I've found that many restaurant wine buyers work hard at finding great deals. Instead of being embarrassed about ordering from the lower end, I've decided to make the most of their expertise. For example, the least expensive wine on the list at Bouchon, Thomas Keller's Napa Valley bistro, is a **Delas Frères Côtes du Ventoux 2000** from France ($20). It's terrific—juicy, earthy, and leathery. Just the ticket for, say, roast chicken and *pommes frites.*

5. Drink more white wine with cheese. In experiment after experiment, I've discovered that white wine generally tastes better with most cheeses than red; acidity does the trick. My favorite combination: goat cheese and a crisp **Sauvignon Blanc** (also called Fumé Blanc). **Benziger, Dry Creek, Firestone, Hogue, Honig,** and **Meridian** all make great ones (and Sauvignon Blancs are steals, to boot).

6. Open wine just for myself. There's a bottle of **Domaine Carneros sparkling wine** in my refrigerator, but I've never considered opening it when no one else is around. I'm going to get over that. Each of us deserves the simple pleasure of a glass of good wine. Besides, the rest won't go bad in a day. If you pour out a glass and stopper the bottle immediately, the wine will be fine the next day; put a white back in the refrigerator and it will probably be good for several days to come. Ditto for sparklers: you just need one of those sparkling-wine stoppers that keep the bubbles in ($5 to $10 in most wine shops).

7. Give red wines the carafe treatment. Most of the reds I drink are young. I know they'll taste softer, rounder, and more expressive if I just take a minute to pour them into a carafe or decanter so exposure to the air can open up their flavors. When I did this recently with a **Penfolds "Thomas Hyland" Shiraz** from Australia (about $15), the transformation was amazing: the wine actually tasted like it cost a lot more.

8. Stop holding back those "great" bottles. I'm as guilty as anyone of saving wines instead of enjoying them, even though I know it makes little sense. As far as wine is concerned, delayed gratification may be overrated. Wine is meant for drinking. Without waiting for a special occasion, I'm going to invite friends over and open some of those gems I've had stashed away for years. —*Karen MacNeil-Fife*

Five red wines to sip by the fire

Foppiano Zinfandel 2000 *(Dry Creek Valley, CA),* $15. Intriguing boysenberry and briar aromas, then boysenberry, cherry, and blueberry flavors nearly leap out of the glass. A great all-around wine to pair with comfort food.

Laurel Glen "Za Zin" Old Vine Zinfandel 2000 *(Lodi, CA),* $15. You know the concept of dressing up a pair of jeans by wearing pearls? Well, if meatloaf is for dinner, Laurel Glen's Za Zin could well be the pearls. Spicy, licoricey, loads of black cherry flavor.

Gallo of Sonoma Cabernet Sauvignon Reserve 1999 *(Sonoma County),* $13. It's juicy and a bit rustic, with raspberry, dried cranberry, and tobacco flavors. Paired with a simple roast, it could make your evening.

Murphy-Goode "Liar's Dice" Zinfandel 2000 *(Sonoma County),* $20. If you like wines that hedonistically suggest chocolate and vanilla flavors, you'll love this thick, satisfying wine.

Bedford Thompson Mourvèdre 1999 *(Santa Barbara County),* $20. Earth, licorice, tar, blackberries in an intense rendition of this varietal. In a Victorian romance, it would be the guy with the black cape on the black horse who rides through black forests in the black of night. —*K. M.-F.*

New year, new flavors

Readers' recipes
tested in *Sunset's* kitchens

Photographs by James Carrier

Coconut Scones

Kim Case, Portland

Kim Case writes that her nephew calls these jam-filled scones "coconut stones," which is no reflection on their moist and fluffy texture!

PREP AND COOK TIME: About 30 minutes

MAKES: 8 scones

- 1¾ cups **all-purpose flour**
- ½ cup **sweetened flaked coconut**
- ½ cup **rolled oats**
- 3 tablespoons **sugar**
- 2 teaspoons **baking powder**
- ¼ teaspoon **salt**
- ⅓ cup cold **butter,** cut into chunks
- 2 **large eggs**
- ½ cup **milk**
- ¼ cup **raspberry** or cherry **jam**

1. In a large bowl, mix flour, coconut, oats, 2 tablespoons sugar, baking powder, and salt. With your fingers or a pastry blender, rub or cut in butter until mixture forms coarse crumbs.

2. In a small bowl, beat eggs and milk to blend. Stir all but about 1 tablespoon egg mixture into flour mixture just until evenly moistened.

3. Scrape dough onto a lightly floured board and pat into an 8-inch round. Slide round onto a buttered 12- by 15-inch baking sheet and cut into 8 wedges, leaving wedges in place. Brush top of round with reserved egg mixture and sprinkle with remaining tablespoon sugar. Make a 1-inch-diameter depression on top of the wide end of each wedge and fill each with about ½ tablespoon jam.

4. Bake in a 375° regular or convection oven until golden brown, 18 to 20 minutes. Recut scones to separate and serve warm, or transfer to a rack to cool completely.

Per serving: 279 cal., 35% (99 cal.) from fat; 6 g protein; 11 g fat (6.8 g sat.); 39 g carbo (1.7 g fiber); 311 mg sodium; 76 mg chol.

Baked-in jam makes coconut scones a perfect breakfast treat.

Split Pea Dal with Mango

*Kristen Dillon Lummis,
Grand Junction, CO*

One night after Kristen Lummis's second child was born, a friend brought her this delicious and simple dal for dinner. The dish was much appreciated by everyone, including her older child, then two years old.

PREP AND COOK TIME: About 1½ hours

MAKES: 4 to 6 servings

- 1½ cups **dried yellow split peas**
- 8 **whole cloves**
- 1 **cinnamon stick** (2 in.)
- 1½ cups **basmati rice**
- 2 tablespoons **butter**
- 1 teaspoon **ground cumin**
- 1 teaspoon **ground dried turmeric**
- ½ teaspoon **mustard seeds**
- ¼ teaspoon **cayenne**
- ¼ teaspoon **ground coriander**
- ¼ teaspoon **ground ginger**
  Salt
- 1 **mango** (about 14 oz.), peeled and cut into ½-inch chunks
- 1 cup **plain yogurt**

1. In a 4- to 6-quart pan over high heat, bring 5 cups water to a boil. Rinse split peas and remove debris. Add split peas, cloves, and cinnamon stick to boiling water. Reduce heat, cover, and simmer, stirring occasionally, until peas are very soft and starting to break down, 1 to 1½ hours (mixture should be soupy). If peas begin to stick before they're done, add more water ½ cup at a time. Remove and discard cloves and cinnamon stick if desired.

2. Meanwhile, in a 3- to 4-quart pan over high heat, bring 2½ cups water to a boil. Add rice, reduce heat to a simmer, cover, and simmer until rice is tender to bite, about 20 minutes.

3. In a 1- to 1½-quart pan over medium heat, melt butter. Stir in cumin, turmeric, mustard seeds, cayenne, coriander, and ginger and cook until fragrant, 1 to 2 minutes. Stir spice mixture into cooked split peas and add salt to taste.

4. Divide cooked rice evenly among four to six wide, shallow bowls and spoon dal equally onto rice. Add mango and yogurt on the side.

Per serving: 417 cal., 13% (56 cal.) from fat; 19 g protein; 6.2 g fat (2.9 g sat.); 77 g carbo (3.8 g fiber); 96 mg sodium; 13 mg chol.

Parmesan coats cauliflower florets and pasta in a one-pan dinner.

Cauliflower Rotini

Paul Genaux, Bremerton, WA

Paul Genaux learned how to make this simple pasta dish in a cooking class he took in Naples, Italy. Using imported Parmigiano-Reggiano cheese makes a big difference in the flavor of the dish.

PREP AND COOK TIME: 35 minutes

MAKES: 4 servings

- 2 tablespoons **olive oil**
- 4 cloves **garlic,** minced
- 1 head **cauliflower** (1¾ lb.), rinsed, trimmed from core, and separated into 1-inch pieces
- 12 ounces **dried rotini pasta** or another shape about 1 inch long
- 1 cup grated **parmesan cheese** (see notes)

   Salt and **pepper**

1. Pour oil into a 12-inch frying pan with 2-inch-high sides over medium heat. When hot, add garlic and stir until fragrant but not brown, about 1 minute. Add cauliflower and stir to coat, about 1 minute.

2. Stir in pasta and 3½ cups water. Bring to a simmer over high heat, then cover, reduce heat, and cook, stirring often, until pasta is just tender to bite and liquid has reduced to a creamy sauce, 15 to 20 minutes; if mixture begins to stick before pasta is done, add more water ½ cup at a time. Stir in cheese and add salt and pepper to taste.

Per serving: 489 cal., 26% (126 cal.) from fat; 21 g protein; 14 g fat (4.9 g sat.); 69 g carbo (4 g fiber); 390 mg sodium; 16 mg chol.

Mediterranean Bread Bowl with Hummus

Joan Cathey, La Center, WA

This variant of the bread bowl filled with dip is a great appetizer. You can make hummus and marinate peppers up to 1 day ahead; cover each and chill. As a shortcut, use purchased hummus.

PREP TIME: About 25 minutes, plus at least 1 hour to chill

MAKES: 6 to 8 appetizer servings

- 1 cup drained **canned peeled red peppers,** cut into strips
- ⅓ cup coarsely chopped **pitted calamata olives**
- 2 tablespoons **plain yogurt**
- 1 tablespoon **olive oil**
- 1 tablespoon **lemon juice**
- 1 clove **garlic,** peeled and minced
- ¼ teaspoon **dried ground turmeric**
- ¼ teaspoon **cayenne**

   Salt
- 1 round loaf (1 lb.) **rye** or pumpernickel **bread**
- 1½ cups **hummus** (recipe follows; see notes)
- ¼ cup **crumbled feta cheese**

1. In a bowl, mix peppers, olives, yogurt, olive oil, lemon juice, garlic, turmeric, and cayenne to coat; add salt to taste. Cover and chill at least 1 hour and up to 1 day (see notes).

2. With a serrated knife, slice about 1 inch off top of loaf. With the knife, hollow out center of loaf, leaving a shell about 1 inch thick. Cut top slice and bread from middle into chunks.

3. Spread hummus in bottom of bread bowl. Top with pepper mixture and feta. Set on a platter and surround with reserved bread chunks for dipping.

Per serving: 328 cal., 36% (117 cal.) from fat; 9.2 g protein; 13 g fat (2.2 g sat.); 45 g carbo (5.4 g fiber); 722 mg sodium; 3.4 mg chol.

Hummus. Drain 1 can (15½ oz.) **garbanzos,** reserving liquid. In a blender or food processor, whirl garbanzos, 3 tablespoons **tahini** (sesame paste), 2 tablespoons **olive oil,** 1 tablespoon **lemon juice,** 1 peeled clove **garlic,** and 1 teaspoon **ground cumin** until smooth. Thin with a few tablespoons reserved liquid if desired. Add **salt** and **pepper** to taste.

Per serving: 131 cal., 49% (64 cal.) from fat; 3.7 g protein; 7.1 g fat (0.9 g sat.); 14 g carbo (1.6 g fiber); 172 mg sodium; 0 mg chol. ◆

Radish in disguise

IT LOOKS LIKE A LARGE, PALE GREEN TURNIP ON THE OUTSIDE. But cut this watermelon radish open and you'll understand the reason for its name. The flesh glows fuchsia and is rimmed with a thin band of white and tinged with green on the outer edges. The visual characteristics become more striking when you splash thin slices with vinegar—which intensifies the color—and sprinkle them with black sesame seeds.

This Asian radish, also known as rose-heart or shinrimei radish, adds crunch and mild flavor to salads and sandwiches. Look for the California-grown roots through March in farmers' markets and in supermarkets that sell specialty produce. You can order seed packets from Evergreen Y. H. Enterprises (www.evergreenseeds.com or 714/637-5769) or Ornamental Edibles (www.ornamentaledibles.com or 408/929-7333).

—Linda Lau Anusasananan

Sweet-tart Watermelon Radish Salad

Peel 1 **watermelon radish** (about 12 oz.). If radish is wider than 3 inches, cut in half lengthwise. Slice crosswise as thinly as possible. Mix with ⅓ cup **seasoned rice vinegar.** Cover and chill at least 10 minutes or up to 1 hour, stirring occasionally. Sprinkle with 1 teaspoon **black sesame seeds,** if desired. Makes 6 servings.

Napa and red cabbages are dressed with an Asian vinaigrette and crunchy roasted sesame seeds (see page 30).

February

A casual won ton party is easy and fun when everyone helps. Start by making dumplings and won ton, and end with a satisfying bowl of soup.

Wrap party

Throw a won ton party where the guests do all the work

By Linda Lau Anusasananan • Photographs by James Carrier • Food styling by Andrea Lucich

Food plays a major role in Debbie Lee's family history. Her great-grandfather, who came to the United States in the 1800s to work on the railroads, started one of the first Chinese restaurants in Los Angeles. Lee, who lives in Sacramento, revives family traditions with a party where she shows guests how to make won ton and dumplings.

"Making won ton is sort of like origami with food," Lee says. "The party brings back memories of my childhood where we cooked together in the kitchen and just hung out." She learned to make won ton from her mom; she has updated the recipe by substituting ground turkey for pork. The dumplings are a new addition, which Lee learned to make on a recent trip to China. We took Lee's ideas to hold our own cooking party with friends. The result was an easy, delicious success.

Won ton menu

Debbie's Dumplings

Sesame Cabbage Salad

Chinese Broccoli

Won Ton Noodle Soup

Tea

Orange wedges

Chinese almond cookies

The strategy

This casual cooking party suits a small group of six to eight, which can include kids—they love the activity. Lee makes the fillings in advance, then demonstrates how to fill the wrappers. After a few attempts, it's easy for a group to produce more won ton than they can eat at a time. Freeze extras, or send guests home with leftovers as party favors. Start by making the dumplings together, then take a break for an appetizer course of salad and dumplings. (If time is short, serve purchased frozen potstickers or gyoza instead.) After the first course, move on to wrapping the won ton. Or wrap all the dumplings and won ton at once, clean up, and eat both together in one big feast that perfectly reflects this party's spirit of community and cooperation.

Pan-browned dumplings are dipped in soy sauce, vinegar, or chili oil.

"The party brings back memories of my childhood where we cooked together in the kitchen."

Debbie's Dumplings

PREP AND COOK TIME: About 2¼ hours; less time with several people filling dumplings

NOTES: You can prepare through step 2 up to 12 hours ahead; cover and chill. To store up to 3 months, freeze until firm, about 2 hours, then pack airtight in bags. To speed up cooking, use two pans and cook two batches at a time.

MAKES: 4 to 5 dozen; 16 to 20 appetizer servings

- 1   pound **ground turkey**
- 1   **large egg**
- ¾   cup finely chopped **fresh shiitake mushroom caps**
- ¾   cup chopped **napa cabbage**
- ½   cup chopped **water chestnuts**
- ½   cup thinly sliced **green onions**
- 1   tablespoon **cornstarch**
- 2   teaspoons grated **fresh ginger**
      About ¼ cup **soy sauce**
- 1   tablespoon **oyster sauce** (or more soy sauce)
- 2   tablespoons **dry white wine** or gin
- ½   teaspoon **salt**
- ½   teaspoon **sugar**
- ¼   teaspoon **ground white pepper**
      About 60 **gyoza** or potsticker **wrappers** (10 to 32 oz.; varies with thickness)
- 3   to 6 tablespoons **vegetable oil**
      Rice vinegar
      Chili oil

1. In a bowl, mix turkey, egg, mushrooms, cabbage, water chestnuts, green onions, cornstarch, ginger, 3 tablespoons soy sauce, oyster sauce, wine, salt, sugar, and pepper until well blended.

2. To assemble each dumpling, fill a small bowl with water. Place one wrapper on a flat surface; cover remaining wrappers with plastic wrap to keep pliable. Place a scant tablespoon of filling in center of wrapper. With your fingers, moisten edge of wrapper all the way around with water, then bring opposite sides together over filling and pinch edges together only in the center. On front side of dumpling, make two pleats on each side of center, folding to the center, and press all edges to seal (see photos at right). Set dumpling, seam side up so dumpling sits flat, on a lightly floured baking sheet. Cover with plastic wrap while you fill remaining wrappers (see notes).

3. To cook each batch, set a 10- to 12-inch nonstick frying pan over medium-high heat (see notes). When hot, coat pan bottom with 1 tablespoon vegetable oil. Set dumplings, seam up and slightly apart, in a single layer in pan. Cook until bottoms are golden brown, 3 to 5 minutes. Add ⅓ cup water, cover pan tightly, reduce heat to medium-low, and cook until filling is no longer pink in the center (cut to test), 3 to 6 minutes (10 to 11 minutes if frozen). Uncover and, if there is still liquid in pan, continue cooking over medium-high heat until the liquid has evaporated.

4. Using a wide spatula, transfer dumplings to a heatproof platter. Serve, or cover and keep warm in a 200° oven. Repeat to cook remaining dumplings.

5. Serve with soy sauce, rice vinegar, and chili oil for dipping.

Per serving: 101 cal., 36% (36 cal.) from fat; 4.7 g protein; 4 g fat (0.8 g sat.); 9.3 g carbo (0.1 g fiber); 384 mg sodium; 27 mg chol.

THREE EASY STEPS

How to make the dumplings

1. Place 1 scant tablespoon filling in center of wrapper. Moisten wrapper edge with water.

2. Bring opposite sides of wrapper together over filling and pinch together only in center.

3. On dumpling's top, fold two pleats toward center on each side of center; press edges to seal.

Sesame Cabbage Salad

PREP TIME: About 20 minutes, plus at least 1 hour to chill

NOTES: Roasted sesame seeds are sold in some super-markets and in Asian grocery stores. If you can't find them, toast your own: stir in a frying pan over medium heat until golden, 5 to 6 minutes. If desired, assemble salad in a glass bowl to show off the colorful layers.

MAKES: 6 to 8 servings

- 1 **English cucumber** (1 lb.)
- 1 cup thinly slivered **red onion**

  Sesame dressing (recipe follows)
- 4 cups finely shredded **napa cabbage** (8 oz.)
- 4 cups finely shredded **red cabbage** (8 oz.)
- ⅓ cup thinly sliced **green onions**
- ¼ cup chopped **fresh cilantro**
- 2 tablespoons **roasted sesame seeds** (see notes)

1. Rinse and thinly slice cucumber. In a bowl, mix cucumber, onion, and sesame dressing. Cover and chill at least 1 hour or up to 1 day.

2. Up to 1 hour before serving, layer napa cabbage and red cabbage in a large bowl (see notes). Pour marinated cucumber mixture over the top. Sprinkle with green onions, cilantro, and sesame seeds. Just before serving, mix well.

Per serving: 86 cal., 55% (47 cal.) from fat; 1.8 g protein; 5.2 g fat (0.7 g sat.); 9.3 g carbo (1.9 g fiber); 227 mg sodium; 0 mg chol.

Sesame dressing. In a small bowl or 1-cup glass measure, mix ½ cup **rice vinegar**, 2 tablespoons **sugar**, 1 tablespoon **vegetable oil**, 1 tablespoon **Asian** (toasted) **sesame oil**, ¾ teaspoon **salt**, and ¼ teaspoon **ground white pepper**. Makes about ¾ cup.

Chinese Broccoli

PREP AND COOK TIME: About 15 minutes

NOTES: Chinese broccoli is slightly more bitter than the common variety and has smaller florets. It's sold in some supermarkets and in Asian grocery stores.

MAKES: 6 to 8 servings

1. Rinse 1 to 1½ pounds **Chinese broccoli** (*gai lan*) or regular broccoli (see notes). Pull off and discard any yellow or damaged leaves; trim off and discard stem ends. If stalks have a tough, fibrous skin, peel it off. If stalks are thicker than ½ inch, cut lengthwise to that size. Cut stalks, including leaves and florets, into 2- to 3-inch lengths.

2. In a 5- to 6-quart covered pan over high heat, bring about 2 quarts **water** to a boil. Add broccoli and cook, uncovered, just until barely tender to bite, 3 to 5 minutes. Drain. Pour onto a platter.

3. In a small pitcher or bowl, mix 2 tablespoons **soy sauce** and 2 teaspoons **Asian** (toasted) **sesame oil.** Drizzle over broccoli.

Per serving: 23 cal., 52% (12 cal.) from fat; 1.4 g protein; 1.3 g fat (0.2 g sat.); 2.4 g carbo (1.1 g fiber); 268 mg sodium; 0 mg chol.

Pair two-tone layered cabbage salad with dumplings; Chinese broccoli goes well with won ton soup.

Turkey-Shrimp Won Ton

PREP TIME: About 1 hour, faster if several people fill won ton

NOTES: You can assemble the won ton up to 5 hours before making soup; cover and chill. To store up to 6 months, freeze on baking sheets until firm, about 2 hours, then transfer to heavy plastic bags.

MAKES: About 4½ dozen

- 8 ounces **ground turkey**
- 4 ounces **shelled, deveined shrimp,** rinsed and finely chopped
- ¼ cup finely chopped **water chestnuts**
- 2 tablespoons **soy sauce**
- 1 tablespoon **dry white wine** or gin
- 1 teaspoon grated **fresh ginger**
- ½ teaspoon **salt**
- ¼ teaspoon **ground white pepper**
  About 54 **won ton skins** (8 to 12 oz.)
  About 1 tablespoon beaten **egg**

1. In a bowl, mix turkey, shrimp, water chestnuts, soy sauce, wine, ginger, salt, and pepper until well blended.

2. Place one won ton skin on a flat surface; cover remaining skins with a damp towel or plastic wrap to keep pliable. Mound 1 teaspoon filling near lower corner of skin. Fold that corner over filling and roll to tuck point under mound (see photos at left). Moisten the two corners nearest you with beaten egg; pull them toward you and overlap them in front of filling (back corner should point up). Pinch together firmly to seal. Repeat with remaining skins, placing filled won ton slightly apart on lightly floured or cooking parchment–lined 12- by 15-inch baking sheets; cover with plastic wrap (see notes).

3. Cook as directed for won ton noodle soup (recipe at right).

Per won ton: 22 cal., 16% (3.6 cal.) from fat; 1.6 g protein; 0.4 g fat (0.1 g sat.); 2.6 g carbo (0.1 g fiber); 91 mg sodium; 7.8 mg chol.

Won Ton Noodle Soup

PREP AND COOK TIME: About 30 minutes

NOTES: Fresh Chinese noodles are sold in the refrigerator section; if not available, use fresh angel hair pasta.

MAKES: 6 to 8 servings

- 2½ to 3 quarts fat-skimmed **chicken broth**
  About 2 tablespoons **oyster sauce** or soy sauce
  About 1 tablespoon **Asian** (toasted) **sesame oil**
- 1 package (1 lb.) **fresh thin Chinese noodles** (see notes)
  About 4½ dozen **fresh** or frozen **turkey-shrimp won ton** (recipe at left)
- ½ cup thinly sliced **green onions**
- ½ cup coarsely chopped **fresh cilantro**
  Ground white pepper

1. In a 4- to 5-quart covered pan over high heat, bring broth to a boil, then reduce heat to low and keep hot. In a 6- to 8-quart covered pan over high heat, bring 3 quarts water to a boil. Meanwhile, in each of six to eight large, deep bowls, place about 1 teaspoon oyster sauce and ½ teaspoon sesame oil.

2. When water boils, add noodles. Stir to separate; cook just until barely tender to bite, about 2 minutes. Drain.

3. Add 3 to 4 quarts water to unwashed pan; cover and bring to a boil over high heat. Meanwhile, with chopsticks or tongs, divide noodles evenly among bowls; cover with foil to keep warm.

4. When water is boiling, add won ton; stir to separate and cook until filling is no longer pink in the center (cut to test), 3 to 4 minutes (6 minutes if frozen). With a large, flat wire strainer or slotted spoon, lift won ton out and divide evenly among bowls.

5. Ladle hot broth over won ton and noodles. Sprinkle servings with green onions and cilantro. Offer white pepper and more oyster sauce to add to taste.

Per serving: 378 cal., 14% (53 cal.) from fat; 28 g protein; 5.9 g fat (1 g sat.); 50 g carbo (1.9 g fiber); 903 mg sodium; 94 mg chol. ◆

How to make the won ton

1. Mound 1 teaspoon filling near lower corner of won ton skin. Fold that corner over filling.

2. Roll won ton to tuck point under mound. Moisten two corners nearest you.

3. Pull the two corners toward you and overlap one with the other in front of filling (back corner should point up). Pinch to seal.

Bittersweet romance

Dark chocolate desserts are the ultimate indulgence

By Linda Lau Anusasananan and Charity Ferreira
Photographs by James Carrier
Food styling by Karen Shinto

Thin slabs of crisp chocolate praline add an untraditional garnish to a dense chocolate crème brûlée.

It has been the subject of lore and the object of cravings for centuries. Historical and fictional notables from Montezuma to Harry Potter have self-medicated with the stuff to great effect. Chocolate has a power to captivate unlike any other food, and its heady hold shows no signs of abating: our taste for chocolate is growing even darker and more complex.

High-quality dark chocolate is more widely available than ever, from imported standbys like Lindt and Valrhona to domestically produced Guittard (which now offers single-bean varietal chocolates) and Scharffen Berger. Dark chocolates are meant to be savored for their deliciously bitter underlying citrus, caramel, or tobaccolike notes. The same subtle flavors can elevate baked goods; choose a chocolate for baking that you enjoy eating.

These four spectacular desserts—from crème brûlée with a chocolate candy top to a chocolate-caramel cake with a gooey center—demonstrate the allure of chocolate's dark side.

Chocolate Crème Brûlée

PREP AND COOK TIME: About 1 hour, plus 1 to 1¼ hours to chill

NOTES: Karen Krasne, creator of Extraordinary Desserts in San Diego, stretches the definition of crème brûlée with this dark chocolate custard capped with a chunk of crisp chocolate praline. The custard can be made through step 5 up to 2 days ahead; cover and chill.

MAKES: 6 to 8 servings

- 1 **vanilla bean**
- 1 cup **whipping cream**
- 1 cup **milk**
- 6 **large egg** yolks (at room temperature)
- ¾ cup **sugar**

Raspberries, mint, and whipped cream turn a fudgy brownie into an elegant dessert.

- 4 ounces *each* **semisweet** and **bittersweet chocolate** (or 8 oz. of semisweet), chopped
- 1 tablespoon **Amaretto** or other almond-flavored liqueur
- 1 tablespoon **Kahlua** or other coffee-flavored liqueur

  Chocolate praline (recipe follows)

1. Cut vanilla bean in half lengthwise; scrape seeds into a 2- to 3-quart pan. Add vanilla pod, cream, and milk. Stir occasionally over medium-high heat until mixture just begins to boil, 14 to 18 minutes.

2. In a bowl, whisk together egg yolks and sugar. Heat chocolate in a small, microwave-safe glass bowl in a microwave oven at half-power (50%) until soft, 1½ to 2 minutes. Stir until smooth.

3. Lift vanilla pod from cream mixture; rinse and dry for another use or discard. Whisk about ½ cup of the hot cream mixture into egg mixture, then whisk egg mixture into remaining cream mixture. Add hot melted chocolate (if it has cooled to room temperature, reheat briefly in microwave oven just until hot to touch; do not overheat). Pour mixture into a blender and whirl until no chocolate flecks remain. Pour through a fine strainer into a 1- to 2-quart glass measure. Stir in Amaretto and Kahlua.

4. Set six to eight soufflé cups, ramekins, or teacups (½ to ¾ cup) in a 9- by 13-inch baking pan. Fill cups equally with chocolate mixture. Set pan in a 300° regular or convection oven and carefully pour about 1 inch of boiling water into pan around cups.

5. Bake until centers of custards barely jiggle when pan is gently shaken, 30 to 35 minutes. With a slotted spatula, lift cups out. Chill until custards are cold, 1 to 1¼ hours (see notes).

6. Garnish each crème brûlée with a large chunk of chocolate praline. Serve any remaining pieces of praline alongside.

Per serving: 365 cal., 57% (207 cal.) from fat; 5.3 g protein; 23 g fat (13 g sat.); 39 g carbo (1.2 g fiber); 32 mg sodium; 197 mg chol.

Chocolate Praline

PREP AND COOK TIME: About 15 minutes, plus 10 minutes to cool

NOTES: You can make this praline up to 1 week ahead; store airtight at room temperature.

MAKES: 6 to 8 servings

1. Place ¼ cup **slivered almonds** in a 9-inch pie pan. Bake in a 300° regular or convection oven, shaking pan once, until nuts are golden, 10 to 12 minutes. Coat a 12-inch square of foil

1. Chop chocolate into about $\frac{1}{2}$-inch chunks; you should have about 2 cups. In a small, microwave-safe bowl, combine half the chocolate and the butter. Heat in a microwave oven on half-power (50%) just until chocolate is soft and butter is melted, 1 to $1\frac{1}{2}$ minutes. Stir until mixture is smooth. Let stand until just warm to touch.

2. In a bowl, with a wooden spoon, beat eggs, sugar, salt, and vanilla until smooth. Add chocolate mixture and stir until well blended. Add flour, about a third at a time, stirring after each addition just until blended. Add remaining chopped chocolate and mix just until chunks are evenly distributed.

3. Line bottom and sides of a 9-inch square baking pan with cooking parchment, draping over rim a little. Scrape batter into pan; spread level.

4. Bake in a 325° regular or 300° convection oven just until surface develops a thin crust (like the delicate layer of ice that forms on freezing water) and a fingertip pressed very gently in the center leaves a soft impression, 20 to 25 minutes; take care not to overbake.

5. Cool completely in pan on a rack, at least 1 hour. Lift brownie out on parchment, peel off parchment, and set brownie on a board. Cut into 8 squares or wedges or 16 triangles (see notes).

Per serving: 443 cal., 53% (234 cal.) from fat; 6.1 g protein; 26 g fat (14 g sat.); 54 g carbo (1.1 g fiber); 213 mg sodium; 111 mg chol.

Chocolate-Banana Cream Tartlets

PREP AND COOK TIME: About 1 hour, plus at least $1\frac{1}{2}$ hours to chill

NOTES: Crème fraîche adds a tangy edge to the whipped cream, but if it's unavailable, omit it and use $1\frac{1}{4}$ cups whipping cream. The crusts can be made through step 2 up to 1 week ahead; cover airtight and freeze, then uncover to bake. The chocolate mixture (steps 4 and 5) can be made up to 2 days ahead; cover airtight and chill. Use a vegetable peeler to make the thin chocolate curls for garnish, or sprinkle with unsweetened cocoa or chocolate sprinkles.

MAKES: Six 4-inch tartlets

1¼ cups **all-purpose flour**

¾ cup **sugar**

¼ cup **unsweetened cocoa**

¾ teaspoon **salt**

½ cup (¼ lb.) **butter,** cut into chunks

1 **large egg**

5 ounces **bittersweet chocolate,** finely chopped

Top chocolate-banana cream tartlets with white or dark chocolate curls or just a sprinkle of cocoa powder.

lightly with **vegetable oil** (about 1 teaspoon).

2. In an 8- to 10-inch frying pan over medium-high heat, combine ¼ cup **sugar,** 2 tablespoons **butter,** 1 tablespoon **corn syrup,** and 1½ teaspoons **milk.** Stir occasionally until mixture is bubbly and golden, about 5 minutes. Add 1½ teaspoons **unsweetened cocoa** and stir until smooth, then stir in toasted almonds. Pour mixture onto oiled foil and spread about ¼ inch thick. Let cool until solid, about 10 minutes. Break praline into 6 to 8 large chunks.

Per serving: 88 cal., 58% (51 cal.) from fat; 1 g protein; 5.7 g fat (2.1 g sat.); 9.3 g carbo (0.3 g fiber); 33 mg sodium; 7.9 mg chol.

Dark Chocolate-Chunk Brownies

PREP AND COOK TIME: About 40 minutes, plus at least 1 hour to cool

NOTES: Michael Recchiuti, a San Francisco chocolate visionary, prefers to make these moist brownies with a distinct chocolate such as L'Harmonie, a 64 percent dark chocolate blend available from E. Guittard consumer sales (800/468-2462). Serve wedges or squares topped with lightly sweetened, softly whipped cream, chopped fresh mint, and fresh raspberries; or crown pieces with vanilla ice cream and a drizzle of caramel sauce.

MAKES: 8 servings

10 ounces **bittersweet chocolate** (see notes)

½ cup (¼ lb.) **butter,** cut into ½-inch chunks

3 **large eggs**

1 cup **sugar**

¼ teaspoon **salt**

½ teaspoon **vanilla**

¾ cup **all-purpose flour**

$2\frac{1}{4}$ cups **milk**

$\frac{1}{4}$ cup **cornstarch**

4 **large egg** yolks

2 teaspoons **vanilla**

$\frac{3}{4}$ cup **crème fraîche** (see notes)

$\frac{1}{2}$ cup **whipping cream**

2 **ripe bananas** (about 12 oz. total)

Chocolate curls (see notes)

1. In a food processor or a bowl, whirl or mix flour, $\frac{1}{4}$ cup sugar, cocoa, and $\frac{1}{4}$ teaspoon salt until blended. Whirl in butter, or rub in with a pastry cutter or your fingers, until well blended. Add whole egg and whirl or mix just until dough starts to come together in a ball.

2. Scrape dough out onto a well-floured board and knead briefly to bring together. Divide into six equal pieces. With well-floured hands, press a piece of dough evenly over bottom and up sides of each of six 4-inch tartlet pans with removable rims. Place pans on a baking sheet and freeze until firm, at least 30 minutes (see notes).

3. Place baking sheet with tartlet pans directly into a 350° regular or convection oven (do not thaw). Bake until the crusts feel dry to the touch, 15 to 18 minutes. Cool in pans on a rack for 10 minutes, then remove pan rims and gently loosen crusts from pan bottoms with the tip of a sharp knife. Set crusts on rack to cool completely.

4. Meanwhile, in a 2- to 3-quart pan over medium-high heat, bring about 1 inch water to a boil. Place chopped chocolate in a bowl, remove pan from heat, and set bowl over water. Stir occasionally until chocolate is melted and smooth.

5. In a 3- to 4-quart pan over medium heat, whisk 6 tablespoons sugar into milk; bring just to a simmer, stirring often. In a small bowl, whisk cornstarch into egg yolks. Whisk about $\frac{1}{2}$ cup hot milk mixture into yolk mixture, then whisk yolk mixture back into milk mixture. Stir constantly until simmering, then cook, stirring often, until very thick, about 1 minute. Stir in melted chocolate and vanilla. Scrape into a bowl and place a layer of plastic wrap directly on surface. Chill until cold, at least 1 hour (see notes).

6. In a bowl, with a mixer on high speed, whip crème fraîche, cream, and remaining 2 tablespoons sugar until soft peaks form. Peel bananas and cut into $\frac{1}{4}$-inch-thick slices.

7. Spread a generous $\frac{1}{4}$ cup chilled chocolate mixture in the bottom of each tartlet shell. Top with 6 to 8 banana slices (about a third of a banana per tartlet). Spread about 3 tablespoons more chocolate mixture over bananas in each tartlet to cover. Mound about $\frac{1}{3}$ cup whipped cream mixture on each tartlet. Garnish with chocolate curls (see notes). Serve immediately or chill, uncovered, up to 4 hours.

Per tartlet: 785 cal., 56% (441 cal.) from fat; 13 g protein; 49 g fat (28 g sat.); 80 g carbo (2.9 g fiber); 536 mg sodium; 279 mg chol.

Molten Chocolate-Caramel Cake

PREP AND COOK TIME: About 1 hour

NOTES: To have a molten center, this cake should be served immediately, while it's warm. It still has a delicious fudgy texture, though, if made (up to 1 day) ahead; cool cake completely, wrap loosely in plastic wrap, and store at room temperature. Reheat the cooled cake in a 300° oven for 10 minutes just before serving.

MAKES: 6 to 8 servings

7 ounces **bittersweet chocolate,** finely chopped

2 cups plus 2 tablespoons **granulated sugar**

1 cup **whipping cream**

$\frac{1}{4}$ cup ($\frac{1}{8}$ lb.) **butter**

4 **large eggs,** separated

3 tablespoons **all-purpose flour**

Powdered sugar

1. In a bowl set over a pan of barely simmering water (bottom of bowl should not touch water), stir chocolate until melted and smooth. Remove pan from heat but leave bowl over water to keep chocolate warm.

2. In a 3- to 4-quart pan over medium heat, stir 2 cups granulated sugar in 1 cup water until sugar is dissolved. Increase heat to high and boil without stirring until mixture is a deep caramel color, 15 to 20 minutes. When sugar begins to brown around the edges of the pan, swirl pan gently to ensure the mixture caramelizes evenly. Remove from heat and immediately add cream and butter; whisk until smooth. Remove 1 cup caramel sauce and reserve.

3. Remove chocolate from over water and whisk in egg yolks, then whisk mixture into caramel in pan. Whisk in flour.

4. In a bowl, with a mixer on high speed, beat egg whites with remaining 2 tablespoons sugar just until soft peaks form. Fold a third of the egg whites into chocolate mixture, then gently fold in remaining whites until no streaks remain. Scrape mixture into a buttered and floured 8-inch cake pan.

5. Bake in a 325° regular or convection oven until a wooden skewer inserted 2 inches from the side of the pan comes out clean but center of cake is still wet, 20 to 25 minutes.

6. Cool cake in pan on a rack for 5 minutes. Run a knife between cake and pan rim. Invert cake onto a plate, place another plate on top, and turn cake upright. Dust with powdered sugar; serve warm (see notes) with caramel sauce.

Per serving: 527 cal., 46% (243 cal.) from fat; 6 g protein; 27 g fat (15 g sat.); 72 g carbo (0.7 g fiber); 108 mg sodium; 157 mg chol. ◆

For more great chocolate recipes, go to *www.sunset.com/food/chocolate.html*

All about chocolate

BEAN VARIETY AND ORIGIN: Most chocolate is made from a blend of cocoa beans from all over the world. Forastero, the base bean of most blends, is grown in Africa, Brazil, and Asia; it makes up 90 percent of the world's cocoa supply. Now, however, some premium chocolates specify bean variety and origin. Two prestigious tree and bean varieties: Criollo, a prized bean from South and Central America and Southeast Asia; and Trinitario (a hybrid of Criollo and Forastero), originally from Trinidad but now grown in other regions too, such as Venezuela, Ecuador, and Colombia.

PERCENTAGE OF CACAO: Indicates the amount of cocoa mass (or chocolate liquor) plus cocoa butter (the natural fat in the cocoa bean). The cocoa mass itself is naturally made up of about half cocoa butter and half dry cocoa solids, but since the ratio varies among beans, two brands labeled 70 percent cacao may not have the same percentage of cocoa butter. One factor that *is* consistent, however, is that most of the remaining content is sugar, so the higher the cacao percentage, the less sugar in the chocolate.

BITTERSWEET CHOCOLATE: Often called dark chocolate. Bittersweet chocolate must contain at least 35 percent chocolate liquor, and many brands now far exceed that. These chocolates (mostly in the 60- to 75-percent range) have intense flavor and, as the name implies, are not very sweet.

SEMISWEET CHOCOLATE: Often labeled dark, sweet chocolate. FDA identification standards don't distinguish between bittersweet and semisweet chocolate, but generally semisweet is slightly sweeter and has a little less intense chocolate flavor.

Pressed for success

Crisp cafe-style sandwiches make quick meals

By Charity Ferreira

Photographs by Maren Caruso

Pressed sandwiches appear on restaurant and cafe menus in myriad incarnations, from the Italian panini to the Cuban. No wonder—there's nothing quite like toasted bread and rich, melting fillings flattened under a hot press. We pressed our favorite cheeses and other tasty ingredients between a variety of breads to create delicious alternatives to standard grilled cheese. From a sophisticated combination of chocolate and marmalade on sourdough to a crunchy baguette filled with salty prosciutto and oozing teleme cheese, these sandwiches will always impress.

Pressing pointers

- **Pull out some of the middle** of rolls or baguettes before assembling sandwiches.

- **Go easy on fillings;** piling your sandwich too high will cause the filling to squeeze out as the sandwich is compressed.

- **Heat your press on the highest setting** (or heat a dry nonstick frying pan over medium heat) for several minutes before pressing sandwich. Use care with a metal waffle iron, as its exterior will get very hot.

- **Flatten the sandwich slightly** with your hands before placing it in the press.

- **Place sandwich on press** and lower lid when press is hot (in most cases, the lid won't close all the way).

- **Press the lid occasionally while toasting** to compact the sandwich; toast until bread or roll is richly browned, 2 to 6 minutes.

- **Weight the sandwich,** if using a frying pan, by placing a cake pan (smaller than the diameter of your frying pan) over the sandwich and placing a full can or other weight on the cake pan. Turn sandwich with a spatula midway through cooking time; replace the cake pan and weight.

Grill yourself a stack of sandwiches. From the top: Gruyère melt; roasted pepper–fontina panini; bacon and tomatillo; prosciutto, teleme, and fig spread; tuna on focaccia.

Gruyère Melt with Apples

Spread about ¹/₂ tablespoon **honey mustard** on each of 2 slices of **walnut bread;** top one of the slices with a quarter (about 2 oz.) of a **tart apple** such as Granny Smith, thinly sliced, and 2 to 3 slices **Gruyère** or Swiss **cheese** (1 oz.). Place second slice of bread, mustard side down, over filling. Toast as directed in "Pressing Pointers" (at left), about 3 minutes. Makes 1.

Per sandwich: 473 cal., 32% (153 cal.) from fat; 17 g protein; 17 g fat (6.4 g sat.); 62 g carbo (1.2 g fiber); 748 mg sodium; 31 mg chol.

Roasted Pepper–Fontina Panini

Slice a purchased **Italian-style panini** or other sandwich roll (4 oz.) in half; pull out middle of roll. Place about 3 slices **fontina cheese** (2 oz.) on the bottom half of the roll; top with about ¹/₄ cup drained **canned roasted red pepper** strips and 3 rinsed **fresh basil**

leaves. Sprinkle with **salt** and **pepper** and place top of roll over filling. Toast as directed at left, about 6 minutes. Makes 1.

Per sandwich: 373 cal., 43% (162 cal.) from fat; 20 g protein; 18 g fat (11 g sat.); 35 g carbo (1.7 g fiber); 840 mg sodium; 66 mg chol.

Cuban-style Sandwich with Bacon and Tomatillo

Husk, rinse, and thinly slice 1 **tomatillo** (about 2 oz.). Place about 2 slices crisp cooked **bacon** (2 oz. total) on a slice of **country-style white bread** or other white sandwich bread; top with tomatillo slices. Sprinkle with **salt** and **pepper** and top with 3 slices **white cheddar cheese** (1 oz. total). Place another slice of bread over filling. Toast as directed at left, about 3 minutes. Makes 1.

Per sandwich: 357 cal., 45% (162 cal.) from fat; 16 g protein; 18 g fat (8.7 g sat.); 32 g carbo (2.4 g fiber); 683 mg sodium; 41 mg chol.

A panini grill presses sandwiches perfectly.

Spread spiced pumpkin butter and fresh chèvre on egg bread for a stylish midmorning snack.

Equipment tips

We found several good tools in our quest for perfect pressed sandwiches. The **Krups Panini Grill** ($80; available online at *www.napastyle.com*) pressed and toasted the sandwiches two at a time, leaving appealing grill marks on the bread. We got mixed results from a lidded electric grill such as the miniature **George Foreman Grilling Machine** ($20 at Target and other stores) and from an electric sandwich-maker such as the **Salton Sandwich Maker** (about $20 at *www.macys.com*), which seals the edges of the sandwich. Both appliances toasted the bread well but required pressure to compact the sandwiches evenly.

If you don't have specialized equipment, some waffle irons have removable grids that can be turned over to reveal a flat side that is perfect for pressing. We also tried standard waffle irons, which did compact and toast the sandwiches but left square indentations. Rolls and sturdy breads held up to this better than soft sliced breads. A nonstick frying pan with a weighted cake pan (see "Pressing Pointers" on page 36) placed on top of the sandwich works well too.

Prosciutto, Teleme, and Fig Spread on a Baguette

Cut a **baguette** (about 8 oz.) crosswise into thirds; cut each piece nearly in half horizontally. Pull out middle of bread. Spread bottom of each piece with about 1½ tablespoons **fig spread** (recipe follows) or fig jam. Top with 2 to 3 slices **prosciutto** (1 oz. total), then spread other side with **teleme cheese** or brie (about 2 oz.). Close baguette over filling. Toast as directed on page 36, about 4 minutes. Makes 3.

Per sandwich: 388 cal., 44% (171 cal.) from fat; 22 g protein; 19 g fat (7.3 g sat.); 35 g carbo (2.8 g fiber); 1,091 mg sodium; 43 mg chol.

Fig spread. In a 3- to 4-quart pan, combine 1 cup coarsely chopped **dried black mission figs** (stems removed), ½ cup **balsamic vinegar**, ½ cup **water**, 2 tablespoons **sugar**, 2 tablespoons chopped **shallot**, 1 tablespoon grated **lemon** peel, and ¼ teaspoon **salt**; bring to a boil over high heat. Reduce heat, cover, and simmer until figs are slightly soft, about 5 minutes. Remove from heat and let stand, covered, until cool, about 40 minutes. Whirl in a blender or food processor until smooth. Makes about 1 cup.

Per tablespoon: 40 cal., 2% (0.9 cal.) from fat; 0.4 g protein; 0.1 g fat (0 g sat.); 10 g carbo (1.2 g fiber); 38 mg sodium; 0 mg chol.

Tuna on Tomato Focaccia

Slice purchased **tomato focaccia** (1-lb. piece; available in the deli section of most supermarkets) into six 4-inch squares. Spread about 1 tablespoon purchased **tapenade** on tomato side of each of 3 pieces; top each with about 2 tablespoons (⅓ of a drained 6-oz. can) **oil-packed tuna** and ¼ cup rinsed and dried **arugula leaves**. Top with a second piece of focaccia, tomato side down. Toast as directed on page 36, about 6 minutes. Makes 3.

Per sandwich: 577 cal., 34% (198 cal.) from fat; 29 g protein; 22 g fat (3.5 g sat.); 72 g carbo (8 g fiber); 1,830 mg sodium; 9.5 mg chol.

Pumpkin Butter and Goat Cheese on Egg Bread

Spread 1 to 2 tablespoons **pumpkin butter** (available in the jam or preserves section of well-stocked supermarkets) or apple butter on one slice of **egg bread**, such as challah (or use a 3-oz. brioche roll, sliced in half). Spread a second slice with 1 to 2 tablespoons **fresh chèvre** (goat cheese). Press slices together. Toast as directed on page 36, about 3 minutes. Makes 1.

Per sandwich: 160 cal., 24% (39 cal.) from fat; 5.6 g protein; 4.3 g fat (1.9 g sat.); 23 g carbo (1 g fiber); 240 mg sodium; 26 mg chol.

Chocolate, Ricotta, and Marmalade on Sourdough

Spread about 2 teaspoons **orange marmalade** on each of 2 slices **country-style sourdough bread** or sourdough sandwich bread (about 3 by 4½ in.; about ½ in. thick). Spread one of the slices with 2 tablespoons **ricotta cheese** and sprinkle with 2 tablespoons chopped **bittersweet chocolate**. Place second slice of bread, marmalade side down, over filling. Toast as directed on page 36, about 6 minutes. Makes 1.

Per sandwich: 422 cal., 30% (126 cal.) from fat; 12 g protein; 14 g fat (7 g sat.); 66 g carbo (2.8 g fiber); 551 mg sodium; 16 mg chol. ◆

Rim of square pan catches overflow glaze on rich sticky buns.

Square deal

We thought we'd seen just about every baking pan imaginable. Round, fluted, tube, loaf—our test kitchen cupboards are jammed with them all. But it's time to make some space, because we've found a new obsession: a springform pan from Kaiser Bakeware. Of course, we've used springform pans before, but this one is different: it's square. The new shape makes it great for bar cookies, brownies, and cakes, tarts,

The new shape of springform: square.

or quiches that you want to cut into squares to serve a crowd. (The seam between rim and base is not watertight, though, so don't use a very thin batter or a water bath.)

It's just the thing for easy sticky buns, which rise to fill the square pan perfectly. We pour a rich brown-sugar glaze over the top of our sticky buns (instead of caramelizing sugar on the bottom) to take advantage of the lip on the pan base, which catches stray drips. And because the springform is nonstick, cleanup is easy—no sticky sauce welded to the pan. In our tests, eating the extra glaze with a spoon was our *second* favorite thing about this recipe—just behind the pleasure of acquiring new bakeware. *$40. Available at Sur La Table and Williams-Sonoma and through Kaiser Bakeware (www.kaiserbakeware.com or 800/966-3009).*

Rum-Raisin Sticky Buns

PREP AND COOK TIME: About 1½ hours, plus 1 hour to soak raisins
MAKES: 16 sticky buns

- ¼ cup plus 2 tablespoons **dark rum**
- 1 cup **raisins**
  About ½ cup (¼ lb.) **butter**
- 1½ cups **pecan halves**
- 1 cup firmly packed **brown sugar**
- 2 teaspoons **ground cinnamon**
- ¼ teaspoon **salt**
- 1 pound **frozen bread dough,** thawed
- 1 **large egg,** beaten to blend with 1 tablespoon water
- ¼ cup **dark corn syrup**

1. In a bowl, pour ¼ cup rum over raisins; let stand until slightly plumped, at least 1 hour. Butter a 9-inch square springform or regular baking pan.

2. In a food processor, whirl 1 cup pecans, ¼ cup butter, ¼ cup brown sugar, cinnamon, salt, and raisins with rum until finely chopped.

3. On a floured surface, with a floured rolling pin, roll bread dough into a 16- by 8-inch rectangle. (If dough springs back, let rest for 5 minutes, then roll again.) Spread rum-raisin filling over dough, leaving a ½-inch margin bare along one long edge.

4. Starting at opposite edge, roll dough around filling into a cylinder. Brush egg mixture over bare edge, then pinch against cylinder to seal. Cut off ragged ends, then cut cylinder into 16 equal rounds. Space rolls evenly, each on a cut side, in pan. Cover with plastic wrap and let stand until doubled, about 40 minutes.

5. Uncover and brush rolls lightly with egg mixture. Bake in a 350° regular or convection oven until browned, 25 to 30 minutes. Remove pan rim (if using a regular pan, invert rolls onto a wire rack, then invert again onto a rimmed plate).

6. In a 1½- to 2-quart pan over medium-high heat, combine remaining ¾ cup brown sugar, ¼ cup butter, and ½ cup pecans with corn syrup. Stir until mixture is thick and bubbling, 3 to 5 minutes. Stir in remaining 2 tablespoons rum. Pour and scrape evenly over warm buns. If excess glaze pools at base, spoon over tops of buns. Serve warm.

Per sticky bun: 303 cal., 45% (135 cal.) from fat; 4.1 g protein; 15 g fat (4.6 g sat.); 42 g carbo (1.6 g fiber); 260 mg sodium; 29 mg chol.

—Kate Washington

Perfect potatoes

Potatoes are subject to water woes. When you boil them unpeeled, their skins tend to break and let water soak in, making this already humble vegetable mushy and unattractive. To avoid waterlogged spuds, don't boil them at all; cook them gently in water slightly below the temperature of an active boil. The potatoes take a little longer to cook, but in most cases you get a watertight casing and succulent interior. Use this method to discover what a treat carefully cooked potatoes are in their skins, with butter and parsley,

or how good a warm potato salad can be when the only liquids in it are flavorful oil and vinegar, not water the potatoes have absorbed.

Slow-cooked potatoes. Scrub **thin-skinned white or red potatoes** (1 to 2 in. wide). Place them, no more than two layers deep, in a pan and cover them by about 1 inch of water. Set over high heat; just before water boils, reduce heat to maintain water temperature at 185° to 195° (when a few bubbles pop up from pan bottom regularly but surface of water is smooth). Cook, uncovered, just until potatoes are tender when pierced: for

1-inch diameter, about 25 minutes; 1½ inches, 35 to 40 minutes; and 2 inches, about 50 minutes. Serve, or turn off heat and leave in water up to 30 minutes.

—*Jerry Anne Di Vecchio*

Brussels sprouts rate more than a holiday appearance. They thrive throughout the cool season; enjoy them now, in their prime.

Sprouts undone

Brussels sprouts are one of winter's sleeper vegetables. It's all in the cooking: undress the sprouts, peeling off the leaves one by one, and sauté them quickly with shallots and herbs to bring out their true sweet, nutty character.

Sautéed Brussels Sprout Leaves

Rinse and drain 12 ounces **brussels sprouts.** Cut about ¼ inch off the stem end of each sprout and begin peeling off the leaves. When difficult to peel farther, trim off another ¼ inch and continue removing leaves. Repeat to peel all leaves from sprouts; discard cores. Set a 10- to 12-inch frying pan over medium-high heat; when hot, add 1 tablespoon **olive oil,** ¼ cup chopped **shallots,** brussels sprout leaves, 2 tablespoons chopped **parsley,** and 1 teaspoon **fresh** or ½ teaspoon dried **thyme** leaves. Stir until sprout leaves are bright green and slightly wilted but still crunchy, about 3 minutes. Add **salt** and **pepper** to taste. Makes 3 or 4 servings. —*Linda Lau Anusasananan*

Winning fruits in Las Vegas

Five years ago, the Master Gardeners of Southern Nevada started a fruit tree orchard on a 1-acre site near Las Vegas. Ever since then, a corps of 15 volunteers has carefully maintained the orchard's 450 fruit trees using organic gardening practices. They have also amassed a wealth of information that can be of great help to desert gardeners, especially those in Nevada's Clark County (Sunset climate zone 11) who want to grow fruits successfully in their own yards. The following varieties are recommended by the master gardeners, based on the trees' performance and productivity in the trial orchard. February is a good month to plant bare-root fruit trees and grapevines; peak harvest months are listed.

APPLES. 'Anna': Large fruit with sweet flesh; August harvest. Plant with 'Dorsett Golden' for cross-pollination.

'Pink Lady': Medium-size fruit with sweet-tart flesh, good fresh or cooked; August. Plant with 'Granny Smith' for cross-pollination.

APRICOTS. 'Blenheim': Medium fruit has very sweet flavor, excellent for drying; late July.

'Gold Kist': Medium fruit has good flavor, bears large crop; early July.

NECTARINES. 'Arctic Star': Medium fruit with sweet white flesh; mid-June.

'Desert Dawn': Medium fruit has excellent flavor; May.

PEACHES. 'Fairtime': Large freestone fruit with sweet white flesh; September.

'Summerset': Large freestone fruit has yellow flesh with excellent flavor; September.

PEARS. 'Hood': Large fruit with sweet flesh; August.

'Kieffer': Medium fruit is excellent for cooking and canning; August.

PLUMS. 'Elephant Heart': Medium fruit with sweet flesh; July.

'Sugar': Small fruit with sweet flesh; July. —*Liz Hartley*

Best wines for battling the winter blues

With all due respect to April, February is undoubtedly the cruelest month. Beat it back with a top-notch dessert wine.

Hogue Late Harvest White Riesling 2001 *(Columbia Valley, WA)*, $8 for 750-ml. bottle. Apricot nectar with grace notes of litchi, vanilla, and spices.

Robert Mondavi Winery Moscato d'Oro 2000 *(Napa Valley)*, $20 for 500-ml. bottle. A surge of beautiful apricot flavor that's very fresh on the palate; don't be afraid to serve it quite cold.

Santa Barbara Winery Late Harvest Sauvignon Blanc 1998 *(Santa Ynez Valley, CA)*, $30 for 375-ml. half-bottle. Gorgeous honey flavors, plus hints of almonds and spice; opulent and irresistible.

Arrowood Select Late Harvest White Riesling 2000 *(Alexander Valley, CA)*, $35 for 375-ml. half-bottle. The essences of peaches and apricots, with just a drizzle of honey flavor.

Chateau St. Jean "Belle Terre Vineyard" Special Select Late Harvest Johannisberg Riesling 2000 *(Alexander Valley, CA)*, $40 for 375-ml. half-bottle. Rich flavors of apricot, peach, caramel, and honey, plus a hint of something exotic and spicy.

—*Karen MacNeil-Fife*

Best martini when in Death Valley

Chemist Tom Malefyt and his colleagues trek there every year and developed this martini to match the setting: hot and dry.

Death Valley Martini. 1. On each of two swizzle sticks, skewer 1 or 2 **pimiento-** or pickled onion–**stuffed green olives**, then 1 **hot chili–stuffed green olive** such as Reese; set a stick in each of two chilled martini glasses. **2.** Pour 1 tablespoon **sweet vermouth** into an ice-filled shaker. **3.** Fill shaker with chilled **Bombay Sapphire dry gin**, cover, and shake just until blended. **4.** Pour into glasses. Let steep 5–15 minutes, according to your taste for heat (sip often to check), then pull off chili-stuffed olive (eat it if you dare).

—*Sara Schneider*

Classic Rockies fare: a cornmeal-coated, savory trout served by Jon Severson and executive sous chef Leo Dominguez).

Mountain trout

DENVER'S BLUE SKY GRILL is dramatic and classically Western—massive stone fireplaces, walls made of logs, and floors fashioned from 100-year-old barn wood. That classicism extends to executive chef Jon Severson's menu: it's pure Rockies, from starters (elk quesadilla, bison chili) to entrées (mountain trout, buffalo rib eye). *1000 Chopper Circle; (303) 405-6090.*

Trout with Browned Butter and Capers

1. On a dinner plate, mix ¼ cup *each* **all-purpose flour** and **yellow cornmeal**, ½ teaspoon **salt**, and ¼ teaspoon **pepper**. Rinse 1 **cleaned, boned whole trout** (8 to 10 oz.), head and tail removed, and pat dry; place in flour mixture and turn to coat.
2. In a 1-quart pan over medium heat, bring ¼ cup (⅛ lb.) **butter** to a simmer; remove from heat. With a spoon, skim off and discard foam, leaving clarified butter behind.
3. Pour 1 tablespoon of clarified butter into a 10- to 12-inch non-stick frying pan over high heat; place trout, skin side down, in pan and cook until browned on the bottom, 2 to 3 minutes. Turn with a wide spatula, reduce heat to medium, and cook until fish is barely opaque but still moist-looking in center of thickest part (cut to test), 2 to 4 minutes longer.
4. Meanwhile, add 1 tablespoon drained **capers** to remaining clarified butter in pan and shake pan often over medium heat until capers pop open, 1 to 2 minutes.
5. Transfer trout, skin down, to a plate. Spoon caper butter over fish and garnish with **lemon** wedges and **parsley** sprigs. Add **salt** and **pepper** to taste. Makes 1 or 2 servings.

—*Linda Lau Anusasananan, Lora J. Finnegan*

Hole-y grail

A quick taste of Seattle's best doughnut shops

By Kate Chynoweth
Photographs by Dan Lamont

Crispy and sweet, golden and tender, a doughnut is the perfect match for a strong cup of coffee. No wonder, then, that Seattle—a city known for good java—has more than its fair share of great doughnut shops. Drawing enthusiastic crowds despite the competition from national chains, each neighborhood hot spot has its own delightful and unique appeal. The independently owned stores listed here are distinguished by their devoted owners, memorable ambience, and, of course, delicious doughnuts.

Daily Dozen Doughnut Co. Owner Barbara Elza started making doughnuts at this lively stand in Pike Place Market 15 years ago, and she fell in love with the job. "It's a big family here," she says. "We know how to have fun." Locals and visitors have a great time watching the "Donut Robot"—a machine invented in the 1930s—turn out fresh, hot miniature doughnuts in plain, sugar, and cinnamon-sugar. The frosted "fancies" tend to disappear quickly. "Kids are stronger than you think," Elza says. "They can really muscle their way to the front." *93 Pike Place Market, #7; (206) 467-7769.*

Family Doughnut Shop. Regulars flock to this hole-in-the-wall shop for tasty doughnuts and friendly banter with owner Tony Oeung and wife Vanna. "It's a pleasure to get to know the customers," says Tony. Of course, the

Lounging is encouraged at Top Pot.

real joy comes from biting into the deep-fried treats he makes fresh every morning. Choose from glazed buttermilk, old-fashioned, and frosted cake doughnuts of every variety, along with fluffy jellies, maple bars, and twists. *2100 N. Northgate Way; (206) 368-9107.*

Sophie's Donuts. Susan Kaplan seeks out the finest ingredients for her doughnuts. The former owner of Seattle's popular Boat Street Cafe, Kaplan recently got into this business with a vision to re-create the doughnuts she loved as a kid. "We use old-fashioned recipes to make the dough from scratch," she says. Visit this tiny shop in Seattle's Eastlake neighborhood for luscious renditions of all the classics, as well as the memorable Bismarck, which is filled with real raspberry jam. True enthusiasts can even sign up for a doughnut-making class. *2238 Eastlake Ave. E.; (206) 323-7132.*

Top Pot. This postmodern designer shop on a quiet, leafy street in Seattle's Capitol Hill neighborhood has lines out the door on weekends. Brothers Mark and Michael Klebeck

opened the place last year with Joel Radin, and all share a nostalgia for the late 1940s; doughnuts are served on vintage plates from that era, and the glass case displays gemlike treats frosted with retro pink or chocolate icing. Old-fashioned cake stands display their newest jelly creation, the Valley Girl Lemon. Watch for their new store, opening next month in downtown Seattle. *609 Summit Ave. E.; (206) 323-7841.* ◆

Toss shrimp and pasta with pesto for a six-ingredient, one-pan dinner.

Midwinter favorites

Readers' recipes tested in *Sunset's* kitchens

Photographs by James Carrier

Shrimp and Pasta with Creamy Pesto Sauce

Nancy Stringer, San Diego

Nancy Stringer uses frozen cooked shrimp and prepared pesto for this easy-to-assemble dish. To thaw shrimp quickly, place under cold running water for 5 minutes.

PREP AND COOK TIME: About 15 minutes

MAKES: 3 to 4 servings

- 12 ounces **dried penne pasta**
- 1 pound **frozen cooked shrimp** (35 to 40 per lb.), thawed (see note above)
- ½ cup **prepared pesto**
- ¼ cup **whipping cream**
- ¼ cup fat-skimmed **chicken broth**
- 3 tablespoons chopped drained **oil-packed dried tomatoes**
- **Salt** and **pepper**

1. In a 4- to 6-quart pan over high heat, bring about 3 quarts water to a boil. Add pasta and cook, stirring occasion- ally, until tender to bite, 7 to 12 min- utes. Drain and return to pan.

2. Add shrimp, pesto, cream, broth, and dried tomatoes to pasta; stir over medium heat until hot and evenly incor- porated, 2 to 3 minutes. Add salt and pepper to taste. Pour into serving dish or divide among individual bowls.

Per serving: 655 cal., 33% (216 cal.) from fat; 39 g protein; 24 g fat (5.9 g sat.); 69 g carbo (2.8 g fiber); 534 mg sodium; 243 mg chol.

Cream of Garlic Soup

Marcia Trujillo Burns, Twain Harte, CA

Marcia Trujillo Burns added garlic to her favorite cream soup after sampling a similar soup at a restaurant. She gar- nishes her creation with bacon, crou- tons, or parmesan cheese.

PREP AND COOK TIME: About 1 hour

MAKES: About 6 cups; about 4 servings

- ¼ cup (⅛ lb.) **butter**
- 1 cup minced **white onion**
- 1 cup diced (about ¼ in.) **celery**
- 1 head **garlic,** cloves separated, peeled, and minced
- ¼ cup **all-purpose flour**
- 1 **red thin-skinned potato** (about 8 oz.), peeled and diced
- 3 cups fat-skimmed **chicken broth**
- 1 pint **half-and-half**
- ⅛ teaspoon **white pepper**
- **Salt**

1. In a 4- to 6-quart pan over medium- low heat, melt butter. Add onion, celery, and garlic and stir frequently until veg- etables are very soft but not brown, about 15 minutes. Stir in flour and cook 2 minutes, stirring constantly.

2. Add diced potato and chicken broth and stir over medium-high heat until boiling; reduce heat and simmer until potato pieces are very tender when pierced, about 20 minutes. Add the half-and-half and stir until hot. Add white pepper and salt to taste.

Per serving: 364 cal., 62% (225 cal.) from fat; 13 g protein; 25 g fat (16 g sat.); 23 g carbo (3 g fiber); 257 mg sodium; 75 mg chol.

Braised Chicken with Lemons

Margaret Anderson, Laguna Hills, CA

The fruit on Margaret Anderson's lemon tree inspired her to come up with this flavorful braised chicken dish.

PREP AND COOK TIME: About 1½ hours, plus at least 1 hour to chill

MAKES: 3 or 4 servings

- 6 **chicken thighs** (about 1¾ lb. total, bone in and skin on)
- ½ cup **balsamic vinegar**
- 1 tablespoon **olive oil**
  About ½ teaspoon **salt**
  About ¼ teaspoon **pepper**
- 1¼ cup chopped **shallots**
- 2 cloves **garlic,** peeled and minced
- 2 **lemons** (about 12 oz. total), rinsed, halved lengthwise, and thinly sliced
- ¼ cup **vermouth** or dry white wine
- 1 teaspoon **herbes de Provence**

1. Rinse chicken and pat dry; trim and discard pockets of fat. In a bowl, mix vinegar, oil, ½ teaspoon salt, and ¼ teaspoon pepper. Add thighs; turn to coat. Cover and chill 1 hour.

2. Set a 5- to 6-quart ovenproof pan with lid over medium-high heat. Lift chicken thighs from marinade (reserve marinade) and arrange in a single layer in pan. Turn as necessary to brown on both sides, 4 to 6 minutes total. Trans- fer chicken to a rimmed plate and lower heat under pan. Add shallots and garlic to pan and stir frequently until shallots are limp, about 5 min- utes. Return chicken to pan and add marinade, lemons, vermouth, and herbes de Provence.

3. Cover pan. Transfer to a 350° regular or convection oven and bake until chicken is very tender when pierced, 30 to 45 minutes. Add salt and pepper to taste. Spoon into bowls to serve.

Per serving: 427 cal., 59% (252 cal.) from fat; 29 g protein; 28 g fat (7.3 g sat.); 21 g carbo (4.4 g fiber); 420 mg sodium; 132 mg chol.

FOOD STYLING: BASIL FRIEDMAN

Grapefruit and avocado dress up a bright and simple salad.

Grapefruit and Avocado Salad

Havilah Stewart, Denver

Havilah Stewart puts smoked almonds in this salad for a salty, complex note. If smoked almonds are unavailable, substitute roasted salted almonds.

PREP TIME: About 15 minutes

MAKES: 12 cups; 4 servings

- 2 **pink grapefruit** (about 1½ lb. total)
- 2 tablespoons **olive oil**
- 2 tablespoons **lime juice**
- 12 ounces **mixed salad greens** (about 2 qt.)
- 1 **firm-ripe avocado**, peeled and sliced
- ⅓ cup chopped **smoked almonds** (see note above)
- ¼ cup thinly sliced **green onions** (white and pale green parts only)

  Salt and **pepper**

1. With a sharp knife, cut peel and outer membrane from grapefruit. Working over a strainer set over a bowl, cut between inner membranes and fruit to release segments into strainer. Squeeze juice from membranes into bowl. Discard peel and membranes.

2. In a large bowl, combine oil, lime juice, and grapefruit juice. Add salad greens and mix gently to coat. Divide evenly among four plates and top with grapefruit segments, avocado, almonds, and green onions. Add salt and pepper to taste.

Per serving: 251 cal., 72% (180 cal.) from fat; 5.2 g protein; 20 g fat (2.5 g sat.); 16 g carbo (3.7 g fiber); 91 mg sodium; 0 mg chol.

Southwestern Black Bean Dip

Andrea Shaw, Laguna Beach, CA

Andrea Shaw makes this seasoned black bean dip for tortilla chips. Top it with shredded cheddar cheese if you like.

PREP AND COOK TIME: About 45 minutes

MAKES: 3 cups; about 6 servings

- 2 cans (15 oz. each) **black beans**, rinsed and drained
- 1 can (14½ oz.) **diced tomatoes with chilies**
- ½ cup chopped **red onion**
- 1 bottle (16 oz.) **beer**
- ½ cup chopped **fresh cilantro**

In a 3- to 4-quart pan over medium-high heat, bring beans, tomatoes, ¼ cup onion, and beer to a boil. Lower heat and cook, stirring occasionally, until most of the liquid is absorbed and remaining liquid is thick, 35 to 45 minutes. If a smooth consistency is desired, whirl in a blender or food processor until smooth. Stir in remaining ¼ cup onion and the cilantro.

Per ½ cup: 107 cal., 6% (6.3 cal.) from fat; 6.2 g protein; 0.7 g fat (0.1 g sat.); 20 g carbo (5.7 g fiber); 509 mg sodium; 0 mg chol. ◆

Love potions

Valentine's Day calls for something, well, lip-smacking—a wine, of any color, that has an extra layer of sensuality about it. Here are three of my favorites that deliver that lushness.

Buttonwood "Trevin" 1997 *(Santa Ynez Valley, CA), $30.* Loads of sumptuous cassis flavors laced with chocolate and vanilla in this red blend. Not cheap, but it tastes like it costs twice the price.

Morgan "Metallico" Chardonnay 2001 *(Santa Lucia Highlands, CA), $20.* One of the new-style beautifully balanced, nonoaked California Chardonnays.

Mumm Cordon Rouge Non-vintage Brut *(Champagne, France), $36.* Light, fresh, and tingling.

—Karen MacNeil-Fife

Make your own super granola with loads of fruits and nuts for a scrumptious start to the day (see page 56).

March

Dried chilies give earthy heat
to steak and bell peppers.

The new rice bowl

Combine easy toppings and versatile rice for worlds of flavor

By Charity Ferreira • Photographs by James Carrier
Food styling by Basil Friedman

Mushrooms, leeks, and white wine make a rice bowl with French sensibilities.

For most of us in the West, a meal composed of rice with a saucy topping of meat and vegetables means Chinese or Japanese cuisine. But as a staple food for more than half the world's population, rice partners well with an unlimited number of flavors, making this convenient dish easily adaptable to many cuisines. Combinations like spicy flank steak and bell peppers in chili sauce, or quickly braised chicken with leeks and mushrooms, can be prepared in about the time it takes to cook the rice. Together they make simple, self-contained meals.

Mexican Flank Steak with Brown Rice

PREP AND COOK TIME: About 1 hour
MAKES: 4 servings

- 1 pound **beef flank steak,** fat trimmed
- 3 **dried New Mexico** or California **chilies** (each about 5 by 2 in.), rinsed, stemmed, seeded, and cut into 1-inch pieces
- 6 tablespoons **lime juice**
- 1 tablespoon minced **garlic**
- 1/2 teaspoon **cayenne**

  About 1/2 teaspoon **salt**
- 2 cups **brown rice**
- 1 tablespoon **vegetable oil**
- 1 pound **red** and **yellow bell peppers** (about 2), rinsed, stemmed, seeded, and thinly sliced lengthwise
- 1 **red onion** (8 oz.), peeled and slivered lengthwise
- 1/4 cup chopped **fresh cilantro**

1. Rinse beef and pat dry; cut across the grain into 1/8-inch-thick slices and place in a bowl. In a blender, cover dried chilies with 3/4 cup boiling water; let stand until chilies are soft, about 15 minutes. Add lime juice, garlic, cayenne, and 1/2 teaspoon salt and whirl until smooth. Pour over beef, cover, and chill for 30 minutes.

2. In a 3- to 4-quart pan over high heat, bring 4 cups water and the brown rice to a boil. Cover, reduce heat to low, and simmer until liquid is absorbed and rice is tender to bite, about 45 minutes.

3. Meanwhile, pour oil into a 10- to 12-inch frying pan over high heat. When the oil is hot, lift beef from marinade with a slotted spoon (reserve marinade) and add to pan. Stir until meat is no longer pink, about 3 minutes. Transfer beef to a rimmed plate or bowl. Add peppers and onion to pan; stir frequently until limp, 5 to 6 minutes. Return beef to pan along with reserved marinade; bring to a boil and cook, stirring once or twice, for 1 minute.

4. Spoon rice into four wide, shallow bowls and top equally with beef, vegetables, and sauce. Sprinkle with cilantro. Add more salt to taste.

Per serving: 625 cal., 23% (144 cal.) from fat; 33 g protein; 16 g fat (4.8 g sat.); 89 g carbo (7.6 g fiber); 393 mg sodium; 57 mg chol.

Chicken, Leeks, and Mushrooms with Wild Rice

PREP AND COOK TIME: About 45 minutes
NOTES: Packaged wild rice blends are available in most supermarkets; look for one without seasoning.
MAKES: 4 servings

- 1 1/2 cups **unseasoned wild rice blend** (see notes)

  About 1/2 teaspoon **salt**
- 1 pound **boned, skinned chicken thighs**
- 2 **leeks** (about 1 lb. total)
- 1 tablespoon **olive oil**
- 1 clove **garlic,** peeled and minced
- 8 ounces **fresh shiitake mushrooms,** rinsed, stemmed, and sliced; or common mushrooms, rinsed, stem ends trimmed, and sliced
- 3/4 cup **dry white wine**
- 1/4 cup **whipping cream**
- 1 tablespoon **soy sauce**

  Pepper

1. In a 3- to 4-quart pan over high heat, bring 3 1/2 cups water, the rice, and 1/2 teaspoon salt to a boil. Cover, reduce heat to low, and simmer until liquid is absorbed and rice is tender to bite, about 45 minutes.

2. Meanwhile, rinse chicken and pat dry; cut into 1-inch chunks. Trim and discard root ends, tough green tops, and tough outer layers from leeks. Split leeks in half lengthwise and rinse well under running water, flipping layers to release grit; thinly slice crosswise.

3. Pour oil into a 10- to 12-inch frying pan over medium-high heat. When hot, add chicken and stir until no longer pink in the center (cut to test), about 7 minutes. With a slotted spoon, transfer chicken to a rimmed plate or bowl. Reduce heat to medium and add leeks and garlic to pan; stir until leeks are limp, about 5 minutes. Add mushrooms and stir until mushrooms are browned and have released their juices, about 5 minutes. Add wine and bring to a simmer, scraping bottom of pan to release any browned bits.

4. Return chicken to pan. Add cream and soy sauce and simmer, stirring occasionally, until liquid is slightly thickened, 2 to 3 minutes. Add salt and pepper to taste.

5. Spoon rice into four wide, shallow bowls and top equally with chicken, vegetables, mushrooms, and sauce.

Per serving: 486 cal., 24% (117 cal.) from fat; 30 g protein; 13 g fat (4.5 g sat.); 55 g carbo (2.1 g fiber); 666 mg sodium; 111 mg chol.

Seafood in Red Curry with Sticky Rice

PREP AND COOK TIME: About 30 minutes

NOTES: Thai red curry paste, which is not the same as Asian red chili paste, is sold in the Asian food section of many well-stocked supermarkets and in Asian grocery stores.

MAKES: 4 servings

1½ cups **short-grain white rice**

1 cup **coconut milk**

½ cup fat-skimmed **chicken broth**

1 tablespoon **Thai red curry paste** (see notes)

1 tablespoon **Asian fish sauce** (*nuoc mam* or *nam pla*)

1 tablespoon firmly packed **brown sugar**

1 pound **asparagus**, rinsed, tough stem ends snapped off, and cut into 1-inch pieces

8 **clams in shells,** suitable for steaming (8 to 12 oz.), scrubbed

8 ounces **bay scallops,** rinsed

8 ounces **shelled, deveined shrimp** (30 to 35 per lb.), rinsed

1 tablespoon **lime juice**

1. In a 3- to 4-quart pan over high heat, bring 2½ cups water and the rice to a boil; cover, reduce heat to low, and simmer until liquid is absorbed and rice is tender to bite, about 25 minutes.

2. Meanwhile, in a 10- to 12-inch frying pan over high heat, stir coconut milk, chicken broth, curry paste, fish sauce, and brown sugar until sugar and curry paste are dissolved and mixture is simmering. Stir in asparagus and clams, cover, and cook for 3 minutes. Add scallops and shrimp, cover, and cook, stirring occasionally, until clam shells have opened and shrimp and scallops are opaque but still moist-looking in the center (cut to test), about 3 minutes longer. Stir in lime juice.

3. Spoon rice into four wide, shallow bowls and top equally with seafood, asparagus, and sauce.

Per serving: 559 cal., 26% (144 cal.) from fat; 33 g protein; 16 g fat (12 g sat.); 71 g carbo (1.7 g fiber); 673 mg sodium; 108 mg chol.

Thai red curry paste turns coconut milk into a savory sauce for seafood and vegetables.

Spiced Vegetables with Basmati Rice

PREP AND COOK TIME: About 45 minutes

MAKES: 4 servings

1½ cups **basmati rice**

4 ounces **green beans,** rinsed, ends trimmed, and cut into 1-inch pieces

2 teaspoons **vegetable oil**

1 **onion** (8 oz.), peeled and chopped

1 clove **garlic,** peeled and minced

1 tablespoon minced **fresh ginger**

1 teaspoon **ground cumin**

1 teaspoon **ground coriander**

½ teaspoon **cayenne**

2 cups **cauliflower** florets

1 can (15½ oz.) **crushed tomatoes**

1 can (15½ oz.) **garbanzos,** drained and rinsed

Salt and **pepper**

1. In a 3- to 4-quart pan over high heat, bring 2½ cups water and the rice to

Indian-spiced tomato sauce coats vegetables and garbanzos for an intriguing vegetarian dish.

A rice for every bowl

There are more kinds of rice to choose from on supermarket shelves than ever before, each variety with its own unique texture and flavor. Take advantage of this diversity to vary the personality of your rice bowls.

Long-grain. Its long, slender grains stay separate and distinct when cooked and have a fluffy texture. This is a good rice for pilaf.

Medium-grain. Cooked, the grains are moist and slightly stickier than long-grain rice. This is a good all-purpose rice; it works especially well for rice pudding.

Short-grain. Nearly round uncooked, the grains become soft and sticky when cooked. This is the rice used for sushi.

Arborio. Alternately classified as short- and medium-grain, the grains in question have a white dot in the center; when cooked, they become creamy but maintain a slightly firm texture in the center. This rice is great for risotto.

Aromatic. The best known of the fragrant varieties are Jasmine and Basmati, both delicately flavored, long-grain rices.

Brown. This rice is less processed than its white counterpart: the grains retain their bran layers, giving the rice a light brown color, chewy texture, and nutty flavor.

Wild. This is actually not rice at all; it's the seed of an aquatic grass, which becomes chewy and nutty when cooked. Wild rice is often blended with brown or white rice and sold as a mix.

a boil; cover, reduce heat to low, and simmer until liquid is absorbed and rice is tender to bite, 18 to 20 minutes.

2. Meanwhile, in a 10- to 12-inch frying pan over high heat, bring about 3 cups water to a boil. Add green beans and cook until tender-crisp to bite, about 2 minutes. Drain and rinse under cold running water until cool. Wipe pan dry.

3. Pour oil into pan over medium-high heat. When hot, add onion, garlic, and ginger; stir often until onion is limp, about 5 minutes. Stir in cumin, coriander, cayenne, cauliflower, and 1 cup water. Cover and bring to a simmer;

reduce heat and simmer, stirring occasionally, until cauliflower is tender when pierced, 8 to 10 minutes.

4. Add tomatoes and garbanzos, cover, and simmer, stirring occasionally, to blend flavors, about 10 minutes. Add green beans and stir occasionally until hot, about 2 minutes. Add salt and pepper to taste.

5. Spoon rice into four wide, shallow bowls and top equally with vegetables and sauce.

Per serving: 395 cal., 13% (52 cal.) from fat; 15 g protein; 5.8 g fat (0.4 g sat.); 79 g carbo (7.3 g fiber); 344 mg sodium; 0 mg chol. ◆

More delicious topping ideas

• Cubed chicken and sweet potatoes simmered in coconut milk over aromatic rice, sprinkled with chopped peanuts, toasted coconut, and sliced green onions.

• Broiled salmon or chicken breasts and steamed

vegetables with purchased teriyaki sauce over short-grain rice.

• Black beans simmered with Mexican-seasoned canned tomatoes and chopped cilantro over long-grain rice.

• Sautéed greens such as spinach with purchased Thai peanut sauce over short- or medium-grain rice.

• Sautéed sliced Japanese eggplant and cubed tofu mixed with Asian red chili paste over short-grain rice.

Cheese tasting

For a simple, sophisticated party, pair artisan cheeses with wine

By Linda Lau Anusasananan
Photographs by James Carrier

Gather your friends and taste the latest crop of artisan cheeses; they range from mild to earthy.

Cheesemaking is an old art that has been making a big comeback in the West. Local artisans from Colorado to California are handcrafting cheeses in the Old World tradition, working in small batches and attending to every detail, from what the cows eat to how often the cheeses are turned during the aging process. All this hard work results in complex, flavorful cheeses.

They range from soft-ripened cow-milk cheese full of robust, earthy flavors to aged goat cheese with surprising complexity, and from creamy, buttery-textured blue cheese to aged cheddars. At specialty markets and even large grocery stores now, the selection is getting better and better. This is great news for anyone who likes to entertain with ease. These delicious cheeses make perfect appetizers all on their own—pair a few with some wines for a stylish, no-hassle appetizer party.

The strategy

With just a little advance planning, a cheese- and wine-tasting party is simple to put together. All you really need is great cheese (count on buying 4 to 6 ounces per person), bread or crackers, and wine (about one bottle for every two guests). Everything else is optional, including fresh or dried fruits, toasted or spiced nuts, and other accompaniments.

When purchasing cheese for a party, you can either offer a variety—soft-ripened, cow-milk, goat, blue, and hard cheeses can be mixed and matched with delicious results—or concentrate on one type. The latter approach makes wine pairing a little simpler, but offering a range gives you great potential for a beautiful display and distinctive serving ideas. Let the cheeses warm to room temperature for best flavor and texture. (Use the same strategies to assemble a simple cheese tray that will be part of a larger appetizer spread or—as a cheese course—a stylish way to end dinner.)

Plan ahead: you may need to order artisan cheeses from the cheesemaker or have your market order them. As with anything handmade, supplies of these cheeses may be limited. Our chart on page 51 describes some of our favorites from among the very newest Western cheeses, but explore on your own as well—there's a world of delicious choices at your market.

How to pair cheese and wine

Serve more white wines with cheese. Light, with a crispness that cleanses the palate after rich cheeses, they're often a better choice than reds.

Look for acidity in wines— it's often an asset. Good choices include Sauvignon Blancs, sparkling wines, and dry Rieslings.

Lean toward richly fruity reds. They work well with cheese's salty flavors. Pinot Noirs, Syrahs, and Zinfandels are good bets.

Try different goat cheeses with wine. Overall, they are surprisingly versatile together. Goat cheeses offered the largest number of potential matches in our tasting. The toughest cheeses to pair (goat or otherwise) are earthy and pungent, flavors that can strip down a wine.

Avoid heavily oaked wines, such as super-oaky California Chardonnays. Their buttery richness can be overwhelming with similar qualities in the cheese.

Steer clear of excessively tannic reds, such as Cabernet Sauvignons. Salt and tannin are a train wreck in the mouth, so tannic reds don't work well with most cheeses.

Consider the effect of added flavorings on the wine match. If a cheese is coated in black pepper or herbs, for instance, that can throw off your pairing, so take the characteristics of any flavorings into account when choosing wines.

—*Karen MacNeil-Fife*

The best new cheeses

So what are the standouts among the new artisan cheeses? In a sampling session that was fun as well as flavorful, we picked our favorites from more than 25 and paired them with complementary wines.

	CHEESE	MAKER	TASTE & CHARACTER	SERVING IDEAS	BEST-BET WINE
Blue cheese	**Original Blue**	Point Reyes Farmstead Cheese Co., Point Reyes, CA; www.pointreyescheese.com or (800) 591-6878.	Farmstead blue cheese made with raw Holstein cow milk, aged an average of 6 months. Creamy and full flavored with a slight sharp tang.	Pair with slightly sweet whole-wheat crackers and a chunk of honeycomb or liquid honey for drizzling.	This strongly flavored blue wiped out even port, though we loved it with sweet botrytised or late-harvest whites. Avoid reds and sparklers.
Soft-ripened cow-milk cheeses	**La Petite Crème**	Marin French Cheese Co., Petaluma, CA; www.marinfrenchcheese.com or (800) 292-6001.	Small rounds of mild, creamy, soft-ripened cow-milk cheese, with a velvety texture similar to triple-crème brie.	Spread onto slices of baguette; serve with dried cherries or dates.	Delicious with Riesling, such as Lake Chalice Falcon Vineyard 2002 (Marlborough, New Zealand; $17).
	Poudre Puff	Bingham Hill Cheese Co., Fort Collins, CO; www.binghamhill.com or (970) 472-0702.	Small, fuzzy spheres with melt-in-your-mouth texture and slight pungent bite. Made from cow milk and cream.	Pair with sweet, juicy grapes, or top dried apricots with a bit of cheese and a sprinkling of chopped roasted pistachios.	Try with acidic whites, especially Sauvignon Blanc such as Lawson's Dry Hills (Marlborough, New Zealand; $15).
	Red Hawk	Cowgirl Creamery, Point Reyes, CA; www.cowgirlcreamery.com or (415) 663-9335.	Buttery, aged triple-cream cheese with a red-orange rind produced by brine washing. Made with organic cow milk.	Accompany with ripe Comice pears and toasted hazelnuts.	This cheese was best on its own; its pungent earthiness made it hard to pair with wine.
Semihard to hard aged cow-milk cheeses	**Bandage-Wrapped Cheddar**	Fiscalini Cheese Co., Modesto, CA; www.fiscalinicheese.com or (209) 545-5495.	Firm, raw cow-milk cheddar with pale gold color. Smooth, dry texture becomes flakier as it ages. Aged 18 to 24 months; nutty and tangy to full flavored and salty.	Serve a wedge of this outstanding cheddar with a mellow, spicy-sweet fruit chutney and thin slices of nut or whole-grain bread.	Pinot Noir, such as Dutton-Goldfield Dutton Ranch (Russian River Valley, CA; $35), with lush, earthy tones that complement the cheese.
	Mezzo Secco	Vella Cheese Co. of California, Sonoma, CA; www.vellacheese.com or (800) 848-0505.	Semidry cow-milk cheese, aged 4 to 6 months, with deep, mellow flavors and smooth, slightly crumbly texture. Tastes a bit like a mild, nutty cheddar.	Drizzle shavings with reduced balsamic: stir ½ cup balsamic vinegar in a pan over high heat until reduced to 3 tablespoons, about 3 minutes. Let cool.	Quite flexible; best with earthy reds, such as those from the Rhône, or herbal, crisp whites such as Sauvignon Blanc.
	Queso de Oro	Bravo Farms, Visalia, CA; (559) 734-1282.	Semihard cow-milk farmstead cheese with buttery texture and nutty flavor, made in the style of Edam. Aged 60 to 90 days.	Spread apple butter onto raisin or nut toast and top with a thin slice of cheese, or serve on a crisp, sweet apple slice.	This cheese was nice with sparkling wines, but was otherwise difficult to match.
Fresh goat cheese	**Fresh Chèvre**	Port Madison Farm, Bainbridge Island, WA; (206) 842-4125.	These small rounds of chèvre have a very mild goat flavor; they are clean, fresh, and light tasting, with a smooth, creamy texture.	Drizzle with extra-virgin olive oil, sprinkle lightly with salt and pepper, and serve with baguette slices, toasted or plain.	Choose a mild white such as a Pinot Grigio. This cheese was so mild that it was knocked out by many wines.
Soft-ripened to semihard goat cheeses	**Capricious**	MyTime Ranch, Eureka, CA; (707) 442-3209.	A surprisingly complex semihard, cave-aged farmstead goat cheese; nutty and slightly salty and tangy like Asiago or parmesan, with very mild goat flavor.	Serve thin slices on rye, topped with pickled red cabbage, or pair with golden raisins or sweet apple slices.	Light, fruity wines such as Riesling or Pinot Noir work well with this salty cheese; avoid tannic reds such as Cabernet Sauvignon.
	Golden Rose	White Oak Farmstead, Battle Ground, WA; www.white-oak.com or (360) 576-7688.	Semihard pressed goat cheese, similar to Gouda in flavor and texture. Golden color, slight tang, and smooth, dry-aged texture.	Serve cheese on walnut toast topped with thin apple slices.	Pair with a moderately oaky, restrained Chardonnay, such as Silverado Vineyards 2000 (Napa Valley; $20).
	Marble Mountain	Cypress Grove Chèvre, McKinleyville, CA; www.cypressgrovechevre.com or (707) 839-3168.	This pyramid-shaped, soft-ripened goat cheese has a creamy, mild interior strikingly marbled with vegetable ash, which adds a slight mineral flavor.	For a big visual impact, present this beautiful cheese on its own, with plain crackers or baguette slices.	This cheese was a surprise crossover hit—it worked either with sparklers or with big reds like Merlot or Syrah. ◆

"My husband is a fisherman, so I have the pick of the catch," says Liz Pudwill of Baja Tacos.

Buying Alaskan salmon

The entire Alaska salmon fishery is certified sustainable by the Marine Stewardship Council, so choosing this source for your seafood ensures a guilt-free, pleasurable meal. Fresh Alaska salmon is easiest to find during the peak of the commercial harvest—mid-May to mid-September. Off-season, however, frozen Alaska salmon is a good choice. It's flash-frozen shortly after being caught, so it can be even fresher-tasting than a never-frozen counterpart that has languished during shipping. Sources for flash-frozen Copper River and other Alaskan salmon: **Copper River Seafoods** *(www. copperriverseafood.com or 888/622-1197)* and **Taku Smokeries** *(www. takusmokeries.com or 800/582-5122).*

Wild salmon, Alaska-style

Three delicious ways to enjoy the West's great fish

By Sara Schneider

CASUAL WEEKNIGHT

Salmon Tacos

PREP AND COOK TIME: About 45 minutes

NOTES: The idea for these tacos traveled from Baja California to Cordova, Alaska, with Liz Pudwill, who admits to "borrowing" the recipe from an unsuspecting fisherman. At Baja Tacos, she uses Copper River salmon and serves the tacos on paper plates from a converted red school bus near the harbor. Have the piece of salmon fillet skinned at the seafood market if you like. You can make the salsa and mayonnaise up to 2 days ahead; cover and chill. Bring to room temperature to serve.

MAKES: 8 tacos; 4 to 6 servings

1½ pounds **boned, skinned wild salmon fillet** (see notes)

1 cup **all-purpose flour**

¾ cup **beer**

1 **large egg**

1 tablespoon **Dijon mustard**

   Vegetable oil for frying

   Salt

8 **flour tortillas** (8 in.)

2 cups **finely shredded green cabbage** (about 4 oz.)

   Chipotle mayonnaise (recipe follows)

   Tomatillo salsa (recipe follows)

   Lime wedges

1. Rinse salmon and pat dry; cut the fillet crosswise into ½-inch-wide strips (cut any longer than 6 in. in half). In a bowl, whisk flour, beer, egg, and mustard until well blended.

2. Pour ½ inch oil into a 10- to 12-inch frying pan over high heat. When surface is rippling, one at a time, dip salmon strips in beer batter, turn to coat all sides (or spoon batter over fish), and lay slightly apart in a single layer in hot oil. Cook, turning pieces once with a wide spatula, until batter is golden brown on all sides and salmon is just opaque but still moist-looking in center of thickest part (cut to test), about 3 minutes total. As cooked, transfer to a paper towel–lined 12- by 17-inch baking pan and keep warm in a 200° oven. As there's room in frying pan, coat and cook remaining salmon strips. Add to fish in baking

pan and sprinkle all with salt. Discard remaining batter and the oil in pan; wipe pan clean with paper towels.

3. Set frying pan over medium-high heat. One at a time, lay tortillas in pan and heat, turning once, just until warm, about 30 seconds total for each tortilla. As heated, transfer to a platter or plates and fill each with an eighth of the salmon and ¼ cup shredded cabbage. Add chipotle mayonnaise and tomatillo salsa as desired.

4. Serve with lime wedges to squeeze over tacos and remaining mayonnaise and salsa to add to taste.

Per taco: 550 cal., 44% (243 cal.) from fat; 31 g protein; 27 g fat (4.2 g sat.); 41 g carbo (2.4 g fiber); 335 mg sodium; 97 mg chol.

CHIPOTLE MAYONNAISE. In a blender, whirl 1 cup **mayonnaise,** 1 or 2 **canned chipotle chilies** (to taste), and 3 tablespoons **water** until well blended and smooth. Makes about 1¼ cups.

Per tablespoon: 80 cal., 99% (79 cal.) from fat; 0.1 g protein; 8.8 g fat (1.3 g sat.); 0.4 g carbo (0 g fiber); 69 mg sodium; 6.5 mg chol.

TOMATILLO SALSA. Peel, rinse, and quarter 8 ounces **fresh tomatillos.** Rinse, stem, seed, and coarsely chop 6 ounces **fresh California** or New Mexico **chilies** and 2 **fresh jalapeño chilies** (2 oz. total; use rubber gloves for jalapeños). In a food processor, whirl tomatillos, California chilies, jalapeños, ½ cup coarsely chopped **onion,** and ½ cup coarsely chopped **cilantro** until finely ground. Scrape into a 2½- to 3-quart pan. Stir over medium-high heat until mixture releases some juice and is boiling, then reduce heat and simmer, stirring occasionally, to blend flavors, about 3 minutes. Let cool, then stir in 2 tablespoons **lime juice** and **salt** to taste. Makes about 1¾ cups.

Per tablespoon: 6.1 cal., 15% (0.9 cal.) from fat; 0.2 g protein; 0.1 g fat (0 g sat.); 1.3 g carbo (0.3 g fiber); 0.8 mg sodium; 0 mg chol.

BACKYARD ENTERTAINING

Taku Lodge Basted Grilled Salmon

PREP AND COOK TIME: About 20 minutes, plus at least 1 hour to marinate

NOTES: The grilled salmon at Taku Glacier Lodge is legendary. Visitors can reserve the short floatplane ride up the river from Juneau and enjoy dinner at the lodge (available only in summer). The staff claims to engage in outdoor "combat cooking"—that is, holding back the bears until the salmon is done—but the evening we were there, the only big black beast being held at bay looked an awful lot like a well-fed Labrador retriever. We've reconfigured Taku Lodge's baste ingredients so they can serve as marinade as well.

MAKES: 8 servings

- ½ cup firmly packed **brown sugar**
- ½ cup **dry white wine**
- ¼ cup **lemon juice**
  About ½ teaspoon **salt**
  About ¼ teaspoon **pepper**
- 8 pieces (about 6 oz. each; max. 1¼ in. thick) **boned, skinned wild salmon fillet**
- ¼ cup (⅛ lb.) **butter**
  Lemon wedges

1. In a large, wide bowl or 9- by 13-inch baking dish, stir brown sugar, wine, lemon juice, ½ teaspoon salt, and ¼ teaspoon pepper until sugar is dissolved.

2. Rinse fish and pat dry. Add to marinade and turn to coat. Cover and chill for 1 to 2 hours.

3. Lift salmon from marinade and transfer to a 12- by 17-inch baking pan. Pour marinade into a 1½- to 2-quart pan over medium-high heat; add butter and stir until butter is melted and mixture is simmering, 4 to 5 minutes.

4. Lay salmon, skinned side down, on a generously oiled grill over a solid bed of medium-hot coals or medium-high heat on a gas grill (you can hold your hand at grill level only 3 to 4 seconds). Brush fish generously with the baste; close lid if using a gas grill. Cook until salmon pieces are well browned on the bottom, 3½ to 4 minutes (keep a spray bottle filled with clean water on hand to spritz any flare-ups). With a wide spatula, carefully turn pieces; brush tops with baste and continue to cook, basting often, until the salmon is just opaque but still moist-looking in the center of the thickest part (cut to test), about 5 to 6 minutes longer. Discard any remaining baste.

5. Transfer salmon to a warm platter or plates and garnish with lemon wedges. Add more salt and pepper to taste.

Per serving: 365 cal., 47% (171 cal.) from fat; 36 g protein; 19 g fat (5.3 g sat.); 11 g carbo (0 g fiber); 240 mg sodium; 117 mg chol.

A SPECIAL DISH

Seared Wasabi-Glazed Salmon with "Forbidden" Rice

PREP AND COOK TIME: About 1 hour

NOTES: This striking dish comes from chef Matt Mulder, formerly of Di Sopra (upstairs at the Fiddlehead in Juneau). Black rice, packaged by Lotus Foods under the name "Forbidden Rice," is sold in the Asian-foods section of well-stocked supermarkets and in Asian grocery stores (as is wasabi powder).

MAKES: 4 servings

- 1 tablespoon **Asian (toasted) sesame oil**
- 1 ripe **mango** (1 to 1¼ lb.), pitted, peeled, and coarsely chopped
- 3 tablespoons **rice vinegar**
  About ¼ cup **dry white wine** (optional)
- 4 **jasmine tea bags**
- 1 cup **black** or jasmine **rice** (see notes)
  About ½ teaspoon **salt**
- 2½ tablespoons **wasabi powder** (see notes)
- 1 tablespoon **honey**
- 1⅓ pounds **boned, skinned wild salmon fillet,** cut into four equal pieces
- 2 teaspoons **olive oil**
  Chopped **fresh cilantro** or parsley (optional)

1. Pour sesame oil into a 10- to 12-inch ovenproof frying pan over medium heat. When hot, add mango and stir often just until heated through, 1½ to 2 minutes. Scrape into a blender and add vinegar; whirl until very smooth, then whirl in enough white wine or water to give mixture a very thin, pourable consistency (about ¼ cup). Pour sauce into a small, microwave-safe pitcher. Wipe pan clean.

2. In a 3- to 4-quart pan, combine 2 cups water and the tea bags; bring to a boil over high heat. Remove tea bags and add rice and ½ teaspoon salt; stir, cover, and bring to a simmer. Reduce heat and simmer, covered, until rice is tender to bite, 45 to 55 minutes (about 20 minutes for jasmine rice).

3. Meanwhile, in a small bowl, mix 2½ tablespoons water, wasabi powder, and honey until blended. Rinse and dry salmon.

4. Pour olive oil into the 10- to 12-inch ovenproof frying pan over medium-high heat. When hot, lay salmon pieces in pan, skinned side down; cook, turning once with a wide spatula, until lightly browned on both sides, 3 to 4 minutes total. Remove pan from heat and brush wasabi-honey mixture over tops of salmon pieces, using it all.

5. Transfer pan with salmon to a 350° regular or convection oven. Bake just until fish is opaque but still moist-looking in center of thickest part (cut to test), 7 to 10 minutes.

6. Heat mango sauce in a microwave oven at full power (100%), stirring occasionally, about 2 minutes total. Transfer a piece of salmon to each of four warmed plates; spoon rice equally alongside (or set salmon on rice). Drizzle mango purée around salmon and rice. Garnish with chopped cilantro, if desired, and add more salt to taste.

Per serving: 543 cal., 31% (171 cal.) from fat; 36 g protein; 19 g fat (3.1 g sat.); 57 g carbo (0.8 g fiber); 379 mg sodium; 94 mg chol.

Mango sauce and wasabi glaze enhance seared salmon.

Sustainable seafood's about more than salmon

Consumer choices impact our fish supply and the environment. Issues at a glance:

OVERFISHING. For many popular species, too many boats have gone after too many fish (often catching them before they've had a chance to spawn).

DESTRUCTION OF HABITAT. Some common fishing practices destroy critical features in the environment that wildlife depends on.

BYCATCH. Some methods pull in large volumes of other fish and marine life, which usually die. By some estimates, one-fourth of the world catch is discarded each year.

FARMING. While aquaculture can alleviate overfishing pressure on wild populations, some farms—including salmon—are environmentally destructive: pollution from uneaten feed, pesticides, and antibiotics can destroy habitats; disease from farmed fish can spread to wild populations; and non-native farmed species can escape and threaten native species, in part, by interbreeding with them. Grocery stores and seafood markets are required by the Food and Drug Administration to inform consumers by signs and labeling if farmed salmon contain color additives (to mimic the natural shades of wild salmon). If in doubt about a fish's origins, consumers can ask, "Is it wild?" —*Sara Schneider*

MAKING CHOICES
Are your favorite fish okay to buy?

The answer is complicated. Here are some general guidelines for buying seafood, but learn more from the organizations below. Our favorite substitutes for the fish that we recommend to avoid are striped bass, black cod, and tilapia.

	GOOD CHOICE	CAUTION*	AVOID
Anchovies	✓		
Bass	striped		black sea
Black cod (sablefish)	✓		
Catfish	farmed		
Chilean seabass (Patagonian toothfish)			✓
Clams	farmed	wild	
Cod		Pacific	Atlantic
Crab	Dungeness, most blue	Alaska-caught king, snow	Chesapeake Bay blue
Haddock			✓
Haki	Pacific-caught	Atlantic-caught	
Halibut	Pacific-caught		Atlantic-caught
Herring	✓		
Lingcod	Alaska-caught		all others
Lobster	rock	American (Maine), spiny	
Mackerel	✓		
Mahimahi (dolphinfish)		✓	
Monkfish			✓
Mussels	farmed	wild	
Orange roughy			✓
Oysters	farmed	wild	
Pollock	Pacific		Atlantic
Rainbow trout		farmed	
Red snapper			✓
Rockfish (Pacific snapper, rock cod, perch)			Pacific-caught
Salmon	Pacific-caught: AK & CA		Atlantic-caught, farmed
Sand dabs	✓		
Sardines	✓		
Scallops (sea, bay)		✓	dredged
Shrimp/prawns	trap-caught	U.S.-farmed, wild	imported
Sole (petrale, Dover)		Pacific-caught	Atlantic-caught
Squid	Pacific-caught	Atlantic-caught	
Sturgeon	farmed		wild
Swordfish		Pacific-caught	Atlantic-caught
Tilapia	farmed		
Tuna	troll- or pole-caught	longline- or purse seine–caught	bluefin

*Status in question; ask your purveyor where and how it's caught, and find out more from these sources: Monterey Bay Aquarium Seafood Watch, www.mbayaq.org (click on "Choices for Healthy Oceans") or (831) 647-6873;
National Audubon Society Living Oceans Program, www.audubon.org/campaign/lo; Seafood Choices Alliance, SeaSense database, www.seafoodchoices.com or (866) 732-6673. ◆

Fresh fish

The Copper River salmon fishery is mostly a mom-and-pop industry, using gill-netters that one person can work. The fishery's advanced quality-control program is a primary reason the fish retain their firm texture and rich flavor. As the fish are caught, they are bled and then immediately sorted into small bins and iced; most are quickly transferred to a tender. After they're cleaned, the fish are airlifted to top restaurants and markets across North America.

Asparagus hides under the golden cheese topping of this easy supper dish.

Good eggs

Whip up an airy omelet for a great early spring meal

By Kate Washington
Photograph by James Carrier

My grandmother had a way with egg whites. Not only did she make the best lemon meringue pie in the world, but she also used egg whites to produce a delicious puffed omelet. Somewhere between a frittata and a soufflé, this comforting, old-fashioned dish is perfect for dinner when you don't want to spend a lot of time shopping or cooking.

Grandma's diet was always protein-heavy, so you could count on plenty of eggs and cheese—along with some stray vegetables—lurking in her fridge. These few ingredients are probably in your kitchen now, and they make a luscious dish that will please both grown-ups and kids (vegetables go down easily hidden in a pile of golden, fluffy eggs).

A simple salad with apples is just right with the main dish's sharp cheddar. If you don't have time to whip up a lemon meringue pie for dessert, don't worry: my grandmother always

kept a pink box from the bakery on hand for grandkids with a sweet tooth, so a plate of purchased cookies and a glass of cold milk would be equally faithful to her memory.

Fluffy Omelet with Asparagus

PREP AND COOK TIME: About 30 minutes
NOTES: Other vegetables, such as chopped broccoli or cauliflower, can be used instead of asparagus. The amount of cayenne used here adds flavor and color rather than much spiciness, but if you are very sensitive to heat or are serving this dish to young children, you may want to substitute paprika.
MAKES: 4 servings

  8 ounces **asparagus** (see notes), rinsed and tough ends snapped off

  8 **large eggs,** separated

  1½ cups **shredded sharp cheddar cheese**

  ¼ cup **milk**

  ½ cup **all-purpose flour**

  ½ teaspoon **cayenne** or paprika (see notes)

  ½ teaspoon **salt**

  1 tablespoon **butter**

1. Cut asparagus into ½-inch lengths. In a 1½- to 2-quart pan over high heat, bring 1 quart water to a boil. Add asparagus and cook until bright green and just tender when pierced, about 2 minutes. Drain, rinse with cold water, and drain again.

2. Meanwhile, in a large bowl, mix egg yolks, 1¼ cups cheese, milk, flour, cayenne, and salt until well blended. Stir in asparagus.

3. In another large bowl, with a mixer on medium speed, beat egg whites until stiff peaks form. Spoon about a quarter of the whites into yolk mixture; stir to combine. Scrape yolk mixture into bowl with remaining whites and fold together gently just to combine; do not overmix.

4. In an 11- to 12-inch nonstick, oven-proof frying pan over medium-high heat, melt butter; swirl pan to coat. Pour in egg mixture and smooth top with a heatproof, flexible spatula. Cook until edges appear set and dry and bottom is browned (loosen edges with spatula to check), 7 to 8 minutes.

5. Transfer pan to oven and broil 4 to 6 inches from heat until omelet is puffed, set, and lightly browned, 3 to 5 minutes. Sprinkle evenly with remaining ¼ cup cheese; broil until cheese is melted and bubbling, 1 minute longer. Serve at once from pan, spooning onto plates.

Per serving: 423 cal., 60% (252 cal.) from fat; 27 g protein; 28 g fat (14 g sat.); 16 g carbo (0.9 g fiber); 717 mg sodium; 480 mg chol.

Butter Lettuce Salad with Apples

PREP TIME: About 20 minutes
NOTES: Make the dressing (step 1) before cooking the omelet; prepare lettuce, apple, and parsley while omelet cooks. Mix the salad at the last minute.
MAKES: 4 servings

  3 tablespoons **cider vinegar**

  2 tablespoons chopped **shallot**

  1 tablespoon **coarse-grain mustard**

  3 tablespoons **walnut** or vegetable **oil**
    Salt and fresh-ground **pepper**

  1 head **butter lettuce** (about 10 oz.), leaves separated, rinsed, crisped, and torn into bite-size pieces

  1 **Gala** or other sweet red **apple** (6 oz.), rinsed, cored, and thinly sliced

  2 tablespoons chopped **Italian parsley**

1. In a large bowl, mix vinegar, shallot, and mustard. Whisk in walnut oil until blended; season to taste with salt and pepper.
2. Add lettuce, apple, and parsley; mix gently to coat.

Per serving: 133 cal., 74% (99 cal.) from fat; 1.1 g protein; 11 g fat (1 g sat.); 9.2 g carbo (1.7 g fiber); 50 mg sodium; 0 mg chol. ◆

BEST GRANOLA
Killer cereal

It's taken more than 30 years, but it looks like the '60s may be losing steam. Gun barrels outnumber flower stems, tie-dye no longer merits a Converse high-top color, and it's really starting to seem like Jerry Garcia isn't coming back. But granola is here to stay. We went in search of the best of this generation and found it.

Clementine's Fruit and Nut Granola

1. In a large bowl, mix 6 cups **regular rolled oats,** 2 cups **almonds,** and 1 teaspoon **ground cinnamon.** In a smaller bowl, whisk together 1 cup **honey,** ¾ cup **canola oil,** and 1 tablespoon **vanilla.** Stir honey mixture into oat mixture until well blended. Spread mixture in a lightly oiled 12- by 15-inch baking pan. 2. Bake in a 350° regular or 325° convection oven until golden brown, 20 to 25 minutes. With a wide metal spatula, stir granola, scraping sides and bottom of pan. Reduce heat to 225° and continue to bake 1 hour, stirring several times. Let cool completely in pan, then scrape into an airtight container. 3. In a smaller airtight container, combine ⅔ cup **dried sour cherries,** ⅔ cup **dried cranberries,** and ⅔ cup **slivered dried apricots.** 4. Store fruit and granola at room temperature up to two weeks. Add dried fruit when serving. Makes about 10 cups.

Per 3/4 cup: 442 cal., 45% (198 cal.) from fat; 8.9 g protein; 22 g fat (2 g sat.); 56 g carbo (6 g fiber); 5 mg sodium; 0 mg chol.

Buy a bowlful

SEATTLE: Macrina Bakery & Cafe. Toasty mixture includes hazelnuts, dates, and dried cherries. *2408 First Ave.; (206) 448-4032.*

BERKELEY: Café Fanny. Its claim to fame is organic oat granola, also sold at Bay Area retail locations. *1603 San Pablo Ave.; (510) 524-5447.*

LOS ANGELES: Clementine. Toasted oats and almonds are mixed to order with plump dried fruit at this stylishly wholesome bakery/cafe. *1751 Ensley Ave.; (310) 552-1080.*

TAOS, NEW MEXICO: Dragonfly Café & Bakery. Sweetened with brown sugar and honey, this granola boasts three kinds of nuts, plus pumpkin seeds. *402 Paseo del Pueblo Norte; (505) 737-5859.*

NEAR PARK CITY, UTAH: Deer Valley Bakery. Crunchy seed and nut granola sold by the pound and in smaller packages sized for a snack on the slopes. *At Deer Valley Resort; (435) 645-6623.*
—*Charity Ferreira, with Jim Kravets*

NEW IN THE MARKET
Eye of the dragon

If you've traveled to Asia, you may have eaten a longan—also called dragon's eye. These round, cherry-size fruits have a sweet, juicy succulence that makes them wildly popular in Asia. Now they're grown in Hawaii and can be legally distributed in the West. Look for them in supermarkets, Asian grocery stores, and specialty produce markets through the end of this month. Longans look pretty dull on the outside—a drab, khaki-colored shell encases the marble-shaped fruit. But the pearly, translucent flesh has the texture of a peeled grape and the slight floral, musky sweetness of a delicate wild honey.
—*Linda Lau Anusasananan*

To eat longans

Rinse and drain. From stem end, peel off about half of the thin, crackly shell (you may need a small knife to get it started), then pinch the shell end to pop the sweet, juicy globe in your mouth. Spit out the shiny, dark seed.

Bring out the best with lamb

By Jerry Anne Di Vecchio
Photograph by James Carrier

For everyday wines, I am the buyer; my companion, David, buys for the cellar. In the early 1970s, when prices were exceptionally low for great quality, he took advantage of it. Time flew, and before long, those good-value wines aged and became almost too good to drink—was there ever an occasion important enough? Would we ever drink those bottles before they became absolutely priceless or, worse yet, passed over the hill (or we did)?

Then, in 1999, *Wall Street Journal* wine writers Dorothy J. Gaiter and John Brecher came up with a simple solution: Open That Bottle Night (OTBN). Now, they said, is the time to drink your best wine; make the drinking of it the occasion itself. Liberating! I embellished the concept to Drink Your Best Bottle Dinner (DYBBD), because the finest vintages deserve the company of a great meal, and David bought in.

One of our most recent DYBBDs involved old friends with their own enviable wine resources and a menu that required very few kitchen diversions. The main course was rack of lamb done in two steps, with the double goal of prepping and cooking well ahead of dinner while introducing more flavor to the meat. With braised Belgian endive cloaked in prosciutto and a toasted basmati rice pilaf, the pink chops provided classy support for an elegant Vosne-Romanée Richebourg. They'd be fit company for your best red too.

Twice-marinated lamb offers extra flavor to match a great red wine: try it with a Pinot Noir or Cabernet Sauvignon.

FOOD STYLING: KAREN SHINTO

Two-Step Rack of Lamb

PREP AND COOK TIME: About 30 minutes, plus at least 2 hours to marinate

NOTES: Marinating the racks before and after browning infuses them with extra flavor; it also minimizes last-minute cooking—the racks can stand for up to 4 hours, ready to be finished quickly in a hot oven.

MAKES: 6 servings

    3   **fat-trimmed racks of lamb** (each 1⅓ to 1½ lb., with 8 trimmed rib bones; backbone removed)
    1   cup **dry red wine**
    ½   to 1 cup **port**
    ½   cup **balsamic vinegar**
    ¼   cup minced **shallots** or onion
    1   teaspoon **dried thyme**
    ½   teaspoon fresh-ground **pepper**
        Salt

1. Trim and discard any fat on lamb racks down to about ⅛ inch thick; rinse lamb.

2. In a deep bowl, mix wine, ½ cup port, vinegar, shallots, thyme, and pepper. Add lamb and turn to coat well. Cover bowl airtight and chill for 1 to 4 hours, turning racks occasionally.

3. Lift racks from marinade, draining well; reserve liquid.

4. Place a 10- to 12-inch nonstick frying pan over medium-high heat. When hot, lay lamb racks, one or two at a time (don't crowd), meat side down, in pan. Brown entire meat side, tipping racks back and forth as necessary, 4 to 5 minutes total per rack. Frequently drain and discard any fat in pan to reduce spattering. As browned, return racks to marinade and coat well. Cover airtight and chill another 1 to 4 hours, turning racks occasionally.

5. Lift racks from bowl and lay, bones down (bones can overlap), in a shallow 12- by 17-inch pan. Pour marinade over lamb.

6. Bake in a 450° regular or convection oven until a thermometer inserted into meat in the center of a rack, parallel to rib bones, registers 125° for rare, 15 to 18 minutes, or 135° for medium-rare, 25 to 27 minutes (meat should still give easily when pressed). If marinade evaporates, add about ¼ cup water to pan and tilt to mix, to prevent scorching. Transfer racks to a platter and let stand at least 5 minutes.

7. If desired, add ½ cup port and ¼ cup water to pan; stir over high heat, scraping browned bits free, until mixture is boiling vigorously. Drain any accumulated juices from lamb into pan, then pour pan juices into a small bowl.

8. Cut racks apart into double lamb chops. Serve with pan juices. Add salt to taste.

Per serving: 241 cal., 45% (108 cal.) from fat; 26 g protein; 12 g fat (4.3 g sat.); 5 g carbo (0.1 g fiber); 100 mg sodium; 86 mg chol. ◆

"When you treat yourself, it should be something really special," says Fran, shown here with son Dylan.

Deep, dark secrets

Fran Bigelow, Seattle's most beloved chocolatier, keeps raising the bar

By Charity Ferreira • Photographs by John Granen

In the movie *Chocolat*, a red-caped Juliette Binoche sweeps into a quiet French village, borne by a mysterious breeze that one imagines smells of cocoa and exotic spices, her chocolate-filled valise promising untold pleasures for the town's inhabitants.

Fran Bigelow laughs at the suggested comparison, but then admits, "I guess it was a little bit like that!"

Twenty years ago, after a pastry-making stint in the San Francisco Bay Area, the Seattle native returned to her hometown to open a small shop and make European-quality chocolate desserts. Although her first store was in a somewhat out-of-the-way location on Madison Street, Fran piled 25-cent cocoa-dusted truffles in the front window and customers soon found their way.

Fran compares the development of Americans' awareness of chocolate to the similar evolution in the wine and coffee industries. In 1982, she says, coffee meant MJB and chocolate meant Hershey's. Aware that the chocolates she was making were unlike anything most of her customers had tasted, she tried to connect with everyone who came into her shop, to educate them about what they were tasting. As word spread, Fran continued to add hand-dipped chocolates to her line until she outgrew her small store in 1992.

Today her two retail shops—one in Bellevue, the other in University Village—look like European chocolate salons, minus the hushed, sacred atmosphere. You can buy an elegantly wrapped chocolate assortment or devise an impromptu sundae of Fran's ice creams, dessert sauces, and chocolate-covered cocoa nibs.

It's all about the bean

Though Fran is recognized as one of the premier chocolatiers in the coun-

Though you can order Fran's chocolates by mail, a trip to one of her salons is part of the experience.

lingers on the palate, dark and smooth, not at all bitter.

"Dylan grew up on these truffles," laughs Fran, which might explain why he brought them back last year for the 20th anniversary of Fran's Chocolates. How do these compare with the truffles of his childhood? The quality of the chocolate is far better now, he allows with a grin. "But her original truffles were very good."

Fran's Chocolates, 2594 N.E. University Village, Seattle; (206) 528-9969. 10305 N.E. 10th St., Bellevue; (425) 453-1698. **Mail order:** *www.franschocolates.com or (800) 422-3726.* ◆

Fran's Chocolate Caramel Mousse

This velvety mousse is a good example of how a few high-quality ingredients are all it takes to create a simple, quick dessert. The mousse can be made even more quickly by using an 11-ounce jar of Fran's chocolate caramel sauce; omit step 1 and use the sauce as the base for proceeding with step 2.

1. In a heavy 3- to 4-quart pan over low heat, stir 1¼ cups **sugar** with ½ cup **water** until sugar is dissolved and mixture looks clear. Increase heat to high and boil mixture, without stirring, until dark golden brown, about 10 minutes; occasionally brush sugar crystals down sides of pan with a wet pastry brush, and when mixture begins to caramelize around edge of pan, lift pan and gently swirl to ensure even caramelization. Remove from heat and carefully add ¾ cup **whipping cream** (mixture will bubble up); stir gently until smooth. Let cool for 5 minutes, then stir in 4 ounces finely chopped **bittersweet chocolate** until well blended. Transfer mixture to a large bowl and let cool to room temperature, about 1 hour.

2. Stir 2 tablespoons **Frangelico** or other hazelnut-flavored liqueur into chocolate mixture. In another bowl, with a mixer on high speed, beat 1 cup **whipping cream** to firm peaks. Gently fold about a third of the cream into the chocolate mixture, then fold in remaining cream until no white streaks remain.

3. Spoon mousse into dessert glasses and chill until cold, at least 1 hour, or up to 1 day. Garnish with **berries** or **chocolate shavings** if desired.

try, she continues to experiment and innovate. A local Spanish restaurant recently set her to thinking about sweet smoked paprika, which resulted in macadamia nuts caramelized with the smoky spice and enrobed in chocolate. French gray sea salt made its way into buttery, chocolate-covered caramels topped with a sprinkling of salt crystals. A spicy, concentrated Cabernet reduction joined bittersweet chocolate in a truffle for Michael Chiarello's Napa Style catalog.

But beyond the exotic flavorings she might add to her truffles, the es-

sential element is the bean. "People usually think of chocolate as being one flavor, sort of a sweet, chocolaty flavor," explains Fran's son, Dylan, who recently joined the company after three years at the pioneering Scharffen Berger Chocolate Maker. "This 'bean origin' movement is showing them that chocolate can have hundreds of different flavors."

As proof, Dylan offers a simple cocoa-dusted truffle, which tastes overwhelmingly of its two ingredients: cream and chocolate made from *Hacienda La Conception*, a Carenero bean from Venezuela. It

Pure nuts

New California oils and flours infuse dessert with flavor

In France a few years ago, I browsed happily in every food shop and *supermarché*. The cheese and pâté were lovely, but what really caught my eye were bags of almond flour. I love using nuts in baking, and I've spent way too much time scraping lumps of ground nuts out of my food processor. When I packed to come home, bags of almond flour found themselves nestled among new shoes in my suitcase.

I've long since used up that almond flour, but now I've discovered an American source: California Press, a small producer that cold-presses toasted nuts (almonds, hazelnuts, pecans, pistachios, and walnuts) to make virgin oils and grinds the pressed nuts into light flours. Both products add deep flavor and subtle texture to almost anything, from French crêpes to our very American chiffon-style maple pecan cake.

The oils cost about $17–$24 for 250 ml.; the flours are $17–$19 for 16 oz. They're available at specialty food markets and from California Press (707/944-0343).

Try toasted nut oils in vinaigrettes or drizzled over goat cheese; finely ground nut flour is great for baking, as in our maple pecan cake (above).

Maple Pecan Cake

PREP AND COOK TIME: About 2½ hours

NOTES: If the nut flour is not available, use 1 cup pecans: bake in a 350° oven until golden under skins, about 10 minutes, then whirl in a food processor until finely ground.

MAKES: 8 to 10 servings

- 1 cup **all-purpose flour**
- 1 cup **pecan flour** (see notes)
- 2 teaspoons **baking powder**
- ¼ teaspoon **salt**
- 3 **large egg** yolks, beaten to blend
- ⅔ cup **maple syrup**
- ⅓ cup **pecan** or vegetable **oil**
- 1 tablespoon **brandy**
- 6 **large egg** whites
- ⅓ cup **sugar**
  Maple–cream cheese frosting (recipe follows)
- ½ cup **chopped toasted pecans**

1. Butter and flour a 9-inch cake pan with a removable rim. In a bowl, stir together all-purpose flour, pecan flour, baking powder, and salt.

2. In a small bowl, mix egg yolks, maple syrup, pecan oil, and brandy. Pour into flour mixture; stir to combine.

3. In a large bowl, with a mixer, beat egg whites until soft peaks form. Beat in sugar, a tablespoon at a time, and continue to beat until glossy, about 2 minutes. Stir a quarter of the egg-white mixture into yolk mixture. Scrape into remaining egg-white mixture and fold in gently.

4. Pour batter into prepared pan. Bake in a 350° oven until cake springs back when lightly pressed in the center, 30 to 35 minutes. Transfer in pan to a rack and let cool about 1 hour.

5. Remove pan rim. Cut cake in half horizontally and place bottom layer on a cake plate. Spread half the maple–cream cheese frosting on bottom layer; top with remaining layer. Spread remaining frosting over top (leave sides bare). Sprinkle with chopped pecans.

Per serving: 511 cal., 55% (279 cal.) from fat; 6.2 g protein; 31 g fat (10 g sat.); 56 g carbo (1.1 g fiber); 326 mg sodium; 102 mg chol.

Maple–cream cheese frosting. In a 1- to 1½-quart pan over medium-high heat, bring ¾ cup **maple syrup** to a boil. Reduce heat and simmer, swirling pan occasionally, until reduced by about a third, 10 to 12 minutes. Pour into a glass measure nested in a bowl of ice water and stir constantly until syrup is very thick and barely warm to touch, 3 to 4 minutes. Remove from ice water. In a bowl, with a mixer on low speed, beat 4 ounces **cream cheese** and ½ cup (¼ lb.) **butter,** both at room temperature, until well blended. Beat in ½ cup **powdered sugar**. Scrape in reduced syrup; beat until smooth. Makes 1½ cups.

Per tablespoon: 86 cal., 58% (50 cal.) from fat; 0.4 g protein; 5.5 g fat (3.4 g sat.); 9.2 g carbo (0 g fiber); 54 mg sodium; 16 mg chol.

—*Kate Washington*

Handy rice — when you need just a little

Rice was on our minds this month (see "The New Rice Bowl," page 46), so we couldn't help but fall for this diminutive new rice cooker from National. It produces about 3 cups of cooked rice—just the right amount for one or two people—with the same fail-safe consistency of a larger rice cooker. It's easy to clean and takes up almost no space in the kitchen. In short, it's a convenient way to put a little rice in your life often. *National's 1-cup Mini Rice Cooker (model SR-3NA; about $40) is available online at www.appliances. com and at many Asian grocery and specialty stores such as 99 Ranch Markets (www.99ranch. com) and Uwajimaya (206/624-6248).*

—Charity Ferreira

The real deal

Expensive wines are—naturally—exciting to write about. Cheap wines can be satisfying too: a strange glee comes over you when you find a bottle that costs 70 percent less than it deserves to.

On any given night, however, most of us aren't drinking expensive or cheap wines; we're drinking somewhere in the middle. So for some time now, I've wondered if there's a strategy for finding the best midpriced wines. A couple of months ago, I began tasting more than 160 wines from $10 to $18. While no fail-safe strategies emerged, I came across a number of valuable lessons—and all kinds of interesting wines.

· Great midpriced whites are easier to find than reds. Fresh, snappy whites that aren't aged in oak are especially attractive and available. Sauvignon Blanc, Pinot Gris, and Riesling offer the tastiest deals. To me, most Chardonnays under $18 were dull and flat.

· Among reds, an overabundance of Merlots on the market means they're attractively priced. But the red that gives the biggest bang for the buck right now is Australian Shiraz. (It's nearly impossible to find a stellar Cabernet Sauvignon under $18.)

· Australia and New Zealand in general

Crisp white wines often offer big flavor for little money.

are great sources of terrific midpriced wines. Forget Chile, at least for now, for inexpensive bottles—the Chilean wines in my tasting were generally a little lackluster and flawed.

· The current economic downturn, however depressing, has one bright spot for consumers: wine prices have come down. Though I provide suggested retail prices here, many of these wines are available on sale for less. —*Karen MacNeil-Fife*

Great wines for $18 or less

Whites

Chimney Rock Fumé Blanc 2001 *(Napa Valley), $18.* Sassy grapefruit, melon, and green-tea flavors. Delicious and a little exotic.

Clos du Bois Sauvignon Blanc 2001 *(North Coast, CA), $10.* A good basic white. Fresh, light honeydew melon flavors.

Frog's Leap Leapfrögmilch 2001 *(Napa Valley), $14.* Edgy, spritzy, and crisp. Think Latin food on a warm night.

Glazebrook Sauvignon Blanc 2001 *(Hawkes Bay, New Zealand), $14.* Limy, fresh, and mouthwatering.

Kunde "Magnolia Lane" Sauvignon Blanc 2001 *(Sonoma Valley), $14.* Spearmint, green melons, fresh limes, and peaches. Lovely.

Nautilus Estate Pinot Gris 2002 *(Marlborough, New Zealand), $18.* Lemon meringue pie masquerading as wine. Delicious.

Smith-Madrone Riesling 2001 *(Napa Valley), $17.* Expressive and snappy, with grapefruit and key-lime pie flavors.

Torres Gran Viña Sol Chardonnay 2000 *(Penedès, Spain), $14.* A terrific Chardonnay for the price. Simple vanilla flavors with a touch of crispness.

Twin Islands Sauvignon Blanc 2002 *(Marlborough, New Zealand), $12.* Quintessential New Zealand Sauvignon. Dramatically limy, precise, and sensational—a steal. Try it with goat cheese.

Reds

Domaine la Soumade "Cuvée Prestige" Rasteau Côtes du Rhône Villages 2000 *(France),* $18. Earthy mocha flavors, with hints of plum and black pepper.

Fleur du Cap Merlot 2000 *(Coastal Region, South Africa), $13.* Juicy, smoky, and sleek.

Penfolds "Koonunga Hill" Shiraz/Cabernet Sauvignon 2000 *(South Eastern Australia), $11.* Big and simple, with mouth-filling blackberry and chocolate flavors.

Sebastiani Cabernet Sauvignon 1999 *(Sonoma County), $17.* Powerful and structured, with plush red berry and mocha flavors.

Stonehaven "Limestone Coast" Shiraz 2000 *(Limestone Coast, Australia), $16.* Concentrated—a stellar wine for the price.

Trinchero Family Selection Merlot 2000 *(California), $14.* Ripe blackberries and good dusty tannins. Rustic and appealing.

Quick pizza is even faster if you use leftover cooked chicken: just mix it with the barbecue sauce.

Spring flings

Readers' recipes tested in *Sunset's* kitchens

Photographs by James Carrier

Barbecued Chicken Pizza

Meredith McGowan, Valencia, CA

Meredith McGowan likes devising original combinations to top her family's favorite dish—pizza. McGowan makes dough from scratch, but prebaked pizza crusts—available in many supermarkets—are an easy shortcut.

PREP AND COOK TIME: 45 minutes to 1 hour

MAKES: Two 8-inch pizzas; 2 or 3 servings

- 1 pound **boned, skinned chicken breasts**
- ⅓ cup **prepared barbecue sauce**
  Salt and **pepper**
- 4 slices **bacon** (4 oz. total), cut into 1-inch pieces
- 2 **baked pizza crusts** (7 to 8 in., 5 oz. each; see note above)
- ¼ cup **cream cheese** (2 oz.)
- ¼ cup **canned diced green chilies**
- ½ cup **shredded jack cheese**
- ¼ to ½ teaspoon **hot chili flakes**

1. Rinse chicken and pat dry. Place in an 8-inch baking pan and coat with about 2 tablespoons barbecue sauce. Sprinkle with salt and pepper. Bake in a 350° regular or convection oven until no longer pink at the center of the thickest part (cut to test), about 20 minutes. Let stand until cool enough to handle, then tear into bite-size chunks. In a small bowl, mix with remaining barbecue sauce.

2. Meanwhile, in a 10- to 12-inch frying pan over high heat, stir bacon until browned and crisp, about 5 minutes. With a slotted spoon, transfer bacon to paper towels to drain.

3. Place pizza crusts on a 12- by 15-inch baking sheet. Spread each with about 2 tablespoons cream cheese. Spoon chicken in sauce evenly over both crusts; top with bacon, green chilies, jack cheese, and hot chili flakes.

4. Bake pizzas in a 400° regular or convection oven until cheese is browned and bubbling, 15 to 20 minutes. Transfer to a board and cut into wedges.

Per serving: 720 cal., 36% (261 cal.) from fat; 47 g protein; 29 g fat (12 g sat.); 59 g carbo (4.7 g fiber); 922 mg sodium; 138 mg chol.

Noodles in Spicy Lemon Grass Broth

Karen Biggs, Vancouver, WA

Karen Biggs makes a delicious, simple meal of noodles in a highly seasoned broth. Wear gloves when working with the chilies or wash hands thoroughly afterward. Look for fresh Chinese noodles, either egg-based or plain, in the refrigerator case of many supermarkets or in Asian markets; if you cannot find them, substitute any dried or fresh thin noodle.

PREP AND COOK TIME: About 45 minutes

MAKES: 2 or 3 servings

- 3 stalks **fresh lemon grass** (10 to 12 in. long)
- ½ bunch **cilantro** (about 2 oz.), rinsed
- 5 cups fat-skimmed **chicken broth** or vegetable broth
- ½ cup chopped **green onions** (including tops)
- 6 thin slices (quarter size) peeled **fresh ginger**
- 3 **fresh hot red chilies** (about 2½ in. long), rinsed, stemmed, seeded, and quartered (see note above)
- 3 cloves **garlic**, peeled
- 1 teaspoon **black peppercorns**
- 9 ounces **fresh thin Chinese noodles** (see note above)

1. Rinse lemon grass; cut off and discard tough tops and root ends. Peel off and discard coarse outer layers, then crush the tender inner part with the flat side of a large knife. Coarsely chop ¼ cup cilantro leaves, reserving stems (save extra leaves for other uses).

2. In a 4- to 6-quart pan, combine broth, crushed lemon grass, cilantro stems, ¼ cup green onions, ginger, chilies, garlic, and peppercorns. Bring to a simmer over high heat; cover, reduce heat to maintain a simmer, and cook 30 minutes. Pour through a strainer over a large bowl; discard solids.

3. Meanwhile, in another 4- to 6-quart pan over high heat, bring about 3 quarts water to a boil. Add noodles and cook, stirring occasionally, until tender to bite, 2 to 3 minutes. Drain.

4. Divide noodles between two large soup bowls and ladle broth over noodles. Sprinkle with chopped cilantro and remaining ¼ cup green onions.

Per serving: 332 cal., 7% (23 cal.) from fat; 24 g protein; 2.5 g fat (0.3 g sat.); 53 g carbo (3.8 g fiber); 157 mg sodium; 62 mg chol.

Pork Chops with Mustard and Plum Jam

Janis Dickinson, Long Beach, CA

Her mother's homemade plum jam inspired Janis Dickinson to come up with this pork chop recipe.

PREP AND COOK TIME: About 25 minutes
MAKES: 4 servings

 2 tablespoons **olive oil**
 4 **boned center-cut loin pork chops** (each about ¾ in. thick and 6 oz.)
 1 **onion** (about 8 oz.), peeled and sliced ¼ inch thick
 1 cup **dry white wine**
 2 tablespoons **plum jam**
 1 tablespoon **Dijon mustard**
   Salt and **pepper**

1. Pour oil into a 10- to 12-inch nonstick frying pan over medium-high heat. When hot, add pork chops and cook, turning once, until browned on both sides, about 4 minutes total. Transfer pork chops to a plate.

2. Reduce heat to medium and add onion. Stir frequently until onion is limp, 5 to 8 minutes. Stir in wine, jam, and mustard, and bring to a simmer.

3. Return pork chops to pan and cook until they are barely pink in the center (cut to test), about 5 minutes. Sprinkle with salt and pepper. Transfer chops to plates and spoon sauce over them.

Per serving: 487 cal., 52% (252 cal.) from fat; 35 g protein; 28 g fat (8.4 g sat.); 11 g carbo (0.9 g fiber); 201 mg sodium; 114 mg chol.

Orange Halibut with Quinoa

Jennifer Rinterknecht, Corvallis, OR

By the end of winter, Jennifer Rinterknecht is ready for something bright and vibrant, like this halibut with fruit and the protein-rich grain quinoa. To toast hazelnuts, bake in a 375° oven until golden under skin, about 10 minutes. Pour nuts onto a towel and rub briskly to remove as much skin as possible.

PREP AND COOK TIME: About 30 minutes
MAKES: 3 servings

 1 **avocado** (about 8 oz.)
 1 **orange** (about 8 oz.)
 ¾ cup **quinoa**
   About ½ teaspoon **salt**
 1 pound **boned, skinned halibut,** cut into 3 equal pieces
   Pepper
 1 tablespoon **olive oil**
 1 tablespoon **orange marmalade**

Seared halibut has a tangy marmalade glaze.

 ¼ cup **dried cranberries**
 ⅓ cup chopped toasted **hazelnuts** (about 2 oz.; see note above)

1. Pit and peel avocado and cut into ¼-inch cubes. With a sharp knife, cut and discard peel and white pith from orange. Cut between membranes to release orange segments into a bowl.

2. In a strainer, rinse and drain quinoa. In a 3- to 4-quart pan over high heat, bring 1½ cups water to a boil. Add quinoa and ½ teaspoon salt and adjust heat to maintain a simmer. Cover and cook until water is absorbed and quinoa is tender to bite, about 15 minutes.

3. Meanwhile, rinse halibut and pat dry. Sprinkle lightly all over with salt and pepper. Pour oil into a 10- to 12-inch nonstick frying pan over high heat. When hot, add halibut and cook, turning once, until opaque but still moist-looking at the center of the thickest part (cut to test), about 6 minutes total. Spread about 1 teaspoon marmalade over each piece of fish.

4. Mound quinoa on dinner plates. With a spatula, place a piece of fish on top of quinoa and arrange avocado and orange segments over fish. Sprinkle evenly with cranberries and hazelnuts.

Per serving: 647 cal., 43% (279 cal.) from fat; 41 g protein; 31 g fat (3.6 g sat.); 54 g carbo (7 g fiber); 487 mg sodium; 48 mg chol.

Double-Chocolate Muffins

Heather Henderson, Eugene, OR

The teachers at her children's school claim to suffer withdrawal symptoms for Heather Henderson's homemade muffins when school is out for the summer.

PREP AND COOK TIME: About 45 minutes
MAKES: 18 muffins

 3 **large eggs**
 2 cups **sugar**
 1 cup **vegetable oil**
 ¾ cup mashed **ripe banana**
 ¾ cup **plain yogurt**
 1 teaspoon **vanilla**
 1 cup **whole-wheat flour**
 1 cup **all-purpose flour**
 ½ cup **unsweetened cocoa**
 1 teaspoon **ground cinnamon**
 1 teaspoon **salt**
 1 teaspoon **baking soda**
 ½ teaspoon **baking powder**
 ¾ cup **semisweet chocolate chips**

1. In a large bowl, beat eggs, sugar, oil, banana, yogurt, and vanilla to blend. In a smaller bowl, stir together whole-wheat and all-purpose flours, cocoa, cinnamon, salt, baking soda, and baking powder. Gently stir flour mixture and chocolate chips into egg mixture just until incorporated. Spoon batter evenly into 18 paper-lined muffin cups (¾-cup capacity; fill them all the way to the top).

2. Bake muffins in a 350° regular or convection oven until a wooden skewer inserted into the center comes out with moist crumbs attached, about 25 minutes. Cool 10 minutes and remove from pans. Serve warm or cool.

Per muffin: 308 cal., 47% (144 cal.) from fat; 4 g protein; 16 g fat (3.3 g sat.); 41 g carbo (2.3 g fiber); 232 mg sodium; 36 mg chol. ◆

Give a quick sausage and linguine dish a light and tasty boost by adding soybeans (see page 74).

April

Soufflés made simple

Use our easy techniques to take soufflés to new heights

By Linda Lau Anusasananan • Photographs by James Carrier • Food styling by Susan Devaty

The thought of making anything as fragile-looking as a tall soufflé can terrify cooks. The dish seems magical, but you only need a little basic cooking science to make one—it is nothing more than flavored white sauce folded into beaten egg whites. The whipped egg whites, a network of bubbles, form a structure that captures air. The thick sauce coats the components, stabilizing the soufflé. When heated, the air in the bubbles expands, making the whole mass rise.

To ensure such uplifting results, just follow our easy guidelines for beating the egg whites and blending the batter correctly (see "Soufflé Pointers" at right). And make sure that your guests are at the table when the timer goes off—making a soufflé might not be magic, but its fleeting beauty will pull a disappearing act if you don't serve it at once.

Classic Cheese Soufflé

PREP AND COOK TIME: About 45 minutes

NOTES: You can prepare the dishes, make the sauce (through step 2), shred the cheese, and separate the eggs up to 4 hours ahead; cover separately and chill. Stir sauce over low heat until hot before proceeding.

MAKES: 6 main-dish servings

- ¼ cup (⅛ lb.) **butter**
- ¼ cup **all-purpose flour**
- 1¼ cups **milk**
- ¼ teaspoon **cayenne**
- ¼ teaspoon **salt**
- 1½ cups **shredded sharp cheddar,** pepper jack, or Gruyère **cheese** (6 oz.)
- 6 **large eggs,** separated
- ¼ teaspoon **cream of tartar**

1. Generously butter a 2-quart soufflé dish or six 1- to 1¼-cup soufflé dishes; if using small ones, set them about 2 inches apart in a 10- by 15-inch baking pan.

2. In a 2- to 3-quart pan over medium heat, melt ¼ cup butter. Add flour and stir until mixture is smooth and bubbling. Stir in milk, cayenne, and salt, and continue stirring until sauce boils and thickens, 3 to 4 minutes. Remove from heat.

3. Add cheese and stir until melted. Add egg yolks and stir until the mixture is blended and smooth.

4. In a bowl, with a mixer on high speed, beat egg whites (use whisk attachment if available) with cream of tartar until short, stiff, moist peaks form. With a flexible spatula, fold a third of the cheese sauce into whites until well blended. Add remaining sauce and gently fold in just until blended.

5. Scrape the batter into the prepared soufflé dish (or dishes). If the dish is more than ¾ full, use foil collar (see "Crowning Glory," page 69). If desired, draw a circle on the surface of the soufflé batter with the tip of a knife, about 1 inch in from rim, to help an attractive crown form during baking.

6. Bake in a 375° regular or convection oven until top is golden to deep brown and cracks look fairly dry, 25 to 30 minutes for large soufflé, 15 to 20 minutes for small ones. Serve immediately, scooping portions from single soufflé with a large spoon.

Per serving: 321 cal., 70% (225 cal.) from fat; 16 g protein; 25 g fat (14 g sat.); 7.4 g carbo (0.2 g fiber); 453 mg sodium; 274 mg chol.

Bake cheese soufflé in a classic dish, or use another deep pan or dish of equal volume.

Soufflé pointers

• **Add cream of tartar** to the whites while beating; the acid stiffens and coagulates the egg-white protein, strengthening the walls of the bubbles. Sugar, used in sweet soufflés, also strengthens the bubbles.

• **Use a wire whisk attachment** to introduce air into the whites evenly, creating tiny, strong bubbles.

• **Beat the whites just until stiff** but moist-looking peaks form. If the whites are over-beaten, the walls of the air bubbles will be stretched out; they may burst when heated, collapsing the soufflé.

• **Fold the white sauce gently** but thoroughly into the beaten egg whites, using a flexible spatula. Overmixing, or folding with a heavy hand, may collapse the egg-white bubbles, leaving your soufflé less than ethereal.

• **Bake the soufflé in the right dish size** for the best results (see "Crowning Glory," page 69). Classic soufflé dishes aren't necessary; you can also use deep casseroles or ovenproof bowls, though soufflés baked in bowls with sloping sides won't rise as high as those in straight-sided dishes. Measure your dish's capacity with water to determine its volume.

Corn and Dried Tomato Soufflé with Shrimp-Onion Relish

PREP AND COOK TIME: About 1 hour

NOTES: Use dried tomatoes that are moist, soft, and pliable; if they aren't, soak them in hot water until soft, 5 to 15 minutes, then squeeze out water. Or use oil-packed tomatoes and squeeze out the oil. You can prepare the dishes (step 1), make the sauce (step 2), and separate the eggs up to 4 hours ahead; cover sauce and eggs separately and chill. Stir the chilled white sauce over low heat until hot before proceeding with step 3.

MAKES: 6 main-dish servings

¼ cup (⅛ lb.) **butter**

¼ cup **all-purpose flour**

1¼ cups **milk**

1 teaspoon **dried tarragon**

¼ teaspoon **salt**

1 cup thawed **frozen corn kernels**

⅓ cup finely chopped **dried tomatoes** (see notes)

½ cup **grated parmesan cheese**

8 **large eggs,** separated

¼ teaspoon **cream of tartar**

Shrimp-onion relish (recipe follows; optional)

1. Generously butter a 2½- to 3-quart soufflé dish or six 1½- to 2-cup soufflé dishes. If using small dishes, set them about 2 inches apart in a 10- by 15-inch baking pan.

2. In a 2- to 3-quart pan over medium heat, melt butter. Add flour and stir until mixture is smooth and bubbling. Stir in milk, tarragon, and salt, and continue stirring until sauce boils and thickens, 2 to 3 minutes. Add corn and dried tomatoes and stir until hot, about 1 minute. Remove from heat.

3. Add parmesan cheese and stir until melted. Add egg yolks and stir until mixture is blended and smooth.

4. In a bowl, with a mixer on high speed, beat egg whites (use whisk attachment if available) with cream of tartar until short, stiff, moist peaks form. With a flexible spatula, fold a third of the cheese sauce into whites until well blended. Add remaining sauce and gently fold in just until blended.

5. Scrape batter into prepared soufflé dish (or dishes). If higher than ¾ full, use a foil collar (see "Crowning Glory" at right). If desired, draw a circle on the surface of the soufflé batter with the tip of a knife, about 1 inch in from rim, to help an attractive crown form during baking.

6. Bake large soufflé in a 350° regular or 325° convection oven until top is golden to deep brown and cracks look fairly dry, 35 to 40 minutes. Bake small soufflés in a 375° regular or convection oven, 20 to 25 minutes. Serve immediately, scooping portions from single soufflé with a large spoon. Pass the shrimp-onion relish to spoon over each serving as desired.

Per serving: 300 cal., 60% (180 cal.) from fat; 15 g protein; 20 g fat (10 g sat.); 16 g carbo (1.6 g fiber); 428 mg sodium; 321 mg chol.

Shrimp-Onion Relish

PREP AND COOK TIME: 10 to 15 minutes

NOTES: You can also serve this easy relish over scrambled eggs.

MAKES: 2½ cups

1 tablespoon **olive oil**

2 teaspoons **mustard seeds**

1 cup finely chopped **green onions** (including green tops)

12 ounces **shelled cooked tiny shrimp,** rinsed

Salt and **pepper**

Pour olive oil into an 8- to 10-inch frying pan over medium-high heat. When hot, add mustard seeds and stir often just until they begin to pop, about 30 seconds. Add green onions and shrimp and stir until shrimp are warm, about 1 minute. Season with salt and pepper to taste.

Per tablespoon: 13 cal., 35% (4.5 cal.) from fat; 1.9 g protein; 0.5 g fat (0.1 g sat.); 0.2 g carbo (0.1 g fiber); 19 mg sodium; 17 mg chol.

Serve shrimp relish and asparagus with airy corn and tomato soufflé for brunch or a light supper.

Treat guests to chocolate soufflés— make them partially ahead and bake them just before serving.

Dark Chocolate Soufflé

PREP AND COOK TIME: About 45 minutes

NOTES: You can butter the dishes, prepare the sauce (through step 2), chop the chocolate, and separate the eggs up to 4 hours ahead; cover sauce and eggs separately and chill. Stir sauce over low heat until hot before proceeding.

MAKES: 4 to 6 servings

- 3 tablespoons **butter**
- 3 tablespoons **all-purpose flour**
- 1 cup **milk**
- 1 cup chopped **bittersweet** or semisweet **chocolate** (5 to 6 oz.)
- 4 **large eggs,** separated
- 2 tablespoons **rum** or 1 teaspoon vanilla
- 1/8 teaspoon **cream of tartar**
- 1/4 cup **sugar**

  Lightly sweetened softly **whipped cream**

1. Generously butter four 1- to 1 1/4-cup soufflé dishes or one 1 1/2-quart soufflé dish. If using small dishes, set them slightly apart in a 10- by 15-inch baking pan.

2. In a 2- to 3-quart pan over medium heat, melt 3 tablespoons butter. Add flour; stir until mixture is smooth and bubbling. Stir in milk; continue stirring until sauce boils and thickens, about 2 minutes. Remove from heat.

3. Add chocolate and stir until smooth. Add egg yolks and rum and stir until mixture is blended and smooth.

4. In a bowl, with a mixer on high speed, beat egg whites (use whisk attachment if available) with cream of tartar until foamy. Gradually add sugar and continue beating until short, stiff, moist peaks form. With a flexible spatula, fold a third of the chocolate sauce into whites until well blended. Add remaining sauce and gently fold in just until blended.

5. Scrape batter into prepared soufflé dishes; if higher than 3/4 full, use foil collar (see "Crowning Glory" at left).

6. Bake in a 375° regular or convection oven to desired doneness: For a soft, creamy center, bake until edges feel set and dry but center 1 to 1 1/2 inches of small soufflés or 2 to 3 inches of large one still appear soft and jiggle slightly when dishes are very gently shaken, 12 to 15 minutes for small soufflés, 15 to 20 minutes for large one. For a fully set center, bake until surface appears set and fairly dry, 2 to 3 minutes longer for small soufflés, 5 to 6 minutes longer for large one.

7. Serve at once, scooping portions from single soufflé with a large spoon. Offer whipped cream to add to taste.

Per serving: 329 cal., 57% (189 cal.) from fat; 7.6 g protein; 21 g fat (11 g sat.); 29 g carbo (0.7 g fiber); 147 mg sodium; 170 mg chol. ◆

Crowning glory

Soufflés look most impressive when they rise dramatically over the rim of the dish. To create a beautiful crown on your soufflé, fill the dish about 3/4 full. If it's less full, the soufflé may not rise over the rim. If it's more full, the soufflé may spill over unless you wrap the dish with a foil collar. Here's how to make one.

Cut a 15-inch-wide sheet of foil 4 inches longer than circumference of dish; fold lengthwise in thirds.

Coat one side of the foil strip generously with melted butter, using a pastry brush.

Wrap the foil around outside of dish so that at least 2 inches of foil extend above the rim.

Fold the ends of the buttered foil strip over several times until snug against dish.

A taste of Russia

Throw an easy appetizer party with zakuski

By Kate Washington • Photographs by James Carrier • Food styling by Karen Shinto

Zakuski—Russian appetizers—got their start as just a little something to nibble with vodka. Even though the word means "little bites," zakuski evolved into a lavish spread of hors d'oeuvres. The Old World tradition makes a perfectly modern appetizer party or a casual buffet dinner. Infusing vodkas with aromatics and spices gives cocktail hour an easy new twist (see "Fresh Infusion," below). And Russia's bright spring flavors, such as fresh herbs, sweet beets, and delicate salmon, banish any stereotypes of grim Moscow markets full of cabbage.

A zakuski party can be a flexible mix of homemade and purchased dishes, depending on how much time you want to spend (see "The Strategy," page 72). There are excellent resources in Russian neighborhoods throughout the West, especially in such cities as Seattle, San Francisco, and Los Angeles. The growing enclaves in these cities are renewing the West's long history of Russian settlement from Alaska south down the Pacific coast. Now is the perfect time to celebrate spring with a little bite, a glass of vodka, and a toast with friends.

Onions complement pink peppercorn, saffron-orange, lemon-coriander, and ginger vodkas.

Fresh infusion

Russians are known for drinking vodka straight, but there's also a tradition of flavoring vodkas with herbs and spices. Our infusions range from traditional caraway to updated saffron-orange. Use 2 cups vodka with any of the following. Combine vodka and flavorings in a jar and store at room temperature for at least two days or up to several months. Chill in the freezer before serving.

ANISE VODKA: Add 2 **whole star anise** and 1 tablespoon **anise seeds** to vodka.

CARAWAY VODKA: Add 2 tablespoons **caraway seeds** to vodka.

GINGER VODKA: Add 6 quarter-size slices peeled **fresh ginger** to vodka with 1 teaspoon grated fresh ginger.

HOT CHILI VODKA: Halve 1 rinsed **fresh habanero** or other hot **chili** lengthwise through stem; add half the chili to vodka. Habaneros are extremely hot; if you are sensitive to heat, substitute a milder chili, such as jalapeño.

LEMON-CORIANDER VODKA: Lightly crush 1 tablespoon **coriander seeds** in a mortar or with the bottom of a heavy glass and add to vodka with 1 tablespoon slivered **lemon** peel.

PEPPERCORN VODKA: Lightly crush 1 teaspoon **single-** or multi-**colored peppercorns** in a mortar or with the bottom of a heavy glass; add to vodka.

SAFFRON-ORANGE VODKA: Add ⅛ teaspoon loosely packed **saffron threads** and 1 tablespoon slivered **orange** peel to vodka.

Russian appetizer menu

Infused vodkas*

Pickled spring onions* or purchased pickles

Caviar tartlets*, salmon-herb turnovers*,
or cocktail pelmeni*

Wild mushroom caviar* or purchased spreads

Beet salad* or purchased deli salads

Smoked or cured meats and fish

Russian rye or black bread and crackers

*Recipe provided

For an easy spread, offer
homemade salmon
turnovers and beet salad
alongside purchased
dishes like carrot salad.

Pickled Spring Onions

PREP AND COOK TIME: About 1 hour

NOTES: Spring onions are freshly dug, small-bulbed onions with green stems still attached. They make for tender, mild pickled onions. Look for them in good produce markets or at farmers' markets. If they are unavailable, use pearl onions. You can make the onions up to 2 days ahead; cool, cover, and chill with liquid. Strain and bring to room temperature before serving.

MAKES: 10 to 12 servings as part of an appetizer menu

    1½ cups **distilled white vinegar**
     1 tablespoon **kosher salt**
     1 tablespoon **sugar**
     8 **whole cloves**
     1 teaspoon **hot chili flakes**
     1 **dried bay leaf**
    12 ounces **spring** or pearl **onions** (about 30, 1 to 1½ in. wide; trim any greens before weighing), rinsed (see notes)

1. In a 1½- to 2-quart pan over medium heat, combine vinegar, salt, sugar, cloves, chili flakes, bay leaf, and 1½ cups water. Bring to a simmer and cook for 5 minutes.

2. Meanwhile, peel onions and pull off any thin membrane under peel. Trim root ends.

3. Add onions to vinegar mixture and simmer, stirring occasionally, until just tender when pierced, 10 to 15 minutes. Remove from heat and let cool to room temperature, about 1 hour. Using a slotted spoon, transfer to a serving bowl; discard liquid.

Per serving: 12 cal., 0% (0 cal.) from fat; 0.2 g protein; 0 g fat; 3.1 g carbo (0 g fiber); 164 mg sodium; 0 mg chol.

Caviar Tartlets

PREP TIME: About 15 minutes

NOTES: To make these easy, stylish appetizers, use domestic red, black, or golden caviar or fish roe, or some of each, for visual contrast and appeal. Crisp filo pastry shells, about 1

inch in diameter, are available in well-stocked supermarkets.

MAKES: 45 tartlets

    About 8 ounces **sour cream**
    3 packages (2.1 oz. each) **frozen small filo pastry shells,** thawed (see notes)
    About 4 ounces **caviar** or other fish roe (see notes)
    Fresh chervil leaves or small sprigs fresh dill (optional), rinsed

Spoon about ½ teaspoon sour cream into each filo shell, then ½ to 1 teaspoon caviar. If desired, garnish each tartlet with a leaf of chervil or a small sprig of dill.

Per tartlet: 35 cal., 57% (20 cal.) from fat; 1.1 g protein; 2.2 g fat (0.7 g sat.); 2.8 g carbo (0 g fiber); 64 mg sodium; 17 mg chol.

Salmon-Herb Turnovers

PREP AND COOK TIME: About 1½ hours

NOTES: These pastries are an appetizer-size take on the classic kulebiaka, an elaborate savory pie filled with salmon or sturgeon and rice. The original is made with yeast dough, but purchased puff pastry is an easy shortcut. You can make the filling (steps 1 through 3) up to 3 days ahead; cover and chill.

MAKES: 27 pastries; 10 to 12 servings

    1 cup fat-skimmed **chicken broth**
    ½ cup **basmati rice**
    2 tablespoons **butter**
    ½ cup minced **onion**
    ½ cup finely chopped **mushrooms** (common, exotic, or a mixture)
    ¾ cup **dry white wine**
    8 ounces **boned, skinned salmon fillet,** rinsed, patted dry, and cut into 1-inch chunks
    ½ teaspoon **salt**
    ½ teaspoon fresh-ground **pepper**
    2 tablespoons chopped mixed **fresh herbs** such as chervil, chives, dill, parsley, or tarragon
    3 sheets (each 9 in. square) thawed **frozen puff pastry** (1½ packages, 17.3 oz. each)
    1 **large egg,** beaten to blend with 1 tablespoon water

1. In a 1½- to 2-quart pan, bring chicken broth and rice to a boil over medium-high heat. Reduce heat, cover, and simmer until rice is tender to bite, about 15 minutes.

2. Meanwhile, in a 2- to 3-quart pan over medium heat, melt butter. Add onion and mushrooms and stir often until onion is soft and liquid has evaporated, 7 to 8 minutes. Add wine, increase heat, and bring to a boil; add salmon chunks and reduce heat to maintain a simmer. Cook, stirring often, until salmon is

Caviar tartlets are a colorful, simple appetizer.

broken into flakes and most of the liquid has evaporated, 7 to 10 minutes. Stir in rice, salt, pepper, and herbs.

3. Cut each puff pastry sheet into nine 3-inch squares. On a lightly floured work surface, with a lightly floured rolling pin, roll each square once in each direction to flatten and stretch to approximately 4 inches. Place 1 tablespoon filling in the middle of each square. Brush edges lightly with egg mixture and fold diagonally over filling to make triangles; pinch edges to seal. Arrange pastries ½ inch apart on two cooking parchment–lined 12- by 15-inch baking sheets. Lightly brush the top of each pastry with egg mixture.

4. Bake pastries in a 375° regular or convection oven until golden brown, 20 to 25 minutes. Serve warm.

Per pastry: 194 cal., 56% (108 cal.) from fat; 4.7 g protein; 12 g fat (2.2 g sat.); 16 g carbo (0.6 g fiber); 132 mg sodium; 15 mg chol.

Wild Mushroom Caviar

PREP AND COOK TIME: About 45 minutes

NOTES: You can make this spread up to 1 day ahead; cover and chill. Bring to room temperature and stir before serving. Serve with rye bread or crackers.

MAKES: About 1¾ cups; 10 to 12 servings as part of an appetizer menu

- 1 pound mixed **fresh exotic mushrooms,** such as black trumpet, chanterelle, cremini, and shiitake, and/or common mushrooms
- 3 tablespoons **butter**
- ½ cup minced **onion**
- 1 teaspoon **kosher salt**
  Fresh-ground **pepper**
- ¼ cup **sour cream**
- 2 tablespoons **tarragon-flavored white wine vinegar**
- 1 tablespoon chopped **fresh tarragon**

1. Rinse mushrooms and pat dry with paper towels. Trim and discard any discolored areas and tough stem ends (whole stems for shiitakes). Working in batches, pulse mushrooms in a food processor until finely chopped (or chop with a sharp knife).

2. In a 10- to 12-inch nonstick frying pan over medium heat, melt butter. Add onion and stir often until limp, about 5 minutes. Add chopped mushrooms and sprinkle evenly with salt. Stir often until juices have evaporated and mushrooms are beginning to brown, about 10 minutes; remove from heat. Grind in pepper to taste.

3. In a glass measure, stir together sour cream, vinegar, and tarragon. Pour into mushroom mixture and stir to mix. Serve warm or at room temperature.

Per serving: 47 cal., 74% (35 cal.) from fat; 1.1 g protein; 3.9 g fat (2.4 g sat.); 2.5 g carbo (0.4 g fiber); 196 mg sodium; 9.9 mg chol.

Beet Salad

PREP AND COOK TIME: About 1 hour

NOTES: If you have a mandoline or a Benriner slicer, use the julienne attachment to cut the beets into slender, even matchsticks in step 1. You can make the salad up to 1 day ahead; cover and chill. Before serving, taste and add more rice vinegar if desired. Serve as a canapé topping with rye bread or crackers.

MAKES: About 3 cups; 10 to 12 servings as part of an appetizer menu

- 1½ pounds **beets** (greens trimmed before weighing), rinsed
    About ⅓ cup **sour cream**
- 1 tablespoon chopped **fresh dill**
    Salt and **pepper**
    About 1 tablespoon
    rice vinegar

1. Place beets in an 8-inch square baking pan. Add ½ inch water. Cover pan tightly with foil and bake in a 375° regular or convection oven until beets are just tender when pierced, 45 to 60 minutes. When cool enough to handle, peel and cut into matchstick-size strips (see notes).

2. In a bowl, combine beets and ⅓ cup sour cream and mix gently to coat; if you'd like your salad more moist, stir in a little more sour cream. Stir in dill and salt, pepper, and vinegar to taste.

Per serving: 31 cal., 42% (13 cal.) from fat; 0.8 g protein; 1.4 g fat (0.8 g sat.); 4.2 g carbo (0.4 g fiber); 32 mg sodium; 2.8 mg chol.

Cocktail Pelmeni

PREP AND COOK TIME: About 15 minutes

NOTE: Pelmeni, available frozen at Russian markets, are meat dumplings, usually served boiled in a brothy soup. Frying them in butter turns them into perfect cocktail nibbles.

MAKES: About 50 pelmeni; 10 to 12 servings

In a 10- to 12-inch nonstick frying pan over medium-high heat, melt 2 tablespoons **butter.** When it's foamy, pour in 1 package (1 lb.) frozen **meat** or chicken **pelmeni;** turn occasionally until cooked through (cut to test) and golden brown on at least one side, 6 to 8 minutes. Pour into a serving dish and sprinkle with about 1 tablespoon chopped **fresh dill.** Serve hot, with toothpicks alongside and **sour cream,** if desired, to dip pelmeni in.

No nutritional data is available for pelmeni. ◆

For a dramatic buffet, serve meat dumplings, beet salad, and a whole smoked fish.

Soybeans and carrots dressed with sesame oil and ginger make a quick salad.

The versatile soybean

Healthy and easy to use, these beans are breaking out of their shells

By Linda Lau Anusasananan • Photographs by James Carrier

Whole soybeans, enjoyed in Japan for centuries, have been going incognito in this country for a long time. In Japanese restaurants, as you pore over the sushi list, a bowl of warm, slightly fuzzy pods—called edamame—arrives. You squeeze open the shell and pop out two or three bright green beans with a fresh, nutty flavor—irresistible.

It's hard to stop eating soybeans, so it's a good thing they're good for you. High in fiber, protein, and isoflavones (hormonelike chemicals), they contain no cholesterol and virtually no saturated fat. Studies suggest that they may help reduce the risk of heart disease.

With so much going for them, soybeans can't stay under wraps forever. Fortunately, they're already widely available, cooked in the pod for an instant appetizer or cooked and shelled to use in soups, salads, stir-fries, stews, and pasta dishes. You'll find soybeans in the refrigerator or freezer case in well-stocked supermarkets, as well as in Asian grocery stores. April—national soy month—is the perfect time to start trying them, and here are some recipes that will make converts of us all.

Linguine with Soybeans and Sausage

PREP AND COOK TIME: About 45 minutes
NOTES: Pass additional grated parmesan cheese at the table to add to taste.
MAKES: About 4 servings

- 8 ounces **hot** or mild **Italian sausages,** casings removed
- 1 **onion** (8 oz.), peeled and chopped
- 1 clove **garlic,** peeled and minced
- 1 cup fat-skimmed **chicken broth**
- 1 package (12 oz.) **frozen shelled soybeans** or 2¼ cups refrigerated cooked shelled soybeans
- 8 ounces **dried linguine**
- 3 tablespoons chopped **Italian** or regular **parsley**
- 3 tablespoons **grated parmesan cheese** (see notes)

   Salt and **pepper**

1. Pull sausages into chunks and put in a 10- to 12-inch frying pan over medium-high heat. Add onion and garlic; cook, stirring often to crumble meat, until sausage is browned, 7 to 10 minutes. Add broth and soybeans and bring to a boil; reduce heat to low and simmer, uncovered, stirring occasionally, until beans are hot, 3 to 5 minutes.

2. Meanwhile, in a 5- to 6-quart pan over high heat, bring about 3 quarts water to a boil. Add linguine and stir occasionally until barely tender to bite, 7 to 9 minutes. Drain pasta and return to pan.

3. Add sausage-soybean mixture to linguine and stir over medium heat until hot. Mix in parsley, parmesan cheese, and salt and pepper to taste. Pour into a serving bowl.

Per serving: 621 cal., 42% (261 cal.) from fat; 36 g protein; 29 g fat (8.5 g sat.); 57 g carbo (2.3 g fiber); 511 mg sodium; 46 mg chol.

Spicy Shrimp and Soybean Stir-fry

PREP AND COOK TIME: About 25 minutes
NOTES: To thaw beans quickly, pour into a colander and rinse with hot water. Serve this stir-fry with hot cooked rice.
MAKES: 3 or 4 servings

- ½ cup fat-skimmed **chicken broth** or vegetable broth
- 2 teaspoons **white wine vinegar**
- 2 teaspoons **soy sauce**
- 1 teaspoon **cornstarch**
- ¼ teaspoon **hot chili flakes**
- 1 tablespoon **vegetable oil**
- 1 package (12 oz.) **frozen shelled soybeans,** thawed (see notes), or 2¼ cups refrigerated cooked shelled soybeans
- 1 tablespoon chopped **fresh ginger**
- 1 clove **garlic,** peeled and minced
- 8 ounces **shelled, deveined shrimp** (31 to 35 per lb.), rinsed

   Salt

1. In a 1-cup glass measure, mix broth, vinegar, soy sauce, cornstarch, and chili flakes until smooth.

2. Set a 10- to 12-inch nonstick frying pan over high heat. When hot, add 1 teaspoon oil and the soybeans; stir until beans are hot and their skins are slightly blistered, 2 to 3 minutes. Pour into a bowl.

3. Add remaining 2 teaspoons oil, the ginger, and garlic to pan; stir just until garlic begins to brown, about 15 seconds. Add shrimp and stir until opaque but still moist-looking in center of thickest part (cut to test), 2 to 3 minutes. Return beans to pan. Stir broth mixture and add to pan; stir until sauce boils and thickens. Add salt to taste. Pour into a serving dish.

Per serving: 269 cal., 43% (117 cal.) from fat; 29 g protein; 13 g fat (1.9 g sat.); 12 g carbo (0.1 g fiber); 266 mg sodium; 86 mg chol.

Spicy Tofu and Soybean Stir-fry

Follow recipe for **spicy shrimp and soybean stir-fry** (preceding), but substitute 12 ounces **firm tofu** for the shrimp: Rinse and drain tofu. Cut into ¹⁄₂-inch-thick slices and pat dry with paper towels, then cut into ¹⁄₂-inch cubes. Continue with steps 1 and 2. Add tofu instead of shrimp in step 3 and stir occasionally until tofu is hot and lightly browned, 2 to 3 minutes. Continue as directed.

Per serving: 332 cal., 54% (180 cal.) from fat; 31 g protein; 20 g fat (2.8 g sat.); 15 g carbo (0.1 g fiber); 194 mg sodium; 0 mg chol.

Soybean and Carrot Salad

PREP TIME: About 15 minutes
MAKES: 4 servings

- ¹⁄₄ cup **rice vinegar**
- 1 tablespoon **sugar**
- 1 tablespoon minced **fresh ginger**
- 2 teaspoons **Asian** (toasted) **sesame oil**
- 1 package (12 oz.) **frozen shelled soybeans,** thawed, or 2¹⁄₄ cups refrigerated cooked shelled soybeans
- ³⁄₄ cup shredded **carrot**
- **Salt**

In a bowl, mix rice vinegar, sugar, ginger, and sesame oil. Add soybeans and carrot; mix well. Add salt to taste.

Per serving: 209 cal., 47% (99 cal.) from fat; 16 g protein; 11 g fat (1.6 g sat.); 15 g carbo (0.7 g fiber); 8.4 mg sodium; 0 mg chol. ◆

Crops that thrive in pots

You don't need much space if you plant the right veggies and herbs

By Jim McCausland

Growing in just a few big pots set in a sunny corner of a deck or patio, a compact container garden can reward you with a steady stream of vegetables from spring through fall.

From carrots to zucchini, a surprisingly wide variety can be grown successfully in containers. (Large, space-consuming plants like corn, melons, and pumpkins are still best grown in the ground.)

The basics

Large containers (18 inches or more in diameter) made of thick-walled terra-cotta or plastic work best for vegetables because they allow ample room for root growth, retain moisture well, and provide insulation against day and night temperature extremes.

Fill containers with good potting soil amended with a complete organic or controlled-release fertilizer. Apply fish emulsion or liquid fertilizer (such as 20-20-20 formula) every two weeks for the entire season.

Install supports like stakes, trellises, and tomato cages at planting time. Place pots in a spot where they'll get at least six hours of sun per day. Water whenever the top inch of soil dries out.

For more tips, see *The Bountiful Container*, by Rose Marie Nichols McGee and Maggie Stuckey (Workman Publishing, New York, 2002; $17; www.workman.com or 800/722-7202).

The menu

Beans. Bush-type 'Blue Lake' green bean is a popular choice. Try scarlet runner bean on a trellis or tripod.

Cucumbers. Let lemon cukes trail over the rim or grow up a trellis.

Eggplants. Japanese types work well; we've had excellent success with 'Asian Bride', 'Farmers' Long', and 'Little Fingers'.

Herbs. Plant seedlings of basil, chives, oregano, parsley, rosemary, sage, and thyme. Keep spreaders like lemon balm and mint in their own containers.

Leaf crops. Choose looseleaf lettuce varieties like 'Oak Leaf' or 'Red Sails', or any mesclun. It's hard to beat 'Bright Lights' Swiss chard.

Peas. Bush-type 'Oregon Sugar Pod II', which reaches only 2¹⁄₂ to 3 feet, bears sweet, crisp pods.

Peppers. For large, sweet peppers, try 'Giant Marconi'; for hot peppers, grow 'Habanero', 'Super Cayenne', and 'Thai Dragon'.

Root crops. Plant 'Chantenay #1' or 'Sweetness II' carrots, any kind of radish, and almost any potato (red ones like 'Buffalo' and 'Red La Soda' are especially good).

Tomatoes. Among slicing types, choose determinate varieties like 'Bush Celebrity', 'Pik Red', and 'Solar Set'; for cherry tomatoes, go with 'Sun Gold', 'Sweet Million', and 'Yellow Pear'.

Zucchini. Try a bush type such as 'Eight Ball', 'Raven', 'Ronde de Nice', or 'Spacemiser'.◆

Nouveau napoleons

Crisp layers make savory main and side dishes

By Paula Freschet

Photographs by James Carrier

One Napoléon was a short emperor with big ideas. Another was, until recently, a tall dessert that rose in tiers of flaky pastry and creamy filling. But today, the edible variety goes way beyond dessert. The pastry may be crackly layers of filo dough or crisp, thin potato galettes, the fillings lobster, salmon—even creamy sweet potatoes. And instead of ending a meal, these napoleons have come to power as hot or cold main courses or side-dish consorts. For speedy construction, they all have parts that can be made ahead.

Lobster in a creamy lemon dressing lends a tender texture contrast to flaky filo platforms.

Lobster Salad Napoleons

PREP AND COOK TIME: About 1½ hours
NOTES: You can prepare dressing, pastry, and lobster (through step 2) up to 1 day ahead. Cover dressing and lobster separately and chill; wrap cool pastry stacks airtight and store at room temperature.
MAKES: 4 servings

1 **spiny** or rock **lobster tail** (about 1 lb.), thawed if frozen
  Lemon dressing (recipe follows)
  Filo-parmesan pastry (recipe follows)
2 **firm-ripe tomatoes** (4 to 5 oz. each), rinsed, cored, and thinly sliced
4 cups **arugula** leaves (about 4 oz.), rinsed and crisped
  Salt

1. In a 4- to 5-quart pan over high heat, bring 2 quarts water to a boil. Add lobster and cook until meat is opaque but still moist-looking in center of thickest part (cut to test), 10 to 12 minutes. Drain lobster; immerse in ice water until cool, 1 to 2 minutes, then drain again.

2. Cut shell open and pull out meat from lobster tail. Coarsely chop lobster, put in a bowl, and mix with 2 to 3 tablespoons lemon dressing.

3. Lay a filo pastry rectangle on each of four dinner plates. Arrange half the lobster mixture, tomatoes, then arugula equally on filo. Cover each stack with another rectangle and top equally with remaining lobster, tomatoes, and arugula. Set another pastry, cheese side up, on each stack. Offer more dressing and salt to add to taste.

Per serving: 313 cal., 49% (153 cal.) from fat; 19 g protein; 17 g fat (7.7 g sat.); 20 g carbo (1.1 g fiber); 644 mg sodium; 77 mg chol.

Lemon dressing. In a bowl, mix ¾ cup **mayonnaise,** 1 tablespoon grated **lemon** peel, 3½ tablespoons **lemon juice,** 3 tablespoons finely chopped **fresh tarragon,** and 1½ tablespoons *each* **tarragon wine vinegar** and minced **shallots.** Add **pepper** to taste. Makes 1 cup.

Per tablespoon: 76 cal., 97% (74 cal.) from fat; 0.2 g protein; 8.2 g fat (1.2 g sat.); 0.9 g carbo (0 g fiber); 60 mg sodium; 6.1 mg chol.

Filo-parmesan pastry. You will need 6 sheets of **filo dough** (about 12 by 18 in.), about 3 tablespoons melted **butter,** and 6 tablespoons grated **parmesan cheese.** Lay 1 filo sheet flat (cover remaining with plastic wrap to prevent drying) and brush lightly with butter, then sprin-
kle with 1 tablespoon cheese. Cover with another filo sheet, brush lightly with more butter, and sprinkle with 1 tablespoon cheese. Continue until all the filo is stacked, using the last of the butter and cheese on the top layer. Cut into 12 equal rectangles and transfer to two lightly buttered 10- by 15-inch pans, arranging slightly apart. Bake in a 375° regular or convection oven until golden brown, 8 to 12 minutes. Use warm or cool.

Salmon and Potato Napoleons

PREP AND COOK TIME: About 50 minutes, plus about 2 hours to make potato galettes
NOTES: If you have only one oven, reheat galettes while making vegetable sauce, then keep warm on lowest rack while broiling salmon.
MAKES: 4 servings

1 piece **boned, skinned salmon fillet** (1¼ to 1½ lb.)
  2 teaspoons **olive oil**
  Salt and **pepper**
8 ounces **zucchini,** rinsed and ends trimmed
1 can (14½ oz.) **vegetable broth**
4 ounces **green beans,** rinsed, and ends and strings removed
½ cup **dry white wine**
1 tablespoon **butter**
1 **Roma tomato** (4 oz.), rinsed, cored, and diced

FOOD STYLING: BASIL FRIEDMAN (2)

Crisp potato galettes (recipe follows; see notes)

About 6 tablespoons **sour cream**

1 tablespoon chopped **chives**

1. Rinse salmon and cut across fillet into $\frac{1}{2}$-inch-thick slices. Rub with olive oil. Lay pieces slightly apart in a lightly oiled 10- by 15-inch baking pan and sprinkle with salt and pepper.

2. Cut zucchini into sticks $\frac{1}{2}$ inch thick and 3 inches long. In a 10- to 12-inch frying pan over high heat, bring broth to a boil. Add zucchini and beans; stir occasionally until barely tender when pierced, 1 to 2 minutes. With a slotted spoon, transfer vegetables to a plate. Add wine to broth and boil over high heat until sauce is reduced to $\frac{1}{2}$ cup, 8 to 10 minutes. Add butter, cooked vegetables, and tomato and stir gently until hot, about 1 minute; keep warm.

3. Meanwhile, broil salmon about 3 inches from heat until opaque but still moist-looking in center of thickest part (cut to test), about 4 minutes.

4. Working quickly, lay a hot galette piece on each of four warmed dinner plates. Arrange half the salmon equally on galettes; lay another galette piece on each. Top each equally with remaining salmon, then remaining galette piece and any fragments. Spoon vegetables and sauce around napoleons. Top each with a dollop of sour cream and sprinkle with chives.

Per serving: 543 cal., 48% (261 cal.) from fat; 34 g protein; 29 g fat (8.5 g sat.); 37 g carbo (3.7 g fiber); 176 mg sodium; 101 mg chol.

Crisp Potato Galettes

PREP AND COOK TIME: About 2 hours

NOTES: Don't worry if gaps form as the galettes cook. You can make galettes up to 1 day ahead; store airtight at room temperature. Reheat, uncovered, in a 350° oven for 10 to 15 minutes.

MAKES: 4 servings

 3 **russet potatoes** (8 oz. each), peeled

 About 1 tablespoon **olive** or vegetable **oil**

 Salt

1. Using a mandoline or vegetable slicer, cut potatoes into paper-thin slices (about $\frac{1}{32}$ in. thick). Coat a 10- by 15-inch nonstick pan with 2 teaspoons oil.

2. Cover pan bottom with neat, overlapping layers of potatoes, making layers beside pan rim slightly thicker than those in center of pan. With your fingers, gently rub 1 to 2 more teaspoons oil over the top layer of potatoes.

3. Bake in a 350° oven until potatoes are golden brown (including slices in pan center), 45 minutes to 1 hour; as some areas brown first, cover dark portions lightly with foil. Remove from oven and slide a wide spatula under potatoes to release from pan, but leave in place; (don't worry if the galette cracks). Let cool at least 30 minutes.

4. Return galette to the 350° oven and bake until slightly darker brown and crisp, 15 to 20 minutes. Remove from oven and slide spatula under galette again to be sure it isn't stuck. Sprinkle potatoes with salt and break

into 12 random but similar-size rectangles, saving fragments.

Per serving: 154 cal., 21% (33 cal.) from fat; 2.9 g protein; 3.7 g fat (0.5 g sat.); 28 g carbo (2.6 g fiber); 12 mg sodium; 0 mg chol.

Sweet Potato–Chèvre Napoleons

PREP AND COOK TIME: About $1\frac{1}{3}$ hours, plus 2 hours to make potato galettes

NOTES: You can complete steps 1 through 3 up to 1 day ahead. Chill sweet-potato mixture airtight; cover shallots and store at room temperature. Reheat sweet-potato mixture in a microwave oven, stirring occasionally, for 3 to 4 minutes.

MAKES: 4 servings

 $1\frac{1}{2}$ pounds **sweet potatoes** ($1\frac{1}{2}$ to 2 in. wide)

 12 ounces **shallots** ($\frac{3}{4}$ to 1 in. wide), peeled

 2 tablespoons **olive oil**

 $1\frac{1}{2}$ tablespoons **balsamic vinegar**

 About $\frac{1}{2}$ cup **milk**

 $\frac{3}{4}$ cup **fresh chèvre** (goat cheese)

 2 tablespoons **butter**

 1 teaspoon minced **fresh thyme** leaves or dried thyme

 Salt and **pepper**

 Crisp potato galettes (recipe precedes)

1. Scrub sweet potatoes, pierce each in several places with a fork, and set in an 8- or 9-inch-wide pan. In another pan, mix shallots with oil and vinegar.

2. Bake shallots in a 375° oven, shaking pan occasionally, until deep golden brown, about 45 minutes; bake sweet potatoes until they give very easily when squeezed, about 1 hour.

3. Protecting your hands with a potholder, slit hot sweet potatoes open and scoop flesh into a bowl; discard skins. With a potato masher or a mixer, mash sweet potatoes, $\frac{1}{2}$ cup milk, cheese, butter, and thyme until smooth; for a softer texture, beat in more milk. Season to taste with salt and pepper.

4. Lay a large, hot galette piece on each of four warmed dinner plates. Mound half the hot sweet-potato mixture equally in center of galettes.

5. Lay another galette flat on each sweet-potato mound. Top equally with remaining sweet-potato mixture. Stick remaining galette pieces and any fragments vertically into the sweet-potato mixture; spoon shallots around napoleons.

Per serving: 624 cal., 38% (234 cal.) from fat; 16 g protein; 26 g fat (12 g sat.); 83 g carbo (9.2 g fiber); 264 mg sodium; 39 mg chol. ◆

Not one potato—two. Sweet potatoes mashed with goat cheese are mounded between paper-thin slices of russets.

Polenta's sweeter side

Italian-style cornmeal makes a great breakfast or dessert

By Kate Washington
Photograph by James Carrier

Polenta is best known as a hearty winter side dish, but its sunny yellow color and sweet corn taste make it a natural for spring too. Enhance its flavor with a little sugar in a creamy but light dish for breakfast on a cool spring morning, or use it to add extra crunch to biscotti—perfect with iced coffee on a warm afternoon. Either way, polenta's potential for sweetness and light is just right for the season.

Creamy Breakfast Polenta

PREP AND COOK TIME: About 45 minutes
NOTES: If crème fraîche is unavailable, use lightly sweetened sour cream. We like this soft polenta topped with blackberry jam, but it's equally delicious topped with another jam, fresh fruit, or butter and maple syrup.
MAKES: About 6 cups; 4 to 6 servings

- 3 cups **low-fat (2%) milk**
- 1 cup **polenta**
- 2 tablespoons **sugar**
- ½ teaspoon **salt**
- 4 to 6 tablespoons **blackberry jam** (see notes)
  Lightly sweetened whipped **crème fraîche** (optional; see notes)

1. In a 2½- to 3-quart pan over high heat, bring 3 cups water and the milk to a boil. Reduce heat so liquid is barely boiling. Stirring constantly, pour in polenta in a thin, steady stream, pausing occasionally to break up any lumps. Stir in sugar and salt.

2. Simmer, stirring often, until polenta is soft and creamy to bite, 20 to 40 minutes (if heat is too high, bubbles may "spit" globs of hot polenta out of the pan).

3. Ladle polenta into bowls and top each

On a cool morning, top warm polenta with crème fraîche and jam or berries.

serving with about 1 tablespoon blackberry jam and a dollop of crème fraîche.

Per serving: 292 cal., 8.2% (24 cal.) from fat; 8.2 g protein; 2.7 g fat (1.5 g sat.); 59 g carbo (4.9 g fiber); 262 mg sodium; 9.8 mg chol.

Polenta Biscotti

PREP AND COOK TIME: About 1½ hours
NOTES: Serve these crunchy cookies with espresso, iced tea, or iced coffee as a snack, or with a sweet Muscat wine for a simple dessert. For miniature biscotti, divide the dough into four pieces and shape them into narrower logs; shorten the baking times in steps 5 and 6 by about 5 minutes each.
MAKES: About 3 dozen cookies

- 1 cup **pecan halves**
- ½ cup (¼ lb.) **butter,** at room temperature
- 1 cup **sugar**
- 2 **large eggs**
- 1 teaspoon **vanilla**
- 2 teaspoons grated **lemon** peel
- 2 tablespoons **lemon juice**
- 2½ cups **all-purpose flour**
- ½ cup **polenta**
- 1½ teaspoons **baking powder**
- ½ teaspoon **salt**

1. Spread pecans on a 10- by 15-inch baking sheet. Bake in a 325° oven until

very slightly darker, about 10 minutes. Let cool; leave oven on.

2. Meanwhile, in a large bowl, with a mixer on medium speed, beat butter and sugar until well blended. Add eggs, vanilla, lemon peel, and lemon juice and beat until combined.

3. Add flour, polenta, baking powder, and salt and beat until combined (dough will be sticky). Stir in pecans.

4. Divide dough in half and place portions several inches apart on a baking sheet lined with cooking parchment. Pat each into a log about 10 inches long, 2 inches wide, and 1 inch tall (moisten your hands with cold water if necessary to prevent sticking).

5. Bake until logs start to turn golden at the edges, about 25 minutes. With a wide spatula, transfer to a wire rack and cool for 10 to 15 minutes.

6. With a heavy, sharp knife, cut each log crosswise into ¾-inch-thick slices. Place slices on their side on the cooking parchment–lined sheet. Return biscotti to oven and bake until golden on the bottom, about 20 minutes. Turn them over and continue baking until cookies are crisp and golden on the other side, about 20 minutes longer. Transfer biscotti to a rack to cool. Store airtight up to 2 weeks.

Per cookie: 104 cal., 34% (35 cal.) from fat; 1.7 g protein; 3.9 g fat (1.8 g sat.); 16 g carbo (0.7 g fiber); 82 mg sodium; 19 mg chol. ◆

The right stuff

We like the consistent results of Golden Pheasant polenta, which is widely available. Avoid instant polenta; it cooks quickly, but in our tests was unpleasantly gluey. Regular cornmeal will cook to porridge consistency and will also work fine in the biscotti, but it lacks the distinctive texture of polenta.

Keen on quinoa

Top this versatile grain with a spicy seafood stew

By Charity Ferreira

Photograph by James Carrier

Seafood stew gets a boost from quick, nutritious quinoa.

A quick-cooking, high-protein grain from Peru, quinoa (pronounced *keen*-wah) is available in many supermarkets right alongside rice. Its mild, nutty taste and fluffy but chewy texture make it a good foil for spicy foods. Complement quinoa with the Peruvian flavors of potatoes and seafood in tomato sauce. A salad of sliced avocados, tangerines, and radishes drizzled with a simple vinaigrette makes a refreshing starter or side dish. After dinner, try a tropical banana split: coconut ice cream, sliced bananas, and caramel sauce.

Spicy Seafood Stew

PREP AND COOK TIME: About 50 minutes

NOTES: To have quinoa and stew ready at the same time, start quinoa once you've added the potatoes to the stew (step 1). Small squid (calamari) are sold cleaned and cut into rings at many specialty stores and seafood markets.

MAKES: 4 servings

1 tablespoon **olive oil**

1 **onion** (8 oz.), peeled, halved, and thinly slivered lengthwise

2 cloves **garlic,** peeled and minced

1 can (32 oz.) **diced** or crushed **tomatoes**

8 ounces **red** or white thin-skinned **potatoes** (about 1 in. wide), scrubbed and quartered

1 or 2 **fresh hot green chilies** such as jalapeños, rinsed, stemmed, seeded, and minced

½ teaspoon **ground cumin**

½ teaspoon **chili powder**

½ teaspoon **salt**

12 ounces **shelled, deveined shrimp** (31 to 40 per lb.), rinsed

8 ounces **tilapia** or other white-fleshed fish, rinsed and cut into 1-inch chunks

4 ounces fresh or thawed frozen **calamari rings** (optional; see notes), rinsed

2 tablespoons chopped **fresh cilantro**

Cooked quinoa (recipe follows)

1. Heat oil in a 5- to 6-quart pan over medium-high heat; add onion and garlic and stir often until onion is very limp, 8 to 10 minutes. Add tomatoes, 1½ cups water, potatoes, chilies, cumin, chili powder, and salt; increase heat to high and bring to a boil. Reduce heat, cover, and simmer until potatoes are tender when pierced, 20 to 25 minutes.

2. Stir in seafood, if using. Cover and simmer until shrimp and fish are opaque but still moist-looking in the center of thickest part (cut to test), 3 to 4 minutes. Stir in cilantro. Spoon quinoa onto rimmed plates; top with stew.

Per serving of seafood stew: 262 cal., 24% (62 cal.) from fat; 32 g protein; 6.9 g fat (0.8 g sat.); 19 g carbo (4.4 g fiber); 823 mg sodium; 156 mg chol.

Cooked quinoa. In a 3- to 4-quart pan over high heat, bring 3 cups **water** to a boil. In a strainer, rinse 1½ cups **quinoa** under running water; drain thoroughly. Add quinoa and ¼ teaspoon **salt** to pan with boiling water. Adjust heat to maintain a simmer, cover, and cook until water is absorbed and quinoa is tender to bite, 20 to 25 minutes. Makes 5 cups; about 4 servings.

Per serving: 238 cal., 14% (33 cal.) from fat; 8.4 g protein; 3.7 g fat (0.4 g sat.); 44 g carbo (3.8 g fiber); 156 mg sodium; 0 mg chol. ◆

Go with the grain

Here are other ideas for using quinoa in fast, balanced meals.

• Try the versatile grain as a side dish in place of couscous or rice.

• Combine cooked quinoa with cooked vegetables for a cold or warm salad.

• Toss quinoa with a little balsamic vinegar and some chopped herbs to serve alongside meat, chicken, or fish.

• Use quinoa as a bed for saucy mixtures of meat or vegetables.

Colorful Middle Eastern–style stuffed peppers can be on the table in less than an hour.

The stuff of spring

By Tiffany Armstrong and Kate Washington
Photograph by James Carrier

Retro dishes—like stuffed peppers—might remind us of long hours in the kitchen, but these can be on the table surprisingly fast. Overflowing with lamb and couscous, they're light and satisfying at the same time. Lemony fattoush, a Middle Eastern salad with crunchy pocket-bread chips, matches the mood. And a frothy, milk-based frappé ends the meal on a simple, healthy note.

Mediterranean Lamb- and Couscous-stuffed Peppers

PREP AND COOK TIME: About 35 minutes
MAKES: 4 servings

- 4 **red**, green, and/or yellow **bell peppers** (2 lb. total), rinsed
- 1½ cups chopped **onions**
- 1 tablespoon minced **garlic**
- 1½ teaspoons **fresh thyme** leaves
- 1½ teaspoons minced **fresh mint** leaves
- 1½ teaspoons minced **fresh rosemary** leaves
- 1 teaspoon **olive oil**
- 8 ounces **ground lamb**
- 5 tablespoons **lemon juice**
- 1⅔ cups fat-skimmed **chicken broth**
- 1¼ cups **couscous**
- 1 cup chopped **parsley**
  Salt
- 2 tablespoons crumbled **feta cheese**

1. Slice bell peppers in half lengthwise through stems (retain stems) and remove seeds. Place halves, cut side down, in a 12- by 17-inch baking pan. Bake in a 450° regular or convection oven until lightly browned and tender when pierced, 13 to 18 minutes.
2. Meanwhile, in a 10- to 12-inch frying pan over high heat, stir onions, garlic, thyme, mint, and rosemary in olive oil until onions are limp and beginning to brown, about 5 minutes.
3. Add ground lamb and 3 tablespoons lemon juice. Stir until lamb is browned and crumbly, 2 to 3 minutes.
4. Stir in broth, couscous, and remaining 2 tablespoons lemon juice. Bring to a boil, then cover and remove from heat; let stand until liquid is absorbed and couscous is tender to bite, 3 to 4 minutes. Stir in parsley; add salt to taste.
5. Turn pepper halves over; fill each with about ⅔ cup lamb mixture. Sprinkle feta cheese evenly over filling. Bake until cheese is slightly melted, 3 to 5 minutes. Transfer peppers to a platter.

Per serving: 498 cal., 29% (144 cal.) from fat; 24 g protein; 16 g fat (6.7 g sat.); 65 g carbo (6.6 g fiber); 134 mg sodium; 45 mg chol.

Fattoush

Cut 2 **pocket breads** (7 in.) into 1-inch squares. Put in a zip-lock plastic bag with 2 teaspoons **olive oil;** seal bag and turn to coat. Pour pieces into a 10- by 15-inch baking pan and spread into a single layer. Bake in a 450° oven until crisp and lightly browned, about 5 minutes. Let cool at least 10 minutes. Meanwhile, in a large bowl, mix 2 tablespoons **lemon juice,** 2 tablespoons **extra-virgin olive oil,** ½ teaspoon salt, ¼ teaspoon **coarse-ground pepper,** and ⅛ teaspoon **ground sumac** (optional; available in markets that carry Mediterranean ingredients). Add 3 cups bite-size pieces of rinsed and crisped **romaine lettuce** leaves (about 4 oz.); half an **English cucumber,** rinsed, quartered lengthwise, and cut into ½-inch chunks; 2 cups **cherry tomatoes,** rinsed and stemmed (cut in half if larger than ¾ in.); half a **sweet onion** (8 oz.), thinly slivered; ½ cup **Italian parsley** leaves; 3 tablespoons chopped **fresh mint** leaves; and the pocket-bread chips. Mix gently to coat. Makes 4 servings.

Per serving: 201 cal., 44% (89 cal.) from fat; 51 g protein; 9.9 g fat (1.4 g sat.); 25 g carbo (3.4 g fiber); 466 mg sodium; 0 mg chol.

Nutty frappés

In a blender, combine 1½ cups **ice cubes,** 1½ cups **milk,** and ½ cup **hazelnut syrup** (such as Torani) or Frangelico; whirl at high speed until ice is finely ground and mixture is frothy, about 1 minute. Pour into tall glasses. If desired, sprinkle with finely chopped **unsalted roasted pistachios** (about 1 tablespoon total). Makes 4 servings.

Per serving: 126 cal., 22% (28 cal.) from fat; 3 g protein; 3.1 g fat (1.9 g sat.); 22 g carbo (0 g fiber); 55 mg sodium; 13 mg chol. ◆

FOOD STYLING: KAREN SHINTO

Shepherd's pie

A fresh start for a legendary dish

By Jerry Anne Di Vecchio • Photograph by James Carrier

In days past, when Sunday dinner was routinely a roast with gravy, a meal of leftovers inevitably followed. One appealing roast reincarnation was as shepherd's pie (or "cottage pie")—cold meat and gravy with a top crust of mashed potatoes, baked until browned and bubbly. One reference I came across recently claims that the dish first appeared in the 1870s with the advent of a mincing machine to grind the meat. In *The Boston Cooking-School Cook Book,* by Fannie Merritt Farmer (originally published in 1896 and still surviving as *The Fannie Farmer Cookbook*), the recipe for shepherd's pie is brief to the point of barren and uses roast beef. In other old cookbooks, the meat is often lamb.

Without leftovers from a roast, though, how do you create this comfy dish? My choice is to make a richly browned, deeply flavored onion gravy, poach moist meatballs in it, then nestle the mixture in a wreath of mashed potatoes. I think Fannie would approve.

Spooned around the pie, mashed potatoes offer casual comfort, but they can be piped for a more formal effect.

FOOD STYLING: SUSAN DEVATY

Meatball Shepherd's Pie

PREP AND COOK TIME: About 1¾ hours

NOTES: You can substitute ground turkey for the beef if you like. While you make the brown onion gravy, cook the potatoes: boil, bake, or microwave them. If you have cold leftover cooked potatoes, plain or mashed, reheat them in a microwave oven until steaming, then measure. You can make the gravy and assemble the pie through step 5 up to 1 day ahead; cover and chill. Uncover to continue; bake about 35 minutes if chilled.

MAKES: 6 servings

1½ pounds **ground lean beef** (see notes)

½ cup finely chopped **parsley**

2 tablespoons **Dijon mustard**

2 tablespoons **all-purpose flour**

1 **large egg**

About ½ teaspoon **salt**

About ¼ teaspoon **pepper**

About ½ cup fat-skimmed **beef broth**

Brown onion gravy (recipe follows)

½ cup **dry sherry,** dry white wine, or more fat-skimmed beef broth

6 cups packed peeled hot cooked **potatoes** (see notes)

2 to 3 tablespoons **butter**

½ cup **cream cheese,** at room temperature

½ cup **shredded Gruyère,** Swiss, or parmesan **cheese** (about 2½ oz.)

1. In a bowl, combine ground beef, parsley, mustard, flour, egg, ½ teaspoon salt, ¼ teaspoon pepper, and ½ cup beef broth. Blend well with a fork.

2. In a 4- to 5-quart pan over high heat, bring brown onion gravy to a boil; add sherry and reduce heat to maintain a gentle simmer. Quickly shape beef mixture into 1-inch balls and drop into gravy. When all are in, cover and simmer until meatballs are no longer pink in the center (cut to test), 10 to 12 minutes. With a slotted spoon, transfer meatballs (some of the onions will come too) to a bowl.

3. Boil gravy over high heat, stirring often, until reduced to about 2 cups, 10 to 15 minutes. Season to taste with salt and pepper. Remove from heat and return meatballs and any accumulated juice to gravy; mix gently.

4. Meanwhile, in a large bowl, with a mixer or potato masher, mash potatoes with 2 to 3 tablespoons butter and the

cream cheese until smooth. If desired, add just enough beef broth to moisten potatoes to be able to squeeze them through a pastry bag. Beat in the Gruyère cheese and add salt and pepper to taste.

5. Butter a shallow 3½- to 4-quart casserole. Spread two-thirds of the potato mixture evenly over bottom and up sides. Spoon meatball-gravy mixture into the center. Spoon remaining potato mixture decoratively around edge of meatball mixture, or spoon it into a pastry bag with a 1-inch star or round tip and pipe around the edge.

6. Bake pie in a 400° oven until gravy is bubbling and potatoes are browned, 30 to 35 minutes.

Per serving: 758 cal., 51% (387 cal.) from fat; 34 g protein; 43 g fat (21 g sat.); 56 g carbo (4.6 g fiber); 639 mg sodium; 177 mg chol.

Brown onion gravy. Peel and finely chop 2 **onions** (8 oz. each). In a 4- to 5-quart pan over medium-high heat, stir onions in 2 tablespoons **butter** until richly browned, 13 to 15 minutes. Add 2 teaspoons **sugar** and stir for 2 minutes. Add 3 tablespoons **all-purpose flour** and stir until browned, 1 to 2 minutes. Remove from heat and stir in 3 cups fat-skimmed **beef broth.** Return to high heat and stir until boiling. ◆

Best of the West

Blanc check

BEST SPRING WINES

Here are great West Coast Sauvignon Blancs (a.k.a. Fumé Blancs) for pairing with springtime fare.

Chateau Souverain Sauvignon Blanc 2001 *(Alexander Valley, CA)*, $14. Deliciously sassy, untamed. Lots of green peppercorns and green-tea character.

Chateau St. Jean Sonoma County Fumé Blanc 2001 *(Sonoma County)*, $13. Light notes of vanilla and lemon. Good for richer seafood.

Guenoc Estate Selection Sauvignon Blanc 2001 *(Lake County, CA)*, $14. Bright, peachy, melony flavors. Simple, fresh, and easy to drink.

Preston of Dry Creek "Hartsock" Sauvignon Blanc 2001 *(Dry Creek Valley, CA)*, $18. Exotic lime and lemon-grass aromas and flavors; hints of melons and spearmint. *—Karen MacNeil-Fife*

Baby fresh: enjoy junior varieties of summer veggies now.

Think small this season

Full-size summer vegetables haven't arrived, but their baby

FRESH IDEA counterparts are in markets now. Show off the season's tiny bounty with a platter of pretty crudités.

Baby Crudités with Herb Butter

1. In a blender or food processor, whirl ¼ cup (⅛ lb.) **butter,** 2 tablespoons chopped **fresh chervil** or parsley, 2 tablespoons chopped **fresh chives,** and 1 tablespoon chopped **shallot** until almost smooth. Spoon into a small bowl. **2.** Rinse and prepare vegetables of your choice (about 1½ lb. total), such as **baby artichokes** (trim and discard tough outer leaves; quarter artichokes and steam until tender); **broccolini** (trim stem ends; steam until bright green); **baby carrots** (leave tops on; peel if desired); **baby fennel** (trim and discard stem end and stalks; slice fennel ¼ in. thick); **radishes; sugar snap peas;** or **baby zucchini** (halve lengthwise). **3.** Arrange vegetables on a platter and accompany with herb butter and a bowl of **fine sea salt** for dipping. Makes 4 to 6 servings. *—Kate Washington*

6 great ways to use eggs

If you have too many eggs in one basket after Easter, don't despair. Here's how to enjoy your extra hard-boiled eggs this spring: 1 Substitute chopped eggs for meat in a simple curry with vegetables. 2 Press eggs through a fine strainer to make a pretty garnish for

EASY SNACKS **spinach salad. 3 Thinly slice eggs and place on top of crostini, drizzled with olive oil and sprinkled with sea salt. 4 Layer quartered eggs with tuna, greens, and a simple vinaigrette on a baguette for a Niçoise sandwich. 5 Make a breakfast burrito with chopped eggs, beans, cheese, and salsa wrapped in a flour tortilla. 6 Float sliced eggs on top of a bowl of Japanese-style noodle soup. —K. W.**

Garden-party drinks

It's time to move the party outside. No one does that better than Alexandra and Eliot Angle, authors of *Cocktail Parties with a Twist* and co-owners of Aqua Vitae,

OUTDOOR LIVING a Los Angeles–based event and interior design firm *(www. aquavitaedesign.com or 323/663-1777)*. They designed this tasty no-host bar you can use for your next backyard party. "Inviting guests to make their own drinks is a great icebreaker," says Alexandra, "and you aren't stuck behind the bar all evening." —*Mary Jo Bowling and Sara Schneider*

Decanters

Reuse wine bottles by adding your own labels and filling them with mint-infused syrup or vodka. Fill several ahead, then bring out as needed.

Throws

Drape blankets over chairs for when the evening cools.

YOU WILL NEED:

A. Mint-infused syrup
B. Lime juice
C. Vodka
D. Fresh mint garnish
E. Drink recipes
F. Club soda
G. Lime garnish

How to mix your own drinks

ALCOHOLIC
SoCal

Fill an 8-ounce glass halfway with ice cubes.

Add 2 tablespoons (1 oz.) fresh-squeezed lime juice and 1 tablespoon (½ oz.) mint-infused syrup.

Stir gently.

Add ¼ cup (2 oz.) vodka.

Garnish with fresh mint sprig.

NON-ALCOHOLIC
Limeade

Fill a 12- to 16-ounce glass halfway with ice cubes.

Add 2 tablespoons (1 oz.) fresh-squeezed lime juice and 1 tablespoon (½ oz.) mint-infused syrup.

Stir gently.

Add ¾ cup (6 oz.) club soda.

Garnish with fresh mint sprig.

Photocopy this at 200%, trim at dotted rule, and display in a 4- by 6-inch frame.

MAKE AHEAD:
Mint-infused syrup

In a 3- to 4-quart pan, combine 2 cups **sugar**, 2 cups **water**, and 3 quarts rinsed **fresh mint** leaves (about 4 bunches); stir often over medium-low heat just until simmering. Let stand until cool, about 30 minutes. Pour through a fine strainer into a small pitcher. Chill until cold, about 45 minutes. Makes 3 cups (enough for about 48 drinks; keeps, covered and chilled, up to seven days).

The new spring green

Mâche makes a beautiful salad—and tasty hot dishes too

In the West's luxuriously crowded field of greens, there's another player. Until recently, mâche—also known as lamb's lettuce or corn salad and a longtime staple in France—could be found here mainly in tony restaurants and upscale markets. Now, however, Epic Roots, founded by former chef Todd Koons, is growing it on a large scale in California's Salinas Valley.

Sweet, nutty, and a little bit wild-tasting, mâche is a multitasker. Its delicate round leaves make a fresh background for spring's best veggies, as in the salad here from Koons. But its hearty texture lets mâche work equally well as a cooking green. Use our suggestions below as a starting point for many mâche experiments. *Mâche is available year-round in many markets, including Raley's and some Albertsons, Trader Joe's, and Whole Foods Markets. www.epicroots.com or (415) 331-8271.*

More mâche ideas

• **Wilted salad:** mix with warm sautéed chopped bacon and sliced mushrooms, and a little balsamic vinegar.

• **Pasta:** toss with cooked noodles, garlic sautéed in olive oil, toasted walnuts, and lots of shredded parmesan cheese.

• **Sauce for chicken or fish:** blanch for 30 seconds (keep pushing mâche under water), then purée with white wine vinegar and chopped garlic sautéed in olive oil.

• **Soup:** purée with sautéed onions and some chicken broth, then heat with a white sauce seasoned with fresh-grated nutmeg; top with cooked shrimp or crab.

• **Side dish:** braise in a little chicken broth for about 2 minutes; spritz with lemon juice.

Toss the latest in salad greens: pair mâche with fresh vegetables for a distinctive salad.

Mâche with Spring Vegetables and Lemon Vinaigrette

PREP AND COOK TIME: About 30 minutes

NOTES: You can substitute asparagus for the green beans; cook it for 2 to 3 minutes in step 2.

MAKES: 4 servings

- 2 teaspoons plus ¼ cup **extra-virgin olive oil**

- 1 **red onion** (about 8 oz.), peeled and slivered lengthwise

- 8 ounces **small haricots verts** or other green beans, rinsed, ends trimmed, and any strings pulled off (see notes)

- 8 ounces **baby carrots** (½ in. wide at top), tops trimmed off, and scrubbed, or baby-cut carrots

- 1 cup shelled **fresh peas** (from 1 lb. in shell)

- 2 tablespoons **Meyer** or regular **lemon** juice

- 1 tablespoon **plain yogurt**

- 1 teaspoon **Dijon mustard**

  Fine sea or regular **salt**

  Fresh-ground **black pepper**

- 2 quarts **mâche** (4 oz.), rinsed and crisped

1. Pour 2 teaspoons olive oil into an 8- to 10-inch nonstick frying pan over medium heat; when hot, add onion and stir occasionally until slightly limp, about 8 minutes (onion should be a little crunchy still). Remove from heat and let cool.

2. Meanwhile, in a 3- to 4-quart pan over high heat, bring about 2 quarts water to a boil. Add green beans and cook until tender-crisp to bite, 4 to 5 minutes. With a strainer or slotted spoon, transfer to a colander; rinse under cold running water until cool. Drain and pour into a large bowl. Add carrots to boiling water and cook until tender-crisp, 5 to 6 minutes. Transfer to colander, rinse until cool, drain, and add to bowl. Add peas to boiling water and cook until barely tender to bite, about 3 minutes. Pour into colander and rinse until cool; drain and add to bowl.

3. In a small bowl, mix lemon juice, yogurt, and mustard until blended. Whisk in remaining ¼ cup olive oil and salt and pepper to taste.

4. Add mâche to vegetables in bowl. Drizzle lemon vinaigrette over the top and mix gently to coat. Divide mixture among salad plates and garnish equally with sautéed onion.

Per serving: 240 cal., 64% (153 cal.) from fat; 4.8 g protein; 17 g fat (2.4 g sat.); 21 g carbo (5.3 g fiber); 68 mg sodium; 0.2 mg chol.

—*Sara Schneider*

How to read a wine label

The label on any U.S. wine seems straightforward compared to, say, a French wine. But looks can be deceiving, as they say. The words can mean much or little.

2000
NAPA VALLEY
MERLOT
PRIVATE RESERVE
UNFILTERED

Major grape variety, region, and vintage: By United States law, a wine must be composed of at least 75 percent of the grape named, 85 percent of the grapes must come from the region named, and 95 percent of the wine must be from the vintage named (although states can choose to have stricter laws). These are good regulations. A wine that's 100 percent Cabernet Sauvignon from a single region *may* not be as delicious as a Cab that's blended with a little Merlot or wine grown somewhere else.

"Reserve," "special select," and the like have no legal meaning in the United States. In some cases, they denote a winery's best wine; in others, there is nothing special about it at all. Often, "reserve" is code for saying the wine was made using more oak, which invariably means it's more expensive—but not necessarily better.

"Unfiltered" indicates that the particles weren't strained out; they're settling naturally. The word seems to imply the wine is somehow better, but filtration has no correlation with quality.

Back label: This is the winery's chance to capture your interest. But can all those wines be "rich," "supple," and "soft"? Sadly, in my experience, beyond a general indication of style—"crisp and dry," for instance—back labels are far more about buzzwords than they are about accurate descriptions. There's just no substitute for tasting the wines.

—Karen MacNeil-Fife

For April sipping

Coldstream Hills Sauvignon Blanc 2001 *(Yarra Valley, Australia)*, *$18.* The best Australian Sauvignon Blanc I've ever had—bracingly fresh and clean, with wonderful citrus and spice flavors.

Fleur du Cap Sauvignon Blanc 2001, Unfiltered *(Coastal Region, South Africa)*, *$15.* This is one scrumptious wine—tangy and citrusy, yet creamy, with flavors reminiscent of Key lime pie. A winner with salads and vegetable stir-fries.

Huia Gewürztraminer 2001 *(Marlborough, New Zealand)*, *$17.* Powerful and bone-dry, with a tidal wave of spicy flavor and a rich, creamy texture. Perfect with spicy shrimp.

Kim Crawford Unoaked Chardonnay 2001 *(Marlborough)*, *$18.* Lip-smacking pear tart and light piña-colada flavors, all blissfully unencumbered by oak. Bright, dry, slightly minerally, and a bit racy. A perfect Chardonnay for shellfish.

Robert Mondavi Winery Pinot Noir 2000 *(Carneros, CA)*, *$40.* Pinot Noir is one of the world's most difficult grapes to make into great wine. This one, however, is stellar. Earthy, sensual aromas wrapped up with a ribbon of vanilla and espresso flavors. Wonderful with sautéed mushrooms.

—K. M.-F.

Quick cuts

Perfect julienned carrots or sliced cucumbers make beautiful salads or garnishes, but consistent cutting takes patience—unless you use a mandoline or slicer. Stainless steel models are pricey, but plastic-bodied models, such as the Börner V-Slicer Plus (shown above) and the adjustable Japanese Benriner cutter (our favorite), are just as functional. Their blades slide right through a raw potato for paper-thin slices that fry up into crisp, translucent chips.

The Börner V-Slicer Plus is available at www.amazon.com for about $35. The Benriner cutter, about $35, can be purchased from the Wok Shop in San Francisco (888/780-7171).

Potato Chips

1. Adjust slicer to thinnest setting ($\frac{1}{16}$ or $\frac{1}{32}$ in.) and place over a large bowl of cold **water.** Using the safety guard, slice **russet** or Yukon Gold **potatoes** (peeled or scrubbed) into water. Let soak 10 minutes; rinse slices and blot completely dry with paper towels.

2. Heat 2 inches of **vegetable oil** in a 4- to 5-quart pan over medium-high heat to 380°. Fry potatoes in batches (do not overcrowd pan), stirring occasionally to separate and submerge slices, until crisp and golden, $1\frac{1}{2}$ to 2 minutes for $\frac{1}{32}$-inch-thick slices, $3\frac{1}{2}$ to $4\frac{1}{2}$ minutes for $\frac{1}{16}$-inch-thick slices. Using a slotted spoon, transfer to paper towels to drain. Let oil return to 380° between batches.

3. Sprinkle with **salt** and fresh-ground **pepper.** Makes about 2 appetizer servings per 8-ounce potato.

Per serving: 69 cal., 59% (41 cal.) from fat; 2.5 g protein; 4.6 g fat (0.6 g sat.); 5.3 g carbo (2.6 g fiber); 7.9 mg sodium; 0 mg chol.

—Kate Washington

Kitchen travels

Readers' recipes tested in *Sunset's* kitchens

Photographs by James Carrier

Singapore Chicken Stew

Roxanne Chan, Albany, CA

Roxanne Chan likes the way coconut milk smooths out the assertive spices in this quick chicken dish. If you can't find Chinese five spice, substitute equal parts ground cinnamon, ground cloves, ground ginger, and anise seeds.

PREP AND COOK TIME: About 35 minutes
MAKES: 4 servings

- 1 pound **boned, skinned chicken breasts**
- 2 tablespoons **all-purpose flour**
- ½ teaspoon **salt**
- ½ teaspoon **hot chili flakes**
- ½ teaspoon **Chinese five spice** (see note above)
- 1 tablespoon **vegetable oil**
- 2 cloves **garlic,** peeled and minced
- 1 tablespoon grated **fresh ginger**
- 1 can (13.5 oz.) **coconut milk**
- 1 can (14.5 oz.) fat-skimmed **chicken broth**
- 2 cups lightly packed **washed baby spinach leaves** (about 4 oz.)
- 1 can (14 oz.) **baby corn,** drained
- 2 **Roma tomatoes** (about 8 oz. total), rinsed, cored, and chopped
- ¼ cup sliced **canned water chestnuts**
- ¼ cup thinly sliced **green onions**
- 1 tablespoon **lime juice**
- 3 tablespoons chopped **fresh cilantro** leaves

1. Rinse chicken, pat dry, and cut into 1-inch chunks. In a bowl, mix flour, salt, chili flakes, and five spice. Add chicken pieces and mix to coat.
2. Pour oil into a 4- to 5-quart pan over medium-high heat. Add chicken mixture, garlic, and ginger. Stir frequently

Chicken simmered in coconut milk can be served as a soup or over rice.

until chicken is cooked on the outside but still pink in the center (cut to test), about 3 minutes. Add coconut milk and broth and bring to a simmer. Adjust heat to maintain a simmer, cover, and cook to blend flavors, about 5 minutes.
3. Stir in spinach, corn, tomatoes, water chestnuts, green onions, and lime juice and cook, stirring often, until spinach is wilted, about 3 minutes. Sprinkle with cilantro before serving from pan.

Per serving: 429 cal., 57% (243 cal.) from fat; 33 g protein; 27 g fat (19 g sat.); 18 g carbo (5.2 g fiber); 499 mg sodium; 68 mg chol.

Swedish Salmon Gratin

Jennifer Kirkgaard, Pasadena

Jennifer Kirkgaard added a few of her own innovations to a favorite dish of her Swedish stepmother's.

PREP AND COOK TIME: About 1¼ hours
MAKES: 6 to 8 servings

- 1 can (14.75 oz.) **pink salmon**
- 3 **large eggs**
- 1 cup **milk**
- 2 tablespoons **Dijon mustard**
- 1 tablespoon **sugar**
- 1 teaspoon **salt**
- 2½ pounds **russet potatoes**
- ¼ cup chopped **fresh dill**
- 2 tablespoons **butter,** cut into small chunks
    Pepper

1. Drain salmon. Transfer to a bowl and remove and discard any skin and bones; flake with a fork.
2. In another bowl, whisk eggs, milk, mustard, sugar, and salt until blended.
3. Peel potatoes and cut crosswise

into very thin (¹/₁₆-in.-thick) slices. Arrange about a third of the potato slices over the bottom of a 9- by 13-inch baking dish. Sprinkle half the salmon evenly over potatoes, followed by half the dill. Repeat layers, ending with potatoes. Pour milk mixture over potatoes and distribute butter chunks evenly over the top. Sprinkle generously with pepper and cover dish tightly with foil.

4. Bake in a 375° regular or convection oven until potatoes are tender when pierced, about 45 minutes. Remove foil and continue to bake, uncovered, until golden brown on top, 15 to 20 minutes.

Per serving: 186 cal., 43% (80 cal.) from fat; 17 g protein; 8.9 g fat (3.8 g sat.); 9.1 g carbo (2.9 g fiber); 748 mg sodium; 120 mg chol.

Eggs Baja

Mickey Strang, McKinleyville, CA

Weekend brunch inspired Mickey Strang to create this open-faced egg sandwich.

PREP AND COOK TIME: About 20 minutes

MAKES: 4 servings

- 4 slices **bacon** (about 4 oz. total)
- 4 **large eggs**
  Salt and **pepper**
- 4 slices **sourdough bread** (about 3 by 6 in. and ½ in. thick)
- 1 **firm-ripe tomato** (about 8 oz.), rinsed, cored, and sliced
- 2 **canned whole green chilies**, halved lengthwise
- ½ cup **shredded jack** or cheddar **cheese**
- 2 tablespoons chopped **fresh cilantro** leaves

1. In a 10- to 12-inch nonstick frying pan over medium-high heat, cook bacon, turning once, until crisp, 4 to 5 minutes total. Drain on paper towels. Discard fat; if desired, wipe pan clean.

2. Set pan over medium heat; break eggs into pan and cook to desired doneness, turning once if you like, 2 to 5 minutes for soft yolks. Sprinkle with salt and pepper.

3. Meanwhile, place bread slices on a 12- by 15-inch baking sheet. Broil 6 inches from heat until lightly toasted, 1 to 2 minutes. Turn slices over and top equally with tomato slices, chilies, and cheese. Broil until cheese is melted, 2 to 3 minutes.

4. Top each sandwich with an egg, then a slice of bacon; sprinkle evenly with cilantro. Use a wide spatula to transfer each sandwich to a plate.

A square of this not-too-sweet banana cake and a glass of milk make a perfect snack.

Per serving: 256 cal., 49% (126 cal.) from fat; 15 g protein; 14 g fat (5.6 g sat.); 17 g carbo (1.7 g fiber); 492 mg sodium; 234 mg chol.

Grandma Thury's Banana Cake

Veronica Pape, Reno

Veronica Pape's great-grandmother handed down the recipe for this simple, spicy banana cake that's moistened with sour cream.

PREP AND COOK TIME: About 45 minutes

MAKES: 8 servings

- 2 **large eggs**
- 1 cup **granulated sugar**
- 1 cup **sour cream**
- 1 cup mashed **ripe bananas** (about two; 12 oz. total)
- 1 teaspoon **vanilla**
- 2 cups **all-purpose flour**
- 2 teaspoons **baking powder**
- 1 teaspoon **baking soda**
- ½ teaspoon **salt**
- ¼ teaspoon **ground cinnamon**
- ⅛ teaspoon **ground ginger**
- ⅛ teaspoon **ground cloves**
  Powdered sugar

1. In a large bowl, mix eggs, sugar, sour cream, bananas, and vanilla until well blended. In another bowl, stir together flour, baking powder, baking soda, salt, cinnamon, ginger, and cloves. Stir flour mixture into banana mixture just until well blended. Scrape batter into a buttered and floured 9-inch square baking pan.

2. Bake in a 350° regular or convection oven until top springs back when gently pressed and a skewer inserted in the center of the cake comes out with moist crumbs attached, 30 to 35 minutes. Dust with powdered sugar before cutting into squares; serve warm or cool from pan.

Per serving: 331 cal., 22% (74 cal.) from fat; 6.1 g protein; 8.2 g fat (4.5 g sat.); 59 g carbo (1.3 g fiber); 462 mg sodium; 67 mg chol.

Marinated Garbanzo Salad

Stacy Garcia, Laguna Niguel, CA

This oil-free bean salad is quick to assemble and can be made up to two days ahead.

PREP AND COOK TIME: About 20 minutes, plus at least 2 hours to chill

MAKES: 4 servings

- 2 cans (15 oz. each) **garbanzos**, drained and rinsed
- 1 cup **roasted red peppers**, cut into strips
- ½ cup chopped **red onion**
- 2 stalks **celery**, thinly sliced crosswise
- 2 cloves **garlic**, peeled and minced
- ½ cup chopped **fresh cilantro** leaves
- ½ cup **rice vinegar**
- 2 tablespoons **lemon juice**
- 1 teaspoon **sugar**
  Salt and **pepper**

In a bowl, combine all ingredients, including salt and pepper to taste. Cover and chill at least 2 hours or up to 2 days.

Per serving: 187 cal., 17% (31 cal.) from fat; 8.6 g protein; 3.4 g fat (0.2 g sat.); 32 g carbo (7.1 g fiber); 325 mg sodium; 0 mg chol. ◆

Thai basil adds a nuance of anise flavor to a quick and easy stir-fry of chicken breasts (see page 100).

May

Late-spring dinner for eight

Seared Scallops with Shallots and Coconut Cream*

Yellow Squash and Split Pea Soup with Shrimp*

Garden Greens with Vinaigrette

Wine-Brined Grilled Chicken*

Pea Risotto*

Merlot Strawberries with Vanilla Cream*

Recipe provided

Grilled chicken brined in Sauvignon Blanc pairs well with a similar crisp white wine or a fruity Rhône-style red like Syrah or Granache.

The art of entertaining

A late-spring menu inspired by a Bay Area sculptor is perfect for dinner outdoors

By Charity Ferreira • Photographs by James Carrier • Food styling by Karen Shinto

For as long as he can remember, Kevin Christison has been drawn to both art and food. The 34-year-old bronze sculptor, whose work has been exhibited in the San Francisco Museum of Modern Art as well as numerous galleries and private collections, recalls unscrewing the caps of all the spice jars in the kitchen as a child to inhale the aromas.

Today, Christison's approach to creating—whether he's sculpting in his Oakland, California, studio or cooking dinner for his wife, Amy, and 2-year-old daughter, Lola—is to improvise. "The fun lies in arranging, pairing, and celebrating ingredients," he says. "Just as rewarding is sharing the results with others and feeling that you've nailed it."

For the last few years, the Staglin family, art patrons and owners of Staglin Family Vineyard in Rutherford, California, have teamed up with Christison to offer a wine dinner as an auction item for SFMOMA. The artist, with help last year from cousin Christopher Manning, cooks an elegant meal and serves it to the guests in the winery's garden.

Christison likes simple dishes with high-impact appearance and flavor. His menu here includes seared scallops with coconut crème fraîche and fried shallots; creamy yellow squash and split pea soup garnished with rock shrimp; quartered chickens brined in wine and tarragon, then grilled; and strawberries steeped in wine and topped with rich mascarpone cream.

Kevin Christison (right) and cousin Christopher Manning garnish a salad of garden greens. Staglin Family Vineyard hosts the artist's meal.

Seared Scallops with Shallots and Coconut Cream

PREP AND COOK TIME: About 25 minutes

NOTES: This recipe makes a little more coconut crème fraîche than you need, because a smaller volume is hard to whip; leftovers will keep, covered and chilled, for up to 1 week. We enjoyed them stirred into soups, added to the broth of steamed mussels, and spooned over fruit. You can make the crème fraîche mixture and fry the shallots (steps 1 and 2) up to 1 day ahead. Cover crème fraîche airtight and chill; cover shallots and store at room temperature.

MAKES: 8 appetizer servings

- ½ cup crème fraîche or whipping cream
- ½ cup coconut milk (stir before measuring)
- ½ cup thinly sliced shallots (about 2 oz.)
- ¼ cup vegetable oil
- 8 sea scallops (each about 1 in. wide, about 8 oz. total)
  Salt and pepper

1. In a bowl, with a mixer on high speed, beat crème fraîche and coconut milk until soft peaks form. Cover and chill while preparing shallots and scallops.

2. In an 8- to 10-inch nonstick frying pan over medium heat, stir shallots in oil until crisp and golden, 6 to 10 minutes. With a slotted spoon, transfer to a paper towel to drain.

3. Rinse scallops and pat dry. Sprinkle both sides with salt and pepper. Add scallops in a single layer to frying pan (no need to wash) and cook, turning once, until browned on both sides and barely opaque but still moist-looking in the center (cut to test), 3 to 4 minutes

Easy prep plan

Up to 2 days ahead:
Make mascarpone cream.

Up to 1 day ahead: Mix
coconut crème fraîche and fry
shallots for scallops; make
soup; brine chicken.

Up to 4 hours ahead: Poach
strawberries.

1 hour before serving: Heat
grill; start risotto.

30 minutes before serving:
Begin grilling chicken;
assemble salad.

20 minutes before serving:
Cook scallops.

10 minutes before serving:
Heat soup.

Silky coconut crème fraîche
tops seared scallops
for the first course.

total. Let cool to room temperature,
about 5 minutes.

4. Arrange scallops on a platter and top
each with about 2 teaspoons coconut
crème fraîche. Sprinkle equally with
fried shallots.

*Per serving: 118 cal., 75% (89 cal.) from fat;
5.2 g protein; 9.9 g fat (3 g sat.); 2.2 g carbo
(0.1 g fiber); 51 mg sodium; 14 mg chol.*

Yellow Squash and Split Pea Soup with Shrimp

PREP AND COOK TIME: About 1½ hours

NOTES: This soup is delicious hot or
cold. You can make it up to 1 day ahead;
cool completely, cover, and chill.

MAKES: 8 cups; 8 servings

- 4 **cups diced (¼ in.) yellow summer
  squash (about 1 lb.)**
- 1 **teaspoon olive oil**
  About ¼ teaspoon salt
  About ⅛ teaspoon pepper
- 2 **tablespoons butter**
- 1 **onion (about 8 oz.), peeled
  and diced**
- 5 **cups fat-skimmed chicken broth**
- ½ **cup dry white wine**
- 6 **ounces peeled, deveined rock
  shrimp, thawed if frozen, rinsed**

- 1 **stalk fresh lemon grass
  (10 to 12 in. long)**
- 1 **teaspoon ground cumin**
- ½ **teaspoon ground dried turmeric**
- 1 **cup dried yellow split peas**
- ½ **cup whipping cream**

1. In a 12- by 15-inch baking pan, mix
squash with olive oil; sprinkle with ¼
teaspoon salt and ⅛ teaspoon pepper
and mix to coat. Bake in a 400° regular
or convection oven, stirring occasionally, until squash is tender when
pierced, 15 to 20 minutes.

2. Meanwhile, in a 5- to 6-quart pan
over medium heat, melt butter. Add
onion and stir occasionally until very
limp, 8 to 10 minutes. Add broth and
wine, increase heat, and bring to a sim-

Garnish soup
with nasturtiums
or squash
blossoms.

mer. Add shrimp and simmer, uncovered, just until pink on the outside and
opaque but still moist-looking in center
of thickest part (cut to test), about 2
minutes. With a strainer or a slotted
spoon, transfer shrimp to a bowl.

3. Rinse lemon grass; cut off and discard tough tops and root end. Remove
and discard tough outer layers. With
the flat side of a knife or a mallet, crush
tender inner stalk. Add to pan along
with cumin, turmeric, and split peas.
Bring to a boil over high heat, then
cover, reduce heat, and simmer, stirring occasionally, until peas are very
tender and almost completely broken
down, about 50 minutes.

4. Stir in all but about ¼ cup roasted
squash. In a blender or food processor,
working in batches if necessary, whirl
soup until smooth. Return to pan over
low heat and stir in cream and salt and
pepper to taste. Heat until steaming
(see notes).

5. Ladle soup into bowls and top
equally with shrimp and reserved
roasted squash.

*Per serving: 225 cal., 36% (80 cal.) from fat;
17 g protein; 8.9 g fat (4.9 g sat.); 20 g carbo
(2.4 g fiber); 191 mg sodium; 57 mg chol.*

Wine-Brined Grilled Chicken

PREP AND COOK TIME: About 1 hour, plus 1 day to chill

NOTES: Have butcher remove backs from chickens and quarter birds. You can mince shallots in a food processor.

MAKES: 8 servings

- 2 chickens (about 3½ lb. each), necks and giblets removed, cut into quarters (see notes)
- 1 bottle (750 ml.) Sauvignon Blanc or other dry white wine
- 2 cups minced shallots (see notes)
- 1 cup chopped fresh tarragon
- ¼ cup kosher salt
- 2 tablespoons sugar

1. Rinse chicken and pat dry. Trim off excess fat. In an 11- by 16-inch roasting pan (about 3 in. deep), stir wine, shallots, tarragon, salt, and sugar until salt and sugar are dissolved. Add chicken quarters and turn to coat. Cover and chill for 1 day, turning once.

2. Lift chicken from brine; discard brine. Rinse quarters and pat dry.

3. Lay chicken quarters on a barbecue grill over medium-hot coals or medium heat on a gas grill (you can hold your hand at grill level only 4 to 5 seconds); close lid on gas grill. Cook, turning frequently, until browned on both sides and no longer pink at the bone (cut to test), about 25 minutes. Pile quarters on a platter or place on plates.

Per serving: 424 cal., 51% (216 cal.) from fat; 48 g protein; 24 g fat (6.6 g sat.); 1.3 g carbo (0 g fiber); 389 mg sodium; 154 mg chol.

Pea Risotto

PREP AND COOK TIME: About 40 minutes

NOTES: Start risotto while heating the grill for the chicken; cover and keep warm until you're ready to serve. If using frozen peas, add with last cup broth.

MAKES: 8 cups; about 8 side-dish servings

- 1 tablespoon olive oil
- 1 onion (about 8 oz.), peeled and finely chopped
- 2 cups Arborio or other short-grain white rice
- ½ cup dry white wine

Strawberries steeped in Merlot are a simple, make-ahead dessert.

About 5½ cups fat-skimmed chicken broth
- 8 ounces shelled fresh peas (about 1 lb. in shell), or 1½ cups frozen peas (see notes)
- ½ cup shredded parmesan cheese
  Salt and pepper

1. Pour olive oil into a 5- to 6-quart pan over medium-high heat; when hot, add onion and stir often until limp, about 5 minutes. Add rice and stir until opaque, about 3 minutes.

2. Add wine and stir until absorbed, 1 to 2 minutes. Add 5½ cups broth, about a cup at a time, stirring after each addition until almost absorbed, 25 to 30 minutes total; stir in peas with the second cup of broth. If risotto is thicker than desired, stir in a little more broth. Stir in cheese and add salt and pepper to taste.

Per serving: 264 cal., 17% (46 cal.) from fat; 14 g protein; 5.1 g fat (2 g sat.); 40 g carbo (4.5 g fiber); 225 mg sodium; 7.2 mg chol.

Merlot Strawberries with Vanilla Cream

PREP AND COOK TIME: About 20 minutes, plus 1 hour to cool

NOTES: You can make the mascarpone cream up to 2 days ahead; cover and chill. Whisk briefly before serving.

You can poach the strawberries up to 4 hours ahead; let stand at room temperature. Instead of mascarpone, you can top strawberries with whipped cream.

MAKES: 8 servings

- 8 ounces mascarpone cheese (see notes)
- ½ cup whipping cream
- ⅔ cup sugar
- 1 vanilla bean, split lengthwise
- 2½ cups Merlot or other dry red wine
- 1 teaspoon lemon juice
- 6 cups sliced strawberries

1. Combine mascarpone, cream, and 2 tablespoons sugar; scrape seeds from vanilla bean into mixture (reserve pod). Beat with a mixer on low speed until soft peaks form. Cover and chill.

2. In a 4- to 6-quart pan over medium heat, frequently stir wine, lemon juice, remaining sugar, and vanilla bean pod until mixture is simmering, about 12 minutes. Remove from heat; stir in strawberries. Let cool about 1 hour.

3. Ladle strawberries and liquid into wineglasses or goblets (at least 8 oz.). Top with mascarpone cream.

Per serving: 319 cal., 48% (153 cal.) from fat; 3 g protein; 17 g fat (11 g sat.); 27 g carbo (3 g fiber); 24 mg sodium; 40 mg chol. ◆

Menu for Mom

Rice Salad Niçoise
Quick-Pickled Asparagus
Baguettes and brie
Radishes or olives
Jam Thumbprints

A picnic for Mother's Day

Team up with the kids to make an easy alfresco lunch

By Kate Washington
Photographs by Leigh Beisch

Mother's Day brunch is a tradition, but all too often it means a morning of fighting crowds in a restaurant or an afternoon of cleaning up at home. Instead, head out into the spring sunshine for a peaceful picnic lunch this year.

A simple French-style rice salad and mildly pickled asparagus make a delicious meal, rounded out with baguettes, cheese, and radishes or olives. For dessert, jam thumbprints are the perfect project for little hands. In fact, all the recipes here are kid-tested: without help, our team of two 12-year-olds made the entire menu in less than three hours. The whole meal packs into a basket or backpack to take to a park, on a hike, or just out to the backyard for a relaxed celebration with the family.

For a refreshing picnic drink, add the sparkling orangeade on page 96.

Rice Salad Niçoise

PREP AND COOK TIME: About 1 hour

NOTES: This recipe is already easy, but for a kid-friendly shortcut, purchase cooked rice from a Chinese restaurant; you will need 5 cups.

MAKES: 4 to 6 servings

1½ cups long-grain white rice (see notes)

About ½ teaspoon salt

12 ounces green beans, rinsed

½ cup red wine vinegar

2 tablespoons Dijon mustard

1 clove garlic, peeled and pressed or minced

⅓ cup olive oil

Fresh-ground pepper

¼ cup chopped parsley (see "Cooking with Kids," page 95)

¼ cup thinly sliced fresh chives

12 ounces cherry tomatoes, stemmed and rinsed

2 cans (6 oz. each) solid light tuna in olive oil, drained and broken into large chunks with a fork

1. In a 3- to 4-quart pan, combine rice, ½ teaspoon salt, and 3 cups water. Bring to a boil over high heat, then reduce heat, cover, and simmer until water is absorbed and rice is tender to bite, 20 minutes. Spread rice level in a large baking pan and let cool to room temperature, about 30 minutes.

2. Meanwhile, in a large pan over high heat, bring about 2 quarts water to a boil. Snap ends off green beans and snap or cut beans in half. Add to boiling water and cook just until bright green and tender-crisp to bite, about 2 minutes. Drain, rinse well under cold running water, and drain again.

3. In a small bowl, whisk vinegar, mustard, and garlic until smooth. Add oil and whisk until well blended and thick. Add salt and pepper to taste and 3 tablespoons *each* of the parsley and chives.

4. Spoon rice into a large bowl (with sealable lid, if planning to transport). Pour dressing over rice and mix to coat. Gently stir in beans, tomatoes, and tuna. Sprinkle with remaining herbs.

Per serving: 400 cal., 38% (153 cal.) from fat; 16 g protein; 17 g fat (2 g sat.); 45 g carbo (2.4 g fiber); 585 mg sodium; 20 mg chol.

Quick-Pickled Asparagus

PREP AND COOK TIME: About 45 minutes

NOTES: You can pickle this asparagus (through step 2) up to 2 days ahead; the flavor becomes more intense the longer the asparagus stands in the brine. Serve chilled or at room temperature.

MAKES: 4 to 6 servings

- ¾ cup rice vinegar
- 2 tablespoons salt
- 2 tablespoons sugar
- 2 tablespoons pickling spice
- 1 to 1½ pounds asparagus, rinsed and tough stem ends snapped off

1. In wide 4- to 5-quart pan, combine vinegar, salt, sugar, pickling spice, and 2 cups water. Bring to a boil over high heat, then reduce heat and simmer for 15 minutes.

2. Add asparagus; if liquid doesn't cover it, add water to cover. Simmer, stirring occasionally, until asparagus has faded to dull green and is tender-crisp to bite, 4 to 6 minutes. Remove from heat; add 1 cup ice cubes to stop cooking. Let stand at least 30 minutes (see notes).

3. Drain asparagus and arrange on a platter or seal in a container for transport.

Per serving: 17 cal., 5.3% (0.9 cal.) from fat; 1.9 g protein; 0.1 g fat (0 g sat.); 3.3 g carbo (0.6 g fiber); 194 mg sodium; 0 mg chol.

Jam Thumbprints

PREP AND COOK TIME: About 1 hour

NOTES: We like to use several different flavors of jam for these cookies, such as apricot, plum, raspberry, and strawberry. You can make them up to

Thumbprint cookies make a fun project for young kids.

2 days ahead; store airtight at room temperature.

MAKES: About 16 cookies; 4 to 6 servings

- ½ cup (¼ lb.) butter, at room temperature
- ⅓ cup sugar
- 1 large egg yolk
- 1 teaspoon vanilla
- 1 cup all-purpose flour
- ⅛ teaspoon salt
  About ¼ cup jam (see notes)

1. In a bowl, with a mixer on high speed, beat butter and sugar until smooth. Beat in egg yolk and vanilla until well blended, scraping sides of bowl as necessary.

2. With mixer on low speed, beat flour and salt into butter mixture until well blended. Cover bowl with plastic wrap and chill until dough is firm but still pliable, about 30 minutes.

3. Shape dough into 1-inch balls and place 1 inch apart on a buttered 12- by 15-inch baking sheet. Press your thumb into the center of each cookie to make a ½-inch-deep imprint. Spoon about ½ teaspoon jam into each.

4. Bake cookies in a 325° regular or convection oven until lightly browned on the bottom, 12 to 15 minutes. Transfer to a rack to cool completely.

Per serving: 114 cal., 51% (58 cal.) from fat; 1.1 g protein; 6.4 g fat (3.8 g sat.); 13 g carbo (0.3 g fiber); 82 mg sodium; 29 mg chol. ◆

Cooking with kids

This menu is designed for children of all ages to help with and older ones to produce on their own.

• **Make as much as possible ahead of time.** The best picnic is the one at which neither kids nor grown-ups are exhausted from cooking and cleaning up. Most of our dishes can be made, at least in part, a day or two ahead.

• **Do some basic prep work before asking young children to help you.** They will love making thumbprints in the cookies but might have trouble sitting still for less glamorous tasks like stemming cherry tomatoes.

• **Do steps involving heat yourself** when working with kids under 8. Make sure older ones use caution—and pot holders—at the stove or oven.

• **Give shorter kids a stepladder** or stool to stand on at the counter or stove. If they have to reach up, the chances for spills increase.

• **Use scissors rather than knives** to cut herbs, or simply tear the parsley into pieces. To eliminate any knife work in this menu, press the garlic into the salad dressing.

Best of the West

Dip on a chip

At Mom Is Cooking in San Francisco's Excelsior district, you won't find high style or fancy decor (think red vinyl on the banquettes and beer logos on the walls). But you *will* find some of the best homestyle Mexican food this side of the border, cooked up by Abigail Murillo—the mom of the name. The menu's addictive standout is her boquitos, chips layered with toppings to make an appetizer that combines the best things about nachos, crostini, and seven-layer dip. Make a platter of our easy version of them for Cinco de Mayo, Mother's Day, or whenever you wish Mom were cooking in your kitchen. *Closed Mon. 1166 Geneva Ave.; (415) 586-7000.*

EASY SNACKS

BOQUITOS

- 1 large, sturdy tortilla chip
- 1 tablespoon warm refried pinto or black beans
- 1 teaspoon cooked fresh firm Mexican-style chorizo (to cook 8 oz. chorizo, remove and discard casing; stir chorizo in a frying pan over medium heat until crumbly and browned, 5 to 7 minutes)
- 1 teaspoon guacamole (purchased or homemade)
- 1 teaspoon sour cream or Mexican crema
- 1 teaspoon diced tomato
- 1 fresh cilantro leaf

Layer each chip as shown above.

—Kate Washington

Morning sunshine

Greet Mom with sparkling orangeade this Mother's Day. The drink gets a more delicate flavor from freshly squeezed juice, but in a pinch, feel free to go for made-from-concentrate. The juices and sugar can be combined (step 1) up to 1 day ahead; cover and chill. Add the ice and sparkling water just before serving.

FRESH IDEA

Sparkling Orangeade

1. In a large pitcher (at least 2 qt.), stir 2 cups **orange juice,** ⅔ cup **lime juice,** and ⅔ cup **sugar** until sugar is dissolved. **2.** Add 2 cups **ice cubes** and 1 liter **sparkling water** and stir to blend. **3.** Pour into tall glasses, adding **orange slices** if desired. Makes 2 quarts.

—K. W.

Drink flowers

With aromas evocative of roses, gardenias, apple blossoms, and more, these aromatic white wines are perfect for the season (and are terrific partners for spicy food).

BEST AROMATIC WHITES

Echelon "Esperanza Vineyard" **Viognier 2001** *(Clarksburg, California), $11.* Peach blossoms— juicy and clean. A great change-of-pace wine at an irresistible price.

EXP Viognier 2001 *(Dunnigan Hills, California), $14.* If jasmine could be crossed with piña coladas—rich and silky.

Cline "Oakley" Vin Blanc 2001 *(California), $8.50.* A blend of nine different white grape varietals. Light gardenia and vanilla aroma. Fascinating spicy yet creamy flavors.

Sokol Blosser Evolution, seventh edition, nonvintage *(Oregon), $15.* A blend of nine varietals. Floral and tropical aromas are followed by lime and pear flavors.

Fetzer "Echo Ridge" Johannisberg Riesling 2002 *(California), $8.* Like peach trees in bloom, plus litchi and apricot flavors. Pair with carnitas burritos.

CL "Madonna Vineyard" Gewürztraminer 2000 *(Carneros, California), $15.* Seductive aromas of rose petals, orange-flower water, and vanilla. Limited production, but worth snapping up if you see a bottle.

—Karen MacNeil-Fife

Tortilla tale

Tips from a legendary cook

By Jerry Anne Di Vecchio
Photograph by James Carrier

Elena Zelayeta—a jolly little woman who got stuck in San Francisco as a child in 1910 with her vacationing family when the Mexican revolution broke out—did more than anyone else to bring the lively flavors of Mexico to our everyday tables. By the time I began writing for *Sunset,* in the late 1950s, she was a nationally recognized expert, with an enormously popular downtown restaurant, Elena's Mexican Village, and her own frozen-foods company. Amazingly, she had been blind for decades.

Nevertheless, in her kitchen, Elena led me through the intricacies of huevos rancheros. The key to this dish of eggs layered with beans and chili sauce, she advised, is to have all of the components ready, then fry the eggs and heat the tortillas at the last minute. When she began flipping tortillas directly over a gas flame, though, I gasped. "Well," she said, "this is probably too dangerous for you." Somewhat sheepishly, I took (and still take) a more cautious route to warming the tortillas, and sometimes a purchased shortcut to the sauces.

Mexican-style eggs with both red and green salsas are a quick, flavorful brunch dish.

FOOD STYLING: KAREN SHINTO

Huevos Rancheros Grande

PREP AND COOK TIME: About 20 minutes

NOTES: If desired, stir a can of diced green chilies into the green salsa. Or, instead of salsas, use red and green chili sauces, canned or homemade. Cotija cheese is available in many supermarkets and in Latino grocery stores. You can make the beans up to 3 days ahead; chill airtight. Reheat to use.

MAKES: 6 servings

- 12 **corn tortillas (7 to 8 in.)**
- 2 **tablespoons butter or bacon fat**
- 6 **large eggs**
- 3 **cups finely shredded iceberg lettuce**
  Bacon black beans (recipe follows)
  Canned chunky tomato salsa (see notes), heated
  Canned green (tomatillo) salsa (see notes), heated
- 1½ **cups shredded mild cheddar cheese (about 6 oz.; optional)**
- 6 **tablespoons packed crumbled cotija or feta cheese**
  Sliced avocado (optional)
  Thinly sliced fresh jalapeño chilies (optional)
  Sour cream (optional)
- 2 **limes, rinsed and cut into wedges**
  Salt

1. Stack tortillas, seal in foil, and heat in a 375° oven until hot, 10 minutes.

2. In a 12-inch nonstick frying pan over medium heat, melt butter. Break eggs into pan, slightly apart; cover and cook just until whites are almost firm and yolks are still soft, about 3 minutes.

3. Meanwhile, spread ½ cup lettuce on each plate. Lay tortillas on lettuce and spoon beans over tortillas. With a wide spatula, transfer an egg to each serving. Spoon tomato salsa around one side of eggs, green around the other side. Sprinkle with cheddar cheese, then cotija.

4. Garnish as desired with avocado, jalapeño chilies, sour cream, and lime wedges; add salt to taste. Enclose remaining tortillas in a linen napkin to keep warm, and serve alongside.

Per serving: 414 cal., 41% (171 cal.) from fat; 20 g protein; 19 g fat (7.4 g sat.); 43 g carbo (7.2 g fiber); 664 mg sodium; 236 mg chol.

Bacon black beans. In a 10- to 12-inch frying pan over medium-high heat, stir 4 oz. chopped **bacon** (4 slices) until crisp and brown, 5 to 7 minutes. With a slotted spoon, transfer to paper towels to drain. Spoon all but 2 tablespoons fat from pan (save for huevos, preceding, if desired, or discard) and add 2 minced or pressed **garlic cloves** and 1 cup chopped **onion.** Stir often over high heat until onion is limp, about 3 minutes. Meanwhile, rinse and drain 2 cans (15 oz. each) **black beans;** add to pan along with 1 cup **fat-skimmed chicken broth.** Stir often until most of the liquid is evaporated, 5 to 7 minutes. Stir bacon into beans. If beans have gotten too dry, thin with a little more broth. ◆

Summer's

Lemon basil (*Ocimum basilicum* 'Citriodorum') lends a light, citrus flavor to vinegars, poultry, and vegetable and fish dishes.

favorite herb

Growing and cooking with the tastiest types of basil

By Linda Anusasananan and Sharon Cohoon • Photographs by Thomas J. Story (garden) and James Carrier (food) • Food styling by Basil Friedman

Basil smells like summer. Take a deep whiff of its distinctive spicy-sweet scent and you can almost taste the juicy tomato slices waiting on your plate for a few flavor-filled leaves. No wonder basil is among our favorite annual herbs.

The essential oils that give sweet basil leaves their aroma are made of just a few compounds. Linalool is responsible for the light floral character; eugenol, the clove; and methyl chavicol, the anise. But the ratio of these compounds is different in each type of basil, and consequently so is each variety's perfume. If you grow several kinds of basil, you can select whatever scent complements the food you're preparing.

Use standard sweet basils—the type most commonly stocked at supermarkets—for pesto or other Italian dishes; lemon basils with fish or poultry; anise basil for Thai or other spicy dishes; and red and purple basils for garnish or to add sparkle to salads. But don't restrict yourself; experiment by growing several varieties to familiarize yourself with their fragrances and flavors. Plant basil soon for a summer harvest.

Basil Lemonade

PREP TIME: About 10 minutes

NOTES: All basils add fragrance to lemonade, but colored and scented varieties contribute extra personality. Dark purple basils tint the lemonade a pretty pink but have a milder flavor than green varieties. Lemon basil adds a lemon-drop essence. Cinnamon and Thai basils contribute spicy overtones. You can make the lemonade up to 1 day ahead; cover and chill.

MAKES: 4½ cups; about 4 servings

In a 1½- to 2-quart glass measure or bowl, combine ½ cup rinsed, lightly packed **fresh basil** leaves (see notes) and 3 tablespoons **sugar.** With a wooden spoon, crush leaves with sugar until thoroughly bruised. Add 4 cups **water** and ½ cup freshly squeezed **lemon** juice. Stir until sugar is dissolved, 1 to 2 minutes. Taste and add more sugar if desired. Pour through a fine strainer into ice-filled glasses. Garnish with sprigs of **fresh basil.**

Per serving: 44 cal., 0% (0 cal.) from fat; 0.1 g protein; 0 g fat; 12 g carbo (0.1 g fiber); 0.4 mg sodium; 0 mg chol.

Planting and care

One strategy for making the most of the short basil season is to establish a quick crop by starting with seedlings; most nurseries carry at least a half-dozen varieties.

Wait until nighttime temperatures remain above 55° to plant seedlings or sow seeds directly in the ground. If you want to get a head start, sow seeds indoors four to six weeks before setting out.

• **Plant** in a location that provides at least six hours of direct sun. (In hot locations, light afternoon shade is preferable.) Soil should be neutral (6 to 6.5 pH), rich, and well drained. Space plants 10 to 12 inches apart; seeds about 1 inch apart.

• **Water.** Give plants about 1 inch of water per week. Feed with fish emulsion or a balanced fertilizer when you transplant, then fertilize once or twice during the growing season, such as after a heavy harvest.

• **Check for pests.** Slugs and snails love basil. Encircle young seedlings with a barrier of copper flashing to deter pests.

• **Harvest** generously and frequently. Basil tastes better before it flowers, and it will start flowering after producing about six pairs of leaves. Snip off growing tips often. Cut whole stems. When plants start to get ahead of you, cut them back to the bottom two leaves, and use your harvest to make pesto. Or use the flowering stems in bouquets; Thai basil is especially attractive.

Six tasty basils

Sweet.
A generic term for classic culinary basil. Large, smooth green leaves; white flowers. Scent combines mint, spice, citrus, and anise. 'Genovese', shown here, is a favorite for pesto.

Anise. Also known as licorice or Thai basil. 'Siam Queen' is shown here. Green leaves; purple flowers and stems. Both leaves and flowers have spicy anise scent.

Cinnamon.
Pointed green leaves; reddish stems; lavender flowers. Strong cinnamon scent.

Lemon.
Small light green leaves; white flowers. Sweet lemon scent plus traces of mint and spice. 'Sweet Dani', shown here, is the best-known variety; 'Mrs. Burns' has bigger leaves, stronger scent.

Purple-leafed.
Burgundy- to plum-colored foliage; white to lavender flowers with dark bracts. Mild to peppery taste depending on variety. 'Red Rubin' is shown here. 'Dark Opal' and 'Purple Ruffles' are two other common varieties.

Bush. Also known as Greek or dwarf basil. Tiny leaves on 1-foot-tall plants; white flowers. Stems are soft and succulent, so you can chop up entire sprig, stem and all. Flavor and fragrance vary but tend to be spicy.

Tomato and Basil Orzo Salad

PREP AND COOK TIME: About 20 minutes

NOTES: Serve this warm salad as a main dish for a light lunch or as a dinner companion to grilled steak, chicken, or fish. For a casual appetizer, scoop spoonfuls of the salad into large leaves of fresh sweet basil.

MAKES: 4 to 6 light-entrée servings or 8 to 10 side-dish servings

- 1½ cups dried orzo pasta
- 1¼ pounds firm-ripe tomatoes, at room temperature
- ¾ cup chopped fresh basil leaves
- 1 or 2 cloves garlic, peeled and minced
- 3 tablespoons extra-virgin olive oil
- 2 tablespoons balsamic vinegar
  About ¼ cup grated parmesan cheese
  Salt and pepper

1. In a 3- to 4-quart pan over high heat, bring 1½ to 2 quarts water to a boil. Add orzo and cook until barely tender to bite, 8 to 10 minutes.

2. Meanwhile, rinse and core tomatoes; chop and place in a large bowl. Add basil, garlic, olive oil, and vinegar; mix gently.

3. Drain pasta well and add to tomato mixture. Mix, adding parmesan cheese, salt, and pepper to taste.

Per serving: 255 cal., 32% (81 cal.) from fat; 7.8 g protein; 9 g fat (1.8 g sat.); 37 g carbo (2.6 g fiber); 74 mg sodium; 2.6 mg chol.

Chicken and Basil Stir-Fry

PREP AND COOK TIME: About 25 minutes

NOTES: Thai basil adds an anise nuance, and cinnamon basil contributes notes of spice to this quick stir-fry; however, other basil varieties work well too. Serve with hot cooked rice. Asian fish sauce is available in most supermarkets and in Asian grocery stores.

MAKES: 3 or 4 servings

- 1 pound boned, skinned chicken breast halves
- 1 tablespoon vegetable oil
- 1 tablespoon minced garlic
- 1 tablespoon minced fresh ginger
- ¼ teaspoon hot chili flakes
- ⅔ cup fat-skimmed chicken broth
- 1 tablespoon Asian fish sauce (*nuoc mam* or *nam pla*) or soy sauce
- 2 teaspoons cornstarch
- 3 cups lightly packed fresh basil leaves (see notes), rinsed
  Salt

1. Rinse chicken and pat dry. Cut crosswise into ⅛-inch-thick strips 2 to 3 inches long.

2. Place a 10- to 12-inch nonstick frying pan over high heat; when hot, add oil, garlic, ginger, chili flakes, and the chicken. Stir often until chicken is no longer pink in the center (cut to test), 3 to 4 minutes.

3. In a small bowl, mix broth, fish sauce, and cornstarch until smooth. Add to pan and stir until sauce is boiling, about 1 minute. Add basil leaves and stir just until barely wilted, about 30 seconds. Add salt to taste and pour into a serving bowl.

Per serving: 202 cal., 25% (51 cal.) from fat; 30 g protein; 5.7 g fat (0.9 g sat.); 6.5 g carbo (3.2 g fiber); 239 mg sodium; 66 mg chol.

Orange-Basil Cooler

PREP TIME: About 10 minutes

NOTES: Cinnamon, Thai, and lemon basils add fragrant overtones to this drink, but almost any basil works well, with the exception of red ones, which give a slightly duller color. After adding the orange juice, you can cover mixture and chill up to 1 day if desired.

MAKES: 2 servings

In a 1-quart glass measure or bowl, combine ½ cup rinsed, lightly packed **fresh basil** leaves (see notes) and 2 teaspoons **sugar**. With a wooden spoon, crush leaves with the sugar until thoroughly bruised. Add 1 cup **orange juice** and mix. Pour through a

Fresh basil leaves
scent spicy,
Thai-inspired
chicken stir-fry.

Basil oil adds a fragrant finish to this classic salad of tomatoes, mozzarella, and basil.

Classic Pesto

PREP TIME: About 25 minutes

NOTES: This all-purpose pesto is great to mix with pasta, hot cooked green beans, potatoes, and asparagus; brush it over chicken, shrimp, or pork, and stir it into salad dressings and soups. Pesto darkens rapidly when exposed to air. You can cover the pesto airtight (press plastic wrap directly onto surface) or cover surface with a little extra olive oil. Store up to 1 day in the refrigerator. Or spoon into ice-cube trays, press plastic wrap onto surface, and freeze; when solid, pop cubes from trays and store airtight for up to 6 months in the freezer. Thaw before using. If surface darkens, just stir to blend.

MAKES: 1½ cups

Put 2 or 3 peeled **garlic** cloves and ¼ cup **pine nuts** in a food processor or blender and whirl until coarsely chopped. Rinse and drain 4 cups lightly packed **fresh basil** leaves; gently pat dry. Add basil, 1 cup grated **parmesan cheese** (about 4 oz.), and ¾ cup **extra-virgin olive oil** to garlic mixture; whirl until smooth (if using blender, stop to push basil down into blades as needed). Add **salt** and **pepper** to taste.

Per tablespoon: 92 cal., 88% (81 cal.) from fat; 2.5 g protein; 9 g fat (1.9 g sat.); 1.2 g carbo (0.7 g fiber); 76 mg sodium; 3.2 mg chol.

dry with a towel. In a blender or food processor, combine basil leaves and 1 cup **olive** or vegetable **oil** (see notes). Whirl just until leaves are finely chopped (do not purée).

2. Pour mixture into a 1- to 1½-quart pan over medium heat. Stir occasionally until oil bubbles around pan sides and reaches 165° on a thermometer, 3 to 4 minutes. Remove from heat and let stand until cool, about 1 hour.

3. Line a fine wire strainer with two layers of cheesecloth and set over a small bowl. Pour oil mixture into strainer. After oil passes through, gently press basil to release remaining oil. Discard basil. Serve oil or cover airtight and store in the refrigerator up to 3 months. The olive oil may solidify slightly when chilled, but it will quickly liquefy when it comes back to room temperature.

Per tablespoon: 120 cal., 100% (120 cal.) from fat; 0 g protein; 14 g fat (1.8 g sat.); 0 g carbo; 0 mg sodium; 0 mg chol. ◆

fine wire strainer into two ice-filled glasses (at least 10- to 12-oz. size). Add ½ cup **soda water** to each glass and mix. Garnish coolers with rinsed sprigs of **fresh basil.**

Per serving: 73 cal., 1% (0.9 cal.) from fat; 0.9 g protein; 0.1 g fat (0 g sat.); 18 g carbo (0.2 g fiber); 1.4 mg sodium; 0 mg chol.

Basil Oil

PREP AND COOK TIME: About 10 minutes, plus 1 hour to cool

NOTES: Drizzle this aromatic oil over sliced tomatoes, fresh mozzarella cheese, green beans, potatoes, bread, green salads, and grilled or poached chicken or fish. Choose a mild-flavored oil so it doesn't overwhelm the basil; the oil should take on the flavor and fragrance of the basil you use. For more intense flavor, after step 2, cover and chill oil up to 1 day. Strain (if solidified, let come to room temperature first).

MAKES: About 1 cup

1. Rinse and drain 1½ cups lightly packed **fresh basil** leaves. Pat leaves

FOOD STYLING: KAREN SHINTO

Simple supper menu

Edamame (fresh soybeans)

Rice Noodles with Pork, Spinach, and Peanuts

Beer or oolong tea

Chilled canned litchis with sliced fresh strawberries

Speed wok

Use this versatile Chinese pan to make a quick dinner

By Linda Lau Anusasananan
Photograph by James Carrier

This fast pork stir-fry with noodles is also good with beef.

If I had to limit myself to just one pan, I would choose a wok. In this big bowl-shaped Chinese pan, I can cook just about everything. With its generous surface area, it's great for stir-frying or sautéing. The wok's bowl shape increases its capacity, so you can use it to steam, braise, or deep-fry.

With all these credentials, it's no wonder the wok is standard equipment in many kitchens. The real surprise is that cooks don't use the wok more often to make speedy one-pan dinners like our recipe for rice noodles with pork. This noodle dish takes advantage of the wok's versatility: just stir-fry meat and onions, then add soaked noodles and spinach. Along with purchased edamame for predinner snacking and some fruit for dessert, the result is an easy—and complete—meal.

Rice Noodles with Pork, Spinach, and Peanuts

PREP AND COOK TIME: About 25 minutes

NOTES: Look for Asian rice noodles (also called rice sticks) or bean threads in well-stocked supermarkets or Asian grocery stores. If you don't have a wok, substitute either a 5- to 6-quart pan or 12-inch frying pan with sides at least 2 inches tall; if the pan is too shallow, the noodles may fly out.

MAKES: 3 servings

- 8 ounces dried thin rice noodles (up to 1/4 in. wide; see notes) or dried bean threads
- 1 onion (6 oz.)
- 10 ounces baby spinach leaves (3 qt.)
- 4 ounces bean sprouts
  About 3/4 cup fat-skimmed chicken broth
- 1/4 cup rice vinegar
  About 3 tablespoons reduced-sodium soy sauce
- 1 teaspoon coarse-ground pepper
- 1 tablespoon vegetable oil
- 8 ounces ground lean pork
- 1 tablespoon minced fresh ginger
- 2 cloves garlic, peeled and pressed
- 1/3 cup chopped roasted unsalted peanuts

1. Pour 2 1/2 to 3 quarts boiling water into a large bowl. Add noodles and let stand until soft and pliable, 5 to 15 minutes.

2. Meanwhile, peel and chop onion. Rinse and drain spinach and bean sprouts. In a small bowl, mix 3/4 cup broth, vinegar, 3 tablespoons soy sauce, and pepper.

3. Pour noodles into a colander and drain. If desired, cut noodles into shorter lengths with scissors. Set a 14-inch wok or 12-inch frying pan with 2-inch-tall sides (see notes) over high heat. When hot, add oil and swirl to coat bottom. Crumble pork into pan and stir until lightly browned, 1 to 2 minutes. Add onion, ginger, and garlic; stir often until onion begins to brown, 1 to 2 minutes.

4. Add spinach, noodles, and broth mixture. Mix until noodles are tender to bite and hot, about 3 minutes. If more liquid is desired, stir in 2 to 4 more tablespoons broth. Add bean sprouts and peanuts; mix and add more soy sauce to taste. Pour into a wide serving bowl.

Per serving: 605 cal., 27% (162 cal.) from fat; 26 g protein; 18 g fat (3.7 g sat.); 88 g carbo (8.4 g fiber); 993 mg sodium; 51 mg chol. ◆

Our staffers field-test
tips, recipes, and gear

By the staff of *Sunset*

Sunset goes
camping

L ast summer, some of *Sunset's* editorial staff and their assorted spouses and children staged an off-site meeting, *Sunset*-style: We went camping in the forests of Big Basin Redwoods State Park in the Santa Cruz Mountains. It really was work—while our staff is stacked with hardy veterans of the outdoors, we had to pitch new tents, try out exotic gear, and attempt novel recipes on unfamiliar stoves. But all of us had the time of our lives. In these pages, we'll share advice gleaned from many years of camping, from experts, and from our "off-site"—we did learn a few lessons. Next time summer rolls around we've got our gear ready. We hope you do too.

S'more s'mores

Everyone loves the classic s'mores of childhood. But now that we're older and have the patience to toast our marshmallows to a perfectly crisp, tan shell and gooey interior (no carbonized sugar lumps for us, please), we decided to sandwich them with these updated combinations.

Black forest: Chocolate wafer cookies and cherry jam

The Elvis: Peanut-butter sandwich cookies (twist cookies into two halves), dark or milk chocolate, and sliced bananas

Gianduja: Gaufrette, wafer, or pizelle-style cookies and chocolate-hazelnut spread (Nutella)

Lemon meringue pie: Shortbread cookies and lemon curd

Neoclassic: Digestive biscuits and squares of bittersweet chocolate

Piña colada: Coconut cookies and grilled slices of fresh pineapple

Prefab: Purchased chocolate-topped butter cookies (such as Petit Ecolier)

Thin mint: Chocolate wafer cookies and thin after-dinner mints (such as After Eight)

Other suggestions include using cored apple slices instead of graham crackers, and using peanut butter chocolate cups instead of chocolate squares.

Don't leave home without 'em

- **towels**
- **quarters** (for the shower)
- **headlamp**
- **deck of cards**
- **waterproof tablecloth**
- **tablecloth clips**
- **something to cover wet benches**
- **bungee cords**
- **ice blocks** (last longer than cubes)
- **utility knife**
- **nylon tarps** (lightweight, compact, and come in forest-compatible colors)
- **ground cloth or tarp** (for under the tent)
- **bear barrels** (if in bear country)
- **corkscrew**
  - **whisk broom** (for tent)
  - **comfortable collapsible chairs**
- **firewood** (in case supply is limited where you're going)
- **kindling**
- **extra batteries**
- **sticks for s'mores**
- **DEET-free botanical insect repellent**
- **First-aid kit**
- **Dr. Bronner's soap** (environmentally friendly; use it for everything)
- **cast-iron skillet** (virtually indestructible; cook anything in it)
- **roll-up plastic cutting board**
- **plastic French coffee press**
- **barbecue grill grate** (place it over the campfire for cooking steaks or veggies)
- **hammock**
- **favorite fireside cordial**

Camp food basics

Shopping

- **Buy in small packages.** Bulk just means more to lug.
- **Buy meat vacuum-sealed** (some butchers offer this service) to prevent leaks, or use zip-lock plastic bags.
- **Choose sturdy produce.** Cabbage stays fresh longer than lettuce; apples keep better than strawberries.
- **Purchase bagged vegetables.** Buying them prepped saves time.

Packing

- **Assemble a camping box** with utensils, matches, a small cutting board, and other necessities. Keep it ready to go so you don't forget basics.
- **Decant liquids** such as marinades into plastic bottles.
- **Pack food frozen,** when possible, so it acts like ice and keeps fresh longer.
- **Place fragile greens and herbs at top of ice chest,** not next to ice (greens may freeze).
- **Use paper towels** to cushion pots and pans; they'll also come in handy for cleanup. Plastic bags for leftovers and foil for cooking are also useful.

Cooking

- **Choose quick-cooking items to save fuel.** Camp Stove Pad Thai takes advantage of the short cooking time of rice noodles; to cook meat or vegetables quickly, cut them into small pieces.
- **Cook once, eat twice— or more.** Leftover meats are tomorrow's sandwiches; grilled vegetables are delicious in camp scrambles.
- **Plan something easy for the first night,** like simple grilled steaks or our pad thai.

Cleaning

- **Choose environmentally friendly cleansers** and follow package directions for use and disposal, especially near water sources.
- **Clean as you go,** especially at dinner. You don't want to scrub by flashlight.
- **Recycle boiling water** from pasta or scrambles to soak heavily soiled pans.
- **Relax.** Everything gets dirty when you're camping, so don't sweat it.

Good eats

Breakfast

These easy, boil-in-a-bag scrambled eggs require almost no cleanup. Add whatever tasty extras you have on hand.

Camp Scrambles

AT HOME:

1. To make breakfast for four, pack 1 dozen **eggs, whipping cream, salt,** and **pepper.**

2. Prepare ½ cup additions per serving, such as **cheeses, ham, roasted garlic, roasted red bell peppers, spinach,** or **smoked salmon.**

3. Pack a sturdy zip-lock plastic bag (1 qt.) for each serving; tongs; a large spoon; and a big pan.

IN CAMP:

1. Bring about 4 quarts water to a boil in the pan.

2. Crack 2 to 3 large eggs into each bag. Add 2 tablespoons whipping cream and ⅛ teaspoon *each* salt and pepper. Squeeze bag to blend. Drop in additions to taste and seal bag, expelling as

much air as you can.

3. Lower bags into boiling water, cooking up to three at once. Using tongs and a large spoon, gently turn and squeeze bags until eggs are firm throughout, 5 to 7 minutes total. With tongs, lift bags from water.

4. When cool enough to handle, open bags and pour eggs onto plates.

Lunch

These Vietnamese sandwiches take advantage of leftovers from dinner, but you can use different fixings to make Mexican tortas, Italian panini, or American deli sandwiches.

Vietnamese Subs (Bahn Mi)

AT HOME:

1. Pack split **sandwich rolls** or baguettes; **Asian red chili paste; salad mix** or shredded cabbage; sliced **red onion;** sliced **cucumber;** fresh **cilantro;** and **deli meats** such as ham or chicken.

2. Marinate 1 cup *each* matchstick-size pieces of peeled **jicama** and **carrots** in ½ cup **seasoned rice vinegar** up to three days.

3. Pack fresh and pickled vegetables separately in zip-lock plastic bags.

IN CAMP:

1. Save leftover **beef** or chicken **satay** (or make a double batch;

see dinner menu below).

2. Layer rolls with leftover satay and/or deli meats, chili paste, cilantro, and vegetables. Sprinkle with **salt** and **pepper.**

Dinner

Asian cuisine involves fast, fresh cooking techniques that can produce bold flavors—perfect for camping. Our dinner menu includes an appetizer of easy grilled satay and a simple pad thai, both of which are largely made ahead of time.

Beef or Chicken Satay with Peanut Sauce

AT HOME:

1. Rinse 1 pound **flank steak** or boned, skinned chicken breasts and pat dry. Slice diagonally across the grain into ¼-inch-thick strips.

2. In a zip-lock plastic bag (1-gal. capacity), mix ½ cup **water,** ½ cup **soy sauce,** 2 tablespoons

minced **fresh ginger,** 1 tablespoon **rice vinegar,** 1 tablespoon **sugar,** and 2 teaspoons **Asian red chili paste;** add meat. Cover and chill up to 1 day (if making satay on first day of camping), or seal and freeze up to 1 week ahead. Pack frozen and allow to thaw in ice chest if planning to make the satay on second or third day.

3. Buy 12-inch wooden skewers and **peanut sauce.**

IN CAMP:

1. Lift meat from marinade (discard marinade) and thread each strip on a skewer.

2. Grill over high heat (you can hold your hand at grill level 2 to 3 seconds), turning once, until beef is browned on the outside and still slightly pink in center or chicken is no longer pink in center (cut to test), about 5 minutes.

3. Serve with peanut sauce on the side.

Camp Stove Pad Thai

AT HOME:

1. Buy pad thai sauce, or make your own. Pour 3 tablespoons **vegetable oil** in an 8- to 10-inch frying pan over medium heat. When hot, add ⅓ cup minced **shallots** and 2 teaspoons minced **garlic** and stir until limp, 3 to 4 minutes. Stir in ¼ cup **tamarind concentrate** (or substitute 1 tablespoon dark molasses and increase lime juice to ¼ cup), ¼ cup packed **brown sugar,** 2 tablespoons **Asian fish sauce,** 2 teaspoons **chili powder,** and 2 teaspoons **lime juice;** cook 1 minute. Let cool; chill airtight up to 1 week.

2. Seal 1 cup shredded **carrots,** 1 cup rinsed **bean sprouts,** ¼ cup chopped **cilantro,** ¼ cup chopped **green onions,** and ½ cup chopped **roasted peanuts** in separate plastic bags; chill

vegetables and cilantro.

3. Purchase 1 package (14 oz.) **dried rice noodles, 1 lime,** and 1 pound **frozen cooked shelled shrimp** (pack frozen) or 1 pound firm tofu (cut into 1-in. chunks; seal in a bag and chill).

4. Pack a large pan; a pasta insert or a strainer; a medium pan for sauce; and tongs for combining noodles and sauce.

IN CAMP:

1. Halve and slice lime.

2. In a large pan over high heat, bring 3 quarts of water to a boil. Add noodles and cook until barely tender to bite, 3 to 4 minutes. Drain noodles and rinse well in cool water. Return noodles to pan.

3. In a medium pan over high heat, heat sauce and shrimp or tofu. Add to noodles with carrots, sprouts, cilantro, green onions, and peanuts; mix to coat. Accompany with lime slices. ◆

These pillowy maple-glazed doughnuts are spiced with cardamom.

Doughnut gems

Fluffy, sweet treats are easy to fry at home

By Charity Ferreira
Photographs by James Carrier

There are reasons that freshly made doughnuts are more popular than ever: the techniques are straightforward, and the rewards are sweet. Tender, maple-glazed twists, delicately flavored with cardamom, make a great breakfast. But there's no wrong time of day for fried cake, whether it comes in the form of frosted chocolate doughnuts or lemon–poppy seed doughnut holes. Our guide to deep-frying (see "Fry Right," page 109) makes it simple to turn out treats that are equally delicious as coffee break, dessert, or a weekend brunch with the whole family.

Maple-Glazed Cardamom Twists

PREP AND COOK TIME: About 1 hour, plus at least 2 hours to rise

NOTES: Soften butter in the microwave or at warm room temperature until very soft but not melted. You can make the dough the day before you fry the twists; cover and chill.

MAKES: 24 twists

- 1 package active dry yeast
- 3 tablespoons sugar
- ½ cup milk
- 2 large eggs, lightly beaten to blend
- About 3 cups all-purpose flour
- 1 teaspoon salt
- 1 teaspoon ground cardamom
- ⅓ cup butter, softened (see notes) and cut into chunks
- 6 to 8 cups vegetable oil for frying
- Maple glaze (recipe follows)

1. In the bowl of a standing mixer or another large bowl, stir yeast into ¼ cup warm (110°) water. Let stand until foamy, about 10 minutes. With a wooden spoon, stir in sugar, milk, and eggs (or beat in with paddle attachment); stir or beat in 2¾ cups flour, salt, and cardamom (dough will be soft and sticky). Stir or beat in butter, a few chunks at a time, until well incorporated. *If using a mixer:* Continue to beat at medium-low speed until dough pulls from sides of bowl, 4 to 5 minutes; add up to ¼ cup more flour if necessary. Scrape dough down if it crawls up beater or sides of bowl. Remove beater and scrape clean. Scrape dough onto a well-floured board and knead briefly to bring together. *If mixing by hand:* Scrape dough onto a lightly floured board and knead until smooth and velvety, about 5 minutes, adding more flour as needed to prevent sticking.

2. Return to bowl, cover with plastic wrap, and let stand in a warm place until dough has doubled, 1½ to 2 hours.

3. Scrape dough onto lightly floured board and press gently to expel air. Divide into 24 equal pieces. With floured hands, divide each piece in half. Form each half into a rope about 4 inches long and ½ inch thick. Twist the two ropes together, pinching ends together. Place twists about 1 inch apart on a floured baking sheet and cover with plastic wrap. Let rise until nearly doubled in size, about 30 minutes.

4. Meanwhile, fill an electric deep-fryer to the fill line or pour about 4 inches of oil into a 5- to 6-quart pan and heat to 375° (see "Fry Right," page 109). With a wide spatula, gently slide two twists into oil, one at a time. Cook, turning once, until golden brown on both sides, about 3 minutes total. With a slotted spoon, transfer to paper towels to drain. Repeat to fry remaining twists.

5. When cool enough to handle, dip top half of warm twists in maple glaze. Place on a plate or rack and let stand until glaze is set, about 2 minutes.

Per twist: 173 cal., 40% (70 cal.) from fat; 2.4 g protein; 7.8 g fat (2.1 g sat.); 23 g carbo (0.5 g fiber); 132 mg sodium; 25 mg chol.

Maple glaze. In a bowl, mix 1 cup **powdered sugar**, ½ cup **maple syrup**, and 1 tablespoon **milk** until smooth.

FOOD STYLING: KAREN SHINTO

Decorate dark chocolate doughnuts with nuts, coconut, or sprinkles.

Lemon–Poppy Seed Doughnut Holes

PREP AND COOK TIME: About 1 hour, plus at least 1 hour to chill dough

MAKES: About 24 doughnut holes

- 1½ cups all-purpose flour
- 3 tablespoons poppy seeds
- 1 tablespoon grated lemon peel
- 1½ teaspoons baking powder
- ½ teaspoon salt
- 2 large eggs
- ½ cup sugar
- ¼ cup buttermilk
- 3 tablespoons butter, melted
- 1 teaspoon vanilla
- 6 to 8 cups vegetable oil for frying
  Lemon glaze (recipe follows)

1. In a bowl, mix flour, poppy seeds, lemon peel, baking powder, and salt. In a small bowl, whisk eggs, sugar, buttermilk, melted butter, and vanilla to blend. Stir into dry ingredients until well blended. Chill until firm, at least 1 hour or up to 3 hours.

2. Scrape dough onto a generously floured surface. With floured hands, roll dough into 1-inch balls. Place doughnut holes on a floured baking sheet.

3. Meanwhile, fill an electric deep-fryer to the fill line or pour about 4 inches of oil into a 5- to 6-quart pan; heat to 375° (see "Fry Right," below). Using a slotted spoon to pick up one or two doughnut holes at a time, gently lower three or four holes into oil and cook, turning once, until golden brown, 3 to 4 minutes (to check timing, cut first doughnut hole to test). Using slotted spoon, transfer doughnut holes to paper towels to drain. Repeat to fry remaining holes.

4. When cool enough to handle, roll each hole in glaze to coat. Place on a plate and let stand until glaze is set, about 2 minutes.

Per doughnut hole: 131 cal., 32% (42 cal.) from fat; 1.6 g protein; 4.7 g fat (1.2 g sat.); 21 g carbo (0.3 g fiber); 102 mg sodium; 22 mg chol.

Lemon glaze. In a bowl, mix ¼ cup **lemon juice** and 2 cups **powdered sugar** until smooth.

Chocolate Cake Doughnuts

PREP AND COOK TIME: About 1 hour, plus at least 1 hour to chill dough

MAKES: About 16 doughnuts (3 in. each)

- 2½ cups all-purpose flour
- 1 cup unsweetened Dutch-process cocoa
- 2 teaspoons baking powder
- ½ teaspoon salt
- 4 large eggs
- 1½ cups sugar
- ⅓ cup buttermilk
- 3 tablespoons butter, melted
- 6 to 8 cups vegetable oil for frying
  Mocha glaze (recipe follows)

1. In a bowl, mix flour, cocoa, baking powder, and salt. In a small bowl, whisk eggs, sugar, buttermilk, and melted butter to blend. Stir into dry ingredients until well blended. Chill until cold, at least 1 hour or up to 3 hours.

2. Scrape dough onto a generously floured surface. With floured hands, pat dough out to about ½ inch thick. With a 3-inch doughnut cutter, cut out doughnuts. Pat together scraps of dough and cut again. (Alternately, shape dough into ropes about 5 inches long and ½ inch thick; join rope ends to form doughnuts.) Place doughnuts on a well-floured baking sheet.

3. Meanwhile, fill an electric deep-fryer to the fill line or pour about 4 inches of oil into a 5- to 6-quart pan; heat to 375° (see "Fry Right," below). Place one doughnut at a time onto a wide spatula and gently slide into oil, frying up to three at a time. Cook, turning once, until puffy and cooked through, 3 to 4 minutes total (to check timing, cut first one to test). With a slotted spoon, transfer doughnuts to paper towels to drain. Repeat to fry remaining doughnuts.

4. When cool enough to handle, dip the top half of each doughnut in warm mocha glaze and place on a plate. Let stand until glaze is set, about 5 minutes.

Per doughnut: 360 cal., 50% (180 cal.) from fat; 5.3 g protein; 20 g fat (6.7 g sat.); 44 g carbo (1.1 g fiber); 228 mg sodium; 69 mg chol.

Mocha glaze. In a heatproof bowl, combine 6 ounces chopped **semisweet chocolate,** ½ cup **whipping cream,** 1 tablespoon **butter,** 2 teaspoons **corn syrup,** and 1 teaspoon **instant espresso powder.** Bring a few inches of water to a boil in a pan; remove from heat. Place bowl over water and let stand, stirring occasionally, until smooth, about 10 minutes. ◆

Fry right

Deep-frying is easily managed if you keep these guidelines in mind.

• **Make glaze and assemble tools before you begin frying.** Never leave the fryer unattended.

• **Fry doughnuts in neutral-flavored oil** such as canola or other vegetable oil. Use enough oil that doughnuts can float freely—4 inches deep is optimal. Don't reuse old oil to fry doughnuts, and don't pour it down the drain to discard. Instead, let oil cool completely, pour into a sealable container, and dispose of it in the trash.

• **Maintain a constant frying temperature of 375°** by using a deep-fryer that regulates oil temperature or a heavy, deep 5- to 6-quart pan and a frying thermometer. If the temperature is too low, doughnuts will absorb more oil and taste soggy and oily. If it's too high, they will brown before they cook through.

• **Remember that oil temperature changes slowly**—it may take several minutes to respond to an adjustment in the temperature of the burner. If the temperature drops below 375°, wait until it climbs back up before adding the next batch of doughnuts. If oil gets too hot, lower heat and wait for temperature to drop.

• **Fry no more than two or three doughnuts at a time** (or three or four holes) to allow enough oil to circulate and maintain the oil temperature.

Fresh-ground cumin and coriander seeds add a burst of flavor to lamb loin chops.

JAMES CARRIER (2); FOOD STYLING: KAREN SHINTO

Flavor tips

• **Buy spices whole** and grind them as you need them, since they deteriorate quickly once ground.

• **Smell bulk spices**—they should be fresh and aromatic.

• **Toast spices before using them:** either heat in a pan in a 300° oven, stirring occasionally, or stir in a frying pan over medium heat, until aromatic.

• **Grind spices with a mortar and pestle or in an electric grinder.** A coffee grinder works well; just make sure you have one for spices, another for coffee.

• **Make sure the container is sealed** if you're buying a premade blend, such as curry powder; exposure to air degrades aroma and flavor.

More pairings

Intensify a primary flavor: dust roasted fennel with ground fennel seeds.

Add a new dimension: cook carrots with cumin seeds; sprinkle beets with ground anise seeds; add a pinch of saffron threads to sautéed onions.

Make an everyday dish exotic: Season chicken with Thai curry or garam masala, an Indian mixture similar to curry.

A little spice in your life

Cooks have been wielding spices for centuries, from preserving foods with them to masking smells and flavors in meats that were less than fresh. Almost every culture eventually developed distinct conventions, from the fiery curries of India to paprika-permeated goulash in Hungary.

At Elisabeth Daniel restaurant in San Francisco, chef-owner Daniel Patterson imports a tradition from Morocco: *ras-el-hanout,* or "top of the shop." Each spice shop there custom-mixes up to 125 spices for vegetables, poultry, and meats. Patterson coats lamb with a Moroccan ras-el-hanout blend for complex, fascinating flavors. "But using spices does not have to be difficult or exotic," says Patterson. He offers tips, and a simple rub for lamb, to make vibrant spices an easy custom in your kitchen.

Spiced Lamb Chops

PREP AND COOK TIME: About 30 minutes

NOTES: Accompany these pungent cumin- and coriander-spiced lamb chops—two per serving—with couscous flavored with grated lemon peel and cooked carrots (see "More Pairings" at right).

MAKES: 4 servings

1½ tablespoons ground toasted cumin seeds (see tips above, right)

1½ tablespoons ground toasted coriander seeds

8 lamb loin chops (each 1 to 1¼ in. thick and about 4 oz.), fat trimmed

Salt and fresh-ground black pepper

1 tablespoon olive oil

1. In a small bowl, mix cumin and coriander.

2. Rinse lamb and pat dry. Sprinkle chops generously on both sides with salt and pepper, then coat both sides with spice mixture, patting so it adheres.

3. Pour olive oil into a 12-inch ovenproof frying pan over medium-high heat. When hot, set lamb chops slightly apart in pan; cook, turning once, until well browned on both sides, 3 to 4 minutes total (take care not to scorch spices).

4. Transfer pan to a 325° regular or convection oven and bake until an instant-read thermometer inserted horizontally into center of lamb reaches 125° for rare, 7 to 8 minutes, or 135° for medium-rare, 9 to 10 minutes.

Per serving: 284 cal., 44% (126 cal.) from fat; 36 g protein; 14 g fat (4 g sat.); 2 g carbo (1 g fiber); 119 mg sodium; 111 mg chol.

—*Sara Schneider*

Bran new benefits

The pale gold oil made from the bran and germ of rice has a higher smoke point than most other vegetable oils, so it doesn't scorch as fast in cooking. Its health-promoting properties are impressive as well, from poly- and mono-unsaturated fatty acids to antioxidants. A familiar ingredient in Asia, the mellow-tasting rice bran oil is now bottled here by the California Rice Oil Company. It's available in many supermarkets and natural-food stores for about $7 (16.9 oz.). *www. californiariceoil.com* or (415) 382-0373.
—*Jerry Anne Di Vecchio*

How to choose the right one

Restaurant wine lists can make even the most confident host uneasy. The pressure of having to choose a single wine that everyone at the table will love—and that will go with everyone's food—is frightening. It doesn't help that many wine lists are huge. You have one chance, out of, say, 500 or more choices, to pick the "right" wine. Through the years, I've come up with a few ways to increase my own comfort level.

· **Order two relatively inexpensive wines,** especially if there are four or more people in your party. Have the wines served at the same time and encourage everyone to try both with the different dishes they've ordered. This takes the pressure off being "right."

· **Ask what wine on the list the chef loves to drink.** Generally, his or her taste pairs instinctively with many dishes on the menu. (In my opinion, this strategy produces better results than asking what the server likes.)

· **Abdicate entirely.** One of the best ways to learn about new wines is to leave the decision entirely to a knowledgeable sommelier or server. Tell him or her what kind of wine you'd like, in what price range: "Please bring me a really crisp, light white for about $30," for example.

· **Give yourself an adventure budget to practice with.** The best way to expand the range of wines you know is to try new ones. Once a month, maybe, when you're out with family or close friends, build your "wine-list muscle" by ordering something you're unfamiliar with. You'll look impressively knowledgeable when you order the same bottle at the next meal you have to host.

Eventually, you'll get to the point where a restaurant's wine list is as easy to deal with as its menu.

Mother's Day inspiration

You may think she wants chocolate or flowers, but a terrific wine might just bowl her over.

Gloria Ferrer Sonoma Brut nonvintage *(Sonoma County, CA), $18.* In the make-her-feel-special department, here's a frothy sparkler with light cream, fresh apple, and snappy lemon-zest flavors—and it won't break the bank.

Smith-Madrone Riesling 2001 *(Napa Valley), $17.* Elegant and expressive (maybe like your mom?). Great fresh citrus and apricot flavors, with a hint of anise.

Cristom "Mount Jefferson" Pinot Noir 2000 *(Willamette Valley, OR), $25.* Sensual dark cherry and earthy aromas and flavors, with hints of spiced tea and espresso—full of personality.

Wolf Blass "Red Label" Shiraz–Cabernet Sauvignon 1998 *(South Australia), $12.* Make her dinner (roast chicken would be perfect), set the table nicely, and pour her a glass of this juicy red with briary ripe-blackberry flavors.
—*Karen MacNeil-Fife*

Tired of the standard gift bag? Try simple round labels instead—we used ¾-inch and 1-inch circles—to put a festive message right on the bottle. Tint the labels with colored markers.
—*Jil Peters*

Fresh favorites

Readers' recipes tested in *Sunset's* kitchens

Photograph by James Carrier

Seared Tuna with Papaya Salsa

Gail Durant, Sisters, OR

A fresh tropical fruit salsa is a welcome addition to peppery ahi tuna steaks in this easy but stylish dish.

PREP AND COOK TIME: About 15 minutes

MAKES: 2 servings

- 1 firm-ripe papaya (about 1 lb.)
- ¼ cup finely diced red onion
- 1 fresh jalapeño or serrano chili, rinsed, stemmed, seeded, and minced
- 2 tablespoons chopped fresh cilantro leaves
- 1 tablespoon lime juice
  Salt
- 2 ahi tuna steaks (each 5 to 6 oz. and about 1 in. thick)
- 2 teaspoons olive oil
  Coarsely ground black pepper

1. Peel and seed papaya; cut into ½-inch cubes.

2. In a bowl, mix papaya, onion, chili, cilantro, and lime juice. Add salt to taste. Set aside while preparing fish or cover and chill up to 4 hours.

3. Rinse fish and pat dry. Coat both sides of steaks with oil and sprinkle all over with salt and pepper. Heat a 10- to 12-inch nonstick frying pan over high heat; add fish and cook, turning once, until opaque on both sides but still pink in the center (cut to test), 4 to 6 minutes total. Transfer steaks to plates and spoon salsa over servings.

Per serving: 248 cal., 21% (53 cal.) from fat; 31 g protein; 5.9 g fat (1 g sat.); 18 g carbo (1.9 g fiber); 55 mg sodium; 57 mg chol.

Ahi tuna and papaya salsa pair up for a quick, light weeknight meal.

Grilled Chicken and Pasta Salad

Helen Schussler, Las Vegas

Helen Schussler combined some of her favorite flavors in this cool main-dish noodle salad. It makes a great casual one-bowl dinner or a perfect dish for a potluck or buffet.

PREP AND COOK TIME: About 45 minutes

MAKES: 6 to 8 servings

- 1½ pounds boned, skinned chicken breasts
- ¾ cup lime juice
- 3 tablespoons olive oil
- 3 tablespoons Asian (toasted) sesame oil
- 3 tablespoons soy sauce
- 1 tablespoon sugar
- 3 cloves garlic, peeled and chopped
- 2 tablespoons minced fresh ginger
- 1 pound dried angel hair pasta
- 1 pound mixed red and yellow bell peppers, rinsed, cored, stemmed, seeded, and diced
- 1 cucumber (about 10 oz.), peeled and chopped
- ½ cup chopped parsley
- ¼ cup chopped green onions (white and pale green parts only)
- ¼ teaspoon hot chili flakes

1. Rinse chicken and pat dry; place in a bowl. In another bowl, combine lime juice, olive oil, sesame oil, soy sauce, sugar, garlic, and ginger. Pour about

¼ cup of the mixture over chicken, reserving remainder. Chill chicken for 30 minutes.

2. Lift chicken from marinade (discard used marinade) and lay over a solid bed of medium coals or medium heat on a gas grill (you can hold your hand at grill level only 4 to 5 seconds); close lid on gas grill. Cook, turning chicken as needed to brown evenly, until no longer pink in the center of the thickest part (cut to test), 6 to 8 minutes total. Transfer to a board and let stand until cool enough to handle, then cut across the grain into 1-inch-wide slices.

3. Meanwhile, in a covered 6- to 8-quart pan over high heat, bring about 3 quarts water to a boil. Add the pasta and cook, stirring occasionally, until tender to bite, 4 to 6 minutes. Drain pasta and rinse under cold running water until cool.

4. In a large bowl, combine pasta, reserved lime-juice mixture, chicken, bell peppers, cucumber, parsley, green onions, and chili flakes; mix to coat. Serve immediately or cover and chill up to 1 day.

Per serving: 421 cal., 24% (99 cal.) from fat; 28 g protein; 11 g fat (1.7 g sat.); 51 g carbo (2.5 g fiber); 421 mg sodium; 49 mg chol.

Honey-Melon Salad

Joyanne McDaniel, Bothell, WA

Joyanne McDaniel combined aromatic herbs from her garden with sweet melon in this simple and refreshing fruit salad. If you don't have access to fresh lemon verbena or another lemon-scented herb such as lemon thyme, fresh basil leaves will impart a different but equally complementary flavor to the salad.

PREP TIME: About 20 minutes

MAKES: 4 to 6 servings

- 1 **honeydew melon (3½ to 4 lb.)**
- 2 **tablespoons chopped or slivered fresh lemon verbena leaves or fresh basil leaves (see note above)**
- 2 **tablespoons chopped or slivered fresh mint leaves**
- 3 **tablespoons rice vinegar**
- 2 **tablespoons honey**

- ½ **teaspoon orange extract or 2 tablespoons orange juice**
- ⅛ **teaspoon salt**

1. Peel and seed melon; cut into 1-inch chunks.

2. In a bowl, mix lemon verbena, mint, vinegar, honey, orange extract, and salt. Add melon and mix to coat. Serve immediately or cover and chill up to 4 hours.

Per serving: 68 cal., 1% (0.9 cal.) from fat; 0.7 g protein; 0.1 g fat (0 g sat.); 17 g carbo (1.3 g fiber); 62 mg sodium; 0 mg chol.

Chilled Cucumber Soup with Crab

Christine Datian, Las Vegas

Christine Datian makes this easy, creamy soup in the morning so that it is chilled by lunchtime. Garnish the soup with a sprinkle of cayenne or chopped fresh dill.

PREP TIME: About 30 minutes, plus at least 2 hours to chill

MAKES: 6 cups; 4 servings

- 4 **cucumbers (about 2¼ lb. total), peeled, seeded, and chopped**
- 2 **cups plain yogurt**
- ¾ **cup sour cream**
- ½ **cup chopped green onions (white and pale green parts only)**
- ¼ **cup chopped fresh dill**
- 1 **clove garlic, peeled and minced**
- 2 **tablespoons olive oil**
- 1 **tablespoon lemon juice**
- 1 **teaspoon Dijon mustard**
  Salt and pepper
- 6 **ounces shelled cooked crab**

1. In a blender or food processor, in batches if necessary, whirl cucumbers, yogurt, sour cream, green onions, dill, garlic, olive oil, lemon juice, and mustard until smooth. Add salt and pepper to taste. Transfer to a bowl, cover, and chill until cold, at least 2 hours and up to 6 hours.

2. Ladle chilled soup evenly into bowls. Top each serving with about ¼ cup crab.

Per serving: 304 cal., 56% (171 cal.) from fat; 17 g protein; 19 g fat (7.8 g sat.); 18 g carbo (1.4 g fiber); 267 mg sodium; 68 mg chol. ◆

STEVE GUNTHER

Stellar fruit

Supermarket star fruit is just expensive parsley, says Alex Silber, owner of **Papaya Tree Nursery** in Granada Hills. Its five-pointed golden yellow slices look pretty garnishing a plate, but they're nearly tasteless. Silber says it's because commercial growers don't choose the best varieties and often pick the fruit green.

A homegrown, fully ripe 'Arkin', 'Florita', 'Golden Star', or 'Kary', on the other hand, provides a delightful flavor, he says. The fruit is juicy and sweet-tart like an orange, and smells like flowers. Star fruit, also called carambola (*Averrhoa carambola*), is surprisingly easy to grow in frost-free areas of Southern California. Once established, trees can survive temperatures as low as 28° for a brief period. The tree likes good drainage, full sun (though it can tolerate less), regular irrigation (soil should be moist but not wet), and protection from wind. It's not a heavy feeder, but it is susceptible to chlorosis in alkaline soils, so it needs chelated iron regularly.

In Southern California, trees generally reach 8 to 15 feet tall, densely clothed in small green leaves, and bear fruits heavily twice a year. The winter crop is especially appreciated, says Fullerton gardener Patricia Sawyer, who has grown 'Arkin' for nearly 10 years. "It's like having a decorated Christmas tree in the yard."

Papaya Tree Nursery: open by appointment, (818) 363-3680. Pacific Tree Farms in Chula Vista: mail order available, (619) 422-2400. Laguna Hills Nursery: (949) 830-5653. — Sharon Cohoon

Orange-flavored Mexican crema dresses a do-it-yourself salad array of fresh chopped vegetables and fruits (see page 118).

June

Southwest feast

Vegetarian tamale tarts and mango crisp make a great meal for friends

By Linda Lau Anusasananan • Photographs by James Carrier
Food styling by Karen Shinto

Moving from textile art to food seemed natural to Donna Knopf, creator of Vegetas, a company that produces a line of healthy vegetarian products in Tempe, Arizona. "Designing and developing recipes is still a highly creative process. I've simply transferred my creativity," Knopf says. "Food is my new medium."

In the vegetarian menu she created for us, Knopf applies her instinct for good taste and design. She adds a little twist to make each dish her own. For instance, she layers tamale ingredients in dried cornhusks to make savory tarts. Her Mexican chopped salad combines contrasting flavors and textures— juicy-sweet melon, creamy avocados, crunchy jicama—in a fresh presentation: Knopf offers the elements of the salad on a platter so guests can build their own. These creative takes on Southwestern flavors result in a stylish menu that's perfect for casual entertaining or celebrations with friends. *(For more information about Vegetas: www.vegetas.com or 480/966-4486.)*

Party menu

Chili-Spiced Nuts

**Mexican Chopped Salad
with Orange Crema**

**Tamale Tarts with
Pumpkin-Seed Salsa**

Pink lemonade or beer

**Mango Crisp with
vanilla or dulce de leche
ice cream**

Dried cornhusks cradle
layered tamale tarts in
a dramatic presentation.
Left: It's hard to stop
snacking on sweet and
hot chili-spiced nuts.

Tamale Tarts

PREP AND COOK TIME: About 1½ hours

MAKES: 8 servings

Dough

1⅔	cups dehydrated masa flour (corn tortilla flour)
¼	cup sugar
1	teaspoon baking powder
½	teaspoon salt
1	can (14¾ oz.) cream-style corn
⅔	cup frozen corn kernels
1	can (4 oz.) diced green chilies
⅓	cup chopped white onion
¼	cup vegetable oil

Spinach filling

½	teaspoon cumin seeds
½	teaspoon coriander seeds
½	teaspoon dried oregano leaves
1	tablespoon vegetable oil
1	onion (8 oz.), peeled and chopped
1	red bell pepper (8 oz.), rinsed, stemmed, seeded, and chopped
2	cloves garlic, peeled and chopped
1	package (10 oz.) frozen chopped spinach, thawed
8	ounces Roma tomatoes, rinsed and chopped
	Salt
1	cup shredded pepper jack cheese
1	cup shredded Mexican cheese blend or cheddar cheese
	Pumpkin-seed salsa (see page 119)

1. For dough: In a bowl, mix masa flour, sugar, baking powder, and salt. Add cream-style corn, corn kernels, chilies, white onion, and oil; mix until blended.

2. For spinach filling: In a 10- to 12-inch frying pan over medium-high heat, stir cumin seeds, coriander seeds, and oregano in oil until fragrant, about 30 seconds. Add onion, bell pepper, and garlic; stir occasionally until onion is limp, about 3 minutes. Press liquid out of spinach. Add spinach and tomatoes to pan and stir often until liquid has evaporated, 2 to 3 minutes. Add salt to taste.

3. Lightly coat insides of eight ramekins or custard dishes (¾ to 1 cup each) with cooking oil spray (to wrap tarts in cornhusks as pictured, see "Party Tarts," page 118.) Spoon an eighth of the dough (a scant ½ cup) into each dish. With the back of a spoon, spread

Party tarts

You can bake the savory treats directly in ramekins or dress them up in husks. You'll need about 35 **dried cornhusks** (each 4 in. wide; 2½ oz. total; available at Mexican markets or well-stocked supermarkets). Make dough and filling for tamale tarts (through step 2, page 117), then prepare the husks.

Separate husks; discard silks. Soak husks in hot water until pliable, about 20 minutes. Rinse well and drain. Tear with grain into sections 2 to 3 inches wide at large end.

Overlap husk pieces to line eight baking dishes (about 4 in. wide), wide ends in bottom, narrow ends over sides.

Fill each with dough (A); spread and layer (step 3 of recipe). Leave open, or tie into packets (**B**): Tear more husks, with the grain, into ¼- to ½-inch-wide strips (if strips are shorter than 8 inches, tie ends of two short strips together). Gather husks over filling in each dish; tie with a strip (**C**).

Set open-faced tarts or packets in a baking pan, cover, and bake (steps 3 and 4 of recipe).

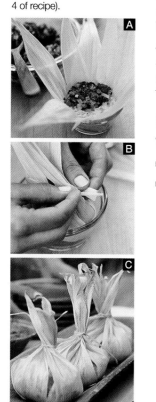

Guests can create their own salads from fresh, colorful fruits and vegetables, served with a creamy orange dressing.

dough over bottom and partially up sides of dish; it should be about ¼ inch thick. Evenly layer an eighth of each of the pepper cheese, spinach filling, and Mexican cheese blend over dough. Arrange dishes on a 10- by 15-inch baking pan. Cover pan with foil.

4. Bake in a 350° oven until tarts are hot in the center, about 30 minutes. Serve with salsa.

Per serving: 392 cal., 46% (180 cal.) from fat; 12 g protein; 20 g fat (6.3 g sat.); 47 g carbo (5 g fiber); 635 mg sodium; 27 mg chol.

Mexican Chopped Salad with Orange Crema

PREP TIME: About 35 minutes

MAKES: 8 servings

- 12 **ounces jicama**
- 12 **ounces English cucumber**
- 1 **pound cantaloupe**
- 1 **pound watermelon**
- 1 **pound honeydew**
- 4 **ounces radishes, rinsed**
- 2 **cups finely shredded red or green cabbage**
- 1 **cup seedless red grapes**
- 1 **firm-ripe avocado (8 to 10 oz.)**
- 2 **tablespoons lemon or lime juice**

- ¾ **cup roasted salted peanuts**
     Orange crema (recipe follows)

1. Cut off and discard peel from jicama; rinse jicama. Rinse cucumber; trim and discard ends. Rinse cantaloupe, watermelon, and honeydew; cut off peels and scoop out seeds. Cut jicama, cucumber, and melons into ½-inch cubes. Trim and discard tops and roots from radishes; rinse radishes and thinly slice. Attractively arrange trimmed produce on a large platter along with cabbage and grapes.

2. Just before serving, pit and peel avocado. Cut into ½-inch cubes and coat with lemon juice; add to platter. Sprinkle with peanuts or offer peanuts alongside. Serve with orange crema.

Per serving: 182 cal., 49% (90 cal.) from fat; 5.7 g protein; 10 g fat (1.7 g sat.); 21 g carbo (5.5 g fiber); 74 mg sodium; 0 mg chol.

Orange Crema

PREP TIME: About 5 minutes

NOTES: Purchase Mexican crema in Latino markets, or substitute crème fraîche or sour cream.

MAKES: 8 servings

In a small bowl, mix ½ cup *each* **mayonnaise,**

thawed **frozen orange juice concentrate,** and **Mexican crema** (see notes). Stir in ¼ cup fresh **lime** juice and 1 teaspoon grated **lime** peel. If making up to 1 day ahead, cover and chill.

Per tablespoon: 50 cal., 82% (41 cal.) from fat; 0.3 g protein; 4.5 g fat (1.2 g sat.); 2.6 g carbo (0.1 g fiber); 27 mg sodium; 7.1 mg chol.

Pumpkin-Seed Salsa

PREP TIME: About 20 minutes

NOTES: Tomatillos, which resemble small green tomatoes covered with a papery husk, are available in many supermarkets and in Latino grocery stores. If fresh ones are not available, use 2 cans (12 oz. each) tomatillos, drained.

MAKES: About 3 cups

- 8 **ounces fresh tomatillos (see notes)**
- 3 **fresh poblano chilies (sometimes mislabeled pasilla) or Anaheim chilies (9 oz. total)**
- 2 **fresh jalapeño chilies (2 oz. total)**
- 1 **clove garlic, peeled**
- ½ **cup sliced green onions**
- ½ **cup coarsely chopped fresh cilantro**
- ½ **cup shelled roasted, salted pumpkin seeds (see notes for chili-spiced nuts, below)**
- ⅓ **cup rice vinegar**
- ¼ **teaspoon ground cumin**
- ¼ **teaspoon dried oregano**
- ¼ **to ½ teaspoon green or red hot sauce**
  Salt

1. Pull off and discard husks and stems from tomatillos; rinse tomatillos well and coarsely chop. Rinse and stem chilies. Remove seeds from poblanos. For a mild salsa, remove seeds from jalapeños. Coarsely chop all chilies.

2. In a food processor or blender, combine tomatillos, poblanos, jalapeños, garlic, green onions, cilantro, pumpkin seeds, vinegar, cumin, and oregano; whirl until smooth. Add hot sauce and salt to taste.

Per tablespoon: 6.8 cal., 26% (1.8 cal.) from fat; 0.3 g protein; 0.2 g fat (0 g sat.); 1.1 g carbo (0.2 g fiber); 4.8 mg sodium; 0 mg chol.

Chili-Spiced Nuts

PREP AND COOK TIME: About 25 minutes

NOTES: Find green hulled pumpkin seeds (*pepitas*) in Latino markets and natural-food stores. Ground chipotle chilies can be found in some supermarkets; cayenne makes a hotter substitute.

MAKES: About 3⅓ cups; 8 to 12 servings

- 1½ **cups pecan halves**
- ¾ **cup pine nuts**
- ¾ **cup hulled raw or roasted pumpkin seeds (see notes)**

- ⅓ **cup shelled roasted or raw pistachios**
- 3 **tablespoons vegetable oil**
- 3 **tablespoons sugar**
- ¾ **to 1¼ teaspoons ground dried chipotle chilies or cayenne (see notes)**
  About ½ teaspoon salt

1. In a large bowl, mix pecans, pine nuts, pumpkin seeds, pistachios, and oil. Add sugar, ¾ teaspoon chilies, and ½ teaspoon salt; mix to coat nuts evenly. Add more chili and salt to taste.

2. Coat a 10- by 15-inch baking pan with cooking oil spray. Spread nuts in pan. Bake in a 325° oven, stirring occasionally, until nuts are browned, 15 to 20 minutes. Cool. Serve or store airtight at room temperature up to 1 week.

Per serving: 219 cal., 78% (171 cal.) from fat; 4.6 g protein; 19 g fat (2.2 g sat.); 9.9 g carbo (1.9 g fiber); 98 mg sodium; 0 mg chol.

Mango Crisp

PREP AND COOK TIME: About 1¼ hours

MAKES: 8 servings

- ⅓ **cup sugar**
- 2½ **tablespoons cornstarch**
- 1 **can (12 oz.; 1½ cups) mango nectar**
- 1 **teaspoon grated lemon peel**
- 1 **tablespoon lemon juice**
- 8 **cups chunks (1 in.) peeled mangoes, fresh (7 to 8 lb. total) or thawed frozen (2½ to 3 lb. total)**
- 1½ **cups regular rolled oats**
- 1½ **cups all-purpose flour**
- 1 **cup roasted macadamia nuts or pecans, coarsely chopped**
- ½ **teaspoon ground ginger**
- ¼ **teaspoon salt**
- ½ **cup maple syrup**
- ½ **cup (¼ lb.) butter, melted**

1. In a 3- to 4-quart pan, mix sugar and cornstarch. Add mango nectar and stir until blended. Stir over high heat until mixture boils, about 3 minutes. Remove from heat and stir in lemon peel and juice. Add mangoes and mix gently to coat. Pour into a shallow 2½- to 3-quart baking dish.

2. In a bowl, mix oats, flour, nuts, ginger, and salt. Add syrup and butter and stir until blended. Distribute mixture evenly over mangoes. Set dish in a foil-lined 10- by 15-inch baking pan.

3. Bake in a 375° oven until topping is golden brown, 30 to 40 minutes. Serve warm or cool.

Per serving: 591 cal., 38% (225 cal.) from fat; 7.2 g protein; 25 g fat (9.3 g sat.); 89 g carbo (4 g fiber); 198 mg sodium; 31 mg chol. ◆

Mango crisp

Strategy

If you take advantage of the make-ahead options, this meal is easy to handle.

Up to 1 week ahead: Make spiced nuts.

Up to 1 day ahead: Assemble tamale tarts (through step 3; cover and chill), make orange crema for salad, and prepare salsa.

Up to 6 hours ahead: Bake mango crisp.

Up to 4 hours ahead: Prepare salad (through step 1; cover and chill).

About 30 minutes ahead: Bake tamale tarts.

Just before serving: Complete salad.

Simple summer menu

By Kate Washington • Photographs by Caroline Kopp

Entertaining in the garden calls for informal, stylish food. In our Italian menu, guests assemble their own crostini and sip pretty Campari-orange sodas (for kids, make Italian sodas with flavored syrup and club soda). Chocolate-pistachio meringues, easily made ahead, are a sweet ending.

Cherry Tomato and Mozzarella Salad

PREP TIME: About 20 minutes

MAKES: 8 appetizer servings

- **4 cups (1¼ lb.) Sweet 100 or Sungold cherry tomatoes (or a mixture), rinsed and stemmed**
- **8 ounces small balls fresh mozzarella cheese (often labeled bocconcini), drained**
- **½ cup loosely packed fresh basil leaves, rinsed**
- **About 2 tablespoons extra-virgin olive oil**
- **Coarse sea salt**

Cut cherry tomatoes in half with a sharp knife. Cut bocconcini in half. Tear basil leaves into small pieces. In a bowl, gently mix cherry tomatoes, mozzarella, and basil. Drizzle with 2 tablespoons olive oil and sprinkle lightly with salt; add more oil and salt to taste.

Per serving: 140 cal., 71% (99 cal.) from fat; 6.9 g protein; 11 g fat (5 g sat.); 4.3 g carbo (1.4 g fiber); 123 mg sodium; 25 mg chol.

Marinated Artichokes

PREP AND COOK TIME: About 1 hour, plus 30 minutes to cool

MAKES: 8 appetizer servings

- **1 lemon (about 4 oz.)**
- **4 pounds regular or baby artichokes**
- **¼ cup extra-virgin olive oil**
- **3 cloves garlic, peeled and coarsely chopped**
- **1 tablespoon grated orange peel**
- **½ teaspoon hot chili flakes**
- **About ½ teaspoon salt**
- **1 teaspoon cracked black peppercorns**
- **2 tablespoons sherry vinegar**
- **2 tablespoons chopped Italian parsley**

1. Grate peel from lemon and reserve; you should have about 1 tablespoon. Cut lemon in half and squeeze juice into a large bowl, discarding any seeds; fill bowl halfway with water.

2. Break off artichokes' coarse green outer leaves down to tender yellow inner leaves (easily pierced with your fingernail). Cut off thorny tips and pare away fibrous green layers from bottoms. Cut each artichoke into quarters lengthwise; with a spoon, scoop out and discard fuzzy centers. Cut quarters into ½-inch wedges (if using baby artichokes, leave quarters whole). As you work, drop pieces into bowl with water and lemon juice.

3. Drain artichokes. In a 10- to 12-inch nonstick frying pan over medium-high heat, stir 2 tablespoons olive oil, garlic, grated lemon and orange peel, and chili flakes until mixture is fragrant, about 2 minutes. Stir in artichokes, ½ teaspoon salt, and cracked pepper. Reduce heat to medium and pour in ½ cup water; cover and cook until water has been absorbed and artichokes are tender when pierced, about 15 minutes.

4. Remove from heat and stir in vinegar and remaining 2 tablespoons olive oil. Pour into a shallow bowl and let cool to room temperature. Before serving, stir in parsley and add more salt to taste.

Per serving: 107 cal., 60% (64 cal.) from fat; 3.1 g protein; 7.1 g fat (1 g sat.); 11 g carbo (4.9 g fiber); 231 mg sodium; 0 mg chol.

Crostini

PREP TIME: About 15 minutes

NOTES: Look for long loaves of Italian country-style bread, about 4 inches across, for making these toasts, or substitute large bâtards or baguettes of French bread.

MAKES: About 32 toasts; 6 to 8 servings

Slice 1 loaf **Italian-style bread** (1 lb.; see notes) crosswise about ¾ inch thick. Brush one side of each slice with **extra-virgin olive oil** and place, oiled side up, on a 10- by 15-inch baking sheet. Broil 4 to 6 inches from heat until golden, about 2 minutes.

Per serving: 214 cal., 38% (81 cal.) from fat; 5 g protein; 9 g fat (1.5 g sat.); 28 g carbo (1.8 g fiber); 331 mg sodium; 0 mg chol.

Chocolate-Pistachio Meringues

PREP AND COOK TIME: 1 hour and 20 minutes, plus at least 4 hours to cool

NOTES: These cookies do not work well on very humid days.

Serve crostini with (left to right): red-and-gold cherry tomato salad; prosciutto with fresh ricotta and roasted red peppers; marinated artichokes; and arugula with parmesan and bresaola, a cured beef. Finish with meringues (in the jar).

MAKES: About 3 dozen cookies

- **4 large egg whites (½ cup), at room temperature**
- **¼ teaspoon salt**
- **¾ cup sugar**
- **4 ounces bittersweet chocolate, chopped (¼ in.), or ¾ cup miniature chocolate chips**
- **¾ cup (about 3 oz.) shelled unsalted roasted pistachios, chopped**
- **1 teaspoon grated orange peel**

1. Line two 10-by-15-inch baking sheets with cooking parchment or silicone baking liners. In a bowl, with an electric mixer at medium-high speed, beat egg whites and salt just until stiff (but not dry) peaks form, 2 to 4 minutes. Reduce speed to medium and add sugar gradually, beating until it has dissolved and whites are glossy and like marshmallow creme in texture, about 3 minutes.

2. With a flexible spatula, gently fold in chocolate, pistachios, and orange peel.

3. Drop mixture in tablespoon portions about 1 inch apart on baking sheets. If desired, swirl the back of a spoon (or your finger) around cookies to shape.

4. Bake in a 250° regular or 225° convection oven until meringues appear set and are just beginning to turn pale gold at edges, about 50 minutes, switching baking sheet positions halfway through baking. Turn off oven and leave cookies inside on sheets until dry in the center (break one to test), at least 4 hours or up to 12. Store airtight at room temperature up to 2 weeks.

Per cookie: 47 cal., 43% (20 cal.) from fat; 1 g protein; 2.2 g fat (0.7 g sat.); 6.5 g carbo (0.3 g fiber); 22 mg sodium; 0 mg chol.

Campari-Orange Sodas

Fill eight tall glasses (at least 12 oz.) with **ice cubes.** Rinse four **oranges** and cut a ¼-inch crosswise slice from the middle of each. Cut each slice in half to form two half-moons. Squeeze juice from one of each of the eight remaining orange halves into each ice-filled glass. Pour ¼ cup (2 oz.) **Campari** into each glass. Fill glasses with **club soda** and garnish rim of each glass with a half-slice of orange. Stir before drinking. Makes 8 servings.

Per drink: 227 cal., 0.8% (1.8 cal.) from fat; 0.8 g protein; 0.2 g fat (0 g sat.); 17 g carbo (0.4 g fiber); 38 mg sodium; 0 mg chol. ◆

Jump-start tomato season

Roast some Romas for full-flavored tomatoes before slicers are ripe on the vine

By Jerry Anne Di Vecchio
Photograph by James Carrier

Romas develop sweet-sharp flavor when roasted with vinegar and ginger.

O n a recent trip through the Italian countryside, we enjoyed numerous picnics on sunny terraces. And though summer hadn't arrived and slicing tomatoes weren't ripe yet, Romas were prominently present—thick-walled and pear-shaped. Raw, these tomatoes are a little flat-flavored and border on mealy. But heat brings out their great character—tangy, succulent, and intense. These are the tomatoes of sauces and pastes for pasta and pizza. They're also marvelous roasted with balsamic vinegar, olive oil, brown sugar, and ginger. (Using the Lucini balsamic and olive oil I discovered near Modena and Livorno, respectively—also available in many supermarkets here—takes me back to Italy.)

Romas take a fair amount of time to soften as they roast, but in the process, they soak up a prodigious amount of flavor from our pungent additions. Serve the roasted halves on crisp toast spread with a mild citrus-flavored cheese for a fine first course; double the portions and add pink curls of prosciutto or thin slices of aromatic salami to make a light lunch dish. A cool, uncomplicated, crisp Italian Pinot Grigio or Orvieto wine is all you need alongside.

Roasted Roma Tomatoes on Toast

PREP AND COOK TIME: $1\frac{1}{2}$ to $1\frac{3}{4}$ hours

NOTES: Make the lemon cheese and olive-oil toast while the tomatoes roast. Or roast the tomatoes (through step 3) and make the lemon cheese up to 2 days ahead; cover separately and chill. Bring to room temperature to serve.

MAKES: 8 appetizer, 4 main-dish servings

- 8 **Roma tomatoes (equal size, 1½ lb. total), rinsed and cored**
- 1 **onion (about 8 oz.), peeled and finely chopped**
- ¾ **cup balsamic vinegar**
- ½ **cup firmly packed brown sugar**
- 2 **tablespoons extra-virgin olive oil**
- 1 **tablespoon minced fresh ginger**
  Lemon cheese (recipe follows)
  Olive-oil toast (recipe follows)
  About 2 cups arugula leaves, stemmed, rinsed, and drained
  Salt

1. Cut tomatoes in half lengthwise. Lay halves cut side up in a single layer in an 8- by 12-inch oval or rectangular casserole (rim should be at least ½ in. higher than tomatoes).

2. In a 1½- to 2-quart pan, combine onion, vinegar, sugar, olive oil, and ginger. Bring to a boil over high heat, stirring often. Pour over tomatoes.

3. Roast in a 400° oven (convection not recommended) until tomatoes are dark brown and sauce is browned and thick-

ened (bubbles will be large and shiny), about 1¼ hours; baste tomatoes with sauce and onions about every 15 minutes at first, then more frequently as mixture begins to thicken, to avoid scorching. Use hot, warm, or at room temperature.

4. Spread lemon cheese equally on oiled sides of the olive-oil toast slices. Set on plates and cover equally with arugula leaves. Spoon tomatoes and juices equally onto toast slices. Add salt to taste.

Lemon cheese. In a food processor or bowl, combine ⅓ cup **cream cheese** (at room temperature), ⅓ cup packed **fresh chèvre** (goat cheese), 2 tablespoons **milk,** and 1 teaspoon grated **lemon** peel. Whirl or beat with a mixer on medium-high speed until blended.

Olive-oil toast. Lay 8 slices of **rustic white bread** such as sourdough or ciabatta (about 3 by 4 in., cut about ½ in. thick) in a single layer in a shallow 10- by 15-inch pan. Bake in a 375° oven until lightly browned on the bottom, 5 to 6 minutes. Turn slices over and brush equally with about 2 tablespoons **extra-virgin olive oil.** Continue baking until golden brown and crisp, 6 to 8 minutes longer. Use warm, or let cool on a rack.

Per piece: 285 cal., 44% (126 cal.) from fat; 6.2 g protein; 14 g fat (5.1 g sat.); 36 g carbo (2.3 g fiber); 261 mg sodium; 17 mg chol. ◆

Cool off with yogurt

Face summer's warm days with a refreshing Indian salad

By Linda Lau Anusasananan
Photograph by James Carrier

Tangy rice salad, topped with crunchy shredded carrots, serves well as a side dish or light lunch.

FOOD STYLING: BASIL FRIEDMAN

Many of our traditional summer salads are dressed with mayonnaise or sour cream. But there's a creamy alternative without all that fat: yogurt. Tangy and rich in protein, nonfat yogurt makes a tasty base for a fresh, healthy salad.

In southern India, the cuisine blazes with chilies and spices. To soothe the palate, cooks often follow hot courses with a yogurt-dressed rice salad. In her home in Cupertino, California, Hema Kundargi serves this refreshing dish as a companion to grilled spice-rubbed chicken. The rice salad and interesting pasta variation that follows also make great vegetarian main dishes for a summer lunch.

Yogurt-Rice Salad

PREP AND COOK TIME: About 35 minutes

NOTES: You can make this salad up to 1 day ahead; cover and chill.

MAKES: 8 side-dish servings

- 1 cup basmati or long-grain white rice
- 1 English cucumber (about 14 oz.)
- 1 zucchini (about 5 oz.)
- 1 Granny Smith apple (about 8 oz.)
- 1 cup chopped white or red onion, rinsed and drained
- 2 cups plain nonfat yogurt
- 1 teaspoon grated fresh ginger
  About 1/2 teaspoon salt
- 1 teaspoon vegetable oil
- 1/4 teaspoon hot chili flakes
- 1/8 teaspoon cracked or coarse-ground pepper
- 3/4 cup shredded carrots

1. In a fine strainer, rinse rice well and drain. In a 2- to 3-quart pan over high heat, bring 3 cups water and the rice to a boil. Reduce heat to medium-high and cook, uncovered, until most of the liquid is absorbed, about 10 minutes. Reduce heat to low, cover, and cook until rice is tender to bite, about 10 minutes longer. Scoop into a large bowl and let cool, stirring occasionally, 15 to 20 minutes.

2. Meanwhile, rinse cucumber, zucchini, and apple. Trim off and discard ends of cucumber and zucchini; cut vegetables into 1/2-inch cubes. Stem and core apple; cut into 1/2-inch cubes. Add cucumber, zucchini, apple, and onion to cool rice.

3. Pour any excess liquid off yogurt. In a bowl, mix yogurt, ginger, and 1/2 teaspoon salt. Add to rice mixture and stir gently to coat.

4. Set a 6- to 8-inch frying pan over medium-high heat; when hot, add oil and chili flakes and stir just until chili begins to darken slightly, 15 to 30 seconds. Add pepper. Pour over rice mixture and stir gently to mix, adding more salt to taste. Spoon into a serving bowl and garnish with shredded carrots.

Per serving: 151 cal., 7% (11 cal.) from fat; 6.9 g protein; 1.2 g fat (0.2 g sat.); 31 g carbo (2.1 g fiber); 204 mg sodium; 1.1 mg chol.

Yogurt-Pasta Salad

PREP AND COOK TIME: About 30 minutes

MAKES: About 8 side-dish servings

Follow recipe for yogurt-rice salad (preceding), but omit rice and use 6 ounces **dried angel hair pasta** instead. For step 1, in a 5- to 6-quart pan over high heat, bring 2 1/2 to 3 quarts water to a boil. Break pasta in half and drop into boiling water; stir to separate strands and cook, uncovered, until barely tender to bite, 5 to 6 minutes. Drain pasta, rinse with cold water, and drain well.

Per serving: 152 cal., 7% (10 cal.) from fat; 7.2 g protein; 1.1 g fat (0.2 g sat.); 29 g carbo (2.4 g fiber); 196 mg sodium; 1.1 mg chol. ◆

Supper menu

Chicken with Pepper Relish

Mixed Greens
with Cherry Tomatoes,
Goat Cheese, and Herbs

Nectarine shortcakes

Casual, colorful chicken

Top chicken breasts with a bright bell-pepper relish

By Charity Ferreira
Photograph by James Carrier

A tumble of colorful bell peppers cooked with olives and capers makes a sweet, tangy relish for that convenient weeknight staple, the boned, skinned chicken breast.

While the chicken and peppers cook, you can make a simple salad: just dress some mixed greens and toss with sweet miniature cherry tomatoes, chopped fresh herbs, and crumbled goat cheese. For dessert, spoon vanilla frozen yogurt into bowls and top with sliced ripe nectarines and shortbread cookies or shortcakes from the bakery. Together, these easy, fresh dishes make a perfect summer dinner.

Chicken with Pepper Relish

PREP AND COOK TIME: About 30 minutes

MAKES: 4 servings

- 4 boned, skinned chicken breast halves (about 6 oz. each)
  Salt and pepper
- 1½ tablespoons olive oil
- ¼ cup chopped shallots
- 2 cloves garlic, peeled and minced
- 1½ pounds red, yellow, and/or orange bell peppers, rinsed, stemmed, seeded, and cut into ½-inch pieces
- 3 tablespoons sherry vinegar
- ¼ cup chopped pitted Spanish-style green olives
- 1 tablespoon drained capers

Quick-cooking bell peppers become a tangy topping for chicken breasts.

1. Rinse chicken and pat dry. Sprinkle breast halves lightly all over with salt and pepper. Heat 1 tablespoon olive oil in a 10- to 12-inch nonstick frying pan over medium heat. Add chicken and cook, turning once, until browned on both sides but still slightly pink in the center of the thickest part (cut to test), about 8 minutes total. Transfer chicken to a plate.

2. Pour remaining ½ tablespoon olive oil into pan. Add shallots and garlic and stir often until fragrant but not browned, 1 to 2 minutes. Add peppers and stir frequently until slightly soft, 1 to 2 minutes. Add vinegar, olives, capers, and the chicken. Cover, lower heat to medium-low, and cook until peppers are soft and chicken is no longer pink in the center of the thickest part (cut to test), 5 to 8 minutes longer. Add salt and pepper to taste. Transfer each breast half to a plate and spoon peppers and juices evenly over warm chicken.

Per serving: 292 cal., 26% (77 cal.) from fat; 41 g protein; 8.5 g fat (1.4 g sat.); 12 g carbo (2.6 g fiber); 414 mg sodium; 99 mg chol.

Mixed Greens with Cherry Tomatoes, Goat Cheese, and Herbs

PREP TIME: About 15 minutes

NOTES: You can adapt this quick salad to complement any weeknight meal.

MAKES: 4 servings

- 2 tablespoons red wine or sherry vinegar
- 2 tablespoons olive oil
- 12 cups mixed baby greens (10 oz.)
- 2 tablespoons chopped fresh herbs such as chives, tarragon, basil, or a combination
- 1 cup miniature cherry tomatoes, such as Sweet 100s (about 8 oz.)
- 4 ounces goat cheese, crumbled
  Salt and pepper

In a large bowl, whisk vinegar and olive oil until well blended. Add greens, herbs, tomatoes, and goat cheese and mix to coat. Add salt and pepper to taste.

Per serving: 186 cal., 73% (135 cal.) from fat; 7.5 g protein; 15 g fat (6.8 g sat.); 6.2 g carbo (1.6 g fiber); 160 mg sodium; 22 mg chol. ◆

Lemon zest

Plant a fast-growing herb with an aromatic zing

By Sharon Cohoon and Kate Washington
Photograph by Thomas J. Story

In the garden, lemon grass forms handsome clumps that reach 3 to 4 feet tall and nearly as wide, with lime green leaves rising from swollen bases. When harvested, the bulbous stems look like scallions, but pale yellow and more fibrous. When you cut them, the stems release essential oils, which immediately perfume the air with the mouthwatering aroma of freshly cut lemon combined with the clean bite of ginger.

Thai and Vietnamese cooks use lemon grass in marinades, stir-fries, curries, and soups. But this fragrant herb isn't limited to Asian cuisine. Make a sugar-syrup infusion to spice up lemonade or to use as the start of a dessert such as Lemon Grass–Coconut Sorbet (left).

Fresh lemon grass can be hard to find at the supermarket. But you can buy a small potted plant now, and you'll grow a large clump of your own by summer's end.

What lemon grass needs

EXPOSURE: Full sun.

SOIL: Rich, with good drainage.

WATER: Ample during growing season; less in winter, when it goes dormant.

FEED: Monthly with half-strength fish emulsion during the growing season.

CLIMATE NOTES: *Cymbopogon citratus* is a perennial in *Sunset* climate zones 12, 13, 16, 17, 23, 24, H1, and H2. Elsewhere, grow it as an annual or treat it like a geranium or other tender perennial by bringing the entire plant or a potted cutting indoors for the winter.

HARVEST: When stems are about $1/2$ inch thick. Push an outside stem to the side, then twist and pull it off. Discard leaves and woody outer layers; save the white inner core.

PLANT SOURCES: Nichols Garden Nursery *(www.nicholsgardennursery.com or 800/422-3985)*. ◆

Lemon Grass–Coconut Sorbet

PREP AND COOK TIME: About 1 hour

NOTES: If you do not have an ice-cream maker, pour lemon grass mixture (after step 3) into a 9- by 13-inch dish and freeze just until firm, 2 to 4 hours. Scrape with a large fork to form a slushy ice; serve at once.

MAKES: About 1 quart; 4 to 6 servings

- 10 stalks fresh lemon grass (about 12 oz.), rinsed
- $1^{1}/_{2}$ cups sugar
- $1/4$ teaspoon salt
- $1/4$ cup lemon juice
- 1 cup coconut milk (stir before measuring)

1. Peel toughest outer layers from lemon grass; discard. Cut into $1/2$-inch lengths. In a 2- to 3-quart pan over high heat, combine lemon grass, sugar, salt, and $2^{1}/_{2}$ cups water. Stir until liquid comes to a boil. Reduce heat; simmer, stirring occasionally, until light golden, about 20 minutes.

2. Pour through a fine strainer into a bowl, pressing on solids; discard solids. Nest bowl in a larger bowl of ice water and stir syrup until cool, about 5 minutes. Stir in lemon juice.

3. Whisk in coconut milk. If mixture is lumpy, pour through a fine strainer.

4. Pour into an ice-cream maker (at least 1 qt.) and freeze. Scoop into bowls or, for a firmer consistency, freeze airtight up to 3 days.

Per serving: 293 cal., 25% (74 cal.) from fat; 1.2 g protein; 8.2 g fat (7.1 g sat.); 58 g carbo (0 g fiber); 104 mg sodium; 0 mg chol.

Almonds and apricots pair up in a cake ideal for summer celebrations.

A piece of cake

With foolproof recipes from *Sunset's* test kitchen, glamorous layer cakes are easier than you think

By Charity Ferreira and Kate Washington
Photographs by James Carrier • Food styling by Karen Shinto

No dessert combines elegance and charm quite like a homemade layer cake. We mark the milestones of our lives, from birthdays to graduations, with cakes, and making a great one from scratch takes just a few minutes longer than stirring up a mix. That small effort not only makes a big difference in flavor and texture, but also makes the celebration that much more special.

The deep, dark chocolate and rich, velvety butter cake we perfected in our test kitchen are great bases on which to layer different fillings and frostings, such as silky buttercream or caramel crème fraîche (see page 130 for seven mouthwatering combinations). From over-the-top toffee crunch to summery berry-lemon, these are special-occasion cakes anyone can create.

Basic Butter Cake

PREP AND COOK TIME: About 1 hour, plus at least 1 hour to cool

NOTES: Soften the butter briefly in a warm place in the kitchen or in a microwave oven until very soft but not melted. For high-altitude adjustments, go to *www.sunset.com/altitude.*

MAKES: Two 9-inch cake layers; 12 to 16 servings

- 1   **cup (½ lb.) butter, softened (see notes)**
- 1½ **cups sugar**
- 3   **large eggs**
- 3   **large egg yolks**
- 1   **tablespoon vanilla**
- 3¼ **cups cake flour**
- 2½ **teaspoons baking powder**
- ¼   **teaspoon salt**
- 1¼ **cups milk**

1. In a bowl, with a mixer on medium-high speed (use the paddle attachment if using a standing mixer), beat butter and sugar until fluffy and pale yellow, 4 to 5 minutes. Add eggs, then yolks, one at a time, beating well after each addition and scraping down sides of bowl as necessary. Beat in vanilla.

2. In another bowl, mix flour, baking powder, and salt. Stir (or beat at low speed) about a third of the flour mixture into butter mixture. Stir in half the milk just until blended. Stir in another third of the flour mixture, then remaining milk, followed by remaining flour. Scrape batter equally into two buttered and floured 9-inch round cake pans and spread level.

3. Bake in a 350° regular or convection oven until a wooden skewer inserted in the center comes out clean, 25 to 30 minutes. Cool on racks in pans for 10 minutes, then invert cakes onto racks and remove pans. Cool completely before frosting.

Per serving: 322 cal., 42% (135 cal.) from fat; 4.8 g protein; 15 g fat (8.5 g sat.); 43 g carbo (0.5 g fiber); 257 mg sodium; 115 mg chol.

Cakewalk

These cake-assembly techniques will give you beautiful results every time.

• **Slice any dome off the bottom layer** to create a level surface for the top layer.

• **Split layers horizontally** for an extra-tall cake, if you like: Make a guide by cutting around layer (1 in. deep), then cut through cake with a serrated knife, steadying top lightly.

• **Stack the layers carefully:** Place bottom layer on cake plate and spread with filling, then gently lower next layers, stepping back after each to be sure it's level and centered.

• **Ensure a perfectly crumb-free exterior** with a crumb coating of frosting underneath. When using buttercream, frost entire cake thinly (1/4 in. or less). Chill cake about 20 minutes, then frost with remaining room-temperature buttercream. (With whipped cream–based frostings, this step is unnecessary.)

• **Use an offset spatula** for best results when frosting, to create either a smooth surface or luscious swirls.

Double-Layer Chocolate Cake

PREP AND COOK TIME: About 1 hour, plus at least 1 hour to cool

NOTES: To melt the chocolate, break it into small pieces and place in a small microwave-safe bowl; cook in a microwave oven at half power (50%), stirring occasionally, until smooth, 2 to 3 minutes.

MAKES: Two 9-inch cake layers; 12 to 16 servings

- ½ cup (¼ lb.) butter, at room temperature
- 1½ cups firmly packed brown sugar
- 3 large eggs
- 4 ounces unsweetened chocolate, melted (see notes)
- 1 teaspoon vanilla
- 2 cups all-purpose flour
- ¾ cup Dutch-processed unsweetened cocoa
- 1 teaspoon baking powder
- 1 teaspoon baking soda
- ¼ teaspoon salt
- 1 cup milk
- ¾ cup sour cream

1. In a bowl, with a mixer on medium speed, beat butter and brown sugar until blended. Beat in eggs. Add melted chocolate and vanilla; beat until combined.

2. In another bowl, stir together flour, cocoa, baking powder, baking soda, and salt. In a small bowl, mix milk and sour cream.

3. Add flour mixture and milk mixture alternately to butter mixture, about a third of each at a time, beating after each addition until incorporated (batter will be very thick). Scrape batter equally into two buttered and floured 9-inch round cake pans and spread level.

4. Bake in a 350° regular or convection oven until a wooden skewer inserted in the center comes out clean, 25 to 30 minutes. Cool on racks in pans for 10 minutes, then invert cakes onto racks and remove pans. Cool completely before frosting.

Per serving: 288 cal., 47% (135 cal.) from fat; 5.2 protein; 15 g fat (8.6 g sat.); 38 g carbo (1.5 g fiber); 272 mg sodium; 64 mg chol.

Foolproof Buttercream

PREP AND COOK TIME: About 30 minutes

NOTES: You can make this frosting up to 1 week ahead; cover airtight and chill. Before using, let buttercream come to room temperature, then beat briefly at medium speed to restore texture. In place of the vanilla in step 4, you can flavor buttercream with 2 to 3 tablespoons liqueur, 6 ounces bittersweet chocolate, melted, or up to ½ cup strained jam of any flavor.

MAKES: About 3½ cups; enough to fill and frost two 9-inch cake layers

- 6 large egg yolks
- ¾ cup sugar
- ½ cup light corn syrup
- 2 cups (1 lb.) unsalted butter, softened (see notes for basic butter cake)
- 2 teaspoons vanilla or other flavoring (see notes)

1. In a bowl, with a mixer at high speed, beat egg yolks until pale yellow, 4 to 5 minutes.

2. Butter a 2-cup glass measure. In a 2- to 3-quart pan, combine sugar and corn syrup. Set over medium-high heat and stir until sugar is dissolved and mixture comes to a rolling boil. Immediately pour into the buttered glass measure.

3. Beating constantly at medium speed, pour syrup in a thin, steady stream into egg yolks (avoiding beaters). Continue beating until mixture is at room temperature, 7 to 10 minutes.

4. Add butter and vanilla. Beat just until smooth.

Per ¼ cup: 334 cal., 75% (252 cal.) from fat; 1.5 g protein; 28 g fat (17 g sat.); 20 g carbo (0 g fiber); 21 mg sodium; 162 mg chol.

Caramel Crème Fraîche

PREP AND COOK TIME: About 45 minutes

NOTES: If you can't find crème fraîche, substitute 1 cup additional whipping cream in step 2.

MAKES: About 4½ cups; enough to fill and frost four 9-inch cake layers

- 1⅓ cups sugar
- 2 cups whipping cream
- 1 cup crème fraîche (see notes)

1. In a 3- to 4-quart pan over medium heat, stir sugar and 1 cup water until sugar is dissolved. Increase heat to high and boil without stirring until mixture is a deep caramel color, 12 to 20 minutes. When sugar begins to brown around edges of pan, swirl gently to ensure that the mixture caramelizes evenly. Remove from heat and immediately add 1 cup cream (mixture may splatter); whisk until smooth. Pour into a large bowl and let cool to room temperature, about 20 minutes.

2. In a bowl, with a mixer on high speed, beat remaining 1 cup cream and the crème fraîche (see notes) until mixture holds medium-soft peaks. Stir about 1 cup cream mixture into caramel until no white streaks remain. Gently fold remaining cream mixture into caramel. When completely incorporated, whisk gently to thicken to spreadable consistency, if necessary. Use immediately, or cover and chill up to 3 hours.

Per ¼ cup: 184 cal., 64% (117 cal.) from fat; 1 g protein; 13 g fat (8.2 g sat.); 16 g carbo (0 g fiber); 18 mg sodium; 41 mg chol.

Coconut

Chocolate-orange

Toffee crunch

Berry-lemon

Seven great cakes

Layer-cake combinations are limited only by your imagination. Here are some of our favorites. Follow our "Cakewalk" tips on page 128 to assemble them.

Chocolate-raspberry cake. Split the layers of the **double-layer chocolate cake,** making four total. Spread each of the first three with **raspberry jam** (about ⅓ cup on each). Stir 3 tablespoons **raspberry-flavored liqueur,** such as Chambord, into **foolproof buttercream** to frost cake. Garnish with rinsed **fresh raspberries** (about 6 oz. total). Makes 12 to 16 servings.

Per serving: 642 cal., 56% (360 cal.) from fat; 6.7 g protein; 40 g fat (24 g sat.); 70 g carbo (2.3 g fiber); 298 mg sodium; 205 mg chol.

Toffee crunch cake. Split the layers of the **double-layer chocolate cake,** making four. Fold 2 cups finely crushed **toffee candy** (such as Heath Bars; about 12 oz. total) into 2 cups **caramel crème fraîche;** spread a third of the mixture on each of the first three cake layers. Frost the outside of the cake with remaining caramel crème fraîche; sprinkle top with about ½ cup chopped toasted **almonds.** Makes 12 to 16 servings.

Per serving: 665 cal., 60% (396 cal.) from fat; 7.8 g protein; 44 g fat (18 g sat.); 64 g carbo (2 g fiber); 352 mg sodium; 109 mg chol.

Chocolate-orange cake. Stir 1 tablespoon grated **orange** peel and 2 tablespoons **Grand Marnier,** other orange-flavored liqueur, or thawed frozen orange juice concentrate into **foolproof buttercream.** Spread bottom layer of **double-layer chocolate cake** with about ⅓ cup **orange marmalade,** then about ¾ cup of the orange buttercream. Top with remaining cake layer and frost with remaining buttercream. Garnish the top of the cake with thin shreds of fresh orange peel. Makes 12 to 16 servings.

Per serving: 603 cal., 60% (360 cal.) from fat; 6.5 g protein; 40 g fat (24 g sat.); 61 g carbo (1.5 g fiber); 294 mg sodium; 205 mg chol.

Orange-caramel cake. Mix 1½ cups **orange marmalade** with 2 tablespoons **Grand Marnier.** Split the layers of the **basic butter cake,** making four. Spread each of the first three with a third of the marmalade mixture, then with ⅔ cup **caramel crème fraîche.** Frost outside of cake with remaining caramel crème fraîche. Chill cake, covered with a large inverted bowl to protect frosting, at least 1 hour and up to 1 day. Makes 12 to 16 servings.

Per serving: 608 cal., 43% (261 cal.) from fat; 6 g protein; 29 g fat (18 g sat.); 81 g carbo (0.6 g fiber); 294 mg sodium; 160 mg chol.

Chocolate-raspberry

Berry-lemon cake. Beat 2 cups chilled **whipping cream** and ¼ cup **sugar** until soft peaks form; gently fold in 1 tablespoon grated **lemon** peel. Spread the bottom layer of the **basic butter cake** with ¼ cup **raspberry** or blackberry **jam,** then with 1 cup purchased **lemon curd.** Top with second cake layer. Frost with the lemon whipped cream. Mound the top of the cake generously with **fresh berries** of your choice. Makes 12 to 16 servings.

Per serving: 489 cal., 46% (225 cal.) from fat; 6.6 g protein; 25 g fat (14 g sat.); 63 g carbo (1.1 g fiber); 285 mg sodium; 148 mg chol.

Almond-apricot cake. Spread the bottom layer of the **basic butter cake** with about ¼ cup **apricot jam.** Shape 7 ounces of **almond paste** into a flat disk and place on a sheet of plastic wrap; cover with a second sheet of plastic and roll out into a 9-inch round. Peel off top layer of plastic and invert almond paste onto bottom layer of cake; peel off remaining plastic wrap and trim off any uneven edges. Spread bottom of top cake layer with about ¼ cup apricot jam; set layer, jam side down, on almond paste. Warm ¾ cup apricot jam in a

microwave oven or over low heat on the stove, then pour through a fine wire strainer; you should have about ½ cup. Beat into **foolproof buttercream;** use apricot buttercream to frost cake. Garnish top or sides with **sliced almonds.** Makes 12 to 16 servings.

Per serving: 426 cal., 38% (162 cal.) from fat; 6.4 g protein; 18 g fat (8.8 g sat.); 61 g carbo (0.7 g fiber); 266 mg sodium; 115 mg chol.

Coconut cake. Fold 1½ cups **sweetened shredded dried coconut** into **basic butter cake** batter in step 2. For frosting, in a large bowl, with a mixer on high speed, beat 3 cups **whipping cream** with 2 tablespoons **sugar** until soft peaks form; fold in 1 tablespoon **light rum.** Split the layers of the coconut butter cake, making four; spread each of the first three with about ¾ cup of the whipped cream. Frost cake with remaining whipped cream, then sprinkle top and sides generously with sweetened shredded dried coconut. Chill at least 1 hour. Makes 12 to 16 servings.

Per serving: 505 cal., 57% (288 cal.) from fat; 6.1 g protein; 32 g fat (20 g sat.); 50 g carbo (1.1 g fiber); 296 mg sodium; 164 mg chol. ◆

Best of the West

Think pink

Admit it: you've drunk it. This year marks the 30th anniversary of the invention of white Zinfandel by Bob Trinchero at Sutter

FRESH IDEA **Home Winery in Napa Valley. Soon sweet white Zin "just exploded," Trinchero says. "In 1980, we had trucks lined up down the highway." His innovation spawned imitators—and it led legions of novice drinkers into the world of wine. Here are five ways to be pretty in pink:**

1 Make a baby-pink sorbet (pictured): stir wine with sugar to taste over low heat until sugar is dissolved; chill until cold, then freeze in an ice cream maker. **2** Use it in a gelatin dessert with berries. **3** Poach pears or peaches in it. **4** Pair it with fiery curries or stir-fries. **5** Pay homage to its '70s roots by using it in a wine cooler.

—*Kate Washington*

Tuna types

The Japanese rate tuna based on fat content and size, the higher-fat species being the most flavorful and tender. Look for troll-, pole-, or rod-and-reel–caught fish.

Big eye (ahi). Deep ruby red flesh and high fat content. Availability can be spotty.

Yellowfin (ahi). Much like big eye, but milder in flavor and slightly leaner and firmer. Widely available.

Albacore (tombo). Leanest and most affordable. Usually served cooked.

Buying tips

• Buy from a shop you trust. The way tuna is handled greatly affects its quality.

• Choose a store with quick product turnover. Japanese markets are often good bets.

• Select the fish with your nose: it should smell ocean-fresh or be odorless.

• Look for firm flesh with uniformly bright color.

• Avoid fish that feels slimy or granular.

• For sashimi (raw fish), ask for *maguro*—a tender cut that runs along the spine near the head—cut into *saku* blocks.

A note on safety

Parasites are rare in tuna (especially sashimi-grade cuts), but to minimize the risk, follow the buying tips above. And to help slow the growth of bacteria, keep fish cold, then sear it on the outside, where bacteria generally occur.

Soy-seasoned salsa sets off seared-rare ahi tuna.

All about tuna

From albacore to ahi, what to buy and how to cook it

Fresh tuna is swimming in many channels these days, from sushi rolls in supermarket delis, to seared ahi on restaurant menus, to sashimi in popular sushi bars. Perhaps because it's often served raw or nearly raw and in Japanese preparations, the fish can be intimidating to the average cook. But it's easy to master the basics. Rodelio Aglibot, executive chef at Koi Restaurant in Los Angeles, shares his tuna expertise and a favorite recipe.

Seared Tuna with Japanese Salsa

PREP AND COOK TIME: About 25 minutes

NOTES: Aglibot uses ponzu, a citrus-seasoned soy sauce, to flavor the salsa. We've mixed soy and lemon juice for an easy alternative.

MAKES: 2 servings

- 2 tuna steaks (big eye, yellowfin, or albacore; about 1¼ in. thick, 5 to 6 oz. each)
- 1 teaspoon minced or pressed garlic
  Salt and pepper
- 2 teaspoons vegetable oil
- ¼ cup sake
- 2 tablespoons soy sauce
- ¾ cup finely chopped tomatoes
- 2 tablespoons finely chopped green onion
- 1 tablespoon chopped fresh cilantro
- 1 tablespoon lemon juice
- 6 to 8 slices peeled avocado (3 to 4 oz. total)

1. Rinse tuna; pat dry. Spread garlic on both sides of steaks; sprinkle with salt and pepper. Pour oil into an 8- to 10-inch nonstick frying pan over medium-high heat. When hot, add tuna. Cook, turning once, until lightly browned on both sides, about 1 minute per side. Pour sake and 1 tablespoon soy sauce around steaks; remove from heat. Let cool, turning fish often.

2. Meanwhile, in a small bowl, mix tomatoes, green onion, cilantro, lemon juice, and remaining tablespoon soy sauce.

3. Lift tuna from sake mixture, reserving juices. Cut fish across the grain into ¼-inch-thick slices and lay on plates. Garnish with the salsa and avocado slices. If desired, spoon pan juices equally over tuna (otherwise discard).

Per serving: 340 cal., 48% (162 cal.) from fat; 32 g protein; 18 g fat (3.2 g sat.); 9.5 g carbo (1.9 g fiber); 1,093 mg sodium; 48 mg chol.

—Linda Lau Anusasananan

To vintner Robert Mondavi, the world is a better place with good wine.

Vintage vision

Robert Mondavi, patriarch of the wine company that bears his name, turns 90 this month. In a career that has spanned more than six decades, Mondavi has played a key role in making good wine a way of life for many people in this country. His company now produces a mind-boggling 9.3 million cases a year. Sitting at a spare wooden desk in his small, photograph-filled Napa Valley office, Mondavi shared a few thoughts with me.

Q: When did you begin loving wine?

A: My mother served me wine and water from the time I was 3 years old. I've always looked at it as liquid food. Later, at Stanford University, I thought I'd become a lawyer or businessman, but my father came to me and said he thought there was a big future in the fine-wine business. I realized he was right. Wine has been with civilized man from the beginning. For me, that made the industry inspiring and challenging.

Q: How did you come to go to Stanford University, when your parents were poor and the country had just come out of the Depression?

A: My brother and I had saved $15,000 by working many years nailing fruit crates together. At one point, when my father's business wasn't doing well, he asked me to loan him the money and he'd send me to any college I wanted to go to. Of course I chose Stanford!

Q: So far, what has been your single greatest professional contribution?

A: Convincing the world that California wines belong in the company of the finest wines in the world.

Q: Many wine drinkers and makers in the rest of the world think California wines are too big, powerful, and oaky. What do you think?

A: Those are the kinds of wines I've always tried *not* to make. I want to make wines that harmonize with food—wines that almost hug your tongue with gentleness. When you make a wine like that, you know you've really achieved something.

Q: When you began, there were no wine critics and wine scores. What do you think about the role of critics today?

A: Critics have done the wine industry a lot of good overall. However, the problem is they often imply that their view or evaluation of a wine is the only one, and I disagree. Also, many consumers consider a critic to be like God Almighty. I say to consumers: instead of relying totally on critics, drink what you like and like what you drink.

Q: You have always put wine with food; now you are connecting both to art as well. The first pairing is easy to understand, but where does art fit in?

A: If you go back to the Greeks and Romans, they talk about all three—wine, food, and art—as a way of enhancing life. I've always wanted to improve on the idea of living well. In moderation, wine is good for you—mentally, physically, and spiritually. What else are we living for?

—Karen MacNeil-Fife

Mondavi stars

The Robert Mondavi wine company makes scores of different wines. Here are three of our favorites from its flagship winery in the Napa Valley.

Robert Mondavi Chardonnay 2001 *(Carneros), $25.* Refined, elegant, and sleek, with hints of butter and roasted nuts.

Robert Mondavi Pinot Noir Reserve 2001 *(Napa Valley), $50.* Sensual, soft, and languorous on the palate, with deep, earthy notes.

Robert Mondavi Stags Leap District Cabernet Sauvignon 2000 *(Stags Leap District), $50.* Beautiful cassis and tobacco aromas open up to a firm, concentrated Cabernet—the classic "iron fist in a velvet glove." Lay it away for a few years.

—K. M.-F.

Bright June flavors

Readers' recipes tested in *Sunset's* kitchens

Photographs by James Carrier

Ham, cheese, and tomatoes are layered with Italian bread in this crusty strata.

Sicilian-style Strata

Roxanne Chan, Albany, CA

Because they can be assembled ahead and baked at the last minute, stratas make great brunch entrées. Roxanne Chan also likes to serve this at lunch or dinner.

PREP AND COOK TIME: About 1¼ hours, plus at least 1 hour to chill

MAKES: 8 servings

- 1 loaf (1 lb.) crusty, Italian-style bread, cut into 1-inch cubes
- 4 ounces thick-sliced prosciutto or ham, diced
- ¼ cup chopped canned roasted red peppers
- ¼ cup thinly sliced green onions
- ½ cup grated parmesan cheese
- 1 can (14½ oz.) diced tomatoes
- ¼ cup pitted black olives, coarsely chopped
- ½ cup shredded mozzarella cheese
- 6 large eggs
- 3 cups milk
- 2 teaspoons dried Italian seasoning blend
- ½ teaspoon salt
- ½ teaspoon pepper
- ¼ cup chopped parsley
- 2 tablespoons drained capers

1. Spread half the bread cubes level in a lightly oiled 9- by 13-inch baking dish. Top evenly with prosciutto, peppers, green onions, and parmesan cheese. Spread remaining bread cubes level on top, followed by tomatoes with juices, olives, and mozzarella.

2. In a bowl, whisk eggs, milk, Italian seasoning, salt, and pepper to blend. Pour over layered ingredients. Cover and chill at least 1 hour or up to one day.

3. Bake in a 325° regular or convection oven until center of strata is set and top is lightly browned, 40 to 50 minutes. Sprinkle evenly with parsley and capers. Let stand 10 minutes, then cut into squares. Serve warm or at room temperature.

Per serving: 362 cal., 35% (126 cal.) from fat; 21 g protein; 14 g fat (6 g sat.); 37 g carbo (2.5 g fiber); 1,179 mg sodium; 193 mg chol.

Smoked Salmon Spread

Betty Jean Nichols, Eugene, OR

Betty Jean Nichols serves this creamy spread with crackers or baguette slices.

PREP TIME: About 20 minutes, plus at least 12 hours total to chill

MAKES: 3 cups; 10 appetizer servings

- 1½ cups cottage cheese
- 8 ounces smoked salmon
- 2 tablespoons dry white wine (optional)
- 2 tablespoons lemon juice
- 2 teaspoons Dijon mustard
- 2 tablespoons chopped fresh dill
- Salt and pepper

1. Line a strainer with cheesecloth and set over a bowl. Place cottage cheese in strainer, cover, and chill at least 8 hours or up to 1 day. Discard liquid.

2. Finely dice about a third of the salmon; coarsely chop remainder. In a blender or food processor, whirl drained cottage cheese, coarsely chopped salmon, wine, lemon juice, and mustard until smooth. Stir in diced salmon, dill, and salt and pepper to taste.

3. Spoon mixture into a bowl, cover, and chill at least 4 hours or up to 2 days.

Per serving: 61 cal., 36% (22 cal.) from fat; 8.1 g protein; 2.4 g fat (1.1 g sat.); 1 g carbo (0 g fiber); 606 mg sodium; 9.9 mg chol.

Strawberry-Yogurt Pie

Andee Zetterbaum, Stockton, CA

Andee Zetterbaum made this tangy no-bake pie for her mother's birthday one year during a heat wave.

PREP AND COOK TIME: About 20 minutes, plus at least 6 hours to chill

MAKES: 6 to 8 servings

- 1 quart fresh strawberries, rinsed and hulled
- 6 tablespoons sugar
- 1 envelope (1/4 oz.) unflavored gelatin
- 2 cups plain whole-milk yogurt
- 1/2 teaspoon vanilla
- 1/2 teaspoon grated orange peel
- 1 graham cracker pie crust (9 in.)
- 1/2 cup miniature or regular chocolate chips

1. Coarsely chop about half the strawberries, to equal 1 1/2 cups chopped berries (reserve remaining ones for garnish). In a 2- to 3-quart pan over medium heat, stir chopped strawberries, sugar, and gelatin until gelatin and sugar are dissolved and mixture is boiling. Remove from heat and stir in yogurt, vanilla, and orange peel until well blended (chunks of strawberries will be visible). Pour into pie crust.

2. Chill until set, at least 6 hours, or cover with plastic wrap and chill up to 1 day. Just before serving, sprinkle chocolate chips evenly over top of pie. Slice remaining strawberries. Cut pie into wedges; serve with sliced berries.

Per serving: 258 cal., 35% (90 cal.) from fat; 4.6 g protein; 10 g fat (4.1 g sat.); 38 g carbo (3.3 g fiber); 165 mg sodium; 7.4 mg chol.

noked
mon spread

Deviled Potato Salad with Sausage

Lenore Klass, Koloa, HI

Lenore Klass came up with this recipe to use leftover barbecued sausages and Maui sweet onions. She liked the result so much that now she regularly broils sausages and onions to make this potato salad.

PREP AND COOK TIME: About 1 hour

MAKES: 6 to 8 servings

- 8 ounces green beans, rinsed, ends trimmed, and cut in 1-inch pieces
- 3 pounds Yukon Gold or thin-skinned potatoes, scrubbed and cut into 1-inch chunks
- 2 tablespoons olive oil
- 2 tablespoons brown sugar
- 1 sweet onion such as Maui, Vidalia, or Oso (about 8 oz.), peeled and sliced crosswise 1 inch thick
- 2 fully cooked sausages (about 10 oz. total)
- 1/4 cup mayonnaise
- 1 1/2 tablespoons Dijon mustard
- 1/4 cup balsamic vinegar
- 1/3 cup pitted black olives, coarsely chopped
- 1/4 cup minced parsley
  Salt and pepper

1. In a 6- to 8-quart pan over high heat, bring 3 quarts water to a boil. Add beans and cook until crisp-tender, 1 to 2 minutes. Remove beans from water with a slotted spoon or strainer and rinse under cold running water until cool. Return water to a boil. Add potatoes, reduce heat as necessary to maintain a simmer, and cook until potatoes are tender when pierced, 15 to 20 minutes. Drain.

2. Meanwhile, in a small bowl, mix olive oil and brown sugar. Place onion slices and sausages on a baking sheet and brush generously with brown sugar mixture. Broil 6 inches from heat until onions and sausages are lightly browned and onions are tender when pierced, 8 to 10 minutes. Let stand until cool enough to handle. Coarsely chop onion. Slice sausages 1/2 inch thick.

3. In a large bowl, combine beans, potatoes, onion, sausages, mayonnaise, mustard, vinegar, olives, and parsley. Mix gently to coat, adding salt and pepper to taste. Serve warm, or chill until cold, about 2 hours.

Per serving: 299 cal., 63% (189 cal.) from fat; 11 g protein; 21 g fat (5.2 g sat.); 19 g carbo (5.8 g fiber); 629 mg sodium; 33 mg chol.

Steamed Chicken with Black Bean Sauce

Sandra Machan, Newcastle, WA

Sandra Machan's kids love this simple chicken dish so much that she makes it once a week. Chinese salted fermented black beans are sold in Asian markets.

PREP AND COOK TIME: About 20 minutes, plus at least 30 minutes to chill

MAKES: 2 or 3 servings

- 1 pound boned, skinned chicken breasts
- 3 cloves garlic, peeled and minced
- 1 tablespoon cornstarch
- 1 tablespoon soy sauce
- 1 tablespoon oyster sauce
- 1 1/2 teaspoons sugar
- 1 teaspoon vegetable oil
- 1 tablespoon Chinese salted fermented black beans (see note above), rinsed, drained, and minced
- 1/4 teaspoon salt
- 3 cups hot cooked long-grain white rice

1. Rinse chicken and pat dry. Cut across the grain into 1/4-inch-thick slices. In a bowl, mix garlic, cornstarch, soy sauce, oyster sauce, sugar, oil, fermented black beans, and salt until well blended. Add chicken and turn to coat. Cover and chill 30 minutes.

2. Meanwhile, in an 8- to 10-quart pan or a 14-inch wok, set a rack over at least 1 inch of water. Bring to a boil over high heat. Pour chicken and marinade into a shallow, rimmed pan or a heatproof dish that fits into the larger pan and place on rack. Cover the larger pan and steam until chicken slices are opaque in the center (cut to test), about 10 minutes.

3. Carefully lift pan with chicken off rack. Spoon chicken mixture onto plates and serve rice alongside.

Per serving: 422 cal., 9% (37 cal.) from fat; 41 g protein; 4.1 g fat (0.8 g sat.); 52 g carbo (0.7 g fiber); 1,018 mg sodium; 88 mg chol. ◆

Apricots at the peak of their short season are frozen in pie-pan shape ready to pop into a pie crust anytime (see page 144).

July

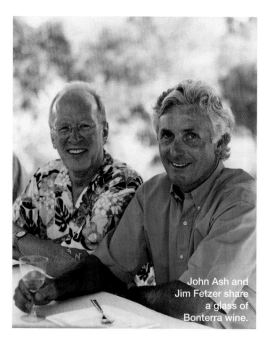

John Ash and Jim Fetzer share a glass of Bonterra wine.

A taste of Mendocino

We gathered visionaries from around the region for a delicious organic meal you can re-create at home

By Linda Lau Anusasananan • Photographs by James Carrier • Food styling by Karen Shinto

"Let's toast to a beautiful day and life," says Matthew Frey, raising his glass. One of 12 brothers and sisters who own Frey Vineyards in Mendocino County, Frey is speaking to fellow food and wine innovators who've gathered to taste the fruits of their labor in a sumptuous supper created by John Ash, culinary director of Fetzer and Bonterra Vineyards. There are salmon and seaweed from the coast; apples, pears, wild mushrooms, and nuts from the land; and wines that reflect the quality of the soil right here in the Bonterra vineyards.

This large, somewhat isolated Northern California county attracts environmentalists and independent thinkers. Frey offers a theory: "All the wild people went west. When

they hit the ocean, they went north." These adventurers made a difference. The Lolonis family, of Lolonis Winery, and Charlie Barra, owner of Barra of Mendocino, started growing grapes without chemical fertilizers and pesticides more than 50 years ago. The method became a movement when the Fetzer and Frey families started farming organically at their estate vineyards in the early 1980s.

"To me, Mendocino means being environmentally aware," says Eric Schramm of Mendocino Mushroom. Ash explains the mind-set: "What we consume has an impact on the whole planet, in how foods are grown, raised, harvested, and distributed. Ultimately, we are the stewards of the land and oceans." His menu, created from Mendocino's organic bounty, makes stewardship a pleasure.

Our guests: John Ash of Fetzer and Bonterra Vineyards, Bob Blue of Bonterra Vineyards, Patrick Cordrey of Oz Farm, Jim Fetzer of Ceago Vinegarden, Matthew Frey of Frey Vineyards, Sue Ellery of Stella Cadente Olive Oil Company, Katherine Roberts Marianchild of Rising Tide Sea Vegetables, Guinness McFadden of McFadden Farm, and Don Schmitt of the Apple Farm.

Sea palm fronds, harvested off the Mendocino coast (and available by mail), garnish soy-roasted salmon.

Party plan

Up to 5 days ahead:
Prepare agrodolce dressing.

Up to 2 days ahead:
Make mushroom pâté.

Up to 1 day ahead:
Bake apple-pear gratin.

Up to 6 hours ahead:
Prepare melon salad through step 3.

Up to 4 hours ahead:
Marinate salmon and prepare cucumbers through step 2.

About 1 hour ahead:
Remove mushroom pâté from refrigerator.

About 30 minutes ahead:
Arrange cherry tomatoes and olives in bowls; slice bread for dipping in olive oil.

About 10 minutes ahead:
Cook fish, dress the cucumbers and the melon salad, and garnish pâté.

About 15 minutes before dessert: Reheat apple-pear gratin if cold.

Mushroom Pâté

PREP AND COOK TIME: About 40 minutes

NOTES: A few dried mushrooms intensify the flavor of the fresh mushrooms in this pâté. If the shelled nuts aren't roasted, bake in a 350° oven until lightly browned, 8 to 10 minutes. You can prepare through step 4 up to 2 days ahead; cool, cover, and chill. Bring to room temperature before serving.

MAKES: 8 to 12 servings

- 1 to 2 ounces dried shiitake, morel, and/or porcini mushrooms (optional; see notes)
- 1 pound fresh shiitake, oyster, cremini, or common mushrooms
- ¼ cup (⅛ lb.) butter
- ½ cup chopped shallots
- 2 teaspoons chopped garlic
- 1½ teaspoons curry powder
- ½ teaspoon ground cumin
- 1 cup unsalted or salted roasted pistachios or almonds (see notes)
- 2 tablespoons extra-virgin olive oil
  - Salt and fresh-ground pepper
- 1 tablespoon minced parsley
  - Sliced baguettes (toasted if desired) or crackers

1. If using dried mushrooms, place in a bowl and cover with 2 cups hot water. Let stand until soft, 15 to 30 minutes. Squeeze mushrooms under water to release any grit, then lift out and rinse thoroughly under running water, gently rubbing to release any remaining grit; discard soaking water. If using shiitakes, trim off and discard tough stems; coarsely chop mushrooms.

Mushroom pâté

2. Meanwhile, rinse fresh mushrooms. If using shiitakes, trim off and discard tough stems. Coarsely chop mushrooms.

3. In a 5- to 6-quart pan over high heat, melt butter. Add fresh and soaked dried mushrooms, shallots, garlic, curry powder, and cumin; stir often until all liquid is evaporated and mixture is lightly browned, 6 to 8 minutes.

4. In a food processor, whirl nuts until finely ground. Add oil and whirl until mixture forms a paste. Add mushroom mixture and whirl until smooth. Add salt and pepper to taste. Mound in a bowl.

5. Sprinkle with parsley. Serve pâté with baguette slices or crackers.

Per serving: 130 cal., 76% (99 cal.) from fat; 3.3 g protein; 11 g fat (3.4 g sat.); 5.7 g carbo (0.6 g fiber); 86 mg sodium; 10 mg chol.

Melon and Goat Cheese Salad with Agrodolce Dressing

PREP AND COOK TIME: About 35 minutes

NOTES: Agrodolce is a sweet-tart Italian mixture of caramelized sugar and vinegar or wine. You can make the dressing up to 5 days ahead; cover airtight and chill. You can prepare the salad through step 3 up to 6 hours ahead; cover and chill. Store nuts airtight at room temperature.

MAKES: 8 servings

- ¾ cup walnut halves
- 1 ripe cantaloupe (about 3 lb.)
- 6 cups tender watercress sprigs (about 6 oz.) or bite-size pieces frisée, rinsed and crisped
- 2 cups huckleberries or blueberries, rinsed
  - Agrodolce dressing (recipe follows)
- 8 to 10 ounces fresh chèvre (goat cheese)
  - Fresh-ground pepper

1. Place walnuts in a 9-inch square or round pan and bake in a 350° regular or convection oven, shaking pan once, until golden brown under skins, about 10 minutes.

2. Meanwhile, cut peel off melon; scoop out and discard seeds. Cut melon into ½-inch-thick crescents.

3. On a large platter or on dinner or salad plates, arrange watercress, melon slices, and berries.

4. Shortly before serving, drizzle about half the agrodolce dressing over fruit on platter or 1 to 2 tablespoons over each serving. Cut chèvre into slices or break into chunks and distribute over salad. Sprinkle with toasted walnuts and pepper to taste. Offer remaining dressing to add to taste.

Per serving: 254 cal., 60% (153 cal.) from fat; 9 g protein; 17 g fat (6.8 g sat.); 18 g carbo (2.5 g fiber); 239 mg sodium; 22 mg chol.

Agrodolce dressing. Put 3 tablespoons **sugar** in a 1- to 1½-quart pan; shake pan often over high heat (do not stir) until sugar is liquefied and amber colored,

Drizzle melon and goat cheese salad with agrodolce, an Italian sweet-and-sour dressing.

ingredients—sake, mirin (sweet sake), onion or radish sprouts, and toasted sesame seeds—can be found in many well-stocked supermarkets and in Japanese grocery stores. If toasted sesame seeds aren't available, stir raw ones in a frying pan over medium heat until golden, about 5 minutes.

MAKES: 8 servings

- ½ **cup soy sauce**
- ½ **cup dry white wine or sake**
- ½ **cup cream sherry or mirin**
- ⅓ **cup chopped green onions**
- ⅓ **cup chopped fresh ginger**
- ¼ **cup sugar**
- 3 **pounds boned salmon fillet**
- 2 **lemons (4 oz. each), rinsed and thinly sliced (ends discarded)**
- 2 **tablespoons olive oil**
- 2 **ounces onion or radish sprouts (1 cup; optional)**

  About ⅛ ounce toasted dried tender sea palm fronds or California nori (optional; see notes)

- 1 **tablespoon toasted sesame seeds (see notes)**

  Crunchy cucumber salad (recipe on page 142)

1. In a 1- to 2-quart pan over high heat, stir soy sauce, wine, sherry, green onions, ginger, and sugar until boiling. Remove from heat and let cool to room temperature, stirring occasionally, about 25 minutes.

2. Meanwhile, with tweezers, pull out tiny pin bones from salmon. Rinse fish and cut into eight equal pieces; arrange in a single layer in a 9- by 13-inch baking dish.

3. Add lemons to cooled soy marinade and pour mixture evenly over fish. Cover and chill fish, turning pieces once, for 1 to 4 hours.

4. Lift fish from marinade and pat dry; discard marinade. Set a 12-inch nonstick ovenproof frying pan (or two 10-inch pans) over medium-high heat; add oil and tilt to coat. Set fish, skin side up, in pan(s) and cook until browned on the bottom, 4 to 5 minutes. With a wide spatula, turn pieces over. Place pan(s) in a 500° regular or convection oven. Bake just until fish is barely opaque but still moist in center of thickest part (cut to test), 3 to 5 minutes.

5. Transfer fish to a large platter or dinner plates. Just before serving, mound sprouts equally on each serving, sprinkle with sea palm fronds and toasted sesame seeds, and mound crunchy cucumber salad alongside salmon (or serve in a separate dish).

Per serving of salmon: 329 cal., 55% (180 cal.) from fat; 31 g protein; 20 g fat (3.9 g sat.); 3.6 g carbo (0.2 g fiber); 359 mg sodium; 90 mg chol.

about 3 minutes. Remove from heat and add ¾ cup **dry red wine** and 3 tablespoons **balsamic vinegar** (mixture will bubble vigorously and sugar will harden). Return to high heat and add 2 teaspoons minced **garlic**, ¾ teaspoon **black peppercorns**, ¾ teaspoon chopped **fresh** or dried **rosemary** leaves, and ½ teaspoon **salt**. Stir often until caramelized sugar melts again and mixture is reduced to about ¾ cup, about 5 minutes. Let stand for at least 2 hours. Pour through a fine strainer set over a small bowl. Whisk in 3 tablespoons **extra-virgin olive oil** and 2 teaspoons fresh **lime** juice. Makes about ¾ cup.

Per tablespoon: 55 cal., 58% (32 cal.) from fat; 0.1 g protein; 3.5 g fat (0.5 g sat.); 3.8 g carbo (0 g fiber); 98 mg sodium; 0 mg chol.

Soy-Roasted Salmon with Cucumbers

PREP AND COOK TIME: About 1 hour, plus at least 1 hour to marinate

NOTES: Toasted dried sea palm fronds—also called sea crunchies—are the leaves, or blades, of the sea palm, an ocean vegetable unique to Northern California, Oregon, and points farther north. The ribbed, noodlelike fronds turn crunchy-chewy when toasted. You can buy them in some natural-food stores and from Rising Tide Sea Vegetables *(www.loveseaweed.com or 707/964-5663).* Or you can substitute California nori: bake it in a 300° oven just until very crisp and slightly browned, 4 to 5 minutes. The other optional

Matthew Frey and
Sue Ellery share
an organic salad.

Locally grown apples and
pears covered with a
biscotti streusel make
a scrumptious dessert.

Crunchy Cucumber Salad

PREP TIME: About 15 minutes, plus at least
1 hour to drain

MAKES: 8 servings

- 2 **pounds English cucumbers**
- 1 **tablespoon kosher or sea salt**
- ½ **cup rice vinegar**
- 3 **tablespoons fresh lime juice**
- 1½ **tablespoons sugar**
- 1 **tablespoon Asian sesame oil**
- ¼ **teaspoon hot chili flakes**
- 1 **cup thinly slivered red onion**
- 1 **tablespoon toasted sesame seeds (see notes for soy-roasted salmon, page 141)**

1. Peel cucumbers, if desired. Cut in half
lengthwise, and with a spoon, scoop out and
discard seeds. Cut cucumbers diagonally into
¼-inch-thick slices.

2. Put cucumbers in a colander set over a
large bowl and mix with salt. Place a weight
over cucumbers (a 1-gal. zip-lock plastic bag
filled with water works well). Cover and chill at
least 1 hour or up to 4 hours. Discard liquid.

3. In a bowl, whisk vinegar, lime juice, sugar,
sesame oil, and chili flakes until well blended.
Mix in drained cucumbers and the slivered
onion. Sprinkle salad with the toasted
sesame seeds.

Per serving: 53 cal., 38% (20 cal.) from fat; 1.8 g
protein; 2.2 g fat (0.3 g sat.); 7.7 g carbo (1.8 g fiber);
247 mg sodium; 0 mg chol.

Apple-Pear Gratin

PREP AND COOK TIME: About 1¼ hours

NOTES: You can make this gratin up to 1 day
ahead; cool, cover, and chill. Reheat, uncovered, in a 350° oven until warm, about 15
minutes.

MAKES: 8 servings

- 1½ **pounds Golden Delicious apples**
- 1½ **pounds firm-ripe Bartlett or Comice pears**
- 1 **lemon (about 6 oz.), rinsed**
- ½ **cup sugar**
- ¼ **cup dried currants**
- 2 **tablespoons rum (optional)**
- 5 **to 6 ounces anise or almond biscotti or shortbread cookies**
- 1 **tablespoon melted butter**
- 1 **teaspoon ground cinnamon**
- ⅔ **cup whipping cream**

  Vanilla ice cream or slightly sweetened softly whipped cream

1. Peel and core apples and pears. Cut fruit
lengthwise into about ½-inch-thick wedges;
place in a large bowl.

2. Grate peel (yellow part only) from lemon,
then ream juice. Add peel and juice to apples
and pears, along with sugar, currants, and
rum; mix gently. Pour into a shallow 2- to 2½-
quart baking dish.

3. Place biscotti in a 1-quart zip-lock plastic
bag and crush lightly with a rolling pin to make
1½ cups coarse crumbs; pour into a small
bowl. Add butter and cinnamon and mix.
Sprinkle crumb mixture evenly over fruit. Pour
cream evenly over topping.

4. Bake in a 375° regular or convection oven
until fruit is tender when pierced and crumb
topping is browned, 30 to 40 minutes. Let
gratin cool at least 10 minutes; serve warm or
cool. Scoop onto plates or bowls and top with
ice cream.

Per serving: 301 cal., 30% (89 cal.) from fat;
3 g protein; 9.9 g fat (4.8 g sat.); 55 g carbo
(5 g fiber); 82 mg sodium; 35 mg chol.

Mendocino for food lovers

Of the restaurants listed, only the Ukiah Brewing Co. & Restaurant is certified 100 percent organic (a complicated goal for a commercial kitchen). We've included other favorites that strongly emphasize organic foods and support local farmers. Reservations are advised. For more information, visit *www.gomendo.com* or call *(866) 466-3636*.

$: average dinner entrées less than $10   **$$:** $10–$20   **$$$:** $20–$30
B=breakfast   **L**=lunch   **D**=dinner

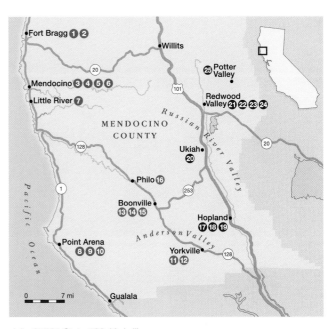

Coastal region

1 Café 1. Sixties-era vegetarian meals served with all the comforts of an old-time diner. *Open daily (B, L; D Thu–Sat only; $$). 753 N. Main St., Fort Bragg; (707) 964-3309.*

2 Mendo Bistro. Try the crab cakes at this casual local favorite. *Open daily (D; $$). 301 N. Main, Fort Bragg; (707) 964-4974.*

3 Cafe Beaujolais. Inventive dinners in a cozy Victorian. Buy brick-oven breads 11–4:30. *Restaurant open daily (D; $$$). 961 Ukiah St., Mendocino; (707) 937-5614.*

4 MacCallum House Restaurant. Housed in an 1882 inn, this restaurant excels in North Coast cuisine. Casual, less expensive plates in the Grey Whale Bar & Café. *Open daily (D; $$$). 45020 Albion St., Mendocino; (800) 609-0492.*

5 Moosse Café. Regional ingredients with an Asian twist in this stylish but casual cafe. *Open daily (L, D; $$). 390 Kasten St., Mendocino; (707) 937-4323.*

6 The Ravens at Stanford Inn by the Sea. Vegetarian restaurant serves creative dishes with produce from its certified organic garden. *Open daily (B, D; $$$). 44850 Comptche-Ukiah Rd. at State 1, Mendocino; (800) 331-8884.*

7 Edge of the Earth. Tiny restaurant with ocean views serves sustainably caught seafood and vegetarian cuisine. *Open Wed–Sun (D; $$). 7750 State 1 N. (next to post office), Little River; (707) 937-1970.*

8 Pangaea. Warm, colorful restaurant serves soulful food from around the world. *Open Wed–Sun (D; $$$). 250 Main St. (State 1), Point Arena; (707) 882-3001.*

9 The Record. Market-deli in a historic newspaper building offers organic goods and sandwiches made with house-roasted meats. *Open daily (B, L; $). 265 Main (State 1), Point Arena; (707) 882-3663.*

10 Oz Farm. Certified organic since 1991, this quiet farm on the Garcia River grows heirloom apples and pears as well as vegetables. *Tours by appointment. Point Arena; (707) 882-3046.*

Anderson Valley/ Yorkville Highlands

11 Le Vin Vineyards. Get a view of the highlands from this hilltop vineyard that produces organic Cabernet and Merlot. *Tours, tasting by appointment. Yorkville; (707) 894-2304.*

12 Yorkville Vineyards and Cellars. Certified organic vineyards produce Bordeaux varieties. *Open daily. 25701 State 128, Yorkville; (707) 894-9177.*

13 Boonville Hotel Restaurant. Craftsman-style roadhouse with restaurant, bar, and lodging. Simple but sophisticated dishes from organic-garden produce. *Call for summer hours ($$$); bar open daily. State 128 at Lambert Lane, Boonville; (707) 895-2210.*

14 Boonville General Store. Deli-cafe serves good salads, pizzas, and sandwiches on house-baked breads. *Closed Wed (B, L; $). State 128, Boonville; (707) 895-9477.*

15 Stella Cadente Olive Oil Company. Bring bottles to fill with olive oil, available for bargain prices at the 3 Wineries Tasting Room. *State 128, across from the Boonville Hotel, Boonville; (707) 895-2848.*

16 The Apple Farm. Heirloom apples, cider, apple-balsamic vinegar, chutney, and apricot jam at a picturesque farm stand. *Open daily. 18501 Greenwood Rd., Philo; (707) 895-2333.*

Russian River Valley

17 Hopland Inn. Victorian inn serves hearty, rustic dishes. *5:30–9 Sun–Tue and 5:30–10 Fri–Sat (D; $$$). 13401 U.S. 101, Hopland; (707) 744-1890.*

18 Bonterra Vineyards. Organic Bonterra wines are available for tasting at Fetzer. Tour the 5-acre organic garden. B&B on site. *Open daily. Fetzer Vineyards, 13601 East Side Rd., Hopland; (707) 744-1250.*

19 Jeriko Estate. Taste organic, estate-grown Chardonnay and Pinot Noir in this large, beautiful new winery. *Open daily. 12141 Hewlitt & Sturtevant Rd., 1 mile north of Hopland; (707) 744-1140.*

20 Ukiah Brewing Co. & Restaurant. The nation's first certified organic brew pub and second organic restaurant serves great hamburgers and beer, along with more creative fare. *Open daily (L, D; $$). 102 S. State St., Ukiah; (707) 468-5898.*

21 Barra of Mendocino at Redwood Valley Cellars. Taste Charlie Barra's interesting Pinot Blanc and Pinot Noir in Redwood Valley Cellars' spacious tasting room. *Open daily. 7051 N. State St., Redwood Valley; (707) 485-0322.*

22 Fife Vineyards. Organic, estate-grown grapes are used in the delicious Zinfandel and Petite Sirah. Spectacular view of Lake Mendocino from picnic tables behind tasting room. *Open daily. 3621 Ricetti Lane, Redwood Valley; (707) 485-0323.*

23 Frey Vineyards. Sulfite-free organic and biodynamic wines. *Tours and tasting by appointment. Redwood Valley; (707) 485-5177.*

24 Lolonis Winery. Catch a ladybug at these vineyards, organic since 1956. *Tours, tasting by appointment. Redwood Valley; (925) 938-8066.*

25 McFadden Farm. Pastoral farm grows herbs, garlic, and grapes. *Tours by appointment. Potter Valley; (800) 544-8230.* ◆

Visit wineries, farms, and restaurants to sample organic Mendocino.

Freeze-ahead apricot pie filling

◀ From freezer to oven

To bake the pie, unwrap frozen filling and place in a 9-inch pie pan lined with an unbaked crust; cover with top crust, crimp edges to seal, and cut small slits in top to vent. Place on a foil-lined baking sheet. Bake pie in a 375° regular or convection oven until top crust is browned and filling is bubbling in the center, $1\frac{1}{4}$ to $1\frac{1}{2}$ hours. (If crust gets too brown before filling is bubbling, cover edges loosely with foil.)

If baking a fresh pie, after mixing filling in step 2, pour directly into unbaked pastry, cover, crimp, and slit. Bake for about 1 hour.

Summer pie, anytime

Like Christmas, apricot season comes but once a year—and it's over about as quickly as Christmas morning. But that season is intense. A corner of my father's almond orchard in California's Central Valley has always been reserved for fruit trees, so every summer we were overwhelmed with stone fruit. In spite of valiant efforts, we just couldn't eat it fast enough.

My mother didn't want to let the fruit go to waste, so she made the apricots into pie filling and froze it. *Sunset* test kitchen manager Bernadette Hart adds the extra tip of freezing the filling in the shape of the pan so it can be dropped right from the freezer into a pastry shell and baked.

Now that I live in San Francisco, I'm no longer troubled by an excess of perfectly ripe summer fruit; I buy it at a farmers' market. But for me, there's no better dessert than apricot pie, with its slightly bitter edge, so I still freeze a couple of fillings every summer, just to have that bittersweet pleasure anytime I like.

Make-Ahead Fruit Pie Filling

PREP TIME: About 20 minutes, plus $1\frac{1}{4}$ hours to bake pie (see above right)

NOTES: To thicken this filling, use a basic ratio of 1 tablespoon of flour for every 2 cups of apricots. Peaches and plums may be juicier; for very juicy fruit, increase flour to up to 1 tablespoon per cup of fruit.

MAKES: Filling for one 9-inch pie

3 pounds firm-ripe apricots, peaches, or plums

About ½ cup sugar

About ¼ cup all-purpose flour

1 tablespoon lemon juice

½ teaspoon ground cinnamon or mace

¼ teaspoon salt

1. Cut each of the apricots lengthwise into quarters (sixths if they're very large), discarding pits. (If using peaches, peel them and cut into thin wedges. If using plums, cut fruit into ½-inch slices.) You should have about 8 cups fruit total.

2. In a large bowl, gently mix fruit, ½ cup sugar, ¼ cup flour (see notes), lemon juice, cinnamon, and salt. Taste fruit and add more sugar if desired (up to ¾ cup total).

3. Line a 9-inch pie pan with a 20-inch-long sheet of foil (there should be about 5 inches of overhang on each side of the pan). Line the foil with a 20-inch-long piece of plastic wrap. Pour fruit into plastic wrap; pull edges together and fold over to seal, then repeat to seal foil over plastic. Freeze up to 3 months, removing from pie pan, if desired, after filling is hard, in about 8 hours.

Per serving of double-crust apricot pie: 296 cal., 33% (99 cal.) from fat; 2.1 g protein; 11 g fat (4.6 g sat.); 47 g carbo (1.8 g fiber); 213 mg sodium; 7.7 mg chol.

—*Kate Washington*

Summer entertaining

Great party ideas from around the world feel at home in the West

Grapefruit Margaritas

PREP TIME: About 5 minutes

MAKES: 1½ quarts; 6 to 8 servings

In a pitcher (at least 2-qt. capacity), combine 3 cups **ruby grapefruit juice** (fresh-squeezed or purchased), 2 cups **tequila,** and 1 cup **triple sec** or other orange-flavored liqueur. Chill until cold, at least 1 hour, or up to 1 day. Pour about ¼ cup **sugar** on a rimmed plate. Cut a **ruby grapefruit** in half and rub rims of double old-fashioned glasses (8 oz.) with cut side of one half to moisten, then dip glass rims in sugar to coat. Fill glasses with **ice cubes.** Pour grapefruit margaritas over ice, taking care not to disturb sugared glass rims.

—Kate Washington

I t doesn't take much to turn a gathering into an event. A simple new drink—like the ruby grapefruit margarita here—does the trick. Just moving the main course outdoors to the grill gets the party started too, as cooks all over the world know. For this special section, we drew on global grilling savvy for menus built around an easy beef brisket from Chile, robata-yaki from Japan, and a couple of gourmet burgers from our own backyards. They all make for superb entertainment. *—Sara Schneider*

In this section

Chilean picnic for 6 to 8

Chicken and Cheese Empanadas

Grilled Salted Beef Brisket or Flank Steak

Sweet Corn and Onion Salad

Petite Peas with Greens

Avocado, Tomato, and Romaine Salad

Country-style Hearth-baked Breads

Chilean Sauvignon Blanc and Cabernet Sauvignon

Sliced-Fruit Platter: Pineapple, Oranges, Apples, Pepinos, and Grapes Splashed with Orange Liqueur

Barbecue, Chilean style

Slow-cooked on your backyard grill, beef brisket makes an easy entrée

By Jerry Anne Di Vecchio • Photographs by James Carrier • Food styling by Susan Devaty

I went to Chile to taste wines, and fell in love with the gracious tradition of dining in the vineyards. We set out one sunny morning on horseback through the Sauvignon Blanc and Cabernet Sauvignon grapes. Just as the heat of the day peaked, we came to a shady eucalyptus grove, where wisps of smoke hinted at cooking.

On a barbecue grill, plump empanadas were heating; on a spit surrounded by low coals, slabs of fresh brisket were turning; and a nearby table was laden with light vegetable salads, crusty breads, and a platter of local fruit, including pale green, purple-streaked pepinos—a South American relative of tomatoes, available at specialty markets here. The

setting itself was a relative of our own wine country; the meal would be perfectly at home in the West.

It was so simple and laced with make-ahead possibilities that I've added it to my roster of easy-entertaining menus. The brisket, a cut of beef we usually braise for tenderness, yields firm but juicy, flavorful slices when cooked over very low heat on a gas barbecue. Or, for quick results, grill flank steak instead. Allow about 1 cup of sliced fruit per person for dessert. As for wines, I recommend the Sauvignon Blanc and Cabernet Sauvignon from those vineyards we traversed, owned by the Undurraga family, who have been making wine for more than 100 years. Their wines are available in some wine shops here.

Creamy chicken- and cheese-filled empanadas and a glass of Sauvignon Blanc keep guests happy while the brisket finishes on the grill. Add some sweet red onion slices for the last few minutes to garnish the beef (opposite).

Chicken and Cheese Empanadas

PREP AND COOK TIME: About 45 minutes

NOTES: You can make the filling for these appetizer pastries (through step 2) up to 1 day before using; cover and chill. You can make the empanadas up to 1 day before serving; let cool, wrap airtight, and chill. Unwrap and reheat on a baking sheet in a 325° oven for 20 minutes.

MAKES: 6 or 8 empanadas

- 1½ **cups coarsely chopped cooked boned, skinned chicken**
- ½ **cup shredded Swiss cheese**
- 2 **tablespoons drained chopped pimientos (2-oz. jar) or chopped roasted red peppers**
- 2 **tablespoons minced onion**
- ½ **teaspoon pepper**
- ½ **cup fat-skimmed chicken broth**
- 1 **tablespoon cornstarch**
- 1 **package (3 oz.) cream cheese, cut into small chunks**
-    **Salt**
- 2 **packages (10 oz. each) refrigerated pizza crust dough**
- 1 **large egg**

1. In a bowl, mix chicken with Swiss cheese, pimientos, onion, and pepper.

2. In a 1½- to 2-quart pan, mix broth with cornstarch. Add cream cheese. Whisk over high heat until mixture is boiling (it will be very thick), 2 to 3 minutes. Scrape over chicken mixture and combine well, adding salt to taste.

3. On a lightly floured board, unroll pizza crust dough. Cut each rectangle crosswise into thirds, for six empanadas, or quarters, for eight pastries. On one end of each piece of dough, mound about 5 tablespoons chicken mixture if making six pastries, about 3 tablespoons for eight. Fold other end of dough over filling to form a rectangle, then fold edges together and pinch to seal.

4. Gently place empanadas, slightly apart, on an oiled 12- by 15-inch baking sheet (you'll need two for eight pastries). In a small bowl, beat egg to blend. Brush generously over each pastry.

5. Bake in a 375° regular or convection

Simple sides—like a salad of avocados, tomatoes, and romaine lettuce—set off the grilled brisket best.

oven until empanadas are very richly browned, 22 to 25 minutes (10 to 12 in convection oven). Transfer to a rack and let cool at least 10 minutes. Serve hot or warm.

Per empanada: 295 cal., 28% (82 cal.) from fat; 19 g protein; 9.1 g fat (4 g sat.); 35 g carbo (1.1 g fiber); 773 mg sodium; 67 mg chol.

Grilled Salted Beef Brisket or Flank Steak

PREP AND COOK TIME: About 5 hours for brisket, 15 minutes for flank steak, plus at least 2 hours to chill in salt

NOTES: A gas barbecue works best to maintain low, even heat to slow-cook the brisket, but for the flank steak use either gas or charcoal. One side of the brisket should be trimmed of all fat, the other side covered with a layer no more than ⅛ inch thick.

MAKES: 8 servings

- 1 **rectangular piece fresh beef brisket (2½ to 3 lb., max. 1½ in. thick; see notes) or 2 beef flank steaks (2½ to 3 lb. total)**
- 2 **tablespoons kosher or coarse salt**
- 2 **tablespoons olive oil**

1. Rinse meat and rub salt evenly onto all sides. Cover and chill for 2 to 3 hours. Rinse meat well and pat dry. Rub all over with oil.

2. *To cook brisket,* turn a gas grill to high, close lid, and heat for 10 minutes. Turn off all but one perimeter burner and reduce heat to medium or low to maintain a temperature of 225° to 250° (check with a grill thermometer or external barbecue thermometer, and open lid as needed to let temperature drop during cooking). Lay brisket, fat side down, on grill as far from flame as possible. Close lid and cook, turning brisket about every 1½ hours, until meat pierces easily with a sharp knife (it will be firm but not hard) and is lightly browned, 5 to 5½ hours total.

To cook flank steak, lay meat on a barbecue grill over a solid bed of hot coals or direct high heat on a gas grill (you can hold your hand at grill level only 2 to 3 seconds); close lid if using a gas grill. Cook, turning once, until flank steaks are done to your liking (cut to test), 7 to 9 minutes total for medium-rare.

3. Transfer meat to a platter and let stand at least 5 minutes. Cut into thin slices.

Per serving of flank steak: 265 cal., 54% (144 cal.) from fat; 27 g protein; 16 g fat (6 g sat.); 0 g carbo; 329 mg sodium; 71 mg chol.

Sweet Corn and Onion Salad

PREP AND COOK TIME: About 15 minutes

NOTES: You can make this simple salad up to 1 day ahead; cover and chill. Sprinkle it with chopped chives and thin slivers of lemon peel for garnish.

MAKES: 6 to 8 servings

- 1 cup finely chopped onion
- 3 tablespoons vegetable oil
- 6 cups corn kernels (fresh or frozen)
- ½ cup fat-skimmed chicken broth
- ¼ cup lemon juice
- 2 teaspoons sugar
  Salt and pepper

1. In a 10- to 12-inch frying pan over medium-high heat, stir chopped onion in oil until lightly browned, 3 to 5 minutes.

2. Add corn and broth; stir until liquid is evaporated, 8 to 9 minutes. Pour into a bowl and add lemon juice, sugar, and salt and pepper to taste. Serve warm or cool.

Per serving: 160 cal., 37% (59 cal.) from fat; 4.5 g protein; 6.5 g fat (0.8 g sat.); 25 g carbo (4 g fiber); 24 mg sodium; 0 mg chol.

Petite Peas with Greens

PREP TIME: 7 to 8 minutes

MAKES: 6 to 8 servings

- ¼ cup sour cream
- 2 tablespoons mayonnaise
- 1 tablespoon white wine vinegar
- 2 cups frozen petite peas, thawed
- 2 cups finely slivered romaine lettuce leaves
  Salt and pepper

1. In a small bowl, mix sour cream, mayonnaise, and vinegar.

2. In a bowl, mix peas and lettuce. Stir dressing into vegetables and add salt and pepper to taste.

Per serving: 75 cal., 53% (40 cal.) from fat; 2.8 g protein; 4.4 g fat (1.4 g sat.); 6.4 g carbo (3 g fiber); 87 mg sodium; 5.2 mg chol.

Avocado, Tomato, and Romaine Salad

PREP TIME: About 15 minutes

NOTES: You can assemble this salad (step 1) and make the dressing (step 2) up to 4 hours ahead. Cover salad and chill; cover dressing and let stand at room temperature.

MAKES: 6 to 8 servings

- 1 firm-ripe avocado (8 oz.), pitted and peeled
  About 3 tablespoons sherry vinegar or balsamic vinegar
- 4 cups bite-size pieces romaine lettuce leaves
- 1 tomato (9 to 10 oz.), rinsed, cored, peeled (if desired), and cut into wedges
- 3 tablespoons extra-virgin olive oil
  About ½ teaspoon salt
  Pepper

1. Thinly slice avocado and arrange slices along one side of a wide, shallow bowl; brush lightly with vinegar. Mound lettuce in center of bowl, and arrange tomatoes opposite the avocado.

2. In a small bowl, mix 3 tablespoons vinegar, olive oil, and ½ teaspoon salt.

3. Pour dressing over salad; mix gently at the table, adding pepper and more salt to taste.

Per serving: 91 cal., 85% (77 cal.) from fat; 1.1 g protein; 8.6 g fat (1.3 g sat.); 4.1 g carbo (1.3 g fiber); 152 mg sodium; 0 mg chol. ◆

Serve vegetables in the form of cool salads for this midsummer meal.

Purchased mochi ice cream is an easy dessert.

Let guests pile their plates with an assortment of grilled skewers and cool soba salad.

Party tips

• **Allow about ½ pound of chicken or seafood** per person, plus about ¼ pound of vegetables. This menu serves 6 to 8 guests, but it adjusts easily to accommodate more.

• **Soak 12-inch wood skewers** in water for 10 minutes before threading.

• **Make the sauces and salads in advance;** chill until serving. You can also thread meat and vegetables on skewers several hours ahead; chill them until ready to grill.

• **Set out several bowls** or ramekins for the dipping sauces. Guests can dip or spoon sauces onto their plates. Alternatively, give each guest a few small, shallow bowls.

• **Arrange grilled skewers** on platters; let guests help themselves.

• **Purchase mochi ice-cream balls** at specialty food stores or Asian markets; buy about two whole ones per person. Just before serving, cut them in half and arrange on a platter with toothpicks.

Japanese grill party

Entertain outdoors with an easy robata-yaki menu

By Charity Ferreira • Photographs by James Carrier • Food styling by Karen Shinto

Robata-yaki, or Japanese barbecue, is perfect for warm-weather entertaining—it's simple, fresh, and meant to be shared with friends along with sake and cold beer.

"Robata-yaki originated in seaside villages in Japan, when fishermen would grill the catch of the day on the boat," says Vernon Cardenas, executive chef at Katana in Los Angeles, a restaurant specializing in Japanese barbecue. Cardenas grills meat, seafood, and vegetable skewers served with flavorful dipping sauces.

Our flexible robata-yaki menu accompanies three of Katana's sauces. Serve ponzu with skewers of seafood, ginger sauce with vegetables, and mustard sauce with chicken, or let guests mix and match. Round out the menu with edamame and spinach and noodle salads. Mochi ice-cream balls—scoops of ice cream thinly covered with chewy pounded-rice dough—make a perfect handheld dessert.

Boiled, salted soybeans slip easily from their pods for an irresistible appetizer.

Boiled Edamame

PREP AND COOK TIME: About 10 minutes

MAKES: 6 to 8 servings

In a 5- to 6-quart pan over high heat, bring about 3 quarts water and 1 teaspoon **salt** to a boil. Add 2 pounds **frozen soybeans in pods** and cook until beans inside pods are tender to bite (break a pod open to test), about 5 minutes. Drain and sprinkle with additional salt to taste. Serve warm or cover and chill up to 4 hours.

Per serving: 13 cal., 92% (12 cal.) from fat; 9.4 g protein; 1.3 g fat (0 g sat.); 9.4 g carbo (6.7 g fiber); 145 mg sodium; 0 mg chol.

Grilled Seafood or Chicken Skewers

PREP AND COOK TIME: About 30 to 45 minutes

MAKES: 6 to 8 servings

1. Rinse 3 to 4 pounds of any combination of the following: **boned, skinned salmon; albacore tuna fillet; boned, skinned chicken breast halves; peeled, deveined shrimp** (20 to 30 per pound); and/or **sea scallops** (about 1 in. wide). Pat dry.

2. Cut salmon or albacore against the grain into ½-inch-wide strips. Cut chicken lengthwise into 1-inch-wide, ½-inch-thick strips. Use a small sharp knife to butterfly shrimp: cut lengthwise along back of shrimp, stopping before you cut all the way through, then spread apart to flatten.

3. Thread one strip of fish or chicken, two scallops, or one shrimp onto each soaked 12-inch wood skewer. Brush lightly with **Asian sesame oil** or vegetable oil.

4. Place on a lightly oiled grill over a solid bed of hot coals or high heat on a gas grill (you can hold your hand at grill level only 2 to 3 seconds); close lid on gas grill. Cook, turning once, until seafood is opaque but still moist-looking in center of thickest part or chicken is no longer pink in the center (cut to test), about 5 minutes for tuna, chicken, and shrimp, 8 to 10 minutes for salmon and scallops. Serve warm with **mustard, ginger,** or **ponzu dipping sauce.**

Per 1-ounce salmon skewer: 59 cal., 59% (35 cal.) from fat; 5.6 g protein; 3.9 g fat (0.7 g sat.); 0 g carbo; 17 mg sodium; 17 mg chol.

Grilled Vegetable Skewers

PREP AND COOK TIME: About 30 to 45 minutes

MAKES: 6 to 8 servings

1. Rinse 1½ pounds **fresh shiitake mushrooms** (2 to 3 in. wide) *or* **Asian eggplant,** or a combination of both. Remove tough stems from shiitakes. Slice eggplant in half crosswise; cut each piece in half lengthwise.

2. If using eggplant, place a rack over about 1 inch water in a 6- to 8-quart pan. Pile eggplant on rack, bring water to a boil over high heat, cover, and steam eggplant until soft, about 5 minutes. Let stand until cool enough to handle.

3. Thread two or three mushrooms (horizontally through cap) or one piece eggplant onto each soaked 12-inch wood skewer. Brush

Dipping sauces

Ginger. In a blender or food processor, whirl ¼ cup coarsely chopped **white onion,** ½ cup peeled, coarsely chopped **ginger,** and ⅓ cup peeled, coarsely chopped **sweet apple** (such as Red Delicious), scraping sides of bowl as necessary, until smooth. Add ¾ cup **soy sauce,** 6 tablespoons **rice vinegar,** 1½ tablespoons **Asian sesame oil,** and ¼ cup sugar. Whirl until smooth. Serve immediately or cover and chill up to 1 week. Whisk before serving. Makes about 2 cups.

Mustard. In a blender, whirl ¾ cup **soy sauce,** 2 tablespoons **water,** ¼ cup **dry mustard,** ¼ cup **toasted sesame seeds,** and ¼ cup **sugar** until smooth. Stir in an additional ¼ cup **toasted sesame seeds.** Serve immediately or cover and chill up to 1 week. Whisk before serving. Makes about 1⅓ cups.

Ponzu. In a 2- to 3-quart pan over high heat, bring to a boil ½ cup **sake** or dry white wine, ½ cup **mirin** (sweet rice wine; available in supermarkets), ½ cup **soy sauce,** ½ cup **rice vinegar,** and ¼ cup **dried bonito flakes** (optional; see notes for cold soba noodle salad, page 152; if omitting bonito flakes, combine all other ingredients in a bowl and chill. Lower heat and simmer 15 minutes. Strain and chill until cold, about 1 hour. Stir in 3 tablespoons **lemon juice.** Serve immediately or cover and chill up to 1 week. Makes 2 cups.

Sesame seeds garnish a bundle of lightly dressed spinach.

½ cup minced green onions

¼ cup dried bonito flakes (optional; see notes)

1. In a 5- to 6-quart pan over high heat, bring about 3 quarts water to a boil. Add noodles and cook until tender to bite, 3 to 6 minutes. Drain noodles and rinse gently under cold running water until cool.

2. Meanwhile, in a large bowl, mix rice vinegar, soy sauce, sesame oil, and wasabi. Pour about half the dressing into a small bowl and reserve. Add noodles to the large bowl; mix to coat. Cover and chill until cold, about 1 hour, or up to 4 hours.

3. Just before serving, add reserved dressing to noodles and mix to coat. Sprinkle salad with green onions and bonito flakes, if using.

Per serving: 302 cal., 15% (46 cal.) from fat; 11 g protein; 5.1 g fat (0.7 g sat.); 58 g carbo (0.2 g fiber); 1,135 mg sodium; 0 mg chol.

Sesame Spinach Salad

PREP AND COOK TIME: About 25 minutes

MAKES: 6 servings

1½ pounds spinach, stemmed and rinsed well

¼ cup sake or dry white wine

2 tablespoons soy sauce

2 teaspoons sugar

2 teaspoons Asian sesame oil

2 tablespoons toasted sesame seeds

1. In a 5- to 6-quart pan over high heat, bring about 3 quarts water to a boil. Add half the spinach and cook until wilted, 1 to 2 minutes. Remove spinach from water with a strainer and place in a large bowl of ice water until cool; lift out and drain. Repeat process to cook and cool remaining spinach.

2. In a large bowl, mix sake, soy sauce, sugar, and sesame oil.

3. Squeeze or roll spinach tightly in a kitchen towel to remove as much water as possible. Place in bowl and mix with dressing to coat. If making salad ahead, cover and chill up to 4 hours.

4. Divide spinach into six cylindrical bundles and squeeze each tightly to compact the leaves. Arrange bundles on a serving plate or in individual small, shallow bowls. Spoon a little of the dressing left in the bowl over each bundle. Sprinkle each bundle with about 1 teaspoon sesame seeds.

Per serving: 62 cal., 45% (28 cal.) from fat; 3.1 g protein; 3.1 g fat (0.4 g sat.); 5.5 g carbo (2.6 g fiber); 409 mg sodium; 0 mg chol. ◆

Choosing sake

Premium sake is served chilled—never warm—to allow its subtle flavors to be appreciated. Sake is brewed in many styles, ranging from light and fragrant to smoky and full bodied. Among light, dry sakes, we liked **Hakusan** and **Sho Chiku Bai Premium Ginjo Sake**. We liked **Momokawa Diamond Junmai Ginjo Medium Dry** as a medium-bodied sake. Plan to spend between $10 and $20 for a good-quality domestic sake, more for an import.

Many brands are sold in 1.5-liter bottles—perfect for a party. If the bottle has a date, buy sake that is less than a year old. Shop for sake at an Asian market or a well-stocked wine store, or buy online at *www.sakeone.com,* which offers detailed sake descriptions.

vegetables lightly with **Asian sesame oil** or vegetable oil.

4. Place on a lightly oiled grill over a solid bed of medium-hot coals or medium heat on a gas grill (you can hold your hand at grill level only 3 to 4 seconds); close lid on gas grill. Cook, turning once, until tender when pierced, 6 to 8 minutes. Serve with **ginger** or **ponzu dipping sauce.**

Per skewer of shiitakes: 15 cal., 60% (9 cal.) from fat; 0.7 g protein; 1 g fat (0.1 g sat.); 1.4 g carbo (0.3 g fiber); 0 mg sodium; 0 mg chol.

Cold Soba Noodle Salad

PREP AND COOK TIME: About 25 minutes, plus at least 1 hour to chill

NOTES: Soba (Japanese buckwheat) noodles and powdered wasabi are available in the Asian food section of well-stocked supermarkets as well as in Asian markets; bonito flakes are available in Asian markets.

MAKES: 6 servings

1 pound soba noodles (see notes)

¼ cup rice vinegar

3 tablespoons soy sauce

2 tablespoons Asian sesame oil

1 tablespoon powdered wasabi (see notes)

Mixed grill

Offer a pair of burgers for a laid-back summer party that fits every taste

By Jerry Anne Di Vecchio
Photographs by James Carrier

Burgers are the perfect solution for casual entertaining: easy, quick to cook, and beloved by almost everyone. But now that more diners are steering clear of red meat, you might not want to offer beef alone. This relaxed party menu gives you a delicious option: a savory salmon burger and a classic ground-beef burger with bacon will satisfy a wide range of guests' tastes.

Both burger mixtures, and their accoutrements, can be made a day in advance. While the grill heats up and the burgers sizzle, set out the homemade condiments and the other usual suspects for embellishment: ketchup, mustard, mayonnaise, tomatoes, onions, and pickles. Add a big green salad and the party is ready to go. For dessert, what could be better than ice cream sundaes? For sundae recipes, see page 155.

Ground salmon makes a light, delicate burger; left, offer an array of condiments to top different burgers.

Double Salmon Burgers

PREP AND COOK TIME: About 35 minutes
MAKES: 4 servings

- 1 pound boned, skinned salmon fillet
- 6 tablespoons fat-skimmed chicken broth or vegetable broth
- ¼ cup fine dried bread crumbs
- 1 tablespoon chopped fresh dill or 1 teaspoon dried dill weed
- ½ teaspoon salt
- 1 large egg
  Vegetable or olive oil
- 4 soft potato rolls or English muffins (4 in. wide), cut in half horizontally
- 4 to 6 tablespoons smoked salmon cream cheese spread
  Butter lettuce leaves, rinsed and crisped
  Cucumber–hearts of palm relish (see "Burger Condiments," page 154)

1. Rinse salmon and pat dry; cut into ½-inch chunks. Pulse several times in a food processor to coarsely grind, scraping down sides once or twice. In a bowl with a fork, mix ground salmon with broth, bread crumbs, dill, salt, and egg until thoroughly blended.

2. Make four foil strips 5 to 6 inches wide by 10 inches long. Fold each strip to form 5- to 6-inch squares, then fold in edges to seal layers. Coat one side of each foil square with vegetable oil. Divide salmon mixture into four equal portions, place a portion on oiled side of each foil square, and shape each into an evenly thick 4-inch-wide round. If making ahead, lay patties (on foil) in a single layer on a plate, cover airtight, and chill up to 1 day.

3. Place salmon patties, still on foil squares, on a barbecue grill over a solid bed of medium coals or medium heat on a gas grill (you can hold your hand at grill level only 4 to 5 seconds); cover barbecue and open vents. Cook patties without turning, until firm when pressed and pale pink in the center (cut to test), about 10 minutes. When patties are almost done, lay rolls, cut side down, on grill and toast until golden, 1 to 2 minutes.

4. Spread the toasted side of each bun half with smoked salmon cream

Burger condiments

Cucumber–hearts of palm relish. In a bowl, combine ½ cup diced (¼ in.) seeded **English cucumber**, ½ cup thinly sliced **canned hearts of palm**, ¼ cup **rice vinegar**, 2 tablespoons chopped **green onions** (including green tops), 2 teaspoons **sugar**, and ½ teaspoon **salt** (or to taste). Mix and let stand at least 5 minutes or cover and chill up to 1 day. Serve with a slotted spoon. Makes about 1 cup.

Horseradish slaw. In a blender or in a bowl with a fork, mix ¼ cup **cream cheese** or Neufchâtel (light cream) cheese with 3 tablespoons fat-skimmed **chicken broth**, 2 tablespoons **prepared horseradish**, and 1 tablespoon **lemon juice.** In a bowl, mix horseradish dressing with 3 cups **finely shredded cabbage** (8 oz.; sometimes labeled angel hair), 1 tablespoon minced **onion**, and **salt** and **pepper** to taste. If making ahead, cover and chill up to 1 day; mix before serving. Makes 1½ cups.

A hearty beef and bacon burger gets extra zip from horseradish slaw.

cheese. Layer bottom of each bun with lettuce and a salmon patty; top with cucumber–hearts of palm relish and set bun tops in place.

Per serving: 442 cal., 41% (180 cal.) from fat; 32 g protein; 20 g fat (5.3 g sat.); 31 g carbo (2 g fiber); 1,143 mg sodium; 130 mg chol.

Beef and Bacon Burgers

PREP AND COOK TIME: About 25 minutes

MAKES: 4 servings

6	tablespoons fat-skimmed chicken broth
2	tablespoons mustard seeds
1	pound ground lean beef
¼	cup fine dried bread crumbs
1	large egg
½	teaspoon salt
4	bacon slices (about 4 oz. total)
4	ounces münster cheese, thinly sliced
4	hamburger buns or rolls (4 in. wide), cut in half horizontally
	About 2 tablespoons mayonnaise
	Horseradish slaw (see "Burger Condiments," above left)

1. In a small microwave-safe bowl or glass measuring cup, combine 2 tablespoons chicken broth and mustard seeds. Heat in a microwave oven on full power (100%) until bubbling, 15 to 30 seconds. Pour into a large bowl and add remaining ¼ cup broth.

2. Add ground beef, bread crumbs, egg, and salt; mix well.

3. Divide beef mixture into four equal portions; shape each into an evenly thick 4-inch-wide round. Wrap a slice of bacon snugly in a ring around edge of each patty, overlapping ends and securing with a toothpick. If making ahead, lay patties in a single layer on a plate, cover airtight, and chill up to 1 day.

4. Lay beef patties on a lightly oiled barbecue grill over a solid bed of medium coals or medium heat on a gas grill (you can hold your hand at grill level only 4 to 5 seconds); cover barbecue and open vents. Cook patties until browned on the bottom, 4 to 6 minutes. Turn with a wide spatula and continue to cook until patties feel firm when pressed and are no longer pink in the center (cut to test), 4 to 7 minutes longer. Cover meat evenly with cheese and lay buns, cut side down, on grill; cover and cook until cheese is melted and buns are toasted, 2 to 3 minutes.

5. Spread toasted sides of each bun with mayonnaise. Set a beef patty on each bun bottom. Pull out toothpicks and discard. Top each with horseradish slaw and cover with bun top.

Per serving: 726 cal., 60% (432 cal.) from fat; 40 g protein; 48 g fat (19 g sat.); 34 g carbo (3.5 g fiber); 1,105 mg sodium; 184 mg chol. ◆

Sundae best

Add quick toppings to ice cream for deliciously easy desserts

By Linda Lau Anusasananan
Photographs by James Carrier

Ice cream means instant dessert. It waits in the freezer, always on call, ready to appear au naturel or dressed up for a celebration. Sauces, fruit, nuts, liqueur, and whipped cream are simple ways to transform even plain vanilla into lavish sundaes. Use our easy homemade sauces or, if time is tight, use purchased toppings. Build sundaes small or repeat layers for a double-dip treat. For a crowd, consider a party-size super sundae that will please everyone. Almost any combination works—you just can't miss with ice cream sundaes.

Nestle a banana split into a cone for a walk-away sundae.

Chocolate-Caramel Peanut Sundae

Place a scoop of **dulce de leche** or vanilla **ice cream** in a large wine glass or small bowl. Drizzle it generously with warm **chocolate sauce** and warm **orange-caramel sauce** (see recipes, opposite page) and sprinkle with **roasted salted peanuts.** Top with lightly sweetened softly **whipped cream** and sprinkle with chopped **chocolate-covered peanut nougat candy bar,** such as Snickers.

Strawberry Shortcake Sundae

Place a layer of ¹/₂-inch chunks of **meringue cookies** or pound cake in a large wine glass or small bowl. Top with a scoop of **vanilla ice cream** and sweetened sliced **strawberries.** Generously drizzle with **simple strawberry sauce** (see recipe, page 156). Top with lightly sweetened softly **whipped cream** and a whole strawberry.

Banana Split in a Cone

Set a large **waffle cone** in a tall glass for support. Cut a peeled small **firm-ripe banana** in half lengthwise; stand one half in cone. Add 1 small scoop *each* of **cherry, pistachio,** and **mango ice cream** (or use 1 large scoop of your favorite). Drizzle with a tiny spoonful of **simple strawberry sauce** (see recipe, page 156) or strawberry jam. Garnish with a small dollop of lightly sweetened softly **whipped cream,** chopped **roasted pistachios,** and a **maraschino cherry.**

Coffee Crunch Sundae

Place a scoop of **coffee ice cream** in a large wine glass, small bowl, or coffee cup. Generously drizzle with warm **chocolate sauce** (see recipe, page 156) and **Kahlúa.** Top with lightly sweetened softly **whipped cream** and sprinkle lightly with chopped **chocolate-covered** or plain **coffee beans.**

Peach-Berry Sundae

Place a scoop of **peach,** mango, or vanilla **ice cream** in a large wineglass or small bowl. Top with sliced peeled **peaches** or mango and **raspberries,** then drizzle with warm **orange-caramel sauce** (see recipe, page 156) and **orange-flavored liqueur.** Top with lightly sweetened **whipped cream** and garnish with finely shredded **orange** peel and a few more raspberries.

Piña Colada Sundae

Place a layer of diced **fresh pineapple** in a large wine glass or small bowl. Top with a scoop of **pineapple-coconut** or vanilla **ice cream.** Generously drizzle with **rum** and warm **orange-caramel sauce** (see recipe, page 156). Top with lightly sweetened softly **whipped cream** and **toasted coconut** (see recipe, page 156). Garnish with a spear of pineapple.

Sundae toppings

Chocolate Sauce

PREP AND COOK TIME: About 6 minutes

NOTES: Store sauce, covered, in the refrigerator for up to 2 weeks. Reheat in microwave oven at half power (50%) until warm, stirring occasionally.

MAKES: About 1⅔ cups

In a 2-cup glass measure, combine 1½ cups **semi-sweet chocolate chips,** ⅔ cup **whipping cream,** and 1 teaspoon **vanilla.** Cook in a microwave oven at half power (50%), stirring every 60 seconds, until smooth, 2 to 3 minutes total. If sauce is too thick, stir in a few more tablespoons cream. Serve warm or cool.

Per tablespoon: 65 cal., 66% (43 cal.) from fat; 0.5 g protein; 4.8 g fat (2.9 g sat.); 6.3 g carbo (0.6 g fiber); 3.2 mg sodium; 6.8 mg chol.

Orange-Caramel Sauce

PREP AND COOK TIME: About 12 minutes

NOTES: Store, covered, in refrigerator up to 2 weeks.

MAKES: About ¾ cup

In a 12-inch frying pan or 5- to 6-quart pan, mix ½ cup **sugar** and ½ cup **orange juice.** Cook over high heat, shaking pan often, until mixture is amber colored and very bubbly, about 8 minutes; do not scorch. Remove from heat and add 1 cup **whipping cream** (mixture will bubble). Return pan to medium heat and stir until caramel is smooth; increase heat and boil vigorously, stirring occasionally, until mixture coats spoon in a thin, even layer, 1 to 2 minutes; sauce thickens when cool. Serve warm or cool. If sauce is thicker than desired, stir in a few more tablespoons whipping cream or reheat in a microwave oven at half power (50%) until warm.

Per tablespoon: 95 cal., 59% (56 cal.) from fat; 0.5 g protein; 6.2 g fat (3.9 g sat.); 10 g carbo (0 g fiber); 7 mg sodium; 22 mg chol.

Simple Strawberry Sauce

PREP AND COOK TIME: About 5 minutes

NOTES: Store, covered, in refrigerator up to 2 days.

MAKES: About 1⅔ cups

Rinse and stem 1 pint **strawberries.** Whirl in a blender or food processor until smooth. Stir in 1 to 2 tablespoons **sugar** to taste.

Per tablespoon: 5.6 cal., 0% (0 cal.) from fat; 0.1 g protein; 0 g fat; 1.3 g carbo (0.3 g fiber); 0.1 mg sodium; 0 mg chol.

Toasted Coconut

PREP AND COOK TIME: About 2 minutes

MAKES: About 1 cup

In a 10- to 12-inch frying pan over medium heat, stir 1 cup **sweetened shredded dried coconut** until golden, 1 to 2 minutes. Let cool; store airtight up to 1 week.

Per tablespoon: 22 cal., 64% (14 cal.) from fat; 0.2 g protein; 1.5 g fat (1.3 g sat.); 2.2 g carbo (0.3 g fiber); 12 mg sodium; 0 mg chol. ◆

FOOD STYLING: BASIL FRIEDMAN

You can't have too much chocolate in this decadent sundae for two or more.

Chocolate Decadence Sundae for a Crowd

In a large bowl, mound scoops of 3 to 5 different varieties of **chocolate** or chocolate chunk **ice cream,** such as chocolate–chocolate chip, chocolate truffle, chocolate chip cookie dough, peanut butter fudge chunk, or rocky road (allow 1 or 2 scoops per serving). Drizzle with warm **chocolate sauce** (see recipe at right). Top with lightly sweetened softly **whipped cream** and one or several **chocolate toppings,** such as chopped chocolate, chopped chocolate-covered toffee, or miniature chocolate sandwich cookies. Eat straight from the bowl, or serve in **chocolate** or sugar **cones** or smaller dishes.

Carmen Miranda Sundae for a Crowd

In a large shallow bowl, mound scoops of several flavors of **ice cream,** such as macadamia brittle, butter pecan, peach, berry cheesecake, or vanilla (allow 1 or 2 scoops per serving). Tuck **banana** spears around edges of bowl. Top with bite-size pieces of 3 to 5 types of **fruit,** such as: pineapple, grapes, kiwi, berries, nectarines, or plums (⅓ to ½ cup per serving). Drizzle generously with warm **orange-caramel sauce** and **simple strawberry sauce** (see recipes at right). Top with lightly sweetened softly **whipped cream** and **toasted coconut** (see recipe at right). Eat straight from the bowl, or serve in small bowls.

Breaking the code

Those tiny stickers on loose fruits and vegetables at the market have a worthy purpose. Besides telling the store's computer database at checkout what the item is and how much it costs, the price lookup code (PLU) tells you how it was grown. Conventionally grown produce carries a four-digit code. On organically grown items, a number 9 precedes that basic code, on genetically modified produce a number 8. The number on a conventionally grown apple, for instance, might be 4133; on an organic apple, 94133; and on a genetically modified one, 84133.

—*Linda Lau Anusasananan*

Where there's smoke

From Chile to Japan, the grill is a cook's tool of choice worldwide (see pages 145 to 156). So, what makes a wine great with grilled foods across an international spectrum? Four factors are especially important: **acidity,** to cut through spicy, smoky flavors; **boldness,** to stand up to them; **spiciness,** to mirror them; and **fruitiness,** to cushion them.

A wine needn't have all four attributes to pair well with grilled foods, but one or more increase the chances of a good marriage. Here are eight great mates from around the world.

Whites

E. Guigal Condrieu 2002 *(Condrieu, Rhône Valley, France), $38.* Exotic honeysuckle, tropical fruit, and nut flavors make this Viognier fascinating with Thai, Indian, and Indonesian dishes.

Fresco Extra Dry Sparkling Wine by Chandon *(Argentina), $12.* With its slightly exotic notes and persistent bubbles, this Argentinean sister of France's Moët & Chandon and California's Domaine Chandon is great with spicy starters.

Nautilus Estate Sauvignon Blanc 2002 *(Marlborough, New Zealand), $17.* A fabulous interplay of spicy green peppercorn and tropical pineapple and mango flavors.

Pierre Sparr Pinot Gris Reserve 2001 *(Alsace, France), $15.* Bold, lush, and creamy, with peach and almond flavors and notes of citrus—perfect for Indian or Southeast Asian seafood.

Reds

Bodegas Agapito Rico Carchelo 2002 *(Jumilla, Spain), $8.* Very fruity, with deep, dark berry flavors and a chocolaty finish. Fabulous with hamburgers.

Condado de Haza 2000 *(Ribera del Duero, Spain), $16.* A powerhouse, with rugged blackberry, black plum, and licorice flavors and an almost syrupy texture. Made for meaty short ribs.

Domaine le Sang des Cailloux Vacqueyras 2001 *(Vacqueyras, Southern Rhône Valley), $25. Le sang des cailloux* means "the blood of the stones"—fitting for this deep, dark, spicy wine with hints of chocolate, espresso, and leather. Red meat required.

Stonehaven Limestone Coast Shiraz 1999 *(Australia), $13.* A big, fleshy Shiraz is always a shoo-in with grilled meats. This one is rich with cocoa, vanilla, and plush blackberry flavors, with a nice grip of tannin. Try it with lamb or beef. —*Karen MacNeil-Fife*

Best of the West

Cool fizz

You think you're strolling into just another cafe when, past the cozy chairs and magazine racks, the aroma hits you: chocolate. Cocoa cafes—such as Portland-based Moonstruck Chocolate Co.—are in, and you'll find baristas blending frothy concoctions like this refreshing chocolate fizz. Visit *www.moonstruckchocolate.com* for cafe locations or to order chocolate and cocoa. —*Kendra Smith*

CHOCOLATE FIZZ **1** In a blender, combine 4 ounces **dark chocolate,** chopped, and ¼ cup **sweetened cocoa** (not instant). In a 1- to 2-quart pan over medium-high heat, bring ½ cup **whole milk** to a boil; pour milk over chocolate mixture and whirl until melted and smooth. **2** Pour in 1½ cups cold **half-and-half** and whirl to blend. **3** Place 1 cup **ice cubes** in a cocktail shaker and add half of the chocolate mixture. Shake until cold and strain into a 16-ounce glass with a few ice cubes in it. **4** Fill glass with club soda and stir. Garnish with **whipped cream** and/or **shaved chocolate.** Makes 2 drinks.

Barbecue sauce gives a different twist to taco salad made with chicken, corn, radishes, and beans (see page 174).

August

Easy summer pastas

Freshen up a pantry staple with seasonal ingredients

By Marcia Smart • Photographs by James Carrier
Food styling by Karen Shinto

Classic pasta reborn: arugula pesto gives farfalle late-summer flavor.

The comfort of a warm bowl, the scent billowing from a savory sauce, and the toothsome bite of perfectly cooked pasta—there's nothing like it. Dried pasta is simple to prepare, inexpensive, and often fortified with folic acid and other nutritious ingredients. Its shape and texture will enhance the flavors you pair it with. Made with durum wheat flour (semolina) and water, dried pasta is sturdy enough to stand up to a variety of sauces.

Our recipes take advantage of summer's bounty of juicy tomatoes, delicate zucchini, sweet peas, crisp beans, and herbs and greens. Visit a farmers' market in your area to gather the tastiest spoils of the season. Serve these fresh pasta dishes with a green salad and crusty bread, and you'll have all you need to satisfy your family or impromptu dinner guests with a bright and flavorful celebration of summer.

Farfalle with Arugula Pesto

PREP AND COOK TIME: About 30 minutes

NOTES: This recipe makes extra arugula pesto; cover and chill up to 1 week (or freeze airtight up to 1 month). Use the leftover pesto for other pasta dishes, stir it into minestrone and other Italian soups, or use it in sandwiches or as a topping for pizza.

MAKES: 4 to 6 servings

- 8 ounces yellow wax beans and/or green beans, rinsed, ends trimmed, and cut into 1-inch lengths
- 12 ounces dried farfalle (bow tie) pasta
  About ¾ cup arugula pesto (recipe follows)
- ¼ cup grated pecorino romano or parmesan cheese
- ½ cup yellow and red cherry tomatoes, stemmed, rinsed, and halved

1. In a 5- to 6-quart pan over high heat, bring 4 quarts water to a boil; add beans and cook just until barely tender to bite, about 1 minute. With a skimmer or slotted spoon, remove from water and transfer to a colander; rinse under cold running water until cool.

2. Bring water back to a boil. Add farfalle and cook until tender to bite, 14 to 16 minutes. Drain.

3. In a large bowl, mix pasta, beans, and ¾ cup pesto. If more sauce is desired, add up to ¼ cup more pesto. Top with cheese and halved cherry tomatoes.

Per serving: 339 cal., 32% (108 cal.) from fat; 12 g protein; 12 g fat (2.4 g sat.); 48 g carbo (2.8 g fiber); 114 mg sodium; 5.6 mg chol.

Arugula pesto. Spread ¾ cup chopped walnuts in a baking pan; bake in a 350° oven until golden under skins, 6 to 8 minutes. Let cool slightly. In a food processor or blender, working in batches if necessary, combine 1 pound rinsed arugula leaves (about 10 lightly packed cups), the toasted walnuts, ½ cup grated pecorino romano or parmesan cheese, ¼ cup lemon juice, ¼ cup extra-virgin olive oil, 1½ teaspoons chopped garlic, and ¼ teaspoon salt. Pulse motor a few times, just until mixture begins to come together. With motor running, slowly pour ¼ cup more extra-virgin olive oil through feed tube or top of blender and whirl until mixture is smooth. Add more salt and fresh-ground pepper to taste. Makes about 2½ cups.

Per tablespoon: 51 cal., 90% (46 cal.) from fat; 1.1 g protein; 5.1 g fat (0.8 g sat.); 1.1 g carbo (0.3 g fiber); 33 mg sodium; 1.1 mg chol.

Orecchiette with Chicken Sausage and Spinach

PREP AND COOK TIME: About 35 minutes

NOTES: Look for high-quality fresh sausage; the casings will be easier to remove. Ricotta salata is available at specialty food stores and some well-stocked supermarkets; if you can't find it, substitute 2 ounces crumbled feta cheese.

MAKES: 4 to 6 servings

- 12 ounces dried orecchiette pasta
- 3 tablespoons butter
- 1 onion (8 oz.), peeled and chopped
- 2 large cloves garlic, peeled and minced
- ¼ teaspoon hot chili flakes
- 8 ounces chicken sausages, removed from casings and crumbled (see notes)
- 1 pound ripe tomatoes, rinsed, cored, and chopped
- 8 ounces baby spinach leaves (about 3 packed cups), rinsed
- 4 ounces ricotta salata cheese, thinly sliced or crumbled (see notes)

1. In a 5- to 6-quart pan over high heat, bring 4 quarts water to a boil. Add pasta and cook, stirring occasionally, until tender to bite, 12 to 15 minutes. Drain.

2. Meanwhile, in a 12-inch frying pan or a 4- to 5-quart pan over medium-high heat, melt butter. Add onion and stir often until lightly browned around the edges, 8 to 10 minutes.

3. Lower heat to medium and add garlic, chili flakes, and crumbled chicken sausages. Stir with a wooden spoon, breaking up sausage if necessary, until meat is beginning to brown, 5 to 10 minutes; if garlic begins to scorch, lower heat.

4. Add tomatoes and spinach; stir until spinach is wilted, about 2 minutes.

5. In a large bowl, mix pasta and sauce to coat; top with ricotta salata.

Per serving: 442 cal., 35% (153 cal.) from fat; 18 g protein; 17 g fat (8.3 g sat.); 55 g carbo (5 g fiber); 726 mg sodium; 66 mg chol.

Spaghetti Carbonara with Pancetta, Leeks, and Peas

PREP AND COOK TIME: About 25 minutes

NOTES: The eggs in this dish are not fully cooked. If you are concerned about bacteria, use yolks from eggs pasteurized in their shells, which are sold at some specialty food stores, or substitute ⅓ cup egg substitute for the raw yolks. Pancetta—an Italian bacon that is cured but not smoked—is available at Italian markets, specialty food stores, and some supermarkets; if you cannot find it, substitute 6 ounces thick-cut bacon.

MAKES: 4 to 6 servings

- 1 leek (about 8 oz.)
- 12 ounces dried spaghetti
- 8 ounces pancetta, diced (½ in.; see notes)
- 1½ cups shelled fresh peas or thawed frozen petite peas
  About ½ cup whipping cream
- 3 large egg yolks (see notes)
- ¾ cup fresh-grated parmesan cheese
- 1 teaspoon salt
- ¼ teaspoon fresh-ground pepper
- 1 tablespoon chopped parsley

Pairing pastas

Different pastas go better with some sauces than others. Here's a guide.

Strands are best with moderately liquid sauces. Familiar **spaghetti** is a classic with tomato sauce. **Bavette** and **tagliolini** are thin, flattened strands that work well with light cream sauces or fresh tomatoes, garlic, basil, and olive oil. **Bucatini** (thick strands) can stand up to a chunkier sauce, while fine **capellini** (often sold as angel hair) goes with thin sauce.

Thick strips, such as **fettuccine, tagliatelle,** and **pappardelle,** are generally best for creamy sauces, such as Alfredo, or thick meat sauces like a rich duck ragu.

Cylinder shapes, either ridged or smooth, hold sauce on the inside and outside. Bake **penne rigate** with tomato sauce or toss it with pesto or a light but chunky sauce. **Rigatoni**— wider than penne, with blunt-cut ends (as opposed to diagonally cut)—is good with chunky sausage, artichoke, or eggplant sauces.

Specialty shapes can match a variety of sauces. Both **farfalle** (bow ties) and **fusilli** (corkscrews) are great in pasta salads; fusilli is also well matched with thin, flavorful sauces that coat the corkscrew linings. **Orecchiette** ("little ears") are round with a slight indentation; toss them with wilted greens or moderately thick sauces.

Halibut, zucchini, and mint make a distinctive, seasonal topping for penne.

1. Trim and discard root end and tough green top from leek; peel off and discard outer layer. Cut leek in half lengthwise and hold each half under cold running water, flipping layers to separate and remove grit. Thinly slice crosswise.

2. In a 5- to 6-quart pan over high heat, bring 4 quarts water to a boil. Add pasta and cook, stirring occasionally, until tender to bite, 8 to 10 minutes. Drain.

3. Meanwhile, in a 12-inch frying pan or 4- to 5-quart pan over medium-high heat, stir pancetta until fat is rendered and pancetta is crisp and brown, about 8 minutes. Transfer to a paper towel–lined plate. Discard all but 2 teaspoons fat from pan.

4. Lower heat to medium and add leek to pan; stir often until limp and slightly golden, 2 to 3 minutes. Stir in peas and cook until warmed through, 2 minutes longer. Reduce heat to low.

5. Whisk together $^{1}/_{2}$ cup cream, egg yolks, cheese, salt, and pepper. Add hot pasta and cream mixture to pan with leek and peas; mix gently to coat. Stir in pancetta. If desired, add a little more cream to thin sauce. Pour into a large bowl and sprinkle with parsley.

Per serving: 551 cal., 49% (270 cal.) from fat; 19 g protein; 30 g fat (13 g sat.); 51 g carbo (3 g fiber); 829 mg sodium; 157 mg chol.

Penne with Halibut, Zucchini, and Mint

PREP AND COOK TIME: About 40 minutes

MAKES: 4 to 6 servings

- **5** tablespoons olive oil
- **1** onion (8 oz.), peeled and chopped
- **1½** pounds zucchini, rinsed and chopped
  About 1 teaspoon kosher salt
- **12** ounces dried penne pasta
- **1½** pounds boned, skinned halibut pieces
  Pepper
- **½** cup dry white wine
- **1** teaspoon grated lemon peel
- **½** cup slivered fresh mint leaves

1. Pour 3 tablespoons olive oil into a 10- to 12-inch frying pan over medium heat. Add onion and stir often until soft, 6 to 8 minutes. Add zucchini and 1 teaspoon salt; cook, stirring occasionally, until zucchini is soft and most of the liquid has evaporated, about 10 minutes longer.

2. Meanwhile, in a 5- to 6-quart pan, bring 4 quarts water to a boil. Add penne and cook until tender to bite, 10 to 12 minutes. Drain.

3. Coat halibut with remaining 2 tablespoons olive oil and sprinkle all over with salt and pepper. Place in a 10- to 12-inch nonstick frying pan over high heat and cook, turning once, until browned on both sides, about 4 minutes total. Pour in wine, reduce heat to maintain a simmer, and cook until fish flakes easily with a fork, about 5 minutes longer. Break halibut into flakes.

4. Stir lemon peel into zucchini mixture. In a large bowl, combine pasta and zucchini mixture. Add flaked halibut and liquid in pan and sprinkle with all but 2 tablespoons mint; mix to coat pasta. Sprinkle with remaining mint.

Per serving: 480 cal., 28% (135 cal.) from fat; 33 g protein; 15 g fat (2.1 g sat.); 49 g carbo (3 g fiber); 399 mg sodium; 36 mg chol. ◆

Melt cheese over eggplant and polenta slices to make a tempting dinner.

Menu

Eggplant Parmesan Stacks

Escarole Salad with Olives

Chianti or Iced Tea

Biscotti and Strawberries to dip into Vin Santo or Tawny Port

Stack it up

Layer polenta and sauce for easy eggplant parmesan

By Linda Lau Anusasananan
Photograph by James Carrier

Most people think eggplant parmesan is a labor-intensive, multistep dish. These quick stacks of roasted eggplant slices and purchased cooked polenta dispel the image; our twist on the classic dish includes tomato sauce and mozzarella for a full helping of savory Italian flavor, but we've cut the long preparation time and the heavy dose of oil and cheese. With a salad and a simple dessert, this is a weeknight menu *con brio*.

Eggplant Parmesan Stacks

PREP AND COOK TIME: About 35 minutes

NOTES: Look for tubes of cooked polenta in the supermarket refrigerator case; they are often stocked near the cheese.

MAKES: 4 servings

- 1 eggplant (1 lb.)
- 1 tube (1 lb.) cooked polenta (see notes)
  Olive oil cooking spray
- 1 onion (8 oz.), peeled and chopped
- 2 cloves garlic, peeled and pressed or minced
- 2 tablespoons chopped fresh basil leaves or 2 teaspoons dried basil
- 1 can (14 oz.) tomato purée
  Salt and pepper
- 1½ cups shredded part-skim mozzarella cheese (6 oz.)

- ⅓ cup grated parmesan cheese
- 4 fresh rosemary sprigs (optional)
- 8 to 12 breadsticks (2 to 3 oz. total)

1. Rinse eggplant and trim off and discard both ends. Cut eggplant crosswise into 8 equally thick slices. Cut polenta crosswise into 8 equal rounds. Lightly coat a 14- by 17-inch baking sheet with olive oil cooking spray. Arrange eggplant and polenta slices in a single layer on sheet. Lightly coat tops of slices with more cooking spray.

2. Bake in a 425° regular or convection oven until eggplant is soft when pressed and polenta is heated through (cut to test), 20 to 25 minutes.

3. Meanwhile, in an 8- to 10-inch nonstick frying pan over medium-high heat, stir onion, garlic, and basil occasionally until onion is lightly browned, 4 to 5 minutes. Add tomato purée and ¼ cup water; simmer uncovered, stirring occasionally, until flavors are blended, 5 to 10 minutes. Add salt and pepper to taste. Cover and keep warm over low heat, stirring occasionally, until eggplant is done.

4. When eggplant is soft, sprinkle mozzarella and parmesan cheeses equally over eggplant and polenta.

Return to oven and bake until cheese is melted, about 2 minutes.

5. On each of four dinner plates, place 1 eggplant slice (use largest slices first) and drizzle with 1 tablespoon sauce; top with 1 polenta slice and 1 tablespoon sauce. Repeat until all slices are used. If desired, garnish each stack with rosemary sprig. Spoon remaining sauce around base of eggplant stacks. Serve with breadsticks.

Per serving: 376 cal., 26% (99 cal.) from fat; 20 g protein; 11 g fat (5.8 g sat.); 49 g carbo (6.9 g fiber); 1,017 mg sodium; 30 mg chol.

Escarole Salad with Olives

PREP AND COOK TIME: About 15 minutes

NOTES: If escarole is unavailable, use another salad green, such as arugula, endive, or lettuce.

MAKES: 4 servings

In a bowl, mix 2 quarts bite-size pieces rinsed and crisped **escarole** (12 oz.; see notes) with ¼ cup **pitted calamata olives**, 2 tablespoons **extra-virgin olive oil**, 1 tablespoon **balsamic vinegar,** and 1 clove **garlic,** peeled and pressed or minced. Add **salt** and **pepper** to taste.

Per serving: 101 cal., 84% (85 cal.) from fat; 1.1 g protein; 9.4 g fat (1.3 g sat.); 4.3 g carbo (2.1 g fiber); 171 mg sodium; 0 mg chol. ◆

In late summer and early fall, the leaves of certain huckleberry bushes color the hillsides bronze.

The hunt for huckleberries

Now's the time to bag berries in the Northwest

By Bonnie Henderson • Photographs by Pete Stone

To witness the frenzy that descends in early August upon the remote mountain town of Trout Lake in southwest Washington, you'd think they were handing out dollar bills. Actually, it's better than that: millions of huckleberry bushes are giving up their tiny, blue-black and maroon fruit on the open slopes around Mt. Adams.

The huckleberry hubbub isn't unique to Trout Lake and its environs; it can be observed throughout the mountainous Northwest. That's probably because for many, "huckleberrying" is like fishing—less about bagging the berry than an excuse to stroll through airy forests or open hillsides. But for those who are more goal-oriented, the rewards are ample: At its peak, a ripe huckleberry packs twice the tart-sweet flavor of its much larger domestic cousin, the blueberry—and it captures the essence of summer in one bite.

Huckleberries were so valued by Northwest tribes that the picking, preserving, and eating of berries was a near-sacramental tradition. It still is: a 1932 handshake agreement between Yakama Chief William Yallup and the supervisor of Gifford Pinchot National Forest continues to preserve a portion of the Sawtooth Berry Fields near Trout Lake for Native American pickers (watch for signs marking reserved areas).

Twelve huckleberry species can still be found in Oregon and Washington, from plump Cascades (*Vaccinium deliciosum*) to luscious purple-black thin-leaved berries (*V. membranaceum*).

Finding bushes is often easy enough (although uncovering the tiny berries on them can be challenging). A few great huckleberrying locations are Oregon's Mt. Hood as well as the Olallie Lake scenic area (*olallie* is Chinook tribal jargon for "berry"), throughout the Cascades, on Mt. Spokane, and on the rugged slopes of the Idaho Panhandle National Forest. The bushes are typically found in old burns, cleared runs of ski areas with plenty of sunlight, or in forests where trees are reestablishing themselves after a long-ago fire (Native Americans used to maintain favorite berry fields by routinely burning them).

Though some Northwest families keep the location of their favorite field a closely held secret, there are plenty of huckleberries for everyone—and plenty of ways to enjoy the bounty. ◆

Huckleberry Streusel Muffins

PREP AND COOK TIME: About 30 minutes

MAKES: 12 muffins

- 2 **cups all-purpose flour**
- ⅓ **cup granulated sugar**
- 1 **tablespoon baking powder**
- ¾ **teaspoon salt**
- 1 **cup milk**
- 1 **large egg**
- 3 **tablespoons butter, melted**
- 2 **teaspoons vanilla**
- 1 **cup fresh (and rinsed) or frozen huckleberries**
  Streusel (recipe follows)

1. In a large bowl, thoroughly mix flour, sugar, baking powder, and salt; make a well in the center of mixture.

2. In a 2-cup glass measure, beat milk, egg, butter, and vanilla. Pour all at once into center of well. Mix gently just until dry ingredients are moistened; batter will be lumpy. Gently stir in huckleberries.

3. Spoon batter equally into 12 paper-lined muffin cups, filling about ¾ full. Sprinkle streusel evenly over batter.

4. Bake in a 425° regular or convection oven until streusel is lightly browned, 18 to 20 minutes. Remove muffins from pan and place on a wire rack to cool.

Streusel. In a food processor or a bowl, whirl or stir 1 cup **all-purpose flour** and ½ cup **brown sugar** until well blended. Add ½ cup **butter,** cut in chunks, and whirl or rub in with your fingers until mixture forms coarse crumbs.

Per muffin: 291 cal., 37% (108 cal.) from fat; 4.6 g protein; 12 g fat (7.1 g sat.); 41 g carbo (1.1 g fiber); 395 mg sodium; 49 mg chol.

—*Charity Ferreira*

FOOD STYLING: BASIL FRIEDMAN

Best picks

Huckleberry season starts in late July at lower elevations and tends to peak mid-August through mid-September. It's easy to stumble upon the shrubs on hiking trails, but the best picking is off-trail. Look for bushes with shiny blue-black or maroon berries.

Rangers advise that you should watch out for animals and poison oak, hike in groups, and carry water and a whistle, for signaling friends. "It's easy to get lost when you're wandering with your head down, looking for berries," reminds Linda Turner, spokesperson for Gifford Pinchot National Forest.

Here's where to get up-to-date tips on the best picking sites at three of the Northwest's huckleberry hot spots.

Mt. Adams Ranger Station. *2455 State 141, Trout Lake, WA; (509) 395-3400.*

Mt. Hood Information Center. *65000 E. U.S. 26, Welches, OR; (503) 622-4822.*

Sandpoint Ranger District. *1500 U.S. 2, Sandpoint, ID; (208) 263-5111.*

Blueberry-coconut slush

Great shakes

Frosty drinks can never be too rich or too cool

By Charity Ferreira
Photograph by James Carrier

Thick milkshakes, fruit smoothies, and icy coffee drinks promise delicious relief from the heat. This summer, treat yourself to one of these cold, creamy concoctions. All you need to enjoy them at home is a blender, a tall glass, and a straw.

Blueberry-Coconut Slush

In a blender, combine 1 cup **pineapple sherbet** or sorbet, 1 cup **frozen blueberries**, $^{3}/_{4}$ cup canned **reduced-fat coconut milk,** and $^{1}/_{4}$ cup **sweetened shredded coconut.** Whirl until smooth and pour into a chilled tall glass (at least 16 oz.). Makes 2 cups; 1 to 2 servings.

Per serving: 266 cal., 33% (89 cal.) from fat; 2.8 g protein; 9.9 g fat (6.6 g sat.); 46 g carbo (3.1 g fiber); 91 mg sodium; 4.8 mg chol.

Chocolate Malted

In a blender, combine 2 cups **chocolate ice cream,** $^{1}/_{3}$ cup **milk,** $^{1}/_{4}$ cup **malted milk powder,** and 3 tablespoons **chocolate syrup.** Whirl until smooth and pour into a chilled tall glass (at least 16 oz.) or two chilled glasses (8 oz. each). Garnish with halved **chocolate-covered malt balls.** Makes 2 cups; 1 to 2 servings.

Per serving: 489 cal., 35% (171 cal.) from fat; 11 g protein; 19 g fat (11 g sat.); 76 g carbo (0 g fiber); 365 mg sodium; 56 mg chol.

Coffee-Caramel Freeze

In a blender, combine 1 cup **coffee ice cream;** $^{1}/_{4}$ cup cold **espresso** (dissolve 2 tablespoons **instant espresso powder** in $^{1}/_{4}$ cup boiling water; let cool) or **strong coffee;** 3 tablespoons **caramel sauce;** and 1 cup **crushed ice.** Whirl until smooth and pour into a chilled tall glass (at least 16 oz.) or two chilled glasses (8 oz. each). Makes 2 cups; 1 to 2 servings.

Per serving: 217 cal., 30% (66 cal.) from fat; 3.1 g protein; 7.3 g fat (4.5 g sat.); 37 g carbo (0 g fiber); 161 mg sodium; 29 mg chol. ◆

Spoon hot stir-fried beef and onion over a bed of cool watercress.

Watercress: clean green

Pools of pure water produce peppery sprigs for summer dishes

By Linda Lau Anusasananan • Photographs by James Carrier

Wearing rubber boots, David Sumida stands ankle-deep in a pond of water carpeted with green. He waves foot-long leafy green stems in the air to make his point: "Watercress is the cleanest vegetable around. There's no mud—it grows on a bed of gravel in springwater. It takes one million gallons of water a day to grow 1 acre of watercress."

Here at Sumida Farm, a 10-acre oasis surrounded by four shopping malls in Oahu's Pearl Harbor basin, Sumida and his sister, Barbara, grow watercress, as the family has done since 1928. Threatened with development, the third generation stubbornly remains. "We're here because it's the best location to grow watercress in. Pure springwater from the Ko'olau Range bubbles from below, but no mountains block the sun," explains Sumida. This indeed seems to be an ideal place: long days of strong Hawaii sun produce bouquet-size bunches of watercress for bright island cuisine.

Although Sumida watercress is available exclusively in local island markets, mainland-grown watercress packs an equally distinctive peppery bite. This pretty leafy green, wherever it's grown, adds punch to salads, soups, and sauces.

Hot Beef and Wilted Watercress Salad

PREP AND COOK TIME: About 30 minutes
NOTES: Serve this main-dish salad with hot cooked rice.
MAKES: 2 servings

- 8 ounces watercress (2 qt.)
- 8 ounces fat-trimmed beef sirloin, about ¾ inch thick
- 3 tablespoons lime juice
- 1½ tablespoons fish sauce or soy sauce
- 1 tablespoon sugar
- 1 teaspoon coarse-ground pepper
- 2 teaspoons vegetable oil
- 1 onion (6 oz.), peeled and thinly sliced
- 2 cloves garlic, peeled and minced
  Salt

1. Rinse watercress and drain well. Pick tender sprigs from tough stems and cut into 3- to 4-inch lengths (you should have about 6 cups sprigs); reserve stems for another use or discard. Arrange watercress sprigs in a shallow bowl or on a rimmed serving plate.

2. Rinse beef and pat dry; trim and discard excess fat. Cut into ⅛-inch-thick slices about 3 inches long.

3. In a small bowl, mix lime juice, fish sauce, sugar, and pepper.

4. Set a 10- to 12-inch frying pan over high heat. When hot, add 1 teaspoon oil and tilt pan to coat bottom. Add onion and stir until lightly browned, about 1 minute. Pour onto watercress.

5. Return pan to high heat. Add remaining 1 teaspoon oil and the beef and garlic; stir often until beef is lightly browned, about 2 minutes. Add lime-juice mixture and stir until it boils. Pour from pan over onions and watercress. At the table, mix gently before serving. Add salt to taste.

Per serving: 293 cal., 34% (99 cal.) from fat; 30 g protein; 11 g fat (2.7 g sat.); 20 g carbo (4 g fiber); 562 mg sodium; 69 mg chol.

Watercress Vichyssoise

PREP AND COOK TIME: About 40 minutes
NOTES: If you use buttermilk, this soup will have a pleasant tang; cream, on the other hand, brings out the flavor of the watercress and potato. Serve soup hot or cold.
MAKES: 6 servings

- 1 pound thin-skinned potatoes
- 1 quart vegetable broth or fat-skimmed chicken broth
- 8 ounces watercress (2 qt.)
- 1½ cups regular or low-fat buttermilk or whipping cream (see notes)
  Salt and pepper

1. Peel potatoes and cut into ¾-inch chunks. In a 3- to 4-quart pan over

FOOD STYLING: KAREN SHINTO (2)

high heat, bring potatoes and broth to a boil; cover, reduce heat, and simmer until potatoes are tender when pierced, 18 to 25 minutes.

2. Meanwhile, rinse and drain watercress. Pick six tender sprigs from stems and reserve. Coarsely chop remaining watercress, including stems; you should have 2½ to 3 cups. Stir chopped watercress into potato-broth mixture and cook just until watercress is bright green and wilted, about 1 minute.

3. Pour half the potato-watercress mixture into a blender and, holding lid closed with a towel, whirl until smooth. Pour into a bowl. Repeat to purée remaining soup; pour into bowl. Stir in buttermilk.

4. To serve soup hot, return to pan and stir over medium heat just until steaming (do not boil). To serve cold, cover and chill until cold, 3 to 4 hours.

5. Ladle into bowls. Add salt and pepper to taste. Garnish with reserved watercress sprigs.

Per serving: 106 cal., 8% (8.1 cal.) from fat; 4.7 g protein; 0.9 g fat (0.3 g sat.); 20 g carbo (1.9 g fiber); 132 mg sodium; 2.5 mg chol.

Double-Cress Salad

PREP TIME: About 10 minutes

NOTES: George Mavrothalassitis of Chef Mavro restaurant in Honolulu developed this simple salad. It's delicious as a companion to fish, chicken, or steak.

MAKES: 4 servings

- 8 ounces watercress (2 qt.)
- 2 tablespoons extra-virgin olive oil
- 1 tablespoon lemon juice
- 1 clove garlic, peeled and pressed
  Salt and pepper

1. Rinse watercress and drain well. Pick tender sprigs from stems and cut into 3- to 4-inch lengths; you should have about 6 cups sprigs. Finely chop enough of the stems to make 2 tablespoons; save remainder for other uses or discard.

2. In a large bowl, mix olive oil, lemon juice, garlic, and chopped watercress

stems. Add watercress sprigs and mix. Add salt and pepper to taste.

Per serving: 68 cal., 94% (64 cal.) from fat; 1.3 g protein; 7.1 g fat (1 g sat.); 1.2 g carbo (1.2 g fiber); 22 mg sodium; 0 mg chol.

Creamy Watercress Dressing

PREP TIME: About 15 minutes

NOTES: This lovely sauce is another good use for the tougher watercress stems and less-than-perfect leaves. If making it up to 1 week ahead, cover and chill (it will darken and thicken slightly). Serve as a salad dressing or as a dip for cold, cooked shrimp, or drizzle over poached chicken breasts.

MAKES: About 1½ cups

- 4 ounces watercress (1 qt.)
- 1 cup mayonnaise
- 2 tablespoons lemon juice
- 2 teaspoons anchovy paste
- 1 clove garlic, peeled
  Salt and pepper

1. Rinse watercress and drain well; pat dry with towels, then coarsely chop.

2. In a blender or food processor, whirl watercress, ½ cup mayonnaise, lemon juice, anchovy paste, and garlic until smooth.

3. Pour into a bowl and whisk in remaining mayonnaise until smooth. Add salt and pepper to taste.

Per tablespoon: 68 cal., 99% (67 cal.) from fat; 0.3 g protein; 7.4 g fat (1.1 g sat.); 0.4 g carbo (0.1 g fiber); 78 mg sodium; 5.5 mg chol.

Halibut with Watercress Pesto

PREP AND COOK TIME: About 45 minutes

NOTES: You can use the coarse watercress stems and any flawed leaves in this peppery pesto. Besides fish, it also complements chicken, sliced cucumbers, and goat cheese.

MAKES: 4 servings

- 4 ounces watercress (1 qt.)
- 3 tablespoons olive oil
- 1½ tablespoons pine nuts
- 1 teaspoon grated lemon peel
- 1 clove garlic, peeled

Watercress pesto does double duty, seasoning fish and salad.

Salt and pepper
- 1½ pounds boned, skinned halibut fillet
- 1 cup cherry tomatoes
  Lemon wedges

1. Rinse watercress and drain well. Pick tender sprigs from stems and cut into 3- to 4-inch lengths; you should have 1½ to 2 cups sprigs. Coarsely chop remaining watercress and stems; you should have ⅓ to ½ cup.

2. In a blender or food processor, whirl chopped watercress, olive oil, pine nuts, lemon peel, and garlic until finely ground. Add salt and pepper to taste.

3. Rinse fish and pat dry. Cut into four equal pieces. Set slightly apart in an oiled 10- by 15-inch baking pan. Reserve 2 tablespoons pesto; spread remaining equally over fish.

4. Bake in a 425° regular or convection oven until fish is barely opaque but still moist-looking in center of thickest part (cut to test), 8 to 12 minutes.

5. Meanwhile, rinse and stem tomatoes; cut each in half. In a bowl, mix watercress sprigs, tomatoes, and reserved pesto. Spoon equally onto four dinner plates.

6. With a wide spatula, transfer fish to plates. Add salt and pepper to taste. Garnish with lemon wedges to squeeze over fish.

Per serving: 304 cal., 47% (144 cal.) from fat; 37 g protein; 16 g fat (2.2 g sat.); 2.3 g carbo (1.4 g fiber); 106 mg sodium; 54 mg chol. ◆

As savory as its name

This easy-to-grow herb complements summer veggies

By Sharon Cohoon and Kate Washington • Photograph by Thomas J. Story

Summer savory *(Satureja hortensis)* is not as well known as its Mediterranean cousins, sage and thyme, but once you taste it with fresh green beans, you'll wonder how you ever did without it. The aromatic leaves of this fast-growing annual have a mild peppery flavor. The taste is a little sharper than thyme, but not as hot as sage, with a pleasant earthiness all its own. Traditionally used to season snap, shelling, and dried beans, savory is also good with peas, lentils, and other legumes. We like it with root vegetables, especially potatoes, as well as summer squash. Savory also complements roast chicken; blend it with butter to rub under the skin before roasting.

Many nurseries carry this plant, but it's not too late to sow a crop. Savory seeds germinate very quickly, and you can begin harvesting leaves when plants are 6 inches high. The Romans considered savory to be an aphrodisiac, so maybe it wouldn't hurt to grow a little extra.

What summer savory needs

EXPOSURE: Full sun.

SOIL: Light, well drained, organically rich.

WATER: Regular.

GROWING TIPS: Sow directly in the ground (or large containers), barely covering seeds with soil. Thin the strongest seedlings to 12 inches apart. Pinch mature plants often to discourage flowering. If plants get floppy, mound soil slightly around their bases.

SEED SOURCES: Territorial Seed Company *(www.territorialseed.com or 541/942-9547);* Seed Savers Exchange *(www.seedsavers.org or 563/382-5990).* ◆

Warm Potato and Green Bean Salad with Summer Savory

PREP AND COOK TIME: About 30 minutes

MAKES: 4 servings

8	ounces green beans, rinsed and ends snapped off
1½	pounds Yukon Gold potatoes, peeled and sliced ¼ inch thick
2	tablespoons minced shallots
2	tablespoons white wine vinegar
¼	cup olive oil
2	tablespoons summer savory leaves, chopped
	Salt and fresh-ground pepper

1. In a 4- to 5-quart pan over high heat, bring 2 quarts water to a boil. Add green beans and cook until bright green and tender-crisp, 1 to 2 minutes. Drain well and rinse with cold water until cool (or plunge in ice water); drain again.

2. In same pan, bring 2 quarts water to a boil over high heat. Add potato slices and cook until tender when pierced, 10 to 12 minutes; drain well and transfer to a large bowl.

3. Meanwhile, in a 1-cup glass measure, combine shallots and vinegar. In a 1- to 1½-quart pan over medium heat, combine olive oil and summer savory. Stir occasionally until savory is limp and slightly darker and oil is fragrant, 10 to 12 minutes. If oil sizzles, reduce heat slightly.

4. Pour half the oil mixture into vinegar mixture and stir to combine; season with salt and pepper to taste. Pour over warm potatoes and mix gently to coat. Top potatoes with green beans and drizzle remaining oil mixture over beans. Serve warm or at room temperature.

Per serving: 262 cal., 48% (126 cal.) from fat; 4.2 g protein; 14 g fat (1.9 g sat.); 33 g carbo (3.4 g fiber); 13 mg sodium; 0 mg chol.

Best of the West

Summer crush

Sometimes the simplest treats can be the most sublime. As the mercury rises this summer, try freezing your favorite fruit juice to make a snow cone. It's a refreshing twist on a summer classic. *(We used the Rival Deluxe Ice Shaver, $30.)*

Juice Snow Cones

Pour fruit juice, such as apricot, cranberry-raspberry, grape, mango, or any other that you prefer, into ice cube trays (unless shaver manufacturer provides a mold for ice). You will need about ½ cup juice—6 standard-size ice cubes—for each snow cone. Freeze until firm, at least 2 hours. Place 5 to 6 juice cubes (or follow manufacturer's recommendations for maximum amount) in a snow-cone maker or ice shaver and process. Lightly spoon shaved ice into a paper cup.

—*Jil Peters, Kate Washington*

Savoring the Okanagan

By Kate Washington and Steve Lorton

Photographs by Robert Leon

Fragrant, ripe peaches mark the peak of summer at Okanagan fruit stands.

August is the peak of the peach harvest season in British Columbia's Okanagan Valley—a long, narrow, glacier-carved basin filled with a string of gorgeous lakes that stretches more than 100 miles north from the U.S. border in central Washington. This valley is Canada's fruit bowl, known especially for its peaches.

Okanagan flavors

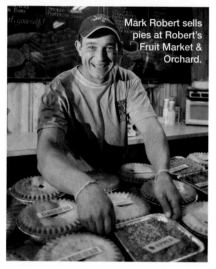

Mark Robert sells pies at Robert's Fruit Market & Orchard.

No. 1 Fruit Stand Peach Cobbler

PREP AND COOK TIME: About 1 hour

NOTES: Mary-Lou Evans makes this easy, homey dessert for her family, including son Bob Evans and daughter Barb Schwabe and her husband, Russ. The family runs the No. 1 Fruit Stand together.

MAKES: 6 to 8 servings

- 3 **pounds ripe peaches**
  About ⅔ cup sugar
- 2 **tablespoons butter, at room temperature**
  About ⅔ cup milk
  About 1½ cups all-purpose flour
- 1 **tablespoon baking powder**
- ¼ **teaspoon salt**
- 1 **teaspoon vanilla**
  Whipping cream or ice cream

1. Peel and pit peaches and slice into ½-inch-thick wedges, dropping slices into a shallow

2½- to 3-quart oval or other baking dish. Gently mix in ⅓ cup sugar; taste, and add a little more sugar if desired.

2. In a bowl, beat butter and remaining ⅓ cup sugar until well blended. Stir in ⅓ cup milk.

3. In another bowl, mix 1½ cups flour, baking powder, and salt. Add to butter mixture with another ⅓ cup milk and stir to combine. Batter should be stiff and sticky; if too dry, add a little more milk; if runny, add flour. Stir in vanilla.

4. Drop batter by tablespoonfuls evenly over prepared fruit (some fruit will show through).

5. Bake in a 350° oven until top is browned and fruit is bubbling, 35 to 40 minutes. Serve warm or at room temperature: scoop into bowls and drizzle cream over each serving if desired.

Per serving: 246 cal., 14% (35 cal.) from fat; 4 g protein; 3.9 g fat (2.2 g sat.); 50 g carbo (2.7 g fiber); 294 mg sodium; 11 mg chol.

Okanagan Green Salad with Fruit and Chèvre

PREP AND COOK TIME: About 30 minutes

NOTES: Andrea McFadden, owner of Okanagan Lavender Herb Farm *(4380 Takla Rd., Kelowna; www.okanaganlavender.com),* developed this recipe with her herbes de Provence (a French dried herb blend). Over time, she says, she started adding more fresh produce, making the salad a great light lunch or dinner dish. If you cannot find herbes de Provence, substitute ½ teaspoon *each* dried thyme, dried rosemary, dried lavender blossoms, and dried marjoram. Use only lavender grown without pesticides.

MAKES: 4 to 6 servings

- ¼ **cup fine dried bread crumbs**
- 2 **teaspoons herbes de Provence (see notes)**
- 1 **log (about 6 oz.) fresh chèvre (goat cheese)**
- 7 **tablespoons extra-virgin olive oil**
- ½ **cup pine nuts**

- ½ **cup fresh raw corn kernels (from 1 ear corn)**
- ¼ **cup white wine vinegar**
- 1 **clove garlic, peeled and minced**
- 1 **teaspoon Dijon mustard**
  Salt and pepper
- 8 **ounces mixed baby salad greens (about 8 cups)**
- 1 **nectarine, rinsed, pitted, and cut into ½-inch chunks**
- ⅓ **cup raspberries, rinsed**
- ⅓ **cup blueberries, rinsed**
  Blossoms from 5 stems fresh lavender (see notes), rinsed

1. On a small rimmed plate, mix bread crumbs and 1½ teaspoons herbes de Provence. Coat chèvre log with 2 tablespoons olive oil, then gently roll the log in bread-crumb mixture. Place on a baking sheet and bake in a 400° regular or convection oven until bread crumbs are golden, 10–12 minutes. Let cool slightly.

2. Meanwhile, spread pine nuts in a small baking pan; toast in same oven until light golden, 3 to 5 minutes. Let cool.

3. Combine corn kernels with 1 cup water in a 1- to 1½-quart pan over high heat; bring to a simmer and cook just until corn kernels are heated through, about 2 minutes. Drain, rinse with cold water, and drain again.

4. In a large bowl, whisk remaining 5 tablespoons olive oil, vinegar, garlic, mustard, and remaining ½ teaspoon herbes de Provence until smoothly blended. Add salt and pepper to taste.

5. Add salad greens, corn kernels, nectarine, raspberries, blueberries, and half the pine nuts and mix gently to coat. Divide among salad plates. Cut chèvre into ½-inch slices or chunks. Top salads evenly with chèvre, remaining pine nuts, and lavender blossoms.

Per serving: 337 cal., 77% (261 cal.) from fat; 9.7 g protein; 29 g fat (7.4 g sat.); 14 g carbo (2.4 g fiber); 171 mg sodium; 13 mg chol. ◆

Summer's bounty

In August you'll find an abundance of peaches and other stone fruit, early apples, and vegetables. Some of the best stands aren't on the main roads; call ahead for directions and to confirm hours—open daily unless noted.

Kaleden: No. 1 Fruit Stand. Copious fresh fruit, vegetables, and jams at a family-run stand. *434 Hwy. 97; (250) 497-8686.*

Okanagan Falls: Matheson Creek Farm. Apples, cherries, and smoothies. *Eastside Rd. 5 miles south of Penticton; (250) 497-8989.*

Penticton Farmers' Market. Gleaming apples, Red Haven peaches, and more. *8:30–noon Sat. Next to Gyro Park (100 block of Main St.); (250) 770-3276.*

Penticton: Spiller's Corner Fruit Stand. Quaint, historic stand. *475 Upper Bench Rd.; (250) 490-4162.*

Summerland: Robert's Fruit Market & Orchard. A variety of fruit, plus preserves (try the apricot) and butter tarts, a Canadian specialty. *On Hwy. 97; (250) 494-5541.*

Blend mayonnaise with basil to top salmon in tomato broth.

Clarifying tomatoes

Their water makes a flavorful backdrop for summer entrées

There's a window of time in August when those tomatoes in your garden that have been poking along in the green stages for months suddenly ripen all at once and you have a rare problem—too many tomatoes on your hands. Here's a beautiful way to clear it up: juice them.

When you purée tomatoes, then strain them through cheesecloth, the red pulp stays behind; what drips through (slowly) is a clear broth that looks like water but tastes like the pure fruit. This tomato "water" is a perfect complement to great summer flavors such as seared scallops on steamed artichoke hearts, grilled chicken breasts topped with chunky black olive tapenade, or our simple grilled salmon with fresh peas. Whatever accompaniment you choose, tomato water lets its colors shine through but packs a wallop of supporting flavor.

Grilled Salmon in Tomato Water

PREP AND COOK TIME: About 30 minutes, plus 12 hours to drain tomatoes

NOTES: The amount of water that tomatoes produce depends on how juicy they are; you may need to adjust the amount you start with. If using thawed frozen peas, omit cooking them; just add with the onions and cherry tomatoes in step 5. Serve the salmon in tomato water, topped with creamy mayonnaise blended with fresh basil and lemon juice; offer crusty bread alongside.

MAKES: 4 servings

5 pounds ripe tomatoes, rinsed, cored, and quartered
   About ½ teaspoon salt

6 ounces purple or white pearl onions (about 1½ cups)

1 cup shelled fresh peas (from 1 lb. in pods) or thawed frozen petite peas

1½ pounds boned, skinned salmon fillet, cut into four equal pieces
   Pepper

¾ cup cherry tomatoes (at room temperature), rinsed and stemmed

1. In a blender, working in batches if necessary, whirl tomatoes with ½ teaspoon salt until smooth. Pour into a strainer lined with two layers of cheesecloth (four if it's loosely woven) and set over a large bowl. Enclose nested containers in plastic wrap and chill, without stirring, at least 12 hours and up to 2 days to drain. Gather cloth edges and twist gently to squeeze out any remaining clear liquid, stopping when any red is released. Pour clear tomato water into a glass measure; you need 3 to 3½ cups. Save red purée for other uses, such as pasta sauce.

2. In a 3- to 4-quart pan over high heat, bring about 2 quarts water to a boil. Add pearl onions and cook just until barely tender when pierced, about 3 minutes. Lift out with a strainer or slotted spoon and rinse under cold running water until cool enough to handle. Trim root end from each onion and squeeze out of peel. Add peas to boiling water and cook until barely tender to bite, 2 to 3 minutes (see notes); drain.

3. Rinse salmon and pat dry. Sprinkle all over with salt and pepper. Lay pieces on a well-oiled grill over a solid bed of hot coals or high heat on a gas grill (you can hold your hand at grill level only 2 to 3 seconds); close lid on gas grill. Cook, turning once, until barely opaque but still moist-looking in center of thickest part (cut to test), 6 to 8 minutes total.

4. Meanwhile, in a microwave oven on full power (100%), heat tomato water until steaming, 2½ to 3 minutes.

5. Set a piece of salmon in each of four wide, shallow bowls. Pour tomato water around fish and distribute onions, peas, and cherry tomatoes in water.

Per serving: 471 cal., 38% (180 cal.) from fat; 41 g protein; 20 g fat (4 g sat.); 34 g carbo (0 g fiber); 445 mg sodium; 100 mg chol.

—Sara Schneider

One grape, two styles: Pinot Gris is intense and elegant, Pinot Grigio light and casual.

Shades of gray

Wine riddle for August: *What white grape has two names and multiple personalities?*
Answer: *Pinot Gris, aka Pinot Grigio—a wine that can so thoroughly change its identity, the CIA would be envious.*

Pinot Gris is a French grape, but it's best known for its Italian personality, as Pinot Grigio. Light and fresh, Pinot Grigio has always been loved for what it is not: it is not complex, intense, or particularly aromatic, flavorful, or long on the palate. Pinot Grigio is, in fact, the ultimate no-frills, no-thought-required quaffer—just the ticket in casual Italian trattorias. Its plain-Jane quality makes it ideal for washing down almost everything.

But in France—the grape's homeland—Pinot Gris is made into a wine that's altogether a different kettle of fish. The most famous French Pinot Gris come from Alsace, possibly the most beautiful wine region in France and, incidentally, the one with the highest concentration of three-Michelin-star restaurants in the country. Here, Pinot Gris is a rich, smooth, powerful wine full of personality, with almond, vanilla, peach, and earthy aromas and flavors. The French drink it with all sorts of substantial dishes, especially pork.

So here's the big picture: think of French Pinot Gris and Italian Pinot Grigio as the bookends. In between are the versions from everywhere else. And they are up-and-coming stars in many places: Oregon, California, New Zealand—even Canada. The key to predicting the nature of any one of them is the name. When it's called Pinot Gris (as it usually is in Oregon), the style is meant to be closer to the French end of the spectrum—that is, the producer is hoping to make a fairly intense, flavorful wine. When it's called Pinot Grigio (as it usually is in New Zealand), the producer is modeling the wine closer to the light, crisp Italian version. In California, you'll find both styles: flamboyant, mouth-filling Pinot Gris and sleek, feathery Pinot Grigios.

Two common themes unite these styles, however: First, most Pinot Gris and Pinot Grigios are very easy on the wallet. Second, most are made without much new oak, so they don't have big, toasty, oaky flavors. Instead, you'll find pure, refreshing citrusy characteristics—perfect for August. —*Karen MacNeil-Fife*

Cool fizz

Amaryll Schwertner, former chef and partner at the recently closed San Francisco restaurant Stars, makes magical drinks out of ordinary fruits and vegetables. Cucumber and mint cool this one down, yogurt smooths it out, and seltzer water jazzes it up.

Persian Carpet

In a blender, whirl 1½ cups coarsely chopped **English cucumber** (for best color, leave peel on), 2 cups **plain whole-milk yogurt,** and 2 teaspoons chopped **fresh mint** leaves until very smooth. Add **kosher** or sea salt to taste (¼ to ½ teaspoon). Fill four tall glasses (16-oz. capacity) halfway with **ice cubes.** Pour yogurt mixture equally into glasses. Slowly fill each glass to the rim with cold **seltzer water.** Garnish with fresh mint sprigs. Makes 4 servings.

Per serving: 75 cal., 44% (33 cal.) from fat; 4.5 g protein; 3.7 g fat (2.4 g sat.); 6.5 g carbo (0.6 g fiber); 172 mg sodium; 15 mg chol.

—*Jerry Anne Di Vecchio*

Great Gris and Grigios

Bethel Heights Pinot Gris 2002 *(Oregon)*, *$12.* Beautiful meadowy, gingery aroma; limey and crisp on the palate. A fresh, dry white that's friendly toward all kinds of foods.

J Pinot Gris 2002 *(Russian River Valley, CA)*, *$18.* Gingery, crisp, and zesty, with a smoothness reminiscent of cream soda and hints of citrus and almonds—exotic and fascinating. Think light curries or Asian-spiced seafood.

Longoria Pinot Grigio 2002 *(Santa Barbara County)*, *$18.*

Floral and spicy, with delicious apricot and peach flavors and hints of almond and vanilla. Long, scrumptious finish.

Nautilus Pinot Gris 2002 *(Marlborough, New Zealand)*, *$18.* Limey and refreshing but creamy at the same time (like a great Key lime pie), with hints of grapefruit, spice, and Mandarin orange. Crisp but not sharp in the mouth. Think grilled vegetables or that favorite Pinot Gris companion: grilled salmon.

Pierre Sparr Pinot Gris Reserve 2000 *(Alsace, France)*,

$15. Powerful and dry, with beautifully dense and concentrated peach and marzipan flavors and hints of almonds, meadows, and vanilla. Irresistible plush texture. Fantastic with a spicy pork dish like grilled kebabs.

Teresa Raiz Pinot Grigio 2001 *(Friuli Venezia Giulia, Italy)*, *$13.* Some Pinot Grigios have more pizzazz than others—like this one, with its lightly spicy aroma and crisp citrus, peach, and almond flavors. A winner with all sorts of light summer salads and pastas. —*K. M.-F.*

Cool off

Readers' recipes tested
in *Sunset's* kitchens

Photographs by James Carrier

Chopped Barbecued Chicken Salad

Tina Williams, Pasadena

A great potluck dish, this salad starts with several prepared or leftover ingredients. As a shortcut, pick up roasted chicken at a market. To transport the salad, bring dressing (step 1) separately; mix all ingredients together in a large bowl (step 2) just before serving. To cook fresh corn kernels, simmer in 1 cup water for 3 to 4 minutes; drain.

PREP TIME: About 20 minutes

MAKES: 4 to 6 main-dish servings

- ¼ **cup prepared barbecue sauce**
- 2 **tablespoons olive oil**
- 2 **tablespoons lime juice**
- 1 **tablespoon red wine vinegar**
- 2 **cans (15 oz. each) kidney beans, drained and rinsed**
- 2 **cups chopped cooked chicken (see notes)**
- 1 **cup cooked fresh or thawed frozen corn kernels (see notes)**
- 1 **cup chopped red bell pepper**
- 1 **cup broken tortilla chips**
- ½ **cup thinly sliced radishes**
- ½ **cup chopped red onion**
- 1 **tomato (about 8 oz.), rinsed, cored, seeded, and diced**
- 8 **ounces mixed baby greens**
  Salt and pepper

1. In a large bowl, mix barbecue sauce, olive oil, lime juice, and vinegar.

2. Add beans, chicken, corn, bell pepper, chips, radishes, onion, tomato, and greens. Mix well. Add salt and pepper to taste.

Per serving: 352 cal., 28% (99 cal.) from fat; 25 g protein; 11 g fat (1.9 g sat.); 39 g carbo (9.1 g fiber); 387 mg sodium; 40 mg chol.

A tangy barbecue-sauce dressing stars in this chicken taco salad.

Cuban Beans and Rice Salad

Linda Lum, Steilacoom, WA

Linda Lum writes that in addition to great flavor, this simple salad has many of the features important to her family—it is nutritious, quick, and economical.

PREP TIME: About 20 minutes

MAKES: 6 cups; about 4 main-dish servings

- 2 **tablespoons lemon juice**
- 2 **tablespoons olive oil**
- 1 **tablespoon balsamic vinegar**
- 1 **teaspoon ground cumin**
- 1 **teaspoon salt**
- ¼ **teaspoon pepper**
- 3 **cups cooked long-grain white rice, cooled**
- 1 **can (15 oz.) black beans, drained and rinsed**
- 8 **ounces firm-ripe tomatoes, rinsed, cored, seeded, and chopped**
- 2 **tablespoons chopped fresh parsley**
- 2 **tablespoons chopped fresh cilantro**
- 1 **firm-ripe avocado (about 9 oz.)**

1. In a large bowl, mix lemon juice, olive oil, vinegar, cumin, salt, and pepper. Stir in rice, beans, tomatoes, parsley, and cilantro.

2. Pit, peel, and dice avocado. Gently stir into salad. Serve immediately or chill up to 4 hours.

Per serving: 364 cal., 37% (135 cal.) from fat; 8.6 g protein; 15 g fat (2.2 g sat.); 50 g carbo (5.2 g fiber); 768 mg sodium; 0 mg chol.

FOOD STYLING: KAREN SHINTO (2)

Hawaiian Smoothies

Margaret Pache, Mesa, AZ

Margaret Pache garnishes this frosty smoothie with orange slices. Coconut sorbet and ice cream are available at some supermarkets; you can also buy the latter by the pint at ice cream shops.

PREP TIME: About 10 minutes

MAKES: Four 8-ounce smoothies

- 1 cup vanilla low-fat yogurt
- 2 cups coconut sorbet or ice cream
- ½ cup pineapple juice, chilled
- 2 large bananas (about 1 lb. total)
- ¼ cup sweetened flaked coconut

In a blender, whirl yogurt, sorbet, pineapple juice, bananas, coconut flakes, and 1 cup crushed ice until smooth. Pour into chilled glasses and serve immediately.

Per smoothie: 314 cal., 32% (99 cal.) from fat; 4.8 g protein; 11 g fat (8.9 g sat.); 53 g carbo (2.5 g fiber); 58 mg sodium; 2.8 mg chol.

Dried Tomato Pesto–Filled Burgers

Karen Rose, Three Forks, MT

These inventive burgers have a layer of tangy dried-tomato pesto in the center. The jalapeño mayonnaise gives them extra zip.

PREP AND COOK TIME: About 45 minutes

MAKES: 6 burgers

- ½ cup shredded parmesan cheese
- 2 tablespoons pine nuts
- 2 tablespoons drained (reserve 2 tablespoons oil) coarsely chopped oil-packed dried tomatoes
- 1 tablespoon tomato paste
- 2 cloves garlic, peeled
- 1½ pounds ground beef round or sirloin
- ⅓ cup beer
- About 1 teaspoon salt
- About 1 teaspoon pepper
- 6 hamburger buns (about 3 oz. each), split in half horizontally
- ¾ cup crumbled feta cheese (4 oz.; optional)
- Jalapeño mayonnaise (recipe follows)

1. In a blender or food processor, whirl parmesan cheese, pine nuts, dried tomatoes, tomato paste, garlic, and 2 tablespoons reserved oil from dried tomatoes until mixture is a chunky paste, scraping down sides of bowl as needed.

2. In a large bowl, mix ground beef with beer, 1 teaspoon salt, and 1 teaspoon pepper until well combined. Divide meat mixture into 12 equal portions and flatten each portion into a 4-inch round.

3. Top each of 6 of the rounds with about 1 tablespoon of the dried-tomato pesto. Top with remaining 6 rounds, pressing edges together to seal.

4. Lay burgers on a barbecue grill over a solid bed of hot coals or high heat on a gas grill (you can hold your hand at grill level only 2 to 3 seconds); close lid on gas grill. Cook burgers, turning once to brown both sides, until meat around filling is no longer pink (cut to test; note that pesto is reddish brown), 6 to 8 minutes total. Also lay bun halves, cut side down, on grill and toast 1 to 2 minutes.

5. With a wide spatula, transfer burgers to bun bottoms. Add salt and pepper to taste. Top each burger with about 2 tablespoons feta cheese, if desired. Cover with bun tops. Serve with jalapeño mayonnaise to add to taste.

Per serving: 601 cal., 40% (243 cal.) from fat; 34 g protein; 27 g fat (8.6 g sat.); 54 g carbo (4 g fiber); 1,414 mg sodium; 76 mg chol.

Jalapeño mayonnaise. In a blender or food processor, whirl 1 rinsed, stemmed, and seeded fresh **jalapeño chili** (1½ oz.) and ¾ cup **mayonnaise** until smooth. Makes about ¾ cup.

Per tablespoon: 100 cal., 99% (99 cal.) from fat; 0.2 g protein; 11 g fat (1.6 g sat.); 0.6 g carbo (0 g fiber); 78 mg sodium; 8.1 mg chol.

Berry Pudding Cake

Gemma Sanita Sciabica, Modesto, CA

This tender cake bakes over sweet berries, creating a juicy, cobblerlike dessert. Serve with whipped cream or vanilla ice cream, if desired.

This juicy cross between a cake and a cobbler uses ripe summer berries.

PREP AND COOK TIME: About 45 minutes

MAKES: About 8 servings

- 2 cups fresh blueberries, rinsed
- 2 cups fresh raspberries, rinsed
- 1¼ cups granulated sugar
- 4 large eggs
- 1 tablespoon olive oil
- 1 tablespoon grated orange peel
- 1 teaspoon vanilla
- 1 cup all-purpose flour
- 1 teaspoon baking powder
- ¼ teaspoon salt
- Powdered sugar

1. In a 9- by 13-inch baking dish, mix blueberries and raspberries with ¼ cup granulated sugar. Spread level.

2. In a bowl, whisk eggs, olive oil, orange peel, vanilla, and remaining 1 cup granulated sugar. Stir in flour, baking powder, and salt until just combined. Pour batter evenly over berry mixture and gently spread to cover berries.

3. Bake cake in a 350° regular or convection oven until top springs back slightly when gently pressed in the center, 28 to 35 minutes. Let cool at least 10 minutes; serve warm or cool. Sprinkle with powdered sugar just before serving, and scoop portions onto plates.

Per serving: 275 cal., 15% (41 cal.) from fat; 5.3 g protein; 4.6 g fat (1 g sat.); 54 g carbo (2.7 g fiber); 167 mg sodium; 106 mg chol. ◆

Pink Lady or Granny Smith apples are paired with walnuts in a rustic galette (see page 185).

September

Porcini-laced meat sauce
and grand meatballs
top spaghetti for a crowd.

Spaghetti Western

Italian American tradition inspires a fun fall dinner

By Charity Ferreira • Photographs by James Carrier
Food styling by Basil Friedman

Time-honored Italian American fare—thick sauces that cling to lanky strands of spaghetti, imbuing them with the concentrated flavors of tomato, olive oil, and garlic—is just the kind of food that everyone loves. It's also an important part of the West's culinary past and present, even if Cal-Ital modernism might seem to have taken over the high-end restaurant scene. But the real old-fashioned thing is just right for casual entertaining.

This hearty spaghetti dinner has authentic roots and flavor. Our earthy, flavorful porcini meat sauce is a variation on a family recipe from Blair Erigero of Stockton, California, whose grandparents brought the recipe when they came to San Francisco from Italy in the 1880s. Erigero remembers that his grandfather sent money home to relatives in Italy, and in return they sent big bags of dried wild mushrooms for his step-grandmother to use in the sauce. A batch of either this sauce or our savory roasted eggplant marinara serves 8 to 12; choose one for a party, or make both for a really big crowd. Either is delicious with tender, juicy meatballs, made from a recipe that three generations of the Gonnella family have served up at the Union Hotel in Occidental, California.

Round out the menu with toasted garlic bread, plenty of parmesan cheese and easygoing red wine, and a simple layered ice cream terrine with spumoni flavors, and you have a homey dinner that's perfect for a crisp fall evening.

Antipasti platter

Put together a family-style first course with three or four of these purchased or easily assembled items.

Canned kidney or white beans tossed with minced garlic and olive oil

Pepperoncini

Roasted bell pepper strips

Mozzarella cheese sticks

Rolled thinly sliced salami or mortadella

Rinsed, trimmed radishes

Olives

Roasted Eggplant Marinara Sauce

PREP AND COOK TIME: About 1½ hours

MAKES: About 12 cups, enough for about 2 pounds spaghetti; 8 to 12 servings

2	pounds eggplant, rinsed, ends trimmed, and cut into ½-inch chunks
3	tablespoons olive oil
3	tablespoons minced garlic
	About ¼ teaspoon salt
	About ¼ teaspoon pepper
1	onion (about 8 oz.), peeled and diced (¼ in.)
3	cans (28 oz. each) crushed or ground tomatoes
2	teaspoons dried basil
1½	teaspoons sugar
1½	teaspoons dried oregano
¾	teaspoon hot chili flakes

1. In a 12- by 15-inch baking pan, mix eggplant with 2 tablespoons oil, 1 tablespoon garlic, ¼ teaspoon salt, and ¼ teaspoon pepper. Bake in a 400° regular or convection oven, stirring once, until eggplant is browned and soft when pierced, 30 to 35 minutes.

2. Pour remaining tablespoon oil into a 5- to 6-quart pan over medium heat. When oil is hot, add onion and remaining 2 tablespoons garlic. Stir frequently until onion is very limp, 5 to 8 minutes.

3. Add tomatoes, basil, sugar, oregano, chili flakes, and roasted eggplant. Cover and simmer, stirring occasionally, until tomatoes have broken down

Assemble the first course with purchased olives, salami, and vegetables.

slightly and mixture is thick, 35 to 40 minutes. Add salt and pepper to taste.

Per serving of sauce: 103 cal., 35% (36 cal.) from fat; 3.1 g protein; 4 g fat (0.5 g sat.); 16 g carbo (3.1 g fiber); 375 mg sodium; 0 mg chol.

Porcini Meat Sauce

PREP AND COOK TIME: About 1¾ hours

MAKES: About 12 cups, enough for about 2 pounds spaghetti; 8 to 12 servings

½	ounce dried porcini mushrooms (about ⅓ cup)
2	tablespoons olive oil
1	pound ground veal or ground beef (sirloin)
1	pound ground pork
2	tablespoons chopped parsley
1	tablespoon minced garlic
3	cans (28 oz. each) crushed or ground tomatoes
¼	teaspoon dried oregano
	About ¼ teaspoon salt
	About ⅛ teaspoon pepper

1. In a small bowl, soak mushrooms in 1 cup hot water until soft, about 15 minutes. Gently rub under water to release grit, then lift out (reserve liquid); finely chop mushrooms.

2. Meanwhile, pour oil into a 6- to 8-quart pan over medium-high heat. When hot, add veal, pork, parsley, and garlic. Stir constantly, breaking meat into small pieces, until browned, 5 to 8 minutes.

3. Stir in tomatoes, oregano, ¼ teaspoon salt, ⅛ teaspoon pepper, and mushrooms; carefully pour in reserved soaking liquid, leaving grit behind. Bring to a boil, then lower heat, cover, and simmer, stirring occasionally, until tomatoes are broken down and sauce is thick, about 1½ hours. Add salt and pepper to taste.

Per serving of sauce: 218 cal., 54% (117 cal.) from fat; 16 g protein; 13 g fat (4.4 g sat.); 9.6 g carbo (1.8 g fiber); 424 mg sodium; 58 mg chol.

Union Hotel Grand Meatballs

PREP AND COOK TIME: About 40 minutes

NOTES: These savory meatballs complement either of our spaghetti sauces.

MAKES: 25 meatballs; 8 to 12 servings

- 3 large eggs
- 3 tablespoons whole milk
- 1½ cups ½-inch chunks sourdough French bread (crusts trimmed)
- 1½ pounds ground beef (sirloin)
- 2¼ cups grated parmesan cheese
- 2 teaspoons Italian seasoning
- ¾ teaspoon salt
- ½ teaspoon pepper

1. In large bowl or the bowl of an electric mixer fitted with the paddle attachment, beat eggs and milk just to blend. Stir in bread and let stand until soft, about 10 minutes. Add ground beef, cheese, Italian seasoning, salt, and pepper and beat on low speed or mix until well blended.

2. Gently shape mixture into 2-inch balls; place meatballs about 1 inch apart on a lightly oiled or foil-lined 14- by 16-inch baking sheet.

3. Bake in a 350° regular or convection oven until no longer pink in the center (cut to test), 20 to 25 minutes.

Per serving: 223 cal., 57% (126 cal.) from fat; 19 g protein; 14 g fat (6.6 g sat.); 3.4 g carbo (0.1 g fiber); 501 mg sodium; 103 mg chol.

Sourdough Garlic Bread

PREP AND COOK TIME: About 10 minutes

NOTES: Pasquale Usorio, proprietor for nearly four decades of Pasquale's Pizzeria in San Francisco, makes a crusty, potent garlic bread that regulars swear by.

MAKES: 12 pieces

In a small bowl, mix ½ cup **olive oil**, 3 tablespoons minced or pressed **garlic**,

and 3 tablespoons chopped **parsley**. Cut two ½-pound loaves of **sourdough French bread** crosswise into thirds, then cut each third in half horizontally. Brush or spoon garlic mixture generously on the cut side of each piece. Sprinkle each piece with about ½ tablespoon grated **parmesan cheese**. Place pieces (cheese side up) on baking sheets and broil 8 inches from heat until well browned, 3 to 4 minutes each. Serve warm.

Per piece: 199 cal., 50% (99 cal.) from fat; 4.5 g protein; 11 g fat (1.9 g sat.); 21 g carbo (1.1 g fiber); 278 mg sodium; 2 mg chol.

Spumoni Ice Cream Terrine

PREP TIME: About 30 minutes, plus at least 9 hours to freeze

NOTES: As you're ready to use each kind of ice cream, soften it in the microwave on high power (100%) in 5-second intervals just until soft enough to spread, but not melting, 5 to 20 seconds.

MAKES: 10 to 12 servings

- 3 cups (1½ pints) strawberry ice cream, softened (see notes)
- 3 cups (1½ pints) pistachio or toasted almond ice cream, softened (see notes)
- 3 cups (1½ pints) chocolate ice cream, softened (see notes)

1. Line a 7- by 9-inch loaf pan (9-cup capacity) completely with two or three pieces of plastic wrap, leaving

This toasted sourdough is for garlic lovers.

several inches of plastic overhanging on all sides.

2. Spread strawberry ice cream in an even layer in the bottom of lined pan; freeze for 30 minutes. Spread pistachio ice cream in an even layer over strawberry; freeze for 30 minutes. Spread chocolate ice cream in an even layer over pistachio; cover with overhanging plastic wrap and freeze until firm, about 8 hours, or up to 1 week.

3. Unwrap terrine and invert pan over a serving plate. Hold on to plastic wrap and lift off pan. Remove plastic wrap. Return to freezer for up to 2 hours, or serve at once. To serve, cut terrine into 1-inch-thick slices (dip knife in hot water and wipe dry between each slice).

Per serving: 280 cal., 51% (144 cal.) from fat; 4.8 g protein; 16 g fat (7.7 g sat.); 29 g carbo (0.2 g fiber); 85 mg sodium; 76 mg chol. ♦

Layer strawberry, pistachio, and chocolate ice cream for a whimsical version of old-fashioned spumoni.

Chicken for all ages

At last, a dinner the whole family will like

By Jerry Anne Di Vecchio
Photograph by James Carrier

Drumsticks and rosemary potatoes bake in the same oven.

Suspicion lurks behind the 10-year-old's question, "What's for dinner?" She's imagining capers in the sauce and arugula in the salad. What parent hasn't despaired of planning dinner that's interesting for the adults and the kids? One simple approach is to start with universally acceptable components—chicken, potatoes, and ice cream, for instance—then make small adjustments to please different tastes. Just add a green salad to our lively meat-and-potatoes combo—who says you can't please 'em all?

Sesame Drumsticks with Crusty Oven Hash

PREP AND COOK TIME: About 1 hour

NOTES: Serve the hot potatoes with sour cream and chopped chives.

MAKES: 4 servings

- 6 cups diced (½ in.) peeled thin-skinned potatoes (about 2½ lb. total)
- 1 onion (about 8 oz.), peeled and chopped
- 1 teaspoon chopped fresh rosemary leaves or ½ teaspoon dried rosemary
- 5 tablespoons plus 2 teaspoons olive oil

  About ½ teaspoon salt

  About ½ teaspoon pepper
- 2 to 3 tablespoons soy sauce

  About ½ cup toasted sesame seeds
- 8 chicken drumsticks (equal size, about 2 lb. total), rinsed and patted dry
- 1½ cups purchased seasoned croutons

1. In a 12- by 17-inch rimmed pan, mix potatoes, onion, rosemary, 3 tablespoons olive oil, ½ teaspoon salt, and ½ teaspoon pepper. Spread into a single layer. Bake on upper rack in a 425° regular or convection oven for 10 minutes.

2. Meanwhile, oil a 10- by 15-inch rimmed pan. In a bowl, mix 2 tablespoons soy sauce and 2 teaspoons oil. Put sesame seeds on a plate. Roll drumsticks in soy mixture (add more soy if needed), then in sesame seeds to coat. Lay drumsticks well apart in pan. When potato mixture has baked 10 minutes, place chicken on lower rack in oven and bake until well browned (180° in center of thickest part), 30 to 35 minutes.

3. When potatoes begin to brown at pan edges, about 10 minutes after adding chicken, turn with a spatula, moving unbrowned ones to edges; spread level. Bake until potatoes are tender when pierced, 15 to 18 minutes longer.

4. While potatoes cook, put croutons into a heavy zip-lock plastic bag and coarsely crush; mix with remaining 2 tablespoons olive oil. When potatoes are done, mix in crushed croutons and bake until browned, 5 to 8 minutes.

5. Arrange chicken on a platter with hash. Add more salt and pepper to taste.

Per serving: 802 cal., 48% (387 cal.) from fat; 40 g protein; 43 g fat (7.9 g sat.); 64 g carbo (8.6 g fiber); 1,106 mg sodium; 97 mg chol.

Flexible Fruit Foster

PREP AND COOK TIME: About 15 minutes

MAKES: 4 servings

- ¼ cup (⅛ lb.) butter
- ¼ cup firmly packed brown sugar
- ⅛ teaspoon ground cinnamon
- 1 tablespoon orange juice
- 3 to 4 firm-ripe bananas (about 1½ lb. total), peeled and cut into 1-inch-thick slices, or 1½ pounds firm-ripe peaches, peeled, pitted, and sliced
- 1 pint vanilla ice cream

  About 2 tablespoons banana- or orange-flavored liqueur

  About 2 tablespoons dark rum

1. In a 10- to 12-inch frying pan over high heat, stir butter and brown sugar until bubbling vigorously. Add cinnamon, orange juice, and fruit; turn fruit often with a spatula until sauce is boiling again and fruit is hot, 1 to 3 minutes.

2. Scoop ice cream equally into four bowls. For the children, spoon fruit and sauce over ice cream. Then, for the adults, pour banana liqueur and rum over fruit in pan and ignite with a match (keep away from vents or flammable materials); shake pan until flame dies. Spoon fruit and sauce over ice cream.

Per serving with liquors: 431 cal., 42% (180 cal.) from fat; 3.6 g protein; 20 g fat (12 g sat.); 58 g carbo (1.8 g fiber); 181 mg sodium; 61 mg chol. ◆

FOOD STYLING: BASIL FRIEDMAN

Tasteful tuna

There's nothing fishy about the Tuna Guys' canned albacore

By Vanessa McGrady
Photograph by John Granen

Operated by John Holt, wife Kathleen, and son Sean—with the help of their boat, *The Kathleen*—the Tuna Guys are a family affair.

When the price of tuna plummeted in 1999, John Holt needed to do something with his catch so it wouldn't all go to waste. The big fish, those 15 pounds and more, got shipped off for export, mostly to Japan. "But the small stuff—we couldn't find a good price for it," he says.

John turned the tide by canning what he couldn't sell—one of the wisest business decisions he'd ever made.

The Tuna Guys' canned albacore, unlike any kind of poultry of the sea, tastes surprisingly like, well, fish. The Gig Harbor–based team—John, wife Kathleen, and son Sean—have found their niche by hand-packing tuna filets and canning them with just a pinch of salt. The tuna creates its own juice—no need to add water or oil, which, at the very least, is what you usually find mixed into the tuna on grocery store shelves.

Most commercial canning companies can't afford to do it the Tuna Guys' way, and the result is a "slurry mush," says John. The Holts' fish retain a firm, fresh flavor. Sure, their product is a little more expensive, but that doesn't hamper its popularity. The Tuna Guys started canning their catch in 1999 and sold 1,000 cases. They tripled that the next year, and now they're selling 18,000 cases a season.

Trolling for tuna

The Holts don't actually do their own canning; that job goes out to a cannery on Vancouver Island, B.C. The family has its hands full fishing and selling. Most of the action happens aboard *The Kathleen*, a 65-foot fishing boat John

built in 1973 and named after his wife. When *The Kathleen* isn't docked in Tacoma, Sean has her crisscrossing the Pacific, wherever the fish are biting. She can carry up to 40 tons of fish.

The fish are troll-caught, meaning that the boat is decked out with big poles, 15 lines dangling from each. Hooks disguised by plastic squid snag fish lured by frozen anchovies. This method is eco-friendly; there are no nets to entangle dolphins.

You can try catching tuna on your own, but keep in mind that they're particular to certain temperatures—John says they won't hang out in places below 59° or above 65°; 62° is optimal —and most of the best fishing is at least 100 miles offshore. "Pick a spot where you're the farthest from anything— that's where you'll find 'em." John recommends fishing charters, which can lead you to the best conditions and provide you with equipment.

After you haul in your catch, the secret to getting the whitest meat is to bleed the fish immediately, then freeze it. "All fish is best to eat when you catch it," John says. If you're lucky enough to snag more than a bellyful, he suggests canning it at home. Or just pick up the phone and order a case of Tuna Guys tuna.

Tuna Guys: www.tunaguys.net or (800) 224-5541.

Kathleen's Tuna Cakes

PREP AND COOK TIME: About 20 minutes

NOTES: Serve these tuna cakes with lemon wedges and your favorite tartar sauce or aioli.

MAKES: 4 cakes; 2 servings

- 1 can (6 oz.) good-quality solid white tuna, drained
- 1 large egg
- 1 cup fresh white bread crumbs
- ¼ cup finely chopped celery
- ¼ cup finely chopped onion
- 2 tablespoons finely chopped red bell pepper
- 1 teaspoon Worcestershire
- ½ teaspoon salt
- ¼ teaspoon pepper
- ¼ teaspoon dry mustard
- 2 tablespoons olive oil

1. In a bowl, flake tuna with a fork. Add egg, bread crumbs, celery, onion, bell pepper, Worcestershire, salt, pepper, and dry mustard; mix until well blended. Shape into four cakes about 3 inches wide and ½ inch thick.

2. Pour olive oil into a 10- to 12-inch frying pan over medium heat. When hot, add cakes, slightly apart, and cook, turning once, until golden brown on both sides, 5 to 6 minutes total. Serve hot.

Per cake: 386 cal., 56% (216 cal.) from fat; 27 g protein; 24 g fat (4.1 g sat.); 15 g carbo (1.2 g fiber); 1,099 mg sodium; 132 mg chol. ◆

Apple season

Celebrate autumn with a rustic open-faced galette

By Kate Washington • Photograph by James Carrier
Food styling by Karen Shinto

Fall announces itself with a hint of coolness in the air and late afternoon's golden light, but its best harbinger is the sudden profusion of juicy apples—pale green, russet, and every color in between. We especially love unusual varieties grown in the West, like Gravenstein and Pink Lady. This new harvest piled up in farmers' markets in early fall turns our thoughts to baking. A free-form galette, rich with caramel and walnuts, is an easy and delicious way to mark the changing of the seasons.

Apple Galette

PREP AND COOK TIME: About 1½ hours, plus about 1 hour to chill dough

NOTES: Serve this tart with vanilla ice cream.

MAKES: 6 to 8 servings

- 1½ **cups all-purpose flour**
- 1 **tablespoon granulated sugar**
- ¼ **teaspoon salt**
- ½ **cup (¼ lb.) plus 2 tablespoons cold butter**
- 1 **large egg yolk, lightly beaten**
- ½ **cup walnuts**
- 2 **pounds tart apples (3 to 5), such as Pink Lady or Granny Smith**
- ½ **cup firmly packed brown sugar**
- ¼ **teaspoon ground nutmeg**
- 1 **large egg, beaten to blend with 1 tablespoon water**

1. In a food processor or large bowl, combine flour, granulated sugar, and salt. Cut ½ cup butter into pieces and add to flour mixture; pulse motor, cut in with a pastry blender, or rub in with your fingers until mixture resembles coarse meal. With motor running (or stirring with a fork after each addition), add egg yolk and 3 to 4 tablespoons cold water, 1 tablespoon at a time; process or stir just until mixture comes together in a ball. Form dough into a flat disk, wrap in plastic wrap, and chill until firm but still pliable, about 1 hour.

2. Meanwhile, spread walnuts in a baking pan and bake in a 375° oven until barely golden under skins, 6 to 8 minutes (leave oven on). Coarsely chop nuts.

3. Peel and core apples; cut each into eight wedges. In a 10- to 12-inch nonstick frying pan over medium heat, melt remaining 2 tablespoons butter. When it's foamy, add apples and stir often until slightly softened and brown at edges, 10 to 12 minutes. Sprinkle brown sugar and nutmeg over fruit and stir until liquid is syrupy and bubbling, about 5 minutes. Stir in walnuts. Remove from heat.

4. Unwrap dough. On a lightly floured surface, with a lightly floured rolling pin, roll into a round about 15 inches in diameter. Line a 12- by 15-inch baking sheet with cooking parchment (or butter the sheet well) and carefully transfer dough round to sheet (edges will hang over sheet).

5. Pour apple mixture onto center of pastry, mounding wedges in a circle about 8 inches wide and 2 inches high. Gently fold edges of dough over apples, pleating as you go, leaving an opening about 4 inches wide in the center. Brush pastry all over with beaten egg.

6. Bake in 375° oven until pastry is golden brown and apples are tender when pierced, 40 to 45 minutes (35 to 40 in a convection oven). Transfer galette (with parchment, if using) to a wire rack to cool. Transfer to a large plate, gently pulling parchment from under tart. Serve slightly warm or at room temperature, cut into wedges.

Per serving: 390 cal., 48% (189 cal.) from fat; 4.9 g protein; 21 g fat (9.8 g sat.); 49 g carbo (2.8 g fiber); 233 mg sodium; 92 mg chol. ◆

Liquid gold

From delicate to robust, honey flavors dishes savory and sweet

By Lisa Taggart and Charity Ferreira
Photographs by James Carrier

It remains one of nature's miracles—that process by which buzzing honeybees transform flower dust into edible gold. Aristotle called the result "the nectar of the gods."

But all honey is not the same. Nuances of flavor and color vary according to the source flower. "It's like wine in that way," says Helene Marshall, who produces honey in the San Francisco Bay Area with her husband, Spencer.

Increasingly, diners—and cooks—are seeking out specific specialty honeys, from delicately perfumed sage to citrusy orange blossom to tangy avocado. Many people are surprised by the range of flavors. Richard Spiegel of Volcano Island Honey Company in Hawaii says most people can't find words to describe the taste of his creamy organic kiawe honey. "It's very light and subtle, but rich and tropical at the same time."

The distinctive flavors of Western honey shine in an equally surprising range of dishes, from salad to dessert.

In general, the darker the honey, the bolder its flavor.

Orange slices—baked on the bottom—end up on top in a rich honey glaze.

Honey-Orange Upside-Down Cake

PREP AND COOK TIME: About 1½ hours

NOTES: Serve this cake with lightly sweetened softly whipped cream.

MAKES: 6 to 8 servings

- ½ cup honey
- ¼ cup orange juice
- 1 unpeeled orange (10 oz.), rinsed and very thinly sliced crosswise (about ⅛ in. thick; discard ends)
- ¾ cup (⅜ lb.) butter, at room temperature
- 1 cup sugar
- 2 large eggs
- 1 tablespoon grated orange peel
- 1½ cups all-purpose flour
- 1 teaspoon baking powder
- ¼ teaspoon salt
- ⅓ cup whole milk

1. In a 9- to 10-inch nonstick, ovenproof frying pan (with sloping sides) over medium-high heat, stir honey and orange juice until boiling. Cook without stirring until mixture is foamy, slightly thickened, and reaches 230° (carefully tilt pan so mixture is deep enough to register on thermometer), 2 to 4 minutes. Chill until thickened, about 15 minutes. Slightly overlap orange slices in concentric circles over syrup.

2. In a large bowl, with a mixer on high speed, beat butter and sugar until smooth. Add eggs one at a time, beating well after each addition. Beat in orange peel.

3. In another bowl, mix flour, baking powder, and salt. Stir half the flour mixture into butter mixture just until incorporated. Stir in milk, then remaining flour mixture, just until incorporated. Carefully scrape batter over orange slices in pan and spread level.

4. Bake in a 350° regular or convection oven until a wooden skewer inserted in the center comes out clean, 35 to 40 minutes for regular, 25 to 30 minutes for convection. Let cool for 5 minutes.

5. Invert a flat plate over pan. Invert cake onto plate and lift pan off, being careful with hot syrup. Let cool completely, then cut into wedges.

Per serving: 442 cal., 39% (171 cal.) from fat; 5 g protein; 19 g fat (11 g sat.); 68 g carbo (1.3 g fiber); 331 mg sodium; 101 mg chol.

Apple and Endive Salad with Honey Vinaigrette

PREP TIME: About 15 minutes

NOTES: Toast pecans in a 350° regular or convection oven until lightly browned, 7 to 10 minutes.

MAKES: 4 to 6 servings

- 2 tablespoons orange blossom or other mild honey
- 2 tablespoons champagne vinegar or white wine vinegar
- 1 tablespoon grape-seed oil or mild olive oil
- 2 heads red or white Belgian endive (about 11 oz. total), rinsed, ends trimmed, and cut lengthwise into ¼-inch-wide slivers
- 1 sweet apple, such as Fuji (about 8 oz.), rinsed, cored, and thinly sliced lengthwise
- ⅓ cup pecan halves, toasted (see notes) and coarsely chopped
- 2 ounces blue cheese, crumbled
  Salt

In a large bowl, mix honey, vinegar, and oil. Add endive, apple, pecans, and blue cheese and mix gently to coat. Add salt to taste.

Per serving: 143 cal., 58% (83 cal.) from fat; 3 protein; 9.2 g fat (2.3 g sat.); 14 g carbo (2.2 g fiber); 135 mg sodium; 7.1 mg chol.

Creamed Honey and Miso–Glazed Salmon

PREP AND COOK TIME: About 25 minutes

NOTES: Creamed (or whipped) honey is sold in well-stocked supermarkets.

MAKES: 4 servings

- 1½ pounds boned, skinned salmon fillet (no more than 1 in. thick), cut into 4 equal pieces
- 3 tablespoons creamed honey (see notes)
- 1½ tablespoons white miso
- 1½ teaspoons lemon juice or rice vinegar
- ½ teaspoon grated peeled fresh ginger
- 1 cup finely shredded daikon (about 6 oz.)

1. Rinse fish and pat dry. In a small bowl, mix honey, miso, lemon juice, and ginger. Brush fish generously all over with honey mixture. Set pieces slightly apart on a 12- by 15-inch baking sheet.

2. Broil salmon 3 to 4 inches from heat, turning once with a wide spatula, until opaque but still moist-looking in center of thickest part (cut to test), 7 to 8 minutes total.

3. Set a piece of fish on each of four plates and mound daikon equally alongside.

Per serving: 378 cal., 45% (171 cal.) from fat; 35 g protein; 19 g fat (3.8 g sat.); 16 g carbo (0.3 g fiber); 345 mg sodium; 100 mg chol

Baked Honey Custards

PREP AND COOK TIME: About 1 hour, plus at least 2 hours to chill

NOTES: Use a dark amber–colored honey.

MAKES: 4 servings

- 4 large egg yolks
- ½ cup honey (see notes)
- 1½ cups whipping cream
- ½ cup whole milk
- 1 teaspoon vanilla
- 2 pitted dates, slivered lengthwise
  Thin strips lemon peel

1. In a bowl, whisk together egg yolks and honey until well blended, then whisk in cream, milk, and vanilla. Pour mixture through a fine strainer into another bowl; discard residue.

2. Pour into four ramekins (¾-cup capacity). Set in a 9- by 13-inch pan (with at least 2-in. sides). Set pan on rack in a 325° oven. Pour boiling water around ramekins almost to top of custards. Cover pan with foil, turning back 1 inch at each corner to release steam.

3. Bake until custards jiggle only slightly in the center when gently shaken, 50 to 55 minutes. With a wide spatula, lift dishes from water and transfer to a rack. Let custards cool completely, then cover and chill until cold, about 2 hours, or up to 2 days. Garnish with slivered dates and lemon peel.

Per serving: 483 cal., 63% (306 cal.) from fat; 5.9 g protein; 34 g fat (20 g sat.); 42 g carbo (0.2 g fiber); 54 mg sodium; 316 mg chol. ◆

Honey sources

Joann's Honey. Nut blends and wildflower. *Reedsport, OR; (877) 846-6392.*

Marshall's Farm Natural Honey. Lavender, wildflower blends, and others. *American Canyon, CA; www.marshallshoney.com or (800) 624-4637.*

McEvoy Ranch. Lavender. *Petaluma, CA; www.mcevoyranch.com or (707) 778-2307.*

Volcano Island Honey Company. *Honoka'a, HI; www.volcanoislandhoney. com or (808) 775-1000.*

Happy-trails mix

Cooler temperatures and fewer crowds make fall the perfect time to head outdoors for a hike. And whether trail snacks are a means to an end or your excursion's *raison d'être,* nothing puts a spring in your step like a handful of something crunchy, salty, and sweet. Tuck one of our favorite trail mixes into your backpack before hitting the path. Combine the ingredients in equal parts—or experiment with your own proportions.

Crunchy Monkey: Peanuts, banana chips, chopped dates, and butterscotch chips.

Morning Buzz: Frosted shredded miniwheat cereal, dried blueberries, almonds, and chocolate-covered espresso beans.

Tutti Frutti: Cashews, golden raisins, chopped dried pineapple, chopped dried papaya, and flaked coconut.

Cherry–Chocolate Chip: Granola, dried cherries, chocolate chips, and almonds. —*Charity Ferreira*

Put up your zukes

FRESH IDEA "The trouble with cooking begins when you decide to take it seriously," writes renowned Italian chef Paul Bertolli, a partner in Oakland, California's **Oliveto Cafe & Restaurant,** in his new book, *Cooking by Hand.* It's a personal and compelling case for taking pleasure in the best simple food, and in the effort required to prepare it, whether a lot—building flavor bit by bit from the bottom of the pot up for an Italian meat broth—or a little, such as preparing his zucchini carpaccio (pictured above). *5655 College Ave.; (510) 547-0835.* Cooking by Hand: *Clarkson Potter, New York; $40; (212) 572-2537. —Sara Schneider*

Chef Paul Bertolli's Zucchini Carpaccio

1 In a bowl, mix $1/4$ cup **champagne vinegar,** 2 tablespoons minced **shallot,** and 1 teaspoon **salt.** Let stand 5 minutes. **2** Whisk in $3/4$ cup **extra-virgin olive oil.** **3** Rinse 2 **small green** and 2 **yellow zucchini** (8 ounces total) and trim off ends. Using a mandoline, slice squash lengthwise $1/16$ inch thick, discarding first and last slices from each. **4** In single-layer batches, steam squash over boiling water until barely tender when pierced, about $1 1/2$ minutes. Arrange warm slices in a single layer in a cooking parchment–lined baking pan and brush tops with vinaigrette. Cover and chill until cold, at least 20 minutes. **5** Arrange slices, mixing colors evenly, on six large plates. Drizzle with a little more vinaigrette and sprinkle with $1/3$ cup toasted **pine nuts** (2 oz.) and $1/2$ cup slivered **fresh basil** leaves. **6** Shave **Parmigiano-Reggiano cheese** over servings to garnish, and drizzle with a little more olive oil. Makes 6 servings.

Big cheese

Pay a tasty visit to Colorado's cheesemakers

By Kyle Wagner

Jim Schott and goats work at Haystack Mountain, producer of chèvre and other cheeses (left).

Move over, Wisconsin. Get real, California. The rising star these days in artisan cheesemaking is Colorado, better known for its steaks than its dairy products.

But that's changing. Northern Colorado has a "microcheesery" that makes award-winning blue cheese and goat cheese, another that makes blue and sheep-milk cheese, and one that produces Camembert. All three sell directly to the public, all welcome visitors (at least on a limited basis), and all are the work of passionate cheesemakers.

"One minute, you're toiling away, thinking that it can't get any harder or more fun, and then the next, you actually turn out to be a cheesemaker," says Jim Schott, a dairyman who owns **Haystack Mountain Goat Dairy** in Niwot, Colorado, about 40 minutes northwest of Denver. "Who would have thought that some small cheesemakers in Colorado would be competing against the century-old cheese guys in Wisconsin?"

Competing they are. In 2002, Haystack Mountain won first place from the American Cheese Society for its green chili–enhanced fresh goat cheese. The same year, **Bingham Hill Cheese Company** in Fort Collins earned a gold medal for its rustic blue cheese in the World Cheese Awards in London.

Crafting winning cheeses in Niwot ...

Schott, a former college professor and educational consultant, started his business with five Nubian goats 12 years ago. Today the herd numbers more than 100 and includes high-producing Saanen goats as well as Cashmeres and Angoras, which provide wool for the hand-knit socks and hats sold at a little table outside the dairy. The woolen goods add to Haystack's homey atmosphere.

Many visitors bring the whole family to see the goats—before they get down to the serious business of buying cheese. Haystack has an annual production of 52,000 pounds of goat cheese, which includes the flavored batches as well as traditional chèvre and feta, and an aged, French-style, pyramid-shaped version with surface-ripened mold.

... and in Fort Collins

Bingham Hill, a producer of cow- and sheep-milk cheeses, is open to visitors four days a week. And although production doesn't take place every day, customers who want to see cheese being made may call ahead to check the schedule. Owners Tom Johnson and his wife, Kristi, who is a former scientist and patent attorney, bubble over like curd-filled vats with recipes for their beloved blue.

MouCo Cheese Company, also in Fort Collins, has been open only since 2001. But co-owner Robert Poland, who started the company with partner Birgit Halbreiter, reports a 250 percent increase in sales over last year. Tours of MouCo, which makes Camembert and another soft-ripened cheese, ColoRouge, are available by appointment. They're worth it: The tour guides are generous with samples, especially Halbreiter, a native of Germany who once worked for one of Europe's largest soft-cheese producers.

All three of Colorado's artisan cheeseries are gaining status among America's foodies. Dean & DeLuca has offered Bingham Hill products in its catalog, Martha Stewart has used Haystack cheese on her TV show, and Cirque du Soleil bought large quantities of MouCo's stock during last year's Denver performances. ◆

Colorado artisan cheesemakers

Bingham Hill Cheese Company. *9–5 Mon–Fri (to see cheesemaking demonstrations, call ahead for specific times). 216 Commerce Dr., Fort Collins; www.binghamhill.com or (970) 472-0702.*

Haystack Mountain Goat Dairy. *Open to visitors noon–2 Tue and Sat. 5239 Niwot Rd., Niwot; www. haystackgoatcheese.com or (303) 581-9948.*

MouCo Cheese Company. *Tours by appointment. 1401 Duff Dr., #300, Fort Collins; www.mouco.com or (970) 498-0107.*

A little heat from Spain

Imported paprikas make a delicious, all-purpose sauce

Paprika is commonly used for its ruddy color rather than for its taste. Now, however, intensely flavored varieties from Spain are arriving in markets here. Their effect on dishes goes beyond cosmetic: They impart distinct flavors, from sweet to hot to smoky.

The velvety red powder, made from finely ground dried peppers, mirrors the character of the pepper used. The drying method also affects the paprika's flavor. Peppers dried in the sun maintain a pure, natural essence; those dried over a wood fire take on complex, smoky overtones. Choose a paprika from our guide at right to make classic Spanish romesco sauce. It's a wonderful accompaniment to a wide range of foods; we love it on pork chops. You can also use Spanish paprikas as you would generic paprika, but expect more intense flavor.

Spanish paprikas are available at specialty markets and from Spanish Table (www.tablespan.com; Berkeley, 510/548-1383; Santa Fe, 505/986-0243; Seattle, 206/682-2827) and Tienda (www.tienda.com or 888/472-1022). —Linda Lau Anusasananan

Romesco Sauce

PREP AND COOK TIME: About 20 minutes

NOTES: Linda Carucci, a cooking teacher, chef, and culinary consultant *(www.lckitchen.com)* from Oakland, California, makes this sauce with a Spanish smoked sweet paprika and cayenne. Taste sauce before adding the cayenne to see if you want more heat. You can use regular paprika, but its flavor won't be as distinctive. You can make the sauce up to 2 days ahead; cover and chill. Alternately, freeze it up to 1 month.

MAKES: About 2½ cups

- 1 cup slivered almonds (4 oz.)
- 4 ounces Italian or sweet French bread
- 1 cup lightly packed fresh basil leaves, rinsed and drained
- 1 jar (7¼ oz.) or 1 cup peeled roasted red peppers
- 2 tablespoons tomato paste
- 2 tablespoons fresh lemon juice
- About 2 tablespoons sherry vinegar or red wine vinegar
- 2 tablespoons brandy (optional)
- 2 tablespoons Spanish or other paprika (see notes)
- 1 tablespoon minced garlic
- About ½ teaspoon kosher salt
- About ⅓ cup clam juice
- ⅔ cup extra-virgin olive oil
- About ½ teaspoon cayenne (if using sweet paprika; see notes)

1. Spread almonds in a 10- by 15-inch baking pan. Bake in a 350° regular or convection oven, shaking pan occasionally, until golden, 8 to 10 minutes.

2. Trim crusts from bread; reserve for another use or discard. Cut bread into 1-inch chunks; you should have about 3 cups.

3. In a food processor, whirl nuts until finely chopped. Add bread, basil, red peppers, tomato paste, lemon juice, 2 tablespoons vinegar, brandy (if desired), paprika, garlic, and ½ teaspoon salt; whirl until peppers are puréed.

4. With motor running, gradually add ⅓ cup clam juice and whirl until incorporated, then gradually add olive oil; process until smooth. Taste, and add cayenne and more salt and vinegar if desired. If thicker than desired, whirl in a little more clam juice. Scrape into a bowl. Let stand about 20 minutes for flavors to blend before serving.

Per tablespoon: 61 cal., 80% (49 cal.) from fat; 1 g protein; 5.4 g fat (0.7 g sat.); 3 g carbo (0.4 g fiber); 59 mg sodium; 0 mg chol. ◆

Paprika guide

There are three types of Spanish paprika available—sweet, bittersweet, and hot—and each comes in sun-dried and smoked forms.

Sweet paprika *(pimentón dulce).* Earthy and mild.

Bittersweet paprika *(pimentón agridulce).* Rich, complex, and slightly smoky.

Hot paprika *(pimentón picante).* Medium-hot but slightly sweet.

In our testing, we found that the romescos made with sun-dried paprikas paired well with light foods: raw vegetables, grilled green onions, roasted potatoes, eggs, shrimp, halibut, salmon, chicken, and pork.

The versions made with smoked paprikas, while also good with the above, tasted even better with hearty, robust fare: beef, lamb, and grilled mushrooms. For smoked paprika, look for *pimentón de La Vera,* made from peppers grown in western Spain.

Chili reception

Every fall in the Southwest and beyond, freelance roasters set up in parking lots and on street corners, tumbling freshly harvested chilies in large mesh drums over roaring propane flames until the peppers' skins are black and blistered. Mild to medium long green chilies, used for rellenos, are sold by the (big) bagful. When you get home, peel 'em, portion 'em, and freeze 'em.

James Campbell Caruso, executive chef of El Farol in Santa Fe, stems the chilies, pinches off the seed clusters, lays the chilies flat on a cutting board, and rubs off the char with a damp terry cloth. (Wear gloves.)

Fold them into an omelet, pile on a burger, or combine with shredded cooked chicken and cheese in a quesadilla.

—*Claire Walter*

Wine is sparkling these days in Monterey County.

Monterey: a region reinvented

Not so long ago, Monterey wine meant no-frills, easy-on-the-pocketbook quaffers. A few large wineries dominated the landscape, and their wines, while serviceable, weren't exactly exciting.

That has changed. Recently I tasted more than 50 wines made within county lines and found some of the most seductive Pinot Noirs I've had in a long time, plus a slew of other superb wines. "Since the early 1990s, there's been a renaissance here," says David Coventry, winemaker for Morgan Winery. "There are now scores of small new wineries that are enticing places for innovative young winemakers who are raising the bar on quality." Coventry's "R & D Franscioni Vineyard" Pinot Gris is sensational, and his "Metallico" Chardonnay is at the forefront of an exciting new lean style of white wine.

Siduri Winery is another star. Adam and Dianna Lee, husband-and-wife owners and co-winemakers, started the winery on a shoestring in 1994. Entirely self-taught, they met in the wine department of Neiman Marcus in Dallas, where both worked as clerks until a passion for Pinot Noir brought them to California.

The much-heralded Pisoni Winery, which is making some of the county's—indeed, the state's—most concentrated Pinot Noirs, is underscoring the talent in the region.

What is it about this place? Descending from the vast arc of Monterey Bay southeast to Hames Valley, about 30 miles north of Paso Robles, Monterey County is big. Much of the land is quite fertile, though, so it's better suited to growing vegetables and fruits than grapevines, which thrive in poorer soils. Such soils are found on the ridges and slopes of the Coastal Range, where they support several smaller, prestigious appellations, including Carmel Valley, Chalone, and the tiny Santa Lucia Highlands.

What these top wine regions share—their secret weapon—is a cool, foggy climate, which means the grapes must hang a long time on the vine before they're ripe. The result is greater flavor intensity. "Think of it in terms of tomatoes," offers Coventry. "A vine-ripened tomato gets more tomatoey the longer it hangs on the vine."

To borrow his point, Monterey's new high-quality Chardonnays are more Chardonnay-like than ever, and the Pinots more Noir. It even seems that the simple quaffers are better than they've ever been.

County picks

Hames Valley Sauvignon Blanc 2002 *(Hames Valley), $18.* Gentle herbal flavors, with aromas of light spearmint and freshly cut grass. A great match for Monterey seafood.

Morgan "R & D Franscioni Vineyard" Pinot Gris 2002 *(Santa Lucia Highlands), $16.* Lip smacking—crisp and creamy at the same time, with vibrant lemon and melon flavors.

Morgan "Metallico" Chardonnay 2002 *(Santa Lucia Highlands), $20.* One of the sensational new Chardonnays being made without any influence of new oak. Soaring with vibrant peach and pear flavors—elegant, plush, and pure.

Paraiso Pinot Noir 2000 *(Santa Lucia Highlands), $18.* Deep, dark, earthy, and satisfying, with juicy blackberry and licorice flavors. Think game or roasted poultry.

Siduri "Pisoni Vineyard" Pinot Noir 2001 *(Santa Lucia Highlands), $50.* Pricey but worth it. Absolutely huge flavors and a gripping, almost syrupy texture. A variety that's often described as feminine, this wine is positively masculine; must have red meat.

Heller Estate Cabernet Sauvignon 2000 *(Carmel Valley), $30.* From beautiful old vineyards close to the Ventana Wilderness, this chocolatey Cabernet has cassis and spicy tobacco aromas and flavors reminiscent of Bordeaux. —*Karen MacNeil-Fife*

Brown sugar and pecans make a distinctive topping for broiled salmon.

Flavorful fall suppers

Readers' recipes tested in *Sunset's* kitchens

Photographs by James Carrier

Praline-Glazed Salmon

Paul Genaux, Bremerton, WA

Paul Genaux devised this recipe from his sister's tale of a New Orleans dish.

PREP AND COOK TIME: About 15 minutes

MAKES: 2 servings

    12 ounces boned, skinned salmon
        fillet, cut into 2 pieces
        About ¼ teaspoon salt
        Pepper
     ¼ cup chopped pecans
      3 tablespoons packed dark
        brown sugar
      2 tablespoons butter, melted
      1 teaspoon lemon juice

1. Rinse salmon and pat dry. Sprinkle all over with salt and pepper. In a small bowl, mix pecans, brown sugar, butter, lemon juice, and ¼ teaspoon salt.

2. Place salmon on a 12- by 15-inch baking sheet. Broil 6 inches from heat for 6 minutes. With a wide spatula, turn fish over. Spoon pecan mixture evenly over fish and broil again, checking frequently to be sure nuts do not scorch, until fish is opaque but still moist-looking in the center of the thickest part (cut to test), 1 to 2 minutes longer.

3. With a wide spatula, transfer fish to serving plate.

Per serving: 581 cal., 60% (351 cal.) from fat; 35 g protein; 39 g fat (12 g sat.); 23 g carbo (0.9 g fiber); 512 mg sodium; 131 mg chol.

Jicama-Apple Salad

Roxanne Chan, Albany, CA

Roxanne Chan created this bright-tasting, tangy salad to go with roasted pork.

PREP TIME: About 15 minutes

MAKES: 6½ cups; 4 to 6 servings

      2 tart green apples (such as Granny
        Smith; about 1 lb. total), rinsed,
        cored, and quartered
      1 pound jicama, peeled and rinsed
     ⅓ cup dried cranberries
      2 tablespoons chopped green onion
      2 tablespoons chopped fresh mint
        leaves
      2 tablespoons minced candied
        ginger
      1 tablespoon lime juice
      1 tablespoon honey

1. With a mandoline or a knife, cut apples and jicama into matchstick-size 2-inch-long strips.

2. In a large bowl, mix all ingredients to coat. Serve immediately or chill up to 3 hours.

Per serving: 118 cal., 3% (3.6 cal.) from fat; 0.7 g protein; 0.4 g fat (0.1 g sat.); 29 g carbo (5.7 g fiber); 8.3 mg sodium; 0 mg chol.

Zucchini Rissoles

Donald Frediani, San Francisco

Donald Frediani's zucchini cakes make a great appetizer when served with tomato sauce; they're also a nice side dish with chicken or fish.

PREP AND COOK TIME: About 40 minutes

MAKES: 12 to 14 cakes; 4 to 6 appetizer servings

      1 pound zucchini, rinsed, ends trimmed
      1 onion (about 8 oz.), peeled
      2 tablespoons olive oil
     ¼ teaspoon salt
     ¼ teaspoon pepper
      1 cup fine dried bread crumbs
      1 large egg
     ½ cup grated dry jack
        or parmesan cheese
      2 tablespoons chopped parsley
      1 tablespoon chopped fresh mint leaves
        About 3 tablespoons vegetable oil

1. Shred zucchini and onion. Pour olive oil into a 10- to 12-inch frying pan over medium-high heat. Add vegetables, salt, and pepper and cook, stirring frequently, until vegetables are soft and any liquid has evaporated, about 8 minutes.

2. Transfer mixture to a large bowl and stir in bread crumbs, egg, cheese, parsley, and mint until incorporated. Let stand until cool enough to handle, about 15 minutes. With well-floured hands, form mixture into patties about 2 inches wide and ½ inch thick.

FOOD STYLING: KAREN SHINTO

Chicken and vegetables top couscous for a satisfying one-dish meal.

3. Wipe pan clean and heat vegetable oil over medium heat. When oil is hot, add patties, three or four at a time. Cook, turning once, until golden brown on both sides, about 6 minutes total. Reduce heat as needed to maintain a constant temperature. With a spatula, transfer to a paper towel–lined baking pan; keep warm in 200° oven. Serve hot.

Per serving: 241 cal., 60% (144 cal.) from fat; 7.3 g protein; 16 g fat (3.6 g sat.); 19 g carbo (1.8 g fiber); 322 mg sodium; 45 mg chol.

Spiced Chicken and Vegetable Couscous

Jennifer Kirk, Tucson

Jennifer Kirk writes that this spiced chicken and vegetable dish is her family's idea of comfort food.

PREP AND COOK TIME: About 1 hour

MAKES: 4 to 6 servings

- 1 pound boned, skinned chicken breasts
  About ⅛ teaspoon salt
  About ⅛ teaspoon pepper
- 2 tablespoons olive oil
- 1 onion (about 8 oz.), peeled and chopped
- 2 cloves garlic, peeled and minced
- 1 teaspoon ground cumin
- 1 teaspoon ground coriander
- ½ teaspoon ground dried turmeric
- ¼ teaspoon cayenne
- 2 cups cauliflower florets (about ½ in.)
- 1 cup baby-cut carrots
- 1½ cups fat-skimmed chicken broth or water
- 1 red bell pepper (about 8 oz.), rinsed, stemmed, seeded, and cut into 1-inch chunks
- 1 zucchini (about 8 oz.), rinsed, ends trimmed, cut into 1-inch chunks

- 2 cans (14.5 oz. each) diced tomatoes
- 1 package (10 oz.) couscous
- 3 tablespoons chopped fresh cilantro leaves

1. Rinse chicken and pat dry; cut chicken into 1-inch chunks and sprinkle with about ⅛ teaspoon salt and ⅛ teaspoon pepper. Heat 1 tablespoon oil in a 12-inch frying pan (with 2-inch-high sides) or a 6-quart pan over medium-high heat. Add chicken and stir often until browned on the outside but still slightly pink in the center (cut to test), 3 to 4 minutes. Transfer chicken to a plate and add remaining tablespoon oil to frying pan.

2. Add onion and garlic to pan and stir often until onion is limp, about 5 minutes. Stir in cumin, coriander, turmeric, and cayenne and cook until spices are fragrant, about 1 minute. Add cauliflower, carrots, and chicken broth; bring to a boil. Lower heat, cover, and simmer until carrots are slightly tender when pierced, 10 minutes. Stir in bell pepper, zucchini, and tomatoes and simmer, uncovered, until zucchini is tender when pierced, 8 to 10 minutes longer. Add salt and pepper to taste.

3. Meanwhile, in a 3- to 4-quart pan over high heat, bring 2 cups water to a boil. Remove from heat, stir in couscous, cover, and let stand until water is absorbed, about 5 minutes.

4. Fluff couscous with fork and spoon onto a large serving platter. Spoon chicken and vegetables over couscous and sprinkle cilantro over the top.

Per serving: 386 cal., 15% (58 cal.) from fat; 29 g protein; 6.4 g fat (1 g sat.); 53 g carbo (5.5 g fiber); 362 mg sodium; 44 mg chol. ◆

Sunset's own heirloom tomato

When Nik Peplenov immigrated to Oregon from southern Russia, he brought along seeds of his favorite heirloom tomato. After friends passed them along to other friends, the tomato found its way into a trial planting conducted by Gary Ibsen, founder of the Carmel TomatoFest. With Peplenov's permission, Ibsen named this tomato 'Sunset's Red Horizon', in honor of *Sunset* magazine.

Fruits are meaty and huge (4 to 5½ inches in diameter and 2 to 3 pounds each). In Ibsen's trials, 'Sunset's Red Horizon' was among the earliest tomatoes to produce, bearing its first fruits about 70 days after being sown and continuing into November. Indeterminate in habit, the plant keeps growing and fruiting as long as the weather allows. The tomato tolerates more shade than most varieties but grows in full sun if the soil is kept evenly moist.

To order seeds of 'Sunset's Red Horizon' for planting in late winter or early spring, visit the Carmel TomatoFest website (www.tomatofest.com). Seed supplies are limited.

—Jim McCausland

Humble beef stew is dressed up for a party with gremolata, polenta, and plenty of black pepper (see page 203).

October

Indian market treasures

How to shop for and cook this flavorful cuisine

By Linda Lau Anusasananan • Photographs by James Carrier • Food styling by Karen Shinto

Food lovers in the West are lucky. We have access to an array of flavors imported by a myriad of people from other places who've re-established their cooking here. Most recently, a large—and growing—number of Asian Indians have opened new restaurants and groceries in neighborhoods from Los Angeles to Vancouver, B.C. The markets range from tiny stores crammed with mysterious-looking packaged goods to spacious, modern supermarkets with beautiful fresh produce and deli foods. All offer fascinating discoveries.

I asked two expert Indian cooks from California—Hema Alur-Kundargi of Cupertino and Laxmi Hiremath of San Ramon—to guide me through two stores near my Bay Area home, point out some of their favorite products, and show me what to do with them. Our shopping trips yielded both interesting ready-to-eat snacks and great ingredients for surprisingly simple everyday dishes (see our guide on page 202). For an intriguing Indian sampler party, combine several of our recipes with ready-to-eat foods. Since both Alur-Kundargi and Hiremath have lived in the West for many years, they had plenty of suggestions for supermarket substitutes for some of the authentic ingredients. You can pull off a party, and get a taste of their country, even if you don't have an Indian market nearby.

Noodle-thin strands of fried garbanzo batter (sev) and a special blend of spices (chaat masala) give this fruit salad a distinctive Indian personality.

Papaya-Kiwi Chaat with Pistachios

PREP TIME: About 30 minutes

NOTES: Instead of the chaat masala Hiremath sprinkles over this salad, you can use ground toasted cumin seeds: stir 1 teaspoon seeds in a frying pan over medium heat until they begin to brown, about 1 minute, then finely grind with a mortar and pestle or whirl in a blender. You can complete step 1 up to 3 hours ahead; cover and chill.

MAKES: 8 servings

- 2½ cups diced (¾ in.) peeled firm-ripe papaya (about 14 oz.)
- 2½ cups diced (¾ in.) peeled firm-ripe kiwi (about 16 oz.)
- ½ cup finely chopped red onion
- 2 fresh red or green jalapeño chilies (1½ oz. total), rinsed, stemmed, and thinly slivered or minced
- 3 tablespoons finely chopped fresh mint leaves
- ½ cup orange juice
- ¼ cup fresh lime juice
- ⅓ cup shelled roasted, salted pistachios
- 1 teaspoon chaat masala (or freshly ground toasted cumin; see notes)
  Salt (optional)
- ⅓ cup sev (optional; see "Discoveries and Deals," page 202)

1. In a wide serving bowl, mix papaya, kiwi, onion, chilies, and mint.

2. Gently stir in orange juice, lime juice, and nuts. Sprinkle with chaat masala (if using cumin, add salt to taste) and sev, if desired.

Per serving: 101 cal., 26% (26 cal.) from fat; 2.4 g protein; 2.9 g fat (0.3 g sat.); 19 g carbo (2.8 g fiber); 30 mg sodium; 0 mg chol.

Try a trio of Indian snacks: samosas (left), potato crisps, and spicy cereal mix (back).

Potato-Chutney Crisps (Sev-puri)

PREP AND COOK TIME: About 25 minutes

NOTES: Sweet-and-sour and spicy-hot chutney over potatoes on a crisp base makes an intriguing appetizer. A sprinkling of sev—fried noodlelike strands of spicy garbanzo batter—adds crunchy texture. The traditional base is a crackerlike fried bread, but Alur-Kundargi prefers crisp sesame crackers or tortilla chips. You can complete step 1 up to 1 hour before serving; let stand at room temperature.

MAKES: 3 dozen appetizers; 10 servings

- 3 **dozen round or triangular tortilla chips (flat ones are best) or thin sesame crackers (1½ to 2 in. wide)**
- ¾ **cup chopped cooked potato**
- ⅓ **cup minced red onion**
- 6 **tablespoons spicy yogurt (recipe follows)**
- 6 **tablespoons tamarind-date chutney (or ¼ cup spiced apple butter mixed with 2 tablespoons lime juice and ⅛ teaspoon *each* cayenne and salt)**
- 3 **tablespoons green chutney (recipe follows)**
- ¾ **cup sev (optional; see notes)**
- 3 **tablespoons chopped fresh cilantro**

1. Arrange chips in a single layer on platters. Mound potato, then onion, equally on chips.

2. Top each chip with about ½ teaspoon *each* spicy yogurt and tamarind-date chutney, ¼ teaspoon green chutney, 1 teaspoon sev, and ¼ teaspoon cilantro.

Per serving: 70 cal., 27% (19 cal.) from fat; 1.3 g protein; 2.1 g fat (0.5 g sat.); 12 g carbo (0.8 g fiber); 198 mg sodium; 0.2 mg chol.

Spicy yogurt. In a bowl, mix 6 tablespoons **plain nonfat yogurt,** and ¼ teaspoon *each* **ground cumin, sugar,** and **salt.** Makes about 6 tablespoons.

Green chutney. In a blender, combine 1 cup coarsely chopped **fresh cilantro;** 2 **fresh jalapeño chilies** (1 oz. total), rinsed, stemmed, and sliced; 1 tablespoon **unsweetened shredded dried coconut;** 1 tablespoon **lime juice;** and ½ teaspoon *each* **sugar** and **salt.** Whirl until smooth, adding just enough **water** (2 to 4 tablespoons) to facilitate blending. Cover and chill up to 1 day. Makes about ⅓ cup.

Toasted or Fried Pappadums

PREP AND COOK TIME: About 1 minute

NOTES: You can buy pappadums—dried lentil wafers—plain or seasoned; sometimes they are even sold in regular supermarkets. Stored airtight, they keep almost indefinitely, ready to use for instant appetizers. When toasted or fried, they become crisp, like potato chips; you can store the cooked wafers airtight up to 1 week.

MAKES: Allow 1 per serving

To toast: Lay **pappadum wafers** (see notes) slightly apart on a baking sheet. Broil 4 to 6 inches from heat until they begin to blister or buckle, 20 to 25 seconds (watch closely—they scorch easily). Turn wafers over and broil again until surface is blistered, 8 to 12 seconds longer. Transfer toasted wafers to a rack.

To fry: Pour about 1 inch of **vegetable oil** into a 10- to 12-inch frying pan over medium-high heat; when oil reaches 375° on a thermometer, adjust heat to maintain temperature. Lay 1 **pappadum wafer** in hot oil; when it puffs up (almost instantly), turn it over, push other side into oil, and cook until puffed and crisp (it doesn't need to brown), 2 to 3 seconds. Transfer to paper towels to drain.

Serve, or cool and wrap airtight.

Per toasted wafer: 27 cal., 6.7% (1.8 cal.) from fat; 2 g protein; 0.2 g fat (0 g sat.); 4.7 g carbo (1 g fiber); 260 mg sodium; 0 mg chol.

Spicy Potatoes

PREP AND COOK TIME: About 25 minutes, plus 1½ hours to marinate

NOTES: Start preparing these sweet-hot garlicky potatoes from Alur-Kundargi (through step 2) about 2 hours ahead so they can marinate in the sauce. Scoop the potatoes into the chapatis or whole-wheat tortillas to eat like burritos; for appetizer portions, cut the bread into wedges and use them to scoop up the potatoes.

MAKES: 8 servings

- 2 **pounds thin-skinned potatoes**
- ¼ **cup minced garlic**
- 2 **tablespoons vegetable oil**
- 1 **cup ketchup**
- 1 **tablespoon pav-bhaji masala, purchased or homemade (recipe follows)**
  Salt
  Indian red chili powder or cayenne
  Chopped fresh cilantro
- 8 **chapatis or whole-wheat tortillas (7 in.)**

1. Peel potatoes and cut into ¾-inch chunks. In a 3- to 4-quart pan over high heat, bring 1 quart water and the potatoes to a boil. Reduce heat, cover, and simmer until potatoes are almost tender when pierced, 7 to 10 minutes. Drain and return to pan.

2. Meanwhile, in a 6- to 8-inch frying pan over medium heat, stir garlic in oil until it begins to turn golden, about 2 minutes. Add ketchup, pav-bhaji masala, and salt and chili powder to taste. Add the seasoned ketchup to potatoes and mix to coat. Cover and let stand about 1½ hours.

3. Pour potatoes into a 10- by 15-inch nonstick baking pan. Bake in a 375° regular or convection oven, stirring occasionally, until potatoes are tender when pierced, 10 to 15 minutes. Scrape into a bowl and sprinkle with cilantro. Serve with chapatis (see notes).

Per serving: 292 cal., 19% (56 cal.) from fat; 6.9 g protein; 6.2 g fat (1 g sat.); 54 g carbo (4.5 g fiber); 744 mg sodium; 0 mg chol.

Pav-bhaji masala. In a small bowl, mix 1 teaspoon **ground coriander,** ¾ teaspoon **ground cumin,** ½ teaspoon **cayenne,** and ¼ teaspoon *each* **ground cardamom** and **ground pepper.**

Scoop potatoes seasoned with ketchup and spices onto chapatis or tortillas for a satisfying snack or lunch.

Spicy Cereal Snack Mix (Chivda)

PREP AND COOK TIME: About 30 minutes

NOTES: Infuse poha (rice flakes) with a spiced oil to make this sweet-hot-sour snack mix, or substitute Western breakfast cereals for the poha, as Alur-Kundargi often does. Store the mix airtight up to 1 week. Similar snack mixes may also be purchased ready-made, but they're often very spicy.

MAKES: About 7½ cups

- 6 **cups thin poha or 3 cups** *each* **toasted rice cereal (such as Rice Krispies) and toasted corn-ball cereal (such as Kix)**
- 3 **fresh jalapeño chilies (2½ oz. total)**
- ¼ **cup vegetable oil**
- 1 **teaspoon cumin seeds**
- ½ **cup roasted unsalted peanuts**
- ¼ **cup roasted unsalted cashews**
- ¼ **cup raisins**
- ¼ **cup dried cranberries**
- 2 **tablespoons lime juice**
- 2 **tablespoons sugar**
- 1 **teaspoon salt**
- ½ **teaspoon garam masala (or ¼ teaspoon** *each* **ground coriander and cumin)**
- ¼ **teaspoon ground turmeric**

1. Spread poha in a 12- by 17-inch baking pan. Bake in a 200° regular or convection oven, stirring occasionally, until flakes are very crisp, about 20 minutes. (If using the cereals, omit this step.)

2. Meanwhile, rinse and dry chilies. Cut each lengthwise into quarters (do not seed). Pour oil into a 5- to 6-quart pan over medium-high heat; when hot, add cumin seeds and stir until they begin to brown, about 30 seconds. Add chilies and stir for 1 minute. Add peanuts, cashews, raisins, and cranberries; stir until fruit is puffy, about 1 minute. Add lime juice, sugar, salt, garam masala, and turmeric; stir until blended.

3. Reduce heat to medium. Add poha or cereal and stir until completely infused with spiced oil and golden throughout, about 6 minutes. Remove and discard chilies. Let mix cool completely. Serve or wrap airtight.

Per ½ cup: 128 cal., 50% (64 cal.) from fat; 2.3 g protein; 7.1 g fat (1 g sat.); 15 g carbo (1.1 g fiber); 208 mg sodium; 0 mg chol.

Tandoori Kebabs

PREP AND COOK TIME: About 1 hour, plus at least 30 minutes to marinate

NOTES: For vegetarian kebabs, Alur-Kundargi uses Indian paneer cheese or nigari (firm-pressed) tofu. You can prepare the kebabs (through step 3) up to 2 hours before grilling; cover and chill.

MAKES: 8 servings

- 2 **cups plain nonfat yogurt**
- 1 **red bell pepper (10 oz.)**
- 1 **red onion (6 oz.)**
- 1 **pound peeled, cored fresh pineapple**
- 1 **pound boned, skinned chicken breast, paneer cheese, or nigari tofu (see notes)**
- 1 **tablespoon tandoori masala, purchased or homemade (recipe follows)**
  Raita (recipe follows)

1. Line a colander with a double layer of cheesecloth or four layers of paper towels; set colander in a sink or over a large bowl. Empty yogurt into lined colander and let drain about 30 minutes.

2. Meanwhile, rinse, stem, and seed bell pepper; cut into 1-inch squares. Peel onion and cut into 1-inch chunks, separating layers. Cut pineapple into 1-inch chunks. If using chicken, rinse and pat dry. Cut chicken, cheese, or tofu into 1-inch chunks.

3. In a large bowl, mix drained yogurt with tandoori masala. If using chicken, scoop out ½ cup yogurt mixture and combine with chicken in a small bowl. Gently mix bell pepper, onion, pineapple, and cheese or tofu, if using, into yogurt mixture in large bowl. Cover and chill at least 30 minutes or up to 2 hours. Thread vegetables, pineapple, and chicken, cheese, or tofu onto metal or soaked wooden skewers, alternating items.

4. Lay kebabs on an oiled grill over a solid bed of hot coals or high heat on a gas grill (you can hold your hand at grill level only 2 to 3 seconds); close lid on gas grill. Cook, turning once, until vegetables are browned on both sides and chicken is no longer pink in the center (cut to test), 8 to 10 minutes. Transfer to a platter. Serve hot or warm, with raita to add at the table.

Per serving with chicken: 156 cal., 7% (11 cal.) from fat; 18 g protein; 1.2 g fat (0.3 g sat.); 18 g carbo (1.7 g fiber); 246 mg sodium; 34 mg chol.

Tandoori masala. In a small bowl, combine 1 teaspoon *each* **ground cumin** and **ground coriander**, ¼ teaspoon *each* **ground cloves** and **cayenne**, and ⅛ teaspoon *each* **ground nutmeg**, **ground pepper**, and **ground cinnamon**; mix well.

Raita. In a bowl, mix ¾ cup **plain nonfat yogurt** with ½ teaspoon *each* **ground cumin**, **sugar**, and **salt**. Gently stir in ¼ cup *each* finely chopped **cucumber**, **tomato**, and **onion**. Makes about 1¼ cups.

Mango Lassi

PREP TIME: About 10 minutes

NOTES: Hiremath uses Alphonso mango pulp to give this cooling drink intense color and flavor without much fiber, but other types of canned or fresh mango may be substituted.

MAKES: About 7 cups; 6 to 8 servings

- 5 **whole green cardamom pods**
- 1 **can (30 oz.) mango pulp (see notes) or 4 cups mashed fresh ripe mango, chilled**
- 1½ **cups plain nonfat yogurt or low-fat buttermilk**
- 12 **ice cubes (1½ in.)**
  About ¼ cup sugar

1. Crush cardamom pods with the flat bottom of a glass or a mortar and pestle; discard hulls. In a blender, whirl seeds until finely ground.

2. Add half the mango pulp, yogurt, and ice cubes to blender, along with 2 tablespoons sugar and ⅓ cup water; whirl until smooth. Add more sugar to taste and water to thin, if desired; whirl briefly to blend. Pour into a pitcher. Repeat with remaining mango, yogurt, and ice, 2 tablespoons sugar, and ⅓ cup water (plus more sugar to taste and water to thin, if desired); pour into the pitcher and stir to blend. Serve at once.

Per serving: 103 cal., 3% (2.7 cal.) from fat; 2.9 g protein; 0.3 g fat (0.1 g sat.); 24 g carbo (0.9 g fiber); 34 mg sodium; 0.9 mg chol.

Tandoori kebabs, marinated in yogurt and spices, then grilled, can be made from chicken, Indian paneer cheese, or tofu. Raita—a yogurt sauce with cucumber and tomato—is a cooling accompaniment.

Discoveries and deals

Indian markets can seem intimidating at first, but Alur-Kundargi and Hiremath led me to foods that are both easy to like and easy to use. I found great bargains for everyday cooking as well. Since spices play a prominent part in this cuisine, they're bountiful, fresh, and cheap at Indian grocery stores. Saffron, especially, is a deal. Many Indians are vegetarians, so the markets carry a huge assortment of dried legumes and well-priced nuts—notably cashews. Here are some of the foods we particularly like. —L. L. A.

Snacks and crisps

Spicy plantain chips.

Samosas (9): Savory filled pastries, frozen or fresh in the deli. Serve with hot ketchup or chutney.

Murukku, chakri, or chakli: Crisp fried cumin-spiked spirals made from a batter of rice, garbanzo, or other flours.

Sev (5, 10): Thick or thin fried strands of spicy garbanzo batter.

Rice chica or khichiyia: Bright- or natural-colored thin disks or extruded wafers of rice, potato, or tapioca flour; when fried, they puff into crisps reminiscent of potato chips.

Pappadums or papads: Paper-thin dried lentil wafers that cook into crisp disks.

Breads (Roti)

Chapati: Tortilla-like flatbread, fresh or frozen.

Naan: Flat rounds or ovals of yeast bread, plain or seasoned.

Paratha: Flaky flatbread rounds.

Cheese

Paneer (3): Fresh, mild, pressed cow's-milk cheese; grill it or use it like firm tofu in curries.

Condiments

Eggplant relish: Eggplant preserved in spices and oil; good with Indian breads. Alur-Kundargi recommends the Patak brand for new-comers (if you want to tone it down slightly, mix ½ cup eggplant relish with 2 tablespoons cream cheese).

Hot ketchup (8): Indian-style ketchup with a spicy kick; Tom Tom is Alur-Kundargi's favorite brand.

Tamarind-date chutney (7): A dark brown, sweet-sour chutney.

Rice

Basmati: Highly aromatic long-grain rice that grows in the foothills of the Himalayas.

Poha (6): Flakes of dried and flattened cooked rice that resemble old-fashioned Ivory soap flakes; they come thick or thin. Use thin poha in snack mixes. Rinse thick poha in a colander until thoroughly moistened and drain; mix with seasoned oils or yogurt for light grain salads (similar to couscous dishes).

Spices

Individual: Saffron; **green** or **black cardamom** (the green is the form that is bleached for white cardamom); **black** and **regular cumin seeds;** and **coriander.**

Blends (1, 4): Garam masala (all-purpose aromatic seasoning; buy a whole-seed version and grind it in a blender or spice grinder for freshest flavor); **chaat masala** (sprinkle over fruit, buttermilk, or potatoes); **pav-bhaji masala** (for vegetable dishes); **tandoori masala** (rub over meats, seafood, and vegetables for grilling); **mukhwa** (roasted seed mixture; use as an after-dinner digestive or breath freshener).

Beverages

Black teas, coffee.

Rose syrup: Sweet, fragrant red syrup; mix with soda water and ice or with cold milk for pink coolers.

Tropical fruit juices: Mango, litchi, guava, and passion fruit.

Sweets

Canned sweetened Alphonso mango pulp (2): The Alphonso variety contains few fibers; Hiremath likes the Ratna brand. Use it for desserts and drinks.

Chikki: Candied nut and seed brittles.

Cookies: Cashew, coconut, almond, and pistachio.

Ice creams: Saffron, saffron-rose, pistachio, mango, litchi, and cashew-raisin; Kwality and Real Ice Cream are good brands. ◆

Shopping

These markets were recommended to us by Indian cooks. Most offer a selection of dry goods, some fresh produce, and refrigerated and frozen offerings. On weekends, many sell freshly baked breads, samosas, desserts, and chaat (snacks). Go to *www.littleindia.us/search/ Grocery.html* for a market list. Many of the ingredients in our recipes can be ordered from the Indian Foods Company (*www.indianfoodsco.com*) or from Namaste.com (*www.namaste.com or 866/438-4642*).

NORTHWEST
India Direct. *16205 N.W. Bethany Court, Ste. 110, Beaverton, OR; (503) 690-0499.*

J.B. Foods. *6607 Main St., Vancouver, B.C.; (604) 321-0224.*

Mayuri Food and Video. *2560 152nd Ave. N.E., Redmond, WA; (425) 861-3800.*

Punjab Food Center Limited. *6635 Main St., Vancouver, B.C.; (604) 322-5502.*

NORTHERN CALIFORNIA
Bharat Bazaar. *3686 El Camino Real, #2203, Santa Clara; (408) 247-4307.*

Dana Bazar. *5113 Mowry Ave., Fremont; (510) 742-0555.*

India Cash & Carry. *1032 E. El Camino Real, Sunnyvale, (408) 735-7383.*

Spice House. *29266 Union City Blvd., Union City; (510) 489-6857.*

VIK Distributors. *726 Allston Way, Berkeley; (510) 644-4412.*

SOUTHERN CALIFORNIA
Bharat Bazaar. *11510 W. Washington Blvd., Los Angeles; (310) 398-6766.*

India Spices and Groceries. *5994 Pico Blvd., Los Angeles; (323) 931-4871.*

SOUTHWEST
India Bazaar. *933 E. University Dr., Tempe, AZ; (480) 784-4442.*

Star stews

Dress up comfort food for autumn entertaining

By Linda Lau Anusasananan
Photographs by James Carrier
Food styling by Susan Devaty

When it's time to throw a party, seemingly humble stews are often overlooked. But take a second glance, because these dishes have many virtues. They can be made ahead, and they take well to either buffet or plated service. With our simple browning technique—which lends color and deep, succulent flavor to the meat—they're easy to cook. Best of all, though, you can add garnishes to transform any stew from comfort food to a stylish party dish. Our two very special stews—a peppery Italian beef stew and a savory Moroccan lamb tagine—stand on their own, but they're true stars when embellished with fresh gremolata or homemade harissa. Add a green salad, and you have a party dinner that's perfect for warming up fall's chilly nights.

Italian Peppered Beef Stew (Peposo)

PREP AND COOK TIME: About 2½ hours

NOTES: John Ash, culinary director of Bonterra and Fetzer Vineyards, adds a generous quantity of garlic and cracked pepper to this beef stew. The gremolata adds a fresh finish of lemon and garlic. Start the polenta about 30 minutes before stew is done. The stew can be prepared through step 2 up to 1 day ahead; cool, cover, and chill. Reheat over medium-high heat, covered, stirring occasionally.

MAKES: 6 servings

- **4** pounds fat-trimmed boned beef chuck or other cut suitable for stewing, rinsed and cut into 1½-inch chunks
- **2** cups dry red wine such as Zinfandel or Merlot

Dig into a hearty one-bowl meal of peppery, succulent beef stew over creamy polenta.

- **2** cans (14½ oz. each) diced tomatoes
- **1** cup chopped fresh basil leaves or 3 tablespoons dried basil
- **18** peeled garlic cloves
- **1** to 1½ tablespoons fresh-cracked or coarse-ground black pepper
  Salt
  Creamy polenta (recipe on page 205; see notes)
  Oven-dried tomatoes (recipe on page 205) or 2 Roma tomatoes, rinsed and sliced crosswise into ¼-inch-thick rounds
  Gremolata (recipe on page 205)

1. Brown beef (see "No-Mess Browning," page 204). Discard fat.

2. Add wine, canned tomatoes (including juices), basil, garlic, and 1 tablespoon cracked pepper to pan with beef. Cover and bring to a boil over high heat, then reduce heat and simmer, stirring occasionally, until beef is very tender when pierced, 1½ to 2 hours. Skim off and discard fat. Add salt and up to ½ tablespoon more cracked pepper to taste.

3. Spoon polenta onto dinner plates or a large shallow bowl or rimmed platter. With a slotted spoon, lift out beef and mound onto center of polenta. Measure remaining pan juices; if less than 3 cups, add water to make that amount, return to pan, and bring to a boil; add salt to taste and pour juices into a serving bowl. Pass pan juices to add over stew servings to taste. Garnish stew with oven-dried tomato slices and gremolata.

Per serving of stew: 504 cal., 41% (207 cal.) from fat; 61 g protein; 23 g fat (8.5 g sat.); 11 g carbo (2.1 g fiber); 463 mg sodium; 197 mg chol.

Preserved lemons and olives garnish spicy Moroccan lamb stew over couscous.

No-mess browning

Browning the meat is the foundation of a good stew, but it can be time-consuming, requiring the meat to be cooked in several batches, or messy, leaving you with an oil-spattered stove. In our technique of sweating the meat, the juices and fat render with the pan covered. Then, after the pan is uncovered, the meat browns in one batch, its juices evaporating and caramelizing. This neat, easy process lends deep flavor to the finished stew. Here's how:

1. Place meat in a heavy-bottomed 5- to 6-quart pan. Add ½ cup water; cover and bring to a boil over high heat. Reduce heat and simmer briskly over medium heat until meat is gray on the outside and has rendered juices and fat, 15 to 20 minutes.

2. Uncover pan, increase heat to high, and stir often until most of the liquid has evaporated, 15 to 20 minutes. Reduce heat to medium-high and stir often until meat juices have caramelized and darkened and meat has browned in the rendered fat, about 5 minutes longer. If drippings and the brown film on pan begin to scorch, reduce heat to medium.

Moroccan Lamb Tagine

PREP AND COOK TIME: About 1¾ hours

NOTES: This stew is adapted from a recipe by Heidi Krahling, chef-owner of Insalata in San Anselmo, California. To add extra layers of flavor, garnish the stew with preserved lemons and harissa (see recipes on page 205, or purchase prepared versions at specialty food stores).

MAKES: 6 servings

    4   **pounds fat-trimmed boned lamb shoulder or other cut suitable for stewing, rinsed and cut into 1½-inch chunks**

    2   **onions (8 oz. each), peeled and thinly sliced**

    4   **cloves garlic, peeled and minced**

    1   **tablespoon *each* paprika and ground cumin**

    1   **teaspoon *each* ground turmeric, ground cinnamon, and minced fresh ginger**

  ½   **teaspoon cayenne**

  ⅛   **teaspoon ground cardamom**

2½   **cups fat-skimmed chicken broth**

    1   **can (14½ oz.) diced tomatoes**

    2   **tablespoons tomato paste**

        Salt and fresh-ground pepper

        Fluffy couscous (recipe on page 205)

  ⅓   **cup pitted kalamata olives**

  ⅓   **cup chopped fresh cilantro**

1. Brown lamb (see "No-Mess Browning" at left). Discard all but 2 tablespoons fat from the pan.

2. Add onions and garlic to pan; stir often over medium heat until onions begin to get limp, 3 to 5 minutes. Add paprika, cumin, turmeric, cinnamon, ginger, cayenne, and cardamom; stir until very fragrant, about 30 seconds. Add broth, tomatoes (including juices), and tomato paste. Bring to a boil over high heat. Reduce heat, cover, and simmer, stirring occasionally, until lamb is tender when pierced, about 1 hour. Skim off and discard any fat. Add salt and pepper to taste.

3. On dinner plates or a large rimmed platter, mound couscous and form a well in the center. With a slotted spoon, transfer lamb and vegetables to well. Measure pan juices; if less than 3 cups, add water to make that amount, return to pan, and bring to a boil over high heat. Add salt to taste. Pour juices into a bowl and pass to add to taste. Scatter olives and cilantro over lamb; garnish as desired (see notes).

Per serving of tagine: 737 cal., 48% (351 cal.) from fat; 80 g protein; 39 g fat (14 g sat.); 13 g carbo (2.2 g fiber); 504 mg sodium; 266 mg chol.

Star makers

These versatile condiments turn everyday dishes into something special.

Creamy Polenta

PREP AND COOK TIME: About 30 minutes

NOTES: If making up to 15 minutes ahead, remove from heat and cover tightly. Shortly before serving, stir over medium heat, adding a little hot water to thin, if needed.

MAKES: 8 cups; 6 to 8 servings

In a 5- to 6-quart pan, mix 1 quart fat-skimmed **chicken broth**, 1 quart **milk**, and 2 cups **polenta**. Stir often over medium-high heat until simmering, 10 to 12 minutes; reduce heat, simmer, and continue to stir until polenta is thickened and smooth and creamy to taste, 15 to 20 minutes. Just before serving, stir in ½ cup **grated parmesan cheese** and **salt** to taste.

Per cup: 370 cal., 16% (58 cal.) from fat; 17 g protein; 6.4 g fat (3.7 g sat.); 60 g carbo (7 g fiber); 211 mg sodium; 22 mg chol.

Oven-Dried Tomatoes

PREP AND COOK TIME: About 3 hours

NOTES: You can make these sweet, slightly chewy tomatoes up to 3 days ahead; cool, cover, and chill. Use them to dress up our Italian peppered beef stew, or place them on salads, sandwiches, or pizza.

MAKES: About 1 cup

Rinse and dry about 1 pound **firm-ripe Roma tomatoes.** Slice crosswise into ¼-inch-thick rounds and pat dry with towels. Coat a 10- by 15-inch baking pan with about 1 tablespoon **olive oil.** Arrange tomato slices in a single layer in pan. Sprinkle lightly with

Immerse lemons in spiced brine to preserve. Use on stews, salads, seafood, and couscous.

salt and **pepper.** Bake in a 200° regular or convection oven until tomatoes are dry but still pliable, 2¼ to 2¾ hours. While still warm, with a wide spatula, loosen slices from pan. Cool completely and store airtight in refrigerator.

Per ¼ cup: 54 cal., 61% (33 cal.) from fat; 1 g protein; 3.7 g fat (0.5 g sat.); 5.3 g carbo (1.5 g fiber); 10 mg sodium; 0 mg chol.

Gremolata

PREP TIME: 5 minutes

NOTES: This mixture adds a lively accent to stews like our Italian peppered beef or to cooked vegetables, meats, or green salads.

MAKES: About ½ cup

In a food processor or with a knife, finely chop 1 peeled **garlic** clove and ½ cup **parsley.** Mix in 1 tablespoon grated **lemon** peel.

Per tablespoon: 2.1 cal., 0% (0 cal.) from fat; 0.1 g protein; 0 g fat; 0.5 g carbo (0.2 g fiber); 1.6 mg sodium; 0 mg chol.

Fluffy Couscous

PREP AND COOK TIME: About 10 minutes

NOTES: Heidi Krahling coats couscous with olive oil before cooking, then adds liquid; this keeps grains separate, producing

a fluffier texture. Start the couscous about 10 minutes before lamb stew is done.

MAKES: 9 cups; 6 to 8 servings

In a large bowl, mix 3 cups **couscous** and 3 tablespoons **olive oil.** Add 1 quart boiling fat-skimmed **chicken broth** and stir gently; cover tightly and let stand until liquid is absorbed and couscous is tender to bite, about 5 minutes. Add ¼ cup **lemon juice** and **salt** and **pepper** to taste; mix and fluff with a large spoon or fork.

Per serving: 323 cal., 15% (50 cal.) from fat; 13 g protein; 5.5 g fat (0.8 g sat.); 54 g carbo (2.2 g fiber); 46 mg sodium; 0 mg chol.

Preserved Lemons

PREP AND COOK TIME: About 20 minutes, plus 5 days to cure

NOTES: You can double Krahling's recipe to have this Moroccan condiment on hand to add a tart, salty, slightly bitter accent to salads, stews, fish, and couscous.

MAKES: 2 lemons

Rinse 2 **lemons** (5 oz. each). Score peels about ¼ in. deep down length of lemons, spacing slashes about 1 inch apart. In a 2- to 3-quart nonreactive pan, combine 2½ cups **water**, 3 tablespoons **kosher salt,** and lemons.

Bring to a boil over high heat, then reduce heat, cover, and simmer until lemon peels are tender when pierced, 12 to 15 minutes. With a slotted spoon, transfer lemons to a pint-size wide-mouthed canning jar; reserve salted water. Add 2 **whole cloves,** 1 **dried bay leaf,** 1 **cinnamon stick** (3 in.), and 2 teaspoons *each* **coriander seeds** and **black peppercorns** to jar. Press lemons down slightly to release juices. Pour enough of the reserved salted water over them to cover completely; seal with lid. When cool, chill at least 5 days, turning jar occasionally (lemons may darken a little), or up to 3 months. To use, lift lemons from liquid, scrape out soft pulp, and sliver or chop peels.

Harissa

PREP TIME: About 30 minutes

NOTES: This homemade Moroccan hot sauce has more complexity than super-hot purchased versions. Our sauce is medium-hot; add more cayenne for extra heat. Make this sauce up to 5 days ahead; cover and chill. Dried ancho chilies are available in well-stocked supermarkets and in Hispanic grocery stores. (Sometimes mistakenly labeled pasillas, anchos are triangular; true pasillas are long and skinny.)

MAKES: About 1 cup

Snap off and discard stems of 2 ounces **dried ancho** or California **chilies** (see notes). Shake out and discard seeds. Rinse chilies and cut or break into about ½-inch pieces. Soak in 1 cup **hot water** until soft, about 20 minutes. Lift chilies out (reserving soaking water) and transfer to a blender or food processor. Add ⅓ cup of the reserved water, 3 tablespoons *each* **lemon juice** and **olive oil,** 1 tablespoon **paprika,** 1½ teaspoons **cayenne,** 1 teaspoon **ground coriander,** 1 teaspoon **salt,** ½ teaspoon **ground cumin,** and ⅛ teaspoon **pepper;** whirl until smooth. If thicker than desired, blend in 2 to 3 more tablespoons reserved water. ◆

Serve saffron-flavored pumpkin bouillabaisse with toasted French bread.

The other pumpkins

Go beyond jack-o'-lanterns and think stews and pilaf

By Charity Ferreira
Photograph by James Carrier

Although there are dozens of varieties, pumpkins fall into two categories: those for carving and those for cooking. The cheerfully ubiquitous jack-o'-lantern pumpkins are great for the front porch, but their flesh tends to be fibrous and bland. The other pumpkins are the ones you'll find all fall at produce and farmers' markets. They're beautiful enough to decorate with, but they're grown to be cooked and eaten like any other winter squash.

Varieties such as Baby Bear and Sugar Pie have dense flesh and delicate flavor. And look for the eggshell-colored Lumina and softball-shaped Orange Smoothie. Whatever variety you choose, these dishes will help you get to know this squash's savory side.

Pumpkin Bouillabaisse

PREP AND COOK TIME: About 1 hour

NOTES: To cut pumpkin into cubes, halve vertically and scrape out seeds. Cut halves into 1-inch-wide wedges. Peel each slice, then cut flesh into cubes.

MAKES: 6 to 8 servings

- 1 pound fennel
- 1 tablespoon olive oil
- 1 onion (about 8 oz.), peeled, halved, and thinly slivered lengthwise
- 2 tablespoons minced garlic
- ½ cup dry white wine
- 4 cups fat-skimmed chicken broth
- 1 bottle (8 oz.) clam juice
- 1 tablespoon Pernod or other anise-flavored liqueur (optional)
- 8 cups cubed (½ in.) pumpkin, such as Sugar Pie or Baby Bear (see notes)
- ¼ teaspoon saffron threads, crumbled
- 1 dried bay leaf
- ½ teaspoon salt
- ¼ teaspoon pepper
- 2 cans (14½ oz. each) crushed or diced tomatoes
- 1 pound halibut, rinsed and cut into 1-inch pieces
- 2 tablespoons chopped parsley
  Rouille (recipe follows)

1. Trim off and discard stalks, root ends, and bruised areas from fennel. Chop and reserve green tops. Rinse heads; cut in half lengthwise, then slice.

2. Heat oil in a 5- to 6-quart pan over medium-high heat; add fennel, onion, and garlic and stir often until soft, 10 to 12 minutes. Add wine; cook until most of liquid has evaporated, about 2 minutes. Add broth, clam juice, Pernod (if using), pumpkin, saffron, bay leaf, salt, and pepper; increase heat to high and bring to a boil. Reduce heat, cover, and simmer just until pumpkin is tender when pierced, 15 to 20 minutes.

3. Add tomatoes; bring to a simmer. Gently stir in fish; simmer until opaque in center (cut to test), 4 to 5 minutes. Stir in parsley. Ladle into bowls and top with 1 tablespoon rouille and fennel tops.

Per serving: 289 cal., 44% (126 cal.) from fat; 20 g protein; 14 g fat (2.1 g sat.); 23 g carbo (2.9 g fiber); 569 mg sodium; 26 mg chol.

Rouille. In a bowl, stir together ½ cup **mayonnaise**, 1 tablespoon **tomato paste**, 2 teaspoons **lemon juice**, 1 minced **garlic clove**, ¼ teaspoon **cayenne**, and **salt** and **pepper** to taste. Makes about ½ cup.

Pumpkin Pilaf

PREP AND COOK TIME: About 1 hour
MAKES: 8 to 10 side-dish servings

- 2 tablespoons olive oil
- 1 cup finely chopped onion
- 2 garlic cloves, peeled and minced
- 2 cups long-grain white rice
- ¼ teaspoon *each* ground cinnamon, ground coriander, ground cumin, ground turmeric, and salt
- ⅛ teaspoon *each* paprika and pepper
- 3 cups fat-skimmed chicken broth
- 1 tablespoon lemon juice
- 3½ cups diced (¼ in.) pumpkin, such as Sugar Pie or Baby Bear (see introduction at left)
- 3 tablespoons dried currants
- 1 tablespoon minced preserved lemon
- ⅓ cup chopped pistachios
- 2 tablespoons chopped fresh cilantro

1. Heat oil in a 10- to 12-inch frying pan (with sides at least 2 in. high) over medium-high heat. When hot, add onion and garlic; stir until limp, about 5 minutes. Add rice, cinnamon, coriander, cumin, turmeric, salt, paprika, and pepper; stir to coat. Add broth, lemon juice, pumpkin, currants, and preserved lemon. Bring to a simmer.

2. Reduce heat to low, cover, and cook until liquid is absorbed and rice is tender to bite, 20 to 25 minutes. Fluff with a fork and stir in pistachios and cilantro.

Per serving: 224 cal., 21% (46 cal.) from fat; 6.8 g protein; 5.1 g fat (0.7 g sat.); 38 g carbo (1.3 g fiber); 84 mg sodium; 0 mg chol.

Pumpkin and Pork Chili

PREP AND COOK TIME: About 1 hour

MAKES: 4 servings

- 1 tablespoon olive oil
- 12 ounces pork tenderloin, rinsed, fat trimmed, and cut into ½-inch cubes
- 1 onion (about 8 oz.), peeled and chopped
- 3 cloves garlic, peeled and minced
- 2 cans (12 oz. each) tomatillos, drained
- 1½ to 3 tablespoons canned diced jalapeño chilies
- 4 cups cubed (½ in.) pumpkin, such as Sugar Pie or Baby Bear (see introduction on page 206)
- 2 cans (15 oz. each) small white beans, drained and rinsed
- 1 teaspoon ground cumin
- ½ teaspoon ground dried chipotle chilies or chili powder
- ¼ teaspoon salt
- ⅓ cup chopped fresh cilantro
- 2 tablespoons lime juice

1. Heat oil in a 5- to 6-quart pan over medium-high heat. When hot, add pork and stir frequently until browned, 2 to 3 minutes. Transfer pork to a plate. Add onion and garlic to pan; stir frequently until onion is limp, about 8 minutes.

2. Meanwhile, in a blender, whirl tomatillos and jalapeños until smooth.

3. Add 1 cup water, tomatillo mixture, pumpkin, beans, cumin, ground chilies, and salt. Reduce heat to maintain a simmer, cover, and cook, stirring occasionally, 10 minutes. Stir in pork. Cook, covered, until pork is no longer pink in the center (cut to test), 10 minutes longer. Add cilantro and lime juice.

Per serving: 378 cal., 18% (68 cal.) from fat; 28 g protein; 7.6 g fat (1.6 g sat.); 48 g carbo (9.8 g fiber); 790 mg sodium; 55 mg chol. ◆

Moist sweet potato pound cake is a treat with homemade butterscotch ice cream on the side.

FOOD STYLING: SUSAN DEVATY

The sweetest endings

By Charity Ferreira • Photograph by James Carrier

Just as pumpkin is used in pie, sweet potatoes find a place in the dessert course in a pound cake with a golden glow.

Sweet Potato Pound Cake

PREP AND COOK TIME: About 2 hours, plus at least 1 hour to cool

NOTES: Choose sweet potatoes with dark red skin and bright orange flesh, often sold as Garnet yams, for this moist pound cake. You can make the sweet potato purée (step 1) up to 2 days ahead; cover and chill. You can bake the cake up to 1 day ahead; wrap tightly and store at room temperature. Serve with scoops of butterscotch ice cream.

MAKES: 6 to 8 servings

- 1¼ pounds Garnet sweet potatoes (see notes)
- ¾ cup (⅜ lb.) butter, at room temperature
- 1¼ cups sugar
- 3 large eggs
- 1 tablespoon grated orange peel
- 1½ teaspoons vanilla
- 1¾ cups all-purpose flour
- 1½ teaspoons baking powder
- ¼ teaspoon mace
- ¼ teaspoon salt

1. Prick sweet potatoes several times with a sharp knife. Place on a 12- by 15-inch baking sheet and bake in a 375° regular or convection oven until very soft when pierced, about 40 minutes. When cool enough to handle, peel sweet potatoes and whirl in a blender or food processor until smooth. You will need 1 cup purée; save any extra for other uses.

2. In a large bowl, with a mixer on medium speed, beat butter and sugar until well blended. Add eggs one at a time, beating to blend after each addition. Beat in 1 cup sweet potato purée, the orange peel, and the vanilla.

3. In another bowl, mix flour with baking powder, mace, and salt. Add the flour mixture to batter; mix on low to incorporate dry ingredients, then beat at medium speed until well blended.

4. Scrape batter into a buttered 4½- by 8½-inch loaf pan.

5. Bake in a 350° regular or 325° convection oven until a wooden skewer inserted into the center comes out clean, 1 hour to 1 hour 15 minutes. Cool in pan on a rack about 15 minutes. Invert cake onto a plate and cool completely, about 1 hour. Cut into ½-inch slices and serve, or wrap tightly and store at room temperature.

Per serving: 465 cal., 39% (180 cal.) from fat; 6.2 g protein; 20 g fat (12 g sat.); 65 g carbo (2.3 g fiber); 377 mg sodium; 128 mg chol. ◆

Creamy potatoes are a great foil for spicy sausages—and you get only one pan dirty.

A case for sausage

Link up with the world's oldest convenience food

By Sara Schneider • Photograph by James Carrier

Sometimes convenience food can be a good thing. Sausages, one of the oldest such foods, bring vibrant flavor to simple cooking. More and more sausage makers in the West have been producing high-quality links. We like to use fresh ones in slow-cooked dishes, such as merguez with scalloped potatoes. Fully cooked sausages make a natural cornerstone for a quick ragout with all the flavor of a long-braised stew.

Merguez Sausages with Scalloped Potatoes

PREP AND COOK TIME: About 1½ hours

NOTES: Harissa-spiced merguez sausages are available from specialty butchers.

MAKES: 6 or 7 servings

- 1 tablespoon butter
- 1½ pounds fresh merguez (spicy beef; see notes) or lamb sausages
- 1 onion (about 8 oz.), peeled and slivered lengthwise
- 5 cloves garlic, peeled and chopped
- 2 cups whipping cream
  About 1¼ cups fat-skimmed chicken broth
- 1½ teaspoons salt
- ½ teaspoon fresh-ground pepper
- 4 pounds Yukon Gold potatoes, peeled, halved, and thinly sliced
  Chopped parsley

1. In a 10- to 12-inch ovenproof frying pan (with sides at least 2½ in. tall) over medium-high heat, melt butter. Add sausages and turn until browned all over, 5 to 8 minutes. Transfer to a plate.

2. Reduce heat to medium, add onion and garlic to pan, and stir occasionally until slightly browned, 5 to 8 minutes. Pour in cream and 1¼ cups broth; stir in salt and pepper. Add potatoes. (Liquid should just cover; if it doesn't, add more broth.) Bring to a simmer over medium-high heat, gently stirring occasionally. Lower heat and barely simmer, uncovered, until potatoes are tender when pierced, about 20 minutes (do not boil).

3. Arrange sausages on potato mixture

and transfer pan to a 350° oven. Bake until cream mixture has thickened and is well browned on top and sausages are cooked through (cut to test), 40 to 45 minutes.

4. Sprinkle with parsley. Serve potatoes and sausages from pan.

Per serving: 731 cal., 60% (441 cal.) from fat; 23 g protein; 49 g fat (25 g sat.); 49 g carbo (3.3 g fiber); 1,667 mg sodium; 145 mg chol.

Sausage and Artichoke Ragout

PREP AND COOK TIME: About 1 hour

NOTES: Serve over soft-cooked polenta.

MAKES: 4 servings

- About 1 tablespoon olive oil
- 1 pound cooked poultry sausages
- 1 onion (about 8 oz.), peeled and thinly slivered lengthwise
- 2 tablespoons minced garlic
- 1 cup dry white wine
- ½ cup fat-skimmed chicken broth
- 2 packages (8 oz. each) frozen artichoke hearts, thawed
- 2 cups chopped Roma tomatoes
- ¾ to 1 cup drained pitted kalamata olives, halved
- 1 tablespoon chopped fresh rosemary
- 1 tablespoon chopped fresh oregano
  Salt and pepper

1. Pour 1 tablespoon oil into a 10- to 12-inch ovenproof frying pan (with sides at least 2½ in. tall) over high heat; when hot, add sausages and turn until browned all over, about 5 minutes. Transfer to a board. Slice on the diagonal ½ inch thick.

2. Meanwhile, add onion and garlic to pan (if no fat is left in pan, add a little more oil) and stir occasionally until they begin to brown, 4 to 5 minutes. Add wine, broth, and artichoke hearts; bring to a boil and stir occasionally until liquid is reduced by about half, 10 to 12 minutes.

3. Add sausages, tomatoes, olives, rosemary, and oregano; bring to a simmer, lower heat, and cook, stirring often, 5 minutes. Add salt and pepper to taste.

Per serving: 433 cal., 46% (198 cal.) from fat; 23 g protein; 22 g fat (4.5 g sat.); 29 g carbo (12 g fiber); 1,275 mg sodium; 111 mg chol. ◆

With toasted bread, a simple, savory soup can be a one-dish meal.

Soup of the evening

Combine greens and beans for a quick, warming dinner

By Kate Washington • Photograph by James Carrier

Since I work around food all day, the last thing I want to do when I go home at night is whip up a cassoulet or lasagna from scratch. That's why this simple, Italian-style soup of greens and beans has become a weeknight staple at my house. I keep a bunch of greens, a few cans of beans, a wedge of parmesan, and some chicken broth on hand for it. (If I'm out of homemade broth, I buy the kind that comes in a carton, which doesn't have the tinny taste of canned.) It's easy to vary the soup with different kinds of beans or greens (though some, such as kale, require longer cooking). It's a minimalist autumn dinner that leaves me free to spend the rest of the evening out of the kitchen.

Chard and White Bean Soup

PREP AND COOK TIME: About 40 minutes

NOTES: If you're using imported parmesan, such as Parmigiano-Reggiano, add a piece of the rind to the soup in step 2 for extra flavor. While the soup simmers, brush some slices of country bread or levain with olive oil and toast them, to serve with the hot soup.

MAKES: 2 1/2 quarts; 4 to 6 servings

1 bunch Swiss chard (about 1 lb.)
1 tablespoon olive oil
1 tablespoon minced garlic
1 quart fat-skimmed chicken broth
2 cans (15 oz. each) cannellini beans, drained and rinsed
    About 1/2 cup fresh-grated parmesan cheese (see notes)
    Salt and fresh-ground pepper

1. Rinse chard well and trim off and discard discolored stem ends; tear leaves from stems. Thinly slice stems crosswise; cut leaves into 1-inch pieces.

2. Pour oil into a 4- to 5-quart pan over medium heat. Add chard stems and garlic; stir often until stems are limp, about 10 minutes. Add chard leaves, broth, and 3 cups water (see notes). Bring to a simmer; cook, stirring occasionally, until chard is tender to bite, 10 minutes longer.

3. Add beans and stir occasionally until hot, 1 to 2 minutes. Stir in 1/2 cup parmesan cheese and add salt and pepper to taste. Ladle into bowls; offer more parmesan to add at the table.

Per serving: 196 cal., 26% (50 cal.) from fat; 17 g protein; 5.6 g fat (1.9 g sat.); 19 g carbo (6.8 g fiber); 526 mg sodium; 6.4 mg chol. ◆

A slice of fall

While persimmons can be used in pies and tarts, you can also enjoy them plain. Choose from 'Hachiya', with a slightly elongated shape and sweet, soft flesh, and 'Fuyu', a squat, tomato-shaped variety that's eaten when crisp. 'Hyakume', or cinnamon persimmon, is a rarer firm variety that's flecked with brown (pictured above).

To eat a ripe 'Hachiya', chill it, cut off the top, and spoon out the flesh. For firm persimmons, peel if desired, seed if necessary, and thinly slice crosswise. Add to salads; tuck them into cheese or ham sandwiches; or dress them with a squeeze of citrus for breakfast.

Persimmons are in markets now. Order 'Hyakume' from Melissa's Produce (www.melissas.com or 800/588-0151).

—Linda Lau Anusasananan

Stock options

A little effort yields big returns in homemade broth

There may be no sure thing in the financial world, but luckily that's not the case in the kitchen. For a small outlay of time and money, homemade chicken stock yields consistently high dividends as a delicious base for soups, stews, sauces, and risottos. Unlike one-dimensional, salty canned broth, stock from scratch lets you add flavor nuances. To save up for stock, throw bones from roasted poultry or raw bones and scraps into a zip-lock plastic bag and freeze until you have a critical mass. It only takes five minutes or so to get homemade stock started and another few minutes to strain it at the end. While the stock is simmering, a warm kitchen is just one more return on your investment.

Basic Chicken Stock

PREP AND COOK TIME: $2^{1}/_{2}$ hours, plus at least 6 hours to chill

NOTES: If you're using large chicken pieces or a whole chicken, chop into smaller pieces with a cleaver. For deeper color in the flavorful brown stock, leave the onion unpeeled.

MAKES: About 3 quarts

- 5 pounds uncooked chicken or turkey pieces and/or bones (skin and fat discarded; see notes), or a mixture of bones from roasted poultry and uncooked meat scraps
- 1 onion (8 oz.), peeled and coarsely chopped (see notes)
- 1 carrot (4 oz.), rinsed and cut into chunks
- 2 stalks celery (4 oz.), leafy tops left on, rinsed and cut into chunks
- ½ cup parsley sprigs, rinsed
- 5 peppercorns (optional)
- 1 dried bay leaf
- 1 sprig fresh thyme, rinsed, or ¼ teaspoon dried thyme

1. In a 6- to 8-quart pan over medium-high heat, combine chicken, onion, carrot, celery, parsley, peppercorns (if using), bay leaf, and thyme. Add cold water just to cover. Bring to a simmer, then lower heat to maintain simmer and cook, occasionally skimming and discarding foam from surface, until liquid is golden and has a deep chicken flavor, about 2 hours. Do not allow stock to boil; the surface should barely be disturbed by small bubbles.

2. If a layer of fat forms on the surface, skim off and discard. If liquid drops below level of chicken and vegetables, add more cold water just to cover.

3. Place a fine strainer over a large bowl nested in ice water in the sink. Ladle or carefully pour stock through strainer. Allow liquid to drip from solids, but do not press to extract more; discard solids. Stir stock occasionally until cool, 10 to 20 minutes; cover and chill until stock is cold and any fat on surface is firm, at least 6 hours, or up to 1 day.

4. With a spoon, skim fat from surface of stock and discard. Cover stock and chill up to 4 days, or pour into jars or ice cube trays and freeze up to 3 months.

Brown chicken stock. Follow directions for basic chicken stock (preceding), but do not peel onion (see notes), and, before beginning step 1, place a single layer of the chicken pieces or scraps, meat side down, in a 6- to 8-quart pan over medium-high heat. Cook without disturbing until meat is well browned, 7 to 10 minutes (take care not to scorch). Using tongs or a long-handled fork (meat may stick; pry it up from pan bottom), turn pieces and cook until second side is browned, about 5 minutes longer. Reduce heat to medium. Pour 2 cups water into pan and stir, scraping pan bottom to loosen browned bits. Adding remaining ingredients, proceed with step 1. —*Kate Washington*

A cellar for the rest of us

When I was younger, it seemed that the world was divided into two kinds of wine drinkers: people like me, who aged wine for about as long as it took to get the bottle home from the store, and people with five-figure, temperature-controlled cellars showcasing thousands of pricey bottles. Short of winning the lottery, I knew I'd never be part of the second group.

But over the years, I've realized that most wine drinkers fall somewhere between these extremes. Thousands of wines are more than most people need or can afford, but a ready stock of, say, 20 to 40 bottles can make wine an easy part of your daily routine.

But which wines should you have? The kinds I'd suggest keeping on hand are somewhat different from the conventional collection. Instead of laying away X number of vintages of Bordeaux, Y number of Burgundies, and so on, buy for current drinking and real-life situations. I've included a list of categories below, but add your own. Keep at least one bottle on hand for each purpose.

For comfort foods. It's Wednesday night, and you're having meatloaf. You might be surprised at how good an unfussy, inexpensive white wine can be: **Adelsheim Pinot Gris 2002** *(Oregon; $16)* has a beautiful lemon-drop, vanilla, and spice character. If you like reds, try **Hedges "CMS" 2000** *(Columbia Valley, WA; $10),* a mouth-filling blend of Cabernet Sauvignon, Merlot, Cabernet Franc, and Syrah.

For company. When friends come by, the perfect wine is one that's easy to drink but has some panache. **Muga Rioja Reserva 1999** *(Rioja, Spain; $17)* has the earthy sensuality of a Burgundy that costs four times as much.

For spicy dishes. Considered exotic just a decade ago, many fiery ethnic dishes are virtually mainstream now. A wine to have on hand as a partner: the super-fruity **Georges Du Boeuf Beaujolais-Villages 2002** *(Beaujolais, France; $8).*

For red-meat meals. Whether it's prime rib or pot roast, meaty dishes need big wines. Try the intense, well-muscled **Chappellet Napa Valley Merlot 2000** *(Napa Valley; $26).*

For a celebration. You don't need to wait for a raise; just getting to Friday night is a victory. It calls for **Domaine Carneros by Taittinger Brut 1999** *(Carneros, CA; $24)*—exquisite, refreshing, and full of frothy bubbles.

For romance. The need is self-explanatory. A hauntingly delicious option is **Taylor Fladgate 20 Year Old Tawny Port** *(Douro Valley, Portugal; $45–$50).* Brown sugar, honey, spices, and toffee all wrapped up into one mesmerizing flavor. (It's not cheap, but an opened bottle will last for months.)

For a last-minute gift. Something generous but not ostentatious is good: **Hamilton's "Stonegarden" Grenache/Shiraz 2000** *(Barossa Valley, Australia; $17).* An absolutely massive and velvety red, evocative of wild berries, cherry preserves, and eucalyptus.

For no reason at all. You need a favorite variety to open on any whim. Try **Annie's Lane Chardonnay 2002** *(Clare Valley, Australia; $13).* Just a hint of oak, with ripe apricot and melon flavors. Best to keep it chilled in the refrigerator, ready to go. —*Karen MacNeil-Fife*

Store wine bottles on their sides or upside down in a fairly cool place that gets no direct sunlight.

Heat of the moment

A convection option is now standard on most new ovens, but it can leave even longtime bakers wondering when to use it. Convection ovens circulate air constantly, eliminating (at least in theory) the hot spots of many regular ovens. This is an asset when you want deep, even color in breads and pastries; crisp skin on poultry; or great browning on roasts. The circulating heat can be a liability for delicate baked goods such as custards. We test all our baking recipes in both regular and convection ovens. We've found that the required temperature and cooking time seldom differ greatly, though our testers report that they start checking for doneness a few minutes early when using convection. If the time or required temperature varies in a convection oven, we note that in the recipe; likewise, if a dish is not suited to convection, we advise using a regular oven. —*K. W.*

CONV. BAKE

October treats

Readers' recipes tested in *Sunset's* kitchens

Photographs by James Carrier

Pumpkin Parfaits

Betty Ray, Vancouver, WA

Betty Ray created this creamy parfait as a light alternative to pumpkin pie.

PREP TIME: About 40 minutes, plus at least 2 hours to chill

MAKES: 4 servings

- 1 jar (7 oz.) marshmallow creme
- 1 package (8 oz.) Neufchâtel (light cream) cheese, at room temperature
- 2 tablespoons thawed frozen orange juice concentrate
- 1 cup canned pumpkin
- ¼ cup maple syrup
- 1½ teaspoons ground cinnamon
- ½ teaspoon ground nutmeg
- ¼ cup chopped toasted pecans
- ¼ cup crumbled gingersnap cookies

1. In a bowl, with an electric mixer on medium speed, beat marshmallow creme, Neufchâtel, and 1 tablespoon orange juice concentrate until smooth.

2. In another bowl, stir together pumpkin, maple syrup, cinnamon, nutmeg, and remaining tablespoon orange juice concentrate. Fold in ¼ cup of the cream cheese mixture until no white streaks remain.

3. Spoon about 3 tablespoons of the remaining cream cheese mixture into each of four dessert or parfait glasses, followed by about 3 tablespoons of the pumpkin mixture. Repeat layers, ending with pumpkin. Chill until cold, at least 2 hours or up to 1 day. Just before serving, sprinkle each parfait with chopped pecans and gingersnap crumbs.

Per serving: 458 cal., 37% (171 cal.) from fat; 8.2 g protein; 19 g fat (9 g sat.); 69 g carbo (1.7 g fiber); 289 mg sodium; 43 mg chol.

Pumpkin is layered with sweetened cream cheese in this inventive parfait.

Blueberry Dream Bars

Judy Wong, Oakland, CA

Judy Wong had never seen a recipe for bar cookies with a blueberry filling, so she decided to come up with one. Dried cherries make a nice alternative. Store airtight at room temperature up to 3 days.

PREP AND COOK TIME: About 1½ hours, plus at least 40 minutes to chill filling

MAKES: 9 bars

- 1 cup sugar
- 8 ounces dried blueberries or dried cherries, finely chopped
- 1 cup all-purpose flour
- 1 cup quick-cooking oats
- ½ teaspoon salt
- ¾ cup (⅜ lb.) butter, cut into chunks
- 1 large egg yolk

1. In a 1- to 2-quart pan, stir together ¼ cup sugar, the blueberries, and 1¼ cups water. Bring to a boil over high heat, then reduce heat to maintain a simmer, cover, and cook, stirring occasionally, until blueberries are soft and most of the liquid is absorbed, about 45 minutes. Chill until cool, about 40 minutes.

2. Meanwhile, in a bowl or in the bowl of a food processor, mix or whirl flour, oats, salt, and remaining ¾ cup sugar until combined. Cut in butter or pulse until mixture forms coarse crumbs. Add egg yolk and mix or pulse until mixture comes together in a crumbly dough. Divide in half. Press half the mixture evenly over bottom of a buttered 8-inch square baking pan. Chill pan and reserved dough while filling cools.

3. Spread blueberry mixture evenly over crust in pan, then sprinkle and pat the remaining half of the dough evenly over the blueberry layer.

4. Bake in a 350° regular or convection oven until top is browned and filling is bubbling around the edges, 35 to 40 minutes. Let cool about 15 minutes, then cut into squares. Serve warm, or let cool completely.

Per bar: 403 cal., 38% (153 cal.) from fat; 3.3 g protein; 17 g fat (10 g sat.); 60 g carbo (4 g fiber); 289 mg sodium; 66 mg chol.

East-West Carrots

Emily Bader, Seattle

Although this dish dates back to Emily Bader's days in Berkeley in the 1970s, she still enjoys it. Miso is a pungent paste made from fermented soybeans. It is available in Asian markets and well-stocked supermarkets.

PREP AND COOK TIME: About 20 minutes

MAKES: 6 servings

- 1½ pounds carrots, peeled and sliced into thin (⅛ to 1/16 in.) rounds
- 1 tablespoon olive oil
- 1 tablespoon lemon juice
- 1 tablespoon cider vinegar
- 2 teaspoons Asian sesame oil
- 2 teaspoons white miso (see note above)
- 2 teaspoons soy sauce
- ¼ cup thinly sliced green onions
- 2 tablespoons minced parsley
- ¼ teaspoon dried tarragon

1. In a 4- to 6-quart pan over high heat, bring about 2 quarts water to a boil. Add carrots and cook just until tender-crisp to bite, 3 to 4 minutes. Drain.

2. Meanwhile, in a large bowl, mix olive oil, lemon juice, vinegar, sesame oil, miso, soy sauce, green onions, parsley, and tarragon. Add warm carrots and mix to coat. Serve, or cover and chill up to 1 day.

Per serving: 85 cal., 44% (37 cal.) from fat; 1.5 g protein; 4.1 g fat (0.6 g sat.); 12 g carbo (3.5 g fiber); 222 mg sodium; 0 mg chol.

Carrot–Sweet Potato Soup

Joanna Zant, Spokane

When Joanna Zant didn't have enough sweet potatoes for a soup recipe, she added carrots, garbanzos, and spices. She serves this flavorful soup with toasted pocket bread and plain yogurt.

PREP AND COOK TIME: About 1 hour

MAKES: About 9 cups; 4 to 6 servings

- 2 teaspoons olive oil
- 1 onion (8 oz.), peeled and chopped
- 2 cloves garlic, peeled and minced
- 1 tablespoon minced fresh ginger
- 2 teaspoons curry powder
- 1 teaspoon ground cumin
- ¼ teaspoon cayenne
- 1 can (15 oz.) garbanzos, drained and rinsed
- 1 pound carrots, peeled and chopped
- 1 sweet potato (about 1 lb.), peeled and cut into 1-inch chunks
- 6 cups fat-skimmed chicken broth
- 3 tablespoons lemon juice
- Salt and pepper

1. Pour oil into a 4- to 6-quart pan over medium-high heat. When hot, add onion, garlic, and ginger; stir often until onion is limp, about 5 minutes. Add curry powder, cumin, and cayenne; cook until fragrant, about 1 minute.

2. Add garbanzos, carrots, sweet potato, and broth; bring to a boil. Reduce heat to maintain a simmer, cover, and cook, stirring occasionally, until vegetables are tender when pierced, 30 minutes.

3. Whirl in batches in a blender or food processor until smooth. Return to pan and stir in lemon juice and salt and pepper to taste. Heat until steaming, then ladle into bowls.

Per serving: 203 cal., 14% (28 cal.) from fat; 13 g protein; 3.1 g fat (0.3 g sat.); 32 g carbo (6.5 g fiber); 188 mg sodium; 0 mg chol. ◆

These marinated carrots make a nice chilled salad or warm side dish.

Chocolate-pumpkin marble cake with chocolate glaze makes a colorful ending for a Thanksgiving feast (see page 220).

November

Familiar foods for the clan: spiced roast turkey (of course), triple mushroom dressing, cranberry chutney, spinach and persimmon salad, mashed potatoes, and creamy gorgonzola broccoli.

A fitting Thanksgiving

Three menus tailored to the size and spirit of your celebration

By Linda Lau Anusasananan • Photographs by James Carrier • Food styling by Susan Devaty

Families come in more sizes than ever these days. Some are big and all in one place; others are divided by distance; many are small to start with. But the joy of Thanksgiving is in celebrating with those you love, no matter what the size of the gathering, so we've designed menus scaled to fit three sizes of holiday feasts.

The first is a large traditional dinner, full of potluck possibilities. The host can roast the turkey; others can bring gorgonzola broccoli casserole or chocolate-pumpkin marble cake. Our medium-size meal, based on an easy-to-roast turkey breast, borrows flavors from another tradition: Persian. Our mini-feast for two includes elegant roast hens on a golden vegetable hash, followed by beautiful persimmon-cranberry tarts. Each is a celebration; together they salute the diversity that makes the West a wonderful place to live.

An Asian dressing enhances a spinach and persimmon salad topped with glazed pecans.

Feast for 12 to 14

For a big family dinner, share the cooking. The hosts can roast the turkey and make their favorite gravy; others bring the rest of this highly portable meal. Add some mashed potatoes to our lineup, and serve a Pinot Noir or Chardonnay.

Spinach and Persimmon Salad

PREP TIME: About 25 minutes

NOTES: The dressing and persimmons for this salad can be prepared up to 4 hours ahead; wrap fruit airtight and chill. Assemble the salad shortly before serving. You'll find glazed pecans in the nut section of your supermarket.

MAKES: 12 to 14 servings

- ¼   **cup rice vinegar**
- 2   **tablespoons orange marmalade**
- 1   **teaspoon Asian sesame oil**
-     **Salt and pepper**
- 5   **quarts baby spinach leaves (1¼ lb.), rinsed and crisped**
- 3   **firm Fuyu persimmons (5 oz. each), peeled and sliced into thin wedges**
- ¾   **cup glazed pecans**

In a large bowl, mix vinegar, marmalade, and sesame oil. Add salt and pepper to taste. Add spinach, persimmons, and pecans. Mix gently to coat with dressing.

Per serving: 85 cal., 33% (28 cal.) from fat; 1.3 g protein; 3.1 g fat (0.3 g sat.); 15 g carbo (3.5 g fiber); 107 mg sodium; 0 mg chol.

Roast Turkey, Plain or Spiced

PREP AND COOK TIME: 2¼ to 3¼ hours, plus 30 minutes to rest

NOTES: You can roast the turkey with just a sheen of oil, or you can add spices for bolder flavor. We've adapted the seasoning rub that Gayle Pirie and John Clark, chef-owners of Foreign Cinema in San Francisco, use on chicken. You can prepare the turkey through step 1 up to 1 day ahead; cover and chill.

MAKES: 12 to 14 servings, with leftovers (allow at least ¾ pound uncooked turkey per person; roast a larger bird for generous leftovers)

- 1   **turkey (14 to 18 lb.)**
      Spice rub (optional; recipe follows)
- ⅓   **to ½ cup vegetable oil**

1. Remove and discard leg truss from turkey. Pull off and discard any lumps of fat. Remove giblets and neck; save for gravy if desired. Rinse turkey inside and out; pat dry. If using spice rub, rub it generously over skin and inside both neck and body cavities. Brush bird with enough oil to coat.

2. Place turkey, breast up, on a V-shaped rack in a 12- by 17-inch roasting pan (pan should be large enough that turkey fits inside).

3. Roast in a 325° regular or convection oven, basting occasionally with oil, or pan drippings if using spice rub, until a thermometer inserted through thickest part of breast to the bone registers 160°, 2 to 3 hours. (See chart at right for different-size birds.)

4. Transfer turkey to a platter. Let rest in a warm place at least 30 minutes, then carve. When you remove the legs, if meat around thigh joints is still too pink, cut drumsticks from thighs and put thighs in a shallow pan in a 450° oven until no longer pink, 10 to 15 minutes.

Per ¼ pound boned cooked turkey with skin, based on percentages of white and dark meat in an average bird: 229 cal., 39% (90 cal.) from fat; 32 g protein; 10 g fat (3 g sat.); 0 g carbo; (0 g fiber); 82 mg sodium; 93 mg chol.

Spice rub. In a 6- to 8-inch frying pan over medium heat, stir 1 tablespoon **fennel seeds** until lightly browned, about 1 minute. Pour into a blender and whirl until finely ground. Add ¾ teaspoon **hot chili flakes** and whirl until coarsely ground. Pour into a small bowl and mix with 3 tablespoons **Madras** or regular **curry powder**, 1½ tablespoons **sugar**, 1 tablespoon **paprika**, and 1 tablespoon **salt**. Makes about ½ cup.

TURKEY TIPS

Oven-roasted whole turkey

See recipe for roast turkey (at left) for directions on preparing the bird; follow this chart for oven temperatures and cooking times to produce a turkey with moist breast meat. After removing the turkey legs, if you find that the meat around the thigh joints is still too pink, cut the drumsticks from the thighs and put thighs in a shallow pan in a 450° oven. Bake until no longer pink, 10 to 15 minutes. Or put on a microwave-safe plate and cook in a microwave oven at full power (100%) for 1 to 3 minutes.

Turkey wt. with giblets	Oven temp.	Inner temp.*	Cooking time**
10–13 lb.	350°	160°	1½–2¼ hr.
14–23 lb.	325°	160°	2–3 hr.
24–27 lb.	325°	160°	3–3¾ hr.
28–30 lb.	325°	160°	3½–4½ hr.

*To measure the internal temperature of the turkey, insert a thermometer through the thickest part of the breast to the bone.

**Times are for unstuffed birds. A stuffed bird may cook at the same rate as an unstuffed one; however, be prepared to allow 30 to 50 minutes more. While turkeys take about the same time to roast in regular and convection heat, a convection oven does a better job of browning the bird all over.

Triple Mushroom Dressing

PREP AND COOK TIME: About 2¼ hours

NOTES: Three kinds of mushrooms make this bread dressing a perennial family favorite of Denise Marshall, owner of the Last Bite, a cooking school in Eagle Point, Oregon. If dried porcini mushrooms are difficult to find, omit them and use more chicken broth in step 5. You can prepare through step 4 up to 1 day ahead; cover and chill.

MAKES: 12 to 14 servings

- 1 **ounce dried porcini mushrooms (about 1 cup; optional—see notes)**
- ¾ **cup hazelnuts**
- 3 **quarts ¾-inch cubes firm white or egg bread (1 lb.)**
- 2 **pounds leeks**
- 1¼ **pounds cremini or common mushrooms**
- 6 **ounces fresh shiitake mushrooms**
- ¼ **cup (⅛ lb.) butter**
- ¾ **cup chopped shallots**
- 1⅓ **cups chopped celery**
- ¾ **cup chopped parsley**
- 2 **tablespoons chopped fresh thyme leaves or 2 teaspoons dried thyme**
- 1½ **tablespoons chopped fresh sage leaves or 1½ teaspoons dried rubbed sage**
  Salt and pepper
- 2 **large eggs**
- ½ **to ¾ cup fat-skimmed chicken broth**

1. Rinse porcini mushrooms and place in a small bowl with 2 cups hot water. Soak until soft, about 20 minutes. Rub porcini to remove any grit; lift out and squeeze liquid into soaking water. Coarsely chop porcini; reserve soaking liquid.

2. Place hazelnuts in a 9-inch pie pan and bake in a 350° regular or convection oven, shaking pan occasionally, until golden under skins, 10 to 15 minutes. Pour into a clean towel and rub to remove

as much skin as possible. Lift nuts from towel, leaving skins behind; coarsely chop nuts.

3. Place half the bread in each of two 12- by 17-inch baking pans. Bake in a 350° regular or convection oven, stirring once, until lightly browned, 12 to 15 minutes. Pour into a large bowl.

4. Trim off and discard dark green tops and root ends from leeks. Cut white stalk in half lengthwise and rinse well, flipping layers to release grit. Coarsely chop. Rinse cremini and shiitake mushrooms; cut off and discard shiitake stems. Thinly slice both types of mushrooms.

5. In a 5- to 6-quart pan over medium-high heat, melt butter. Add shallots, leeks, and cremini and shiitake mushrooms; stir often until mushrooms begin to brown, about 15 minutes. Mix porcini, nuts, celery, parsley, thyme, and sage into mushroom mixture. Stir into bread and add salt and pepper to taste. In a small bowl, beat together eggs, ½ cup of the reserved mushroom-soaking liquid (pour in carefully, leaving grit behind), and ½ cup chicken broth. Pour over bread mixture and mix well. If you prefer a moister texture, add up to ½ cup more mushroom-soaking liquid or broth. Pour into a shallow 3- to 3½-quart baking dish. Cover with a buttered sheet of foil.

6. Bake dressing in a 325° regular or convection oven until hot in the center, 45 minutes to 1 hour; uncover and bake until top is golden, 10 to 20 minutes longer.

Per serving: 206 cal., 41% (84 cal.) from fat; 6.7 g protein; 9.3 g fat (2.8 g sat.); 25 g carbo (2.4 g fiber); 241 mg sodium; 40 mg chol.

Gorgonzola Broccoli Casserole

PREP AND COOK TIME: About 1 hour

NOTES: Denise Marshall elevates classic broccoli in cheese sauce by using gorgonzola. You can prepare the casserole through step 3 up to 1 day ahead; cover and chill. Uncover and continue with step 4.

MAKES: 12 to 14 servings

- 3 **pounds broccoli**
- ¼ **cup (⅛ lb.) butter, plus 1 tablespoon melted**
- ¼ **cup all-purpose flour**
- 2 **cups milk**
- 2 **packages (3 oz. each) cream cheese, cut into ½-inch chunks**
- ½ **cup crumbled gorgonzola or other blue cheese**
- 2 **cups ½-inch cubes French or other firm white bread (3 oz.)**

1. In a 5- to 6-quart pan over high heat, bring about 3 quarts water to a boil. Rinse broccoli and trim off and discard tough stem ends; if skin on stalks is tough, peel stalks. Cut broccoli into 1-inch pieces. Add to boiling water and cook just until barely tender when pierced, 3 to 5 minutes. Drain.

2. Rinse and dry pan. Add ¼ cup butter to pan and melt over medium heat. Stir in flour until smoothly blended; cook until bubbly, about 1 minute. Add milk and stir over medium-high heat until mixture is boiling and thickened, about 3 minutes. Add cream cheese and gorgonzola; whisk until smoothly blended. Stir in broccoli. Pour into a shallow 2½- to 3-quart casserole.

3. In a blender or food processor, whirl bread cubes into coarse crumbs; you should have about 1⅓ cups. In a small bowl, mix crumbs with 1 tablespoon melted butter. Sprinkle evenly over broccoli mixture.

4. Bake in a 350° regular or convection oven until casserole is hot in the center and crumbs are golden, 20 to 30 minutes.

Per serving: 150 cal., 60% (90 cal.) from fat; 5.5 g protein; 10 g fat (6.4 g sat.); 9.9 g carbo (1.9 g fiber); 197 mg sodium; 31 mg chol.

Baked Cranberry-Ginger Chutney

PREP AND COOK TIME: About 1 hour

NOTES: You can make this sauce up to 1 week ahead; cover and chill.

MAKES: About 1¾ cups; 12 to 14 servings

1. Sort 1 package (12 oz.) **fresh** or thawed frozen **cranberries,** discarding any bruised or decayed fruit. Rinse and drain berries.

2. In an 8- or 9-inch square baking dish, mix cranberries, 1 cup **sugar,** ⅓ cup **cider vinegar,** 2 tablespoons chopped **fresh ginger,** 5 **whole cloves,** and 1 **cinnamon stick** (about 3 in.).

3. Bake, uncovered, in a 350° regular or convection oven, stirring occasionally, until berries are tender when pierced and juices are syrupy, 50 to 60 minutes. Lift out and discard cloves and cinnamon if desired. Serve warm or cool.

Per 2 tablespoons: 69 cal., 1% (0.9 cal.) from fat; 0.1 g protein; 0.1 g fat (0 g sat.); 18 g carbo (0.9 g fiber); 0.8 mg sodium; 0 mg chol.

Spicy cranberry chutney can be made several days before Thanksgiving.

Chocolate-Pumpkin Marble Cake

PREP AND COOK TIME: About 1½ hours, plus at least 2 hours to cool

NOTES: Two separate batters are swirled together to create this playful marbled pound cake.

MAKES: 12 to 16 servings

- 1½ cups (¾ lb.) butter, at room temperature
- 3 cups sugar
- 6 large eggs
- 2 teaspoons vanilla
- 1¼ cups canned pumpkin
- 2¾ cups all-purpose flour
- 2 teaspoons baking powder
- 1 teaspoon salt
- ½ teaspoon ground cinnamon
- ¼ teaspoon ground nutmeg
- ⅛ teaspoon ground cloves
- ¾ cup Dutch-processed unsweetened cocoa
- ⅔ cup buttermilk
- Chocolate glaze (recipe follows)
- ½ cup chopped roasted, unsalted peanuts (optional)

1. In a large bowl, with a mixer on medium speed, beat butter and sugar until well blended. Add eggs, one at a time, beating well after each addition. Beat in vanilla. Scrape half the mixture into another bowl.

2. *To make pumpkin batter:* Beat pumpkin into half the butter mixture until well blended. In another bowl, stir together 1¾ cups flour, 1 teaspoon baking powder, ½ teaspoon salt, cinnamon, nutmeg, and cloves. Add flour mixture to pumpkin mixture and beat on low speed or fold in with a flexible spatula just until blended.

3. *To make chocolate batter:* In another bowl, mix remaining 1 cup flour, 1 teaspoon baking powder, ½ teaspoon salt, and the cocoa. Add flour mixture alternately with buttermilk to the other half of the butter mixture (starting and ending with flour mixture), beating after each addition just until blended.

4. Spoon half the pumpkin batter into a buttered and floured 12-cup bundt-cake pan. Drop half the chocolate batter by spoonfuls over (but not entirely covering) the pumpkin batter. Repeat to spoon remaining pumpkin and chocolate batters into pan. Gently run the blade of a butter knife around the center of the pan several times, then draw the knife across the width of the pan in 10 to 12 places to swirl batters.

5. Bake in a 350° regular or 325° convection oven until a wood skewer inserted into center of cake comes out with a few moist crumbs attached, 55 to 60 minutes. Let cake cool 10 minutes in pan, then invert onto a rack, lift off pan, and cool cake completely.

6. Pour warm chocolate glaze over the top of the cake, letting it drip down the sides. Sprinkle glaze with peanuts if desired. Let stand until glaze is set, about 2 hours, or chill about 30 minutes.

Chocolate glaze. In a heatproof bowl or the top of a double boiler, combine 4 ounces chopped **semisweet chocolate,** ½ cup **whipping cream,** 1 tablespoon **butter,** and 1 teaspoon **corn syrup.** Bring an inch or two of water to a boil in a pan that the bowl can nest in or in bottom of a double boiler, then remove from heat. Place chocolate mixture over water and let stand, stirring occasionally, until melted and smooth, about 10 minutes.

Per serving: 498 cal., 47% (234 cal.) from fat; 6.5 g protein; 26 g fat (15 g sat.); 64 g carbo (1.4 g fiber); 464 mg sodium; 138 mg chol.

—Cake recipe by Charity Ferreira

Pumpkin and chocolate swirl together in a handsome cake for a crowd.

Pair juicy brined turkey breast with Persian-style cranberry-orange rice.

move from heat and skim off and discard any fat. Add lemon juice and salt and pepper to taste. Pour into a gravy boat.

6. Slice turkey and serve with cranberry pan juices to add to taste.

Per serving: 418 cal., 34% (144 cal.) from fat; 57 g protein; 16 g fat (5 g sat.); 7.9 g carbo (0 g fiber); 148 mg chol.

Sweet Potato– Banana Purée

PREP AND COOK TIME: About 30 minutes

NOTES: You can make this fruity purée from chef Ron Siegel of Masa's in San Francisco up to 1 day ahead; cool, cover, and chill. Reheat, covered, in a microwave oven on full power (100%), stirring occasionally, about 3 minutes.

MAKES: About 3¼ cups; 6 to 8 servings

- **2 pounds Garnet or Jewel sweet potatoes (often called yams)**
- **1 ripe banana (6 oz.)**
- **2 cups milk**
- **1 piece (3 in.) vanilla bean (or ½ teaspoon vanilla)**
- **2 tablespoons butter (optional)**
- **About 1 tablespoon lemon juice**
- **Salt**

1. Peel sweet potatoes and banana; cut into 1-inch chunks.

2. In a 3- to 4-quart pan, combine sweet potatoes, banana, and milk. Split vanilla bean in half lengthwise; and scrape seeds into pan, then add pod (if using vanilla extract, add it later). Bring mixture to a boil over high heat, then reduce heat, cover, and simmer until sweet potatoes are tender when pierced, 11 to 13 minutes. Remove vanilla pod and discard.

3. Pour sweet potato mixture into a fine strainer set over a bowl; discard milk. In a food processor, purée sweet potato mixture with butter (and vanilla extract if using) until smooth. Stir in lemon juice and salt to taste. Spoon into a bowl.

Per serving: 136 cal., 15% (21 cal.) from fat; 3.5 g protein; 2.3 g fat (1.3 g sat.); 26 g carbo (2.7 g fiber); 41 mg sodium; 8.5 mg chol.

Harvest dinner for 6 to 8

In this elegant dinner, we've surrounded sliced turkey with Persian-inspired flavors: sweet-tart cranberry jus and jewel rice laced with fruit and nuts. Start with a green salad with a lemon-mint vinaigrette, and add buttered steamed green beans and a dry Riesling, Chenin Blanc, or Pinot Noir. Brine the turkey and make the sweet potatoes a day ahead.

Brined Turkey Breast with Cranberry Jus

PREP AND COOK TIME: About 1½ hours, plus 12 hours to brine

NOTES: Brining the turkey makes it juicy and flavorful; using a bone-in, skin-on breast keeps it moist during roasting. Don't brine the breast longer than 24 hours, or it will become too salty. If you're not ready to roast the breast, chill it, uncovered (for crisper skin), up to 1 day after step 2. The sweet-tart pan juices that go with this turkey were inspired by Faz Poursohi, chef and proprietor of the Faz Restaurants in the San Francisco Bay Area.

MAKES: 6 to 8 servings

- **1 cup kosher salt**
- **1 cup sugar**
- **1 bone-in turkey breast (5 to 6 lb.; see notes)**
- **1 tablespoon melted butter**
- **1½ cups fat-skimmed chicken broth**
- **¼ cup frozen cranberry juice concentrate**
- **About 1 tablespoon lemon juice**
- **Salt and pepper**

1. In a large bowl or pan (at least 8 qt.), combine 4 quarts water, kosher salt, and ¾ cup sugar. Stir until salt and sugar are dissolved. Rinse turkey and trim off back, ribs, wing meat, and excess neck skin if attached. Submerge turkey in brine, cover, and chill, turning turkey occasionally, at least 12 hours or up to 24 (see notes).

2. Lift turkey from brine, rinse well, and pat dry; discard brine. Set turkey, skin up, on a rack in a 10- by 15-inch roasting pan. Brush skin with melted butter.

3. Bake in a 375° regular or convection oven until a thermometer inserted through thickest part of breast to bone registers 160°, 1¼ to 1½ hours.

4. Meanwhile, put remaining ¼ cup sugar in an 8- to 10-inch frying pan over high heat; shake pan often until sugar is amber-colored, 2 to 3 minutes. Add ¾ cup broth and the cranberry concentrate; stir over medium-high heat until blended, 1 to 2 minutes. Remove from heat.

5. Transfer turkey to a platter or board; let rest in a warm place about 10 minutes. Add remaining ¾ cup broth to roasting pan and stir to free browned bits. Pour drippings through a fine strainer into cranberry mixture. Add any juices accumulated on platter from turkey. Stir over high heat until boiling. Re-

Cranberry-Orange Jewel Rice

PREP AND COOK TIME: About 1¼ hours

NOTES: This festive rice also comes from Faz Poursohi. It tastes best freshly cooked, but you can prepare the candied peel, almonds, and cranberries through step 3 up to 1 day ahead; cover separately and store at room temperature.

MAKES: 6 to 8 servings

- **2** oranges (10 to 12 oz. each), rinsed
- ½ cup sugar
- ⅓ cup slivered almonds
- **3** tablespoons butter
- ⅔ cup dried sweetened cranberries, chopped
  About ½ teaspoon salt
- **3** cups basmati or other long-grain white rice, rinsed well
- ¼ teaspoon saffron threads
- ⅓ cup chopped roasted, salted pistachios

1. With a vegetable peeler, pare skin (orange part only) from oranges. Cut peel into thin strips; you should have about ½ cup. Reserve fruit for garnish or another use.

2. In a 1- to 1½-quart pan, combine orange peel and 3 cups water. Bring to a boil, then reduce heat and simmer until peel has lost its sharp bitter taste, 3 to 4 minutes; drain. Return peel to pan and add ½ cup water and sugar; bring to a boil, then reduce heat and simmer until peel is shiny and translucent, about 15 minutes. Strain; reserve syrup for another use.

3. Meanwhile, in a 5- to 6-quart nonstick pan over medium heat, stir almonds until golden, 4 to 5 minutes; pour from pan. Add 1 tablespoon butter, 1 tablespoon water, and the cranberries to pan; stir until cranberries are puffy and beginning to brown, 2 to 3 minutes. Remove from pan and wash pan.

4. Add 2 quarts water and ½ teaspoon salt to pan; bring to a boil over high heat. Add rice and boil, uncovered, until slightly translucent but still firm to bite, 5 to 8 minutes. Pour into fine strainer or colander

(lined with cheesecloth if holes are large). Rinse rice and drain well. Rinse and dry pan.

5. Add remaining 2 tablespoons butter to pan over low heat; when melted, tilt pan to coat bottom and about 1 inch up sides. Return rice to pan, drizzle with 2 tablespoons water, cover tightly, and cook over medium-high heat until rice is hot and pan fills with steam, 3 to 5 minutes; reduce heat to very low and cook until tender to bite, 10 to 15 minutes. (If not ready to serve, keep tightly covered, remove from heat, and let stand up to 15 minutes.)

6. With your fingers, crumble saffron into a small bowl. Add ¼ cup hot water and let stand at least 5 minutes. Add saffron mixture, candied orange peel, and cranberries to rice and mix gently. Add salt to taste.

7. Spoon rice onto a platter. Sprinkle with almonds and pistachios.

Per serving: 419 cal., 24% (99 cal.) from fat; 9.7 g protein; 11 g fat (3.3 g sat.); 78 g carbo (1.5 g fiber); 243 mg sodium; 12 mg chol.

Pear-Cherry Pie with Almond Streusel

COOK AND PREP TIME: About 2 hours, plus at least 1½ hours to cool

NOTES: If using a purchased piecrust, bring to room temperature before using. You can make this pie up to 6 hours ahead; let stand at room temperature.

MAKES: 6 to 8 servings

- ½ cup brandy or water
- **1** cup chopped dried sweet or sour cherries
- ⅓ cup granulated sugar
- **2** tablespoons cornstarch
- **1** teaspoon ground coriander
- ¾ teaspoon ground ginger
- ½ teaspoon ground nutmeg
- 1½ quarts thinly sliced peeled firm-ripe Anjou or Comice pears (2 to 2½ lb.)
  Pastry for a 9-inch single-crust pie, homemade or purchased (see notes)
- **1** cup all-purpose flour
- ½ cup firmly packed brown sugar
- **6** tablespoons cold butter
- ½ cup chopped almonds

1. Combine brandy and cherries in a 1- to 1½-quart pan; cover and set over low heat just until hot, about 3 minutes. Remove from heat and let stand until cherries are slightly softened, at least 5 minutes.

2. Meanwhile, in a large bowl, mix granulated sugar, cornstarch, coriander, ginger, and nutmeg. Stir in pears and the cherry mixture.

3. On a lightly floured board, roll pastry into a 12-inch round. Ease, without stretching, into a 9-inch pie pan. Fold excess pastry around edge under itself and flute edge. Pour fruit mixture into pastry.

4. In a food processor or bowl, mix flour and brown sugar. Whirl or rub in butter with your fingers until mixture forms coarse crumbs. Add nuts and whirl or stir just until combined. Squeeze handfuls of the streusel mixture until it sticks together, then coarsely crumble into ½-inch chunks over fruit.

5. Set pan in a foil-lined rimmed baking pan and bake on the bottom rack of a 375° regular or convection oven until juices bubble around edges, 1 to 1¼ hours. If pie browns too quickly (check after 30 minutes), drape dark portions loosely with foil. Let cool on a rack for at least 1½ hours.

Per serving: 500 cal., 36% (180 cal.) from fat; 4 g protein; 20 g fat (8.7 g sat.); 79 g carbo (3.9 g fiber); 192 mg sodium; 28 mg chol.

Festive menu for 2

Thanksgiving dinner doesn't need a turkey to feel like a holiday; small Cornish hens are celebratory too. Slide the fruit tarts into the oven after the hens and hash are done. Add sautéed Swiss chard and pour a Pinot Gris or Chianti. These recipes can easily be adapted for four people.

Watercress and Orange Salad

PREP TIME: About 10 minutes

NOTES: For 4 servings, double the ingredients.

MAKES: 2 servings

- **1** orange (8 oz.)
- **1** tablespoon extra-virgin olive oil
- **1** tablespoon lemon juice
- **1** quart bite-size pieces tender watercress sprigs (3 oz.), rinsed and crisped
- **2** tablespoons chopped roasted, salted almonds
  Salt and pepper

1. With a small, sharp knife, cut ends off orange, deep enough to reveal flesh. Set orange on a cut end on a board. Sice off peel and white pith, down to orange flesh. Holding orange over a strainer set over a small bowl to catch juice, cut between inner membranes and fruit to release segments; drop segments into strainer. Squeeze juice from membranes into bowl; discard membranes.

2. In a large bowl, whisk together olive oil, lemon juice, and 1 table-spoon of the orange juice; reserve remaining juice for another use. Add watercress, orange segments, and almonds. Mix gently. Add salt and pepper to taste and mix again. Mound on plates.

Per serving: 166 cal., 70% (117 cal.) from fat; 3.6 g protein; 13 g fat (1.6 g sat.); 12 g carbo (4.1 g fiber); 95 mg sodium; 0 mg chol.

Roast Hens with Golden Vegetable Hash

PREP AND COOK TIME: About 1½ hours

NOTES: For 4 servings, double the ingredients; use two bags to marinate the Cornish hens, and increase pan size for hens and vegetables to 12 by 17 inches. For better browning with a doubled batch, use a convection oven, or bake vegetables and hens in separate ovens. Garnish birds with fresh sage leaves.

MAKES: 2 servings

- **2** Cornish hens (1½ lb. each)
- ¼ cup balsamic vinegar
- **3** tablespoons olive oil
- **2** tablespoons soy sauce

Our intimate dinner stars Cornish hens with an easy oven-roasted vegetable hash.

occasionally, until vegetables are browned and tender when pierced and hens are browned and meat at thigh bone is no longer pink (cut to test), 45 to 60 minutes.

5. Add salt and pepper to hash to taste. Scoop onto plates or a platter. Arrange hens alongside.

Per serving: 1,018 cal., 61% (621 cal.) from fat; 69 g protein; 69 g fat (17 g sat.); 28 g carbo (6.2 g fiber); 996 mg sodium; 375 mg chol.

Persimmon-Cranberry Tarts

PREP AND COOK TIME: About 30 minutes

NOTES: For 4 servings, double the ingredients. Put the tarts in the oven after the hens and hash come out; they're best eaten within an hour of baking.

MAKES: 2 servings

    2   frozen puff pastry shells,
        thawed
    2   firm Fuyu persimmons
        (5 oz. each) or 1 Fuji apple
        (8 oz.)
    2   tablespoons fresh or
        frozen cranberries, rinsed
    4   teaspoons sugar
    4   teaspoons currant jelly
        Crème fraîche or lightly
        sweetened softly whipped
        cream

1. On a lightly floured board, roll each pastry shell into a 5- to 6-inch round. Set rounds about 2 inches apart on a 12- by 15-inch baking sheet.

2. Peel persimmons or apple; quarter lengthwise, core, and slice ¼ inch thick. Overlap slices attractively on pastries. Sprinkle half the cranberries and sugar evenly over each tart.

3. Bake in a 400° regular or convection oven until richly browned, 20 to 30 minutes. Meanwhile, place jelly in a microwave-safe bowl and heat in a microwave oven on full power (100%) just until melted, 20 to 30 seconds. Brush jelly over hot tarts. Transfer tarts to racks. Serve warm or cool, topped with a dollop of crème fraîche.

Per serving: 441 cal., 37% (162 cal.) from fat; 5 g protein; 18 g fat (2.6 g sat.); 67 g carbo (5.6 g fiber); 123 mg sodium; 0 mg chol. ◆

    1   tablespoon chopped fresh
        sage leaves or 1 teaspoon
        dried rubbed sage
    2   cloves garlic, peeled and
        minced
    1   piece (8 oz.) banana
        squash
    1   Yukon Gold potato (8 oz.)
    1   red bell pepper (8 oz.)
    1   onion (6 oz.)
    6   fresh sage leaves (2 to
        3 in. long) or 1 teaspoon
        dried rubbed sage
        About ¼ teaspoon salt
        About ⅛ teaspoon pepper

1. Remove necks and giblets from hens if present; reserve for another use or discard. Rinse hens and pat dry. In a 1-gallon zip-lock plastic bag, mix vinegar, 1 tablespoon olive oil, soy sauce, chopped sage, and half the garlic. Add hens. Seal bag and chill, turning occasionally, at least 1 hour or up to 1 day.

2. Rinse squash, potato, and bell pepper. Cut off and discard skin from squash. Stem and seed bell pepper. Peel onion. Cut squash, potato, pepper, and onion into ½-inch cubes; put in a 9- by 13-inch

baking pan. Add remaining 2 tablespoons olive oil, remaining garlic, the whole sage leaves, ¼ teaspoon salt, and ⅛ teaspoon pepper; mix well.

3. Lift hens from marinade; discard marinade. Set birds slightly apart, breast up, on a rack in a 10- by 15-inch baking pan. Tie ends of drumsticks loosely together with cotton string.

4. Place vegetables on the top rack and hens on the bottom rack of a 425° regular or convection oven. Roast, stirring vegetables

An Italian family lunch

Four generations share a traditional rustic menu at their family celebration

By Charity Ferreira
Photographs by James Carrier

The Tavellas gather to mix sausage (above); lentil and vegetable soup accompanies the grilled sausage patties (right).

FOOD STYLING: KAREN SHINTO

The Tavella family had always made its own sausage. But when Ernest Tavella married Mary Formento, whose family came from a small town near Turin, Italy, he preferred her mother Lucy's sausage recipe to his own, or so goes family lore. Four generations later, multiple branches of the Tavella family gather at Ernest Tavella's home in Stockton, California, every year on the day after Thanksgiving to eat, drink, and make 100 pounds of pork sausage from Nonna Lucy's recipe.

Early in the morning, the men of the family take turns mixing ground pork shoulder from a local butcher shop with spices and the family's homemade wine as the kids who are too young to help look on. "Making the sausage is definitely a rite of passage," says Christina Tavella Hall, a San Francisco attorney and Ernest Tavella's granddaughter. "Taking your place in the process is a part of growing up."

When the morning's work is done, the family sits down to a hearty lunch that starts with antipasto and bubbling *bagna cauda*. The centerpiece of the meal is the grilled sausage, served with lentil soup and crusty Italian bread. The adults linger over coffee and cook-

ies while the kids play, and then the sausage is divided among the family members to take home and freeze for lasagna, pastas, and soups in the coming year.

The Tavella family's tradition adapts perfectly to smaller gatherings. Our version of their menu will generously serve 8 to 10 people, with plenty of leftover sausage to enjoy after the party.

Tavella Family's Sausage

PREP AND COOK TIME: About 1½ hours

NOTES: Leftover uncooked sausage patties can be wrapped tightly and frozen for up to 3 months. The recipe can be cut in half.

MAKES: 5 pounds sausage; 24 patties

- ¼ cup dry red wine
- 2 teaspoons pickling spice
- 5 pounds ground pork butt (shoulder)
- 2 tablespoons salt
- 1½ tablespoons pepper
- 1½ teaspoons ground cinnamon
- ½ teaspoon ground nutmeg

1. In a 1- to 2-quart pan over high heat, bring wine and pickling spice to a boil. Remove from heat and let cool to room temperature, about 45 minutes. Pour through a strainer into a large bowl; discard solids.

2. Add pork, salt, pepper, cinnamon, and nutmeg to bowl. Mix very thoroughly with your hands to distribute spices evenly.

3. Shape about ⅓ cup (about 3 oz.) pork mixture into an oval-shaped patty about ½ inch thick. Place on a waxed paper–lined baking sheet. Repeat to shape remaining mixture into patties, stacking patties in layers separated by sheets of waxed paper.

4. Lay patties on a grill over medium-hot coals or medium-high heat on a gas grill (you can hold your hand at grill level only 4 to 5 seconds); close lid if

using a gas grill. Cook the sausage patties, turning once, until they are browned on both sides and no longer pink in the center (cut to test), about 8 minutes total. (Alternatively, fry the patties in a 10- to 12-inch frying pan over medium heat, turning as needed, until browned on both sides and no longer pink in the center, 10 to 15 minutes total.) Pile the patties on a platter and serve.

Per patty: 226 cal., 72% (162 cal.) from fat; 15 g protein; 18 g fat (6.4 g sat.); 0.4 g carbo (0.1 g fiber); 629 mg sodium; 66 mg chol.

Bagna Cauda

PREP AND COOK TIME: About 30 minutes

NOTES: Bagna cauda is a buttery dip redolent of garlic and anchovies. The Tavellas make it in an electric skillet right at the table.

MAKES: 8 to 12 servings

- 1½ cups olive oil
- ½ cup butter
- 2 cans (2 oz. each) anchovies, drained, rinsed, and patted dry
- 12 cloves garlic, peeled and crushed with the flat side of a large knife
- 2 heads radicchio (1¼ lb. total), rinsed, cored, and sliced lengthwise ½ inch thick
- 4 heads red or white Belgian endive (12 oz. total), ends trimmed, separated into leaves
- 3 red or yellow bell peppers (1½ lb. total), rinsed, stemmed, seeded, and sliced lengthwise
- 12 green onions, rinsed, root ends and green tips trimmed
- 8 ounces portabella mushrooms, rinsed, stemmed, and sliced
  Sliced crusty Italian bread

1. In a 2- to 3-quart pan or an electric skillet over medium heat, stir olive oil, butter, anchovies, and garlic, breaking up anchovies and garlic slightly with the back of a fork, until butter is melted and mixture is bubbling, about 5 minutes. Remove from the heat and let stand at least 10 minutes or up to 30 minutes.

2. Meanwhile, arrange the radicchio, endive, peppers, green onions, and mushrooms on a serving platter. Reheat butter mixture gently over low heat,

Serve garlic-infused bagna cauda with a variety of raw vegetables for dipping.

then pour into a bowl or ramekin. Alternatively, pour into a 1½- to 2-cup ceramic fondue pan or metal chafing dish in a water-bath jacket. Set over a votive candle or an ignited alcohol or canned solid-fuel flame. Adjust heat to the lowest setting under the fondue pan or to medium under the chafing dish. Pass the platter of vegetables and a bowl filled with the bread for guests to dip in the bagna cauda.

Per serving: 361 cal., 90% (324 cal.) from fat; 4.3 g protein; 36 g fat (8.6 g sat.); 8.4 g carbo (2.3 g fiber); 368 mg sodium; 25 mg chol.

John's Quick Antipasto

PREP TIME: About 10 minutes, plus at least 12 hours to chill

NOTES: Giardiniera is a crunchy mixture of pickled vegetables. You'll find it in jars in the pickle section of the supermarket. Serve this saucy appetizer with crackers or bread for scooping up the chunky mixture.

MAKES: 10 to 12 appetizer servings

- 1 jar (16 oz.) giardiniera, drained (see notes)
- 1 jar (12 oz.) marinated artichoke hearts
- 1 jar (6 oz.) whole button mushrooms, drained
- 1 can (14 oz.) pitted large black olives, drained
- 2 cans (8 oz. each) tomato sauce
- 1 can (7½ oz.) water-packed tuna, drained
- ¼ cup red wine vinegar
  Salt and pepper

In a large bowl, mix the giardiniera, artichoke hearts (including their marinade), mushrooms, olives, tomato sauce, tuna, and vinegar. Cover and chill to blend flavors, at least 12 hours or up to 2 days. Add salt and pepper to taste.

Per serving: 88 cal., 48% (42 cal.) from fat; 5.6 g protein; 4.7 g fat (0.5 g sat.); 7 g carbo (2.9 g fiber); 902 mg sodium; 6.6 mg chol.

Carla's Lentil Soup

PREP AND COOK TIME: About 1 hour

NOTES: If making soup a day ahead, thin with a little water if necessary and reheat before serving.

MAKES: 6 quarts; about 12 servings

- 6 slices bacon (6 oz. total), cut into 1-inch pieces
- 2 onions (1 lb. total), peeled, halved, and thinly sliced
- 2 carrots (8 oz. total), peeled and thinly sliced
- 2 stalks celery (6 oz. total), rinsed and thinly sliced
- 2 cloves garlic, peeled and minced
- 4 cups dried lentils (about 1½ lb.), rinsed and sorted
- ¼ cup chopped parsley
- 1 teaspoon dried thyme
- 1 teaspoon salt
- ½ teaspoon pepper
- 2 dried bay leaves
- 2 cans (28 oz. each) diced tomatoes
- 2 lemons, rinsed and cut into wedges

1. In an 8-quart pan over medium-high heat, stir bacon until browned around edges, about 2 minutes. Add onions, carrots, celery, and garlic to pan and stir frequently until vegetables are very limp, about 10 minutes (lower heat to medium if necessary to prevent scorching).

2. Add lentils, parsley, thyme, salt, pepper, bay leaves, and 9 cups water to pan and bring to a boil. Reduce heat to maintain a simmer, cover, and cook, stirring occasionally, until lentils are very tender to bite, about 20 minutes. Add tomatoes, including juices, and 1 cup water and simmer uncovered for 10 minutes longer.

3. Ladle soup into bowls and serve with lemon wedges for squeezing over individual servings.

Per serving: 323 cal., 25% (82 cal.) from fat; 19 g protein; 9.1 g fat (3.1 g sat.); 44 g carbo (8.9 g fiber); 533 mg sodium; 9.5 mg chol.

Lentil soup is even more delicious when made a day ahead.

Oatmeal–Pine Nut Cookies

PREP AND COOK TIME: About 30 minutes, plus at least 1 hour to chill

NOTES: Lining the baking sheets with cooking parchment makes it easier to remove these thin, crisp cookies.

MAKES: About 5 dozen cookies

- ½ cup (¼ lb.) butter, at room temperature
- 1 cup firmly packed light brown sugar
- 1 large egg
- 1 teaspoon vanilla
- 1 cup all-purpose flour
- ¾ cup regular rolled oats
- ½ cup pine nuts
- ½ teaspoon baking soda
- ¼ teaspoon salt

1. In a bowl, with a mixer on medium speed, beat butter and sugar until smooth. Beat in egg and vanilla until well blended, scraping down sides of bowl as needed. In a small bowl, stir together flour, oats, pine nuts, baking soda, and salt; stir into butter mixture until well blended. Cover and chill until cold, about 1 hour, or up to 1 day.

2. With lightly floured hands, roll dough into 1-inch balls and place about 2 inches apart on cooking parchment–lined or buttered and floured 12- by 15-inch baking sheets (see notes).

3. Bake in a 350° regular or convection oven until well browned, 6 to 10 minutes. Let cookies cool completely on sheets, then remove with a wide spatula. Serve or store airtight up to 2 days.

Per cookie: 47 cal., 45% (21 cal.) from fat; 0.8 g protein; 2.3 g fat (1.1 g sat.); 6.1 g carbo (0.2 g fiber); 38 mg sodium; 7.7 mg chol. ◆

Winter light

Fresh herbs and a special presentation make halibut a casually elegant dinner

By Kate Washington
Photographs by James Carrier

Shaved fennel and oranges add a bright, light note to our winter menu.

FOOD STYLING: KAREN SHINTO

Rich, elaborate meals can be welcome at the holiday season; after a few, though, sometimes we all need a break. This stylish dinner party for six is a relaxing change of pace that shows off the lighter side of winter flavors.

In our main course, halibut pieces are roasted on a bed of sea salt and winter herbs—a fresh, easy adaptation of the classic technique of baking a whole fish in salt. Purchase roasted red peppers and olives for an easy appetizer; while guests nibble, the scent of warm herbs will perfume your home. The fish is done in just 20 minutes; bring the whole dish to the table for a beautiful presentation, and complement it with golden saffron orzo and roasted kale accented with preserved lemon. A salad of fennel and oranges and a red-gold compote of dried cherries and apricots complete the meal.

Fennel-Orange Salad with Green Olives

PREP TIME: 10 minutes

NOTES: Serve this easy salad with the main course, or bring it out at the end of the meal for a refreshing note before dessert.

MAKES: 6 servings

- 4 navel oranges (about 8 oz. each)
- 1 head fennel (about 12 oz.), stalks and discolored ends trimmed and discarded

- 2 tablespoons extra-virgin olive oil
  Salt and fresh-ground pepper
- ½ cup pitted green olives

1. Cut ends off oranges, then cut away peel and outer membrane of fruit in wide strips, following the curve of the orange with the knife. Discard peel; slice fruit crosswise ½ inch thick and arrange slices on a large rimmed plate.

2. Rinse fennel and thinly slice crosswise (or use a mandoline); arrange slices over oranges.

3. Drizzle olive oil evenly over fennel and sprinkle with salt and pepper to taste. Scatter olives over salad.

Per serving: 115 cal., 50% (57 cal.) from fat; 1.8 g protein; 6.3 g fat (0.8 g sat.); 16 g carbo (4.2 g fiber); 298 mg sodium; 0 mg chol.

Halibut Roasted on a Bed of Salt

PREP AND COOK TIME: About 40 minutes

NOTES: We've adapted the technique of baking a whole fish in salt to individual pieces, which are easier to handle and serve. The secret is heating the salt

first: When sprinkled on top, the herbs produce instant aromas that flavor the fish. The heat also cooks the underside of the fish quickly, so the center is done before the edges begin to dry out.

MAKES: 6 servings

- About 5 cups coarse sea salt
- 6 pieces halibut (6 to 8 oz. each; 1½ in. thick), rinsed and patted dry
  Salt and pepper
- 1 tablespoon olive oil
  About 1 cup lightly packed fresh thyme sprigs, rinsed
  About 1 cup lightly packed fresh oregano sprigs, rinsed
- 20 fresh or dried bay leaves
- 1 Meyer or regular lemon, rinsed and thinly sliced crosswise
  Herb oil (recipe follows)

1. Spread salt level (about 1 in. deep) in a 5- to 6-quart oval or 9- by 13-inch rectangular baking dish. Heat in a 450° regular or convection oven until very hot, about 20 minutes.

2. Meanwhile, sprinkle one side of halibut lightly with salt and pepper. Pour olive oil into a 10- to 12-inch nonstick

A relaxed dinner plan

This menu lets guests watch (or help) you put the finishing touches on the meal. Here's how to time it for maximum effect:

A day or two ahead: Make apricot-cherry compote.

The afternoon of the party: Rinse halibut and herbs; put salt in baking dish; make herb oil; measure ingredients for orzo; chop kale and coat with oil (step 1).

Shortly before guests arrive: Make fennel-orange salad; soak saffron for orzo; heat oven to 450°; set out purchased appetizers.

About 40 minutes before serving: Heat salt in oven.

About 30 minutes before serving: Sauté shallots and toast orzo (step 2); brown fish (step 2).

About 20 minutes before serving: Scatter herbs over hot salt, top with fish, and roast; put kale in oven; finish cooking orzo (step 3).

Just before serving: Drizzle a little extra olive oil over salad; stir lemons into kale; spoon orzo into a serving dish.

Present roasted fish on its aromatic bed of herbs and salt.

frying pan over high heat. When hot, place fish pieces in pan, seasoned side down, without crowding; work in batches if necessary. Cook until lightly browned on the bottom, about 2 minutes.

3. Remove baking dish from oven and distribute thyme and oregano sprigs, bay leaves, and all but three of the lemon slices evenly over hot salt (some salt will still be visible). Set halibut pieces browned side up over herbs and salt, spacing evenly. Cut reserved lemon slices in half and place half a slice on each piece of fish.

4. Bake until fish is opaque but still moist-looking in center of thickest part (cut to test), 15 to 20 minutes. Serve with herb oil to drizzle over fish to taste.

Per serving: 207 cal., 27% (55 cal.) from fat; 35 g protein; 6.1 g fat (0.9 g sat.); 0 g carbo; sodium varies; 54 mg chol.

Herb oil. In a blender, combine ¹⁄₂ cup **extra-virgin olive oil** with 2 tablespoons *each* **fresh thyme leaves, fresh oregano leaves,** and **chopped parsley.** Whirl until smooth, then pour through a fine strainer into a bowl, pressing to extract as much oil as possible. Discard residue. Makes ¹⁄₃ cup.

Per tablespoon: 120 cal., 100% from fat; 0 g protein; 14 g fat (2 g sat.); 0 g carbo; 0 mg sodium; 0 mg chol.

Saffron Orzo

PREP AND COOK TIME: About 45 minutes

MAKES: 6 servings

- ¹⁄₄ teaspoon crumbled saffron threads
- 2 tablespoons butter
- ¹⁄₂ cup chopped shallots
- 12 ounces dried orzo pasta
- 2 teaspoons fresh thyme leaves
- 2 teaspoons slivered lemon peel
- 2 cups fat-skimmed chicken broth
- ¹⁄₂ cup dry white wine
- 2 tablespoons lemon juice
- ¹⁄₂ cup grated pecorino romano or parmesan cheese
- Salt and fresh-ground pepper

1. In a glass measure, combine saffron and 1 cup hot water. Let stand for 20 minutes.

2. Meanwhile, in a 3- to 4-quart pan over medium-high heat, melt butter. When it is foamy, add shallots and stir until limp, about 1 minute. Stir in orzo, thyme, and lemon peel. Stir often until some of the orzo is deep golden brown, about 5 minutes.

3. Pour in broth, wine, and saffron water. Bring to a boil, then reduce heat to maintain a simmer. Cover and cook until all the liquid is absorbed and orzo is tender to bite, about 20 minutes.

4. Stir in lemon juice, cheese, and salt and pepper to taste. Spoon into a serving bowl and serve immediately.

Per serving: 307 cal., 20% (60 cal.) from fat; 13 g protein; 6.7 g fat (3.8 g sat.); 45 g carbo (1.6 g fiber); 152 mg sodium; 17 mg chol.

Roasted Kale with Preserved Lemons

PREP AND COOK TIME: About 30 minutes

NOTES: Salty, tart preserved lemons, a staple of North African cooking, are sold in many specialty food stores and markets that stock Middle Eastern or Mediterranean ingredients.

MAKES: 6 servings

1¼	**pounds dinosaur or curly green kale (about 2 bunches), rinsed**
2	**tablespoons olive oil**
	Salt and pepper
3	**tablespoons chopped preserved lemons (see notes) or 1 tablespoon slivered lemon peel**

1. Tear kale leaves away from tough center stems; discard stems. Cut kale into 2-inch pieces and place in a large bowl. Add oil and sprinkle lightly with salt and pepper; mix well to coat. Spoon into a 9- by 13-inch baking dish (kale will fill dish).

2. Bake in a 450° regular or convection oven, stirring occasionally, until top pieces of kale are crisp and remaining are tender to bite, 20 to 25 minutes. Stir in preserved lemons or lemon peel and spoon into a bowl. Serve hot or at room temperature.

Per serving: 69 cal., 64% (44 cal.) from fat; 1.9 g protein; 4.9 g fat (0.7 g sat.); 5.9 g carbo (1.3 g fiber); 218 mg sodium; 0 mg chol.

Apricot-Cherry Compote

PREP AND COOK TIME: About 1 hour, plus at least 2 hours to chill

NOTES: We like to use Sauternes, a botrytized wine with honey and apricot flavors, in this simple but intense dessert. Muscat and other less-expensive white dessert wines produce good results too; don't use fortified

Serve simple but rich-tasting compote with delicate butter cookies.

FOOD STYLING: KAREN SHINTO

wines such as sherry or port. If you can't find crème fraîche, substitute more whipping cream.

MAKES: About 2½ cups; 6 servings

8	**ounces dried apricots**
4	**ounces dried tart cherries**
1	**bottle (375 ml.) Sauternes or other dessert wine (see notes)**
½	**cup whipping cream**
⅓	**cup crème fraîche (see notes)**
1	**tablespoon sugar**

1. Cut dried apricots into ¼-inch strips. In a 3- to 4-quart nonreactive pan, combine apricots, cherries, and 1 cup hot water. Let stand until fruit is slightly soft, about 30 minutes.

2. Pour in Sauternes and bring to a simmer over medium-low heat. Cook, gently stirring occasionally, until cherries are plump, apricots are very soft, and liquid is cloudy and thick, about 30 minutes. Cover and chill until cold, at least 2 hours, or up to 2 days.

3. In a bowl, combine whipping cream, crème fraîche, and sugar; beat with an electric mixer at medium-high speed until soft peaks form. Spoon apricot-cherry

compote into six small bowls. Top each serving with a dollop of whipped cream mixture; offer remaining to add to taste.

Per serving: 284 cal., 35% (99 cal.) from fat; 2.4 g protein; 11 g fat (6.9 g sat.); 48 g carbo (2.9 g fiber); 26 mg sodium; 33 mg chol. ◆

Go nuts

This savory treat makes a fun holiday gift when stored in the right container and with the recipe presented as a festive label.
—*Linda Lau Anusasananan and Jil Peters*

Sweet-Hot Spiced Pecans

1. In a bowl, mix 1/3 cup **sugar**, 3/4 teaspoon **cayenne**, 1/2 teaspoon **salt**, 1/2 teaspoon **ground coriander**, 1/4 teaspoon **ground cinnamon**, and 1/8 teaspoon **ground allspice**. Whisk in 1 **large egg white** and 2 teaspoons **vegetable oil**. Stir in 2 cups **pecan halves**.

2. Spread in a single layer in an oiled nonstick 10- by 15-inch baking pan. Bake in a 300° regular or convection oven, stirring occasionally, until nuts are crisp and lightly browned, 20 to 25 minutes.

3. Let cool about 5 minutes; then with a wide spatula loosen nuts from pan and cool completely. Serve or store airtight at room temperature up to 2 weeks. Makes about 2 cups. ◆

Squeeze lime over toasts topped with soybean spread, cucumber, mint, and chili powder.

3. Place bean mixture in a food processor and whirl until coarsely mashed. Add remaining 3 tablespoons olive oil, 1 tablespoon at a time, whirling until mixture has a spreadable consistency. Season to taste with salt and pepper. Stir in the chopped mint.

4. Slice baguette on a slight diagonal into pieces about ¼ inch thick; reserve ends for another use. Arrange slices on racks on two baking sheets (each 12 by 15 in.). Spray baguette slices lightly with cooking oil spray or brush tops lightly with olive oil. Bake in a 425° regular or convection oven until lightly browned, 6 to 9 minutes.

5. Spread about 1 tablespoon warm or cool soybean mixture on each slice of toast. Rinse cucumber and thinly slice crosswise. Garnish each toast with a cucumber slice, a fresh mint leaf, and a sprinkling of chili powder. Serve with lime or lemon wedges to squeeze over each just before eating.

Per serving: 95 cal., 56% (53 cal.) from fat; 3.4 g protein; 5.9 g fat (0.7 g sat.); 11 g carbo (2 g fiber); 161 mg sodium; 0 mg chol.

FOOD STYLING: KAREN SHINTO

Party bites with style

Try these delicious first acts for holiday entertaining

By Linda Lau Anusasananan • Photographs by James Carrier

The first bite at a party is a preview of what's to come, so impress your guests with these elegant tidbits. Serve one or two selections before dinner, or offer a collection for an appetizer party. Our savory hors d'oeuvres, from stylish tobiko-topped radishes to flavorful shrimp cradled by crunchy endive leaves, will get any gathering off to a wonderful start.

Soybean-Mint Crostini

PREP AND COOK TIME: About 1 hour

NOTES: Donna Knopf, owner of Vegetas *(888/966-9660)* in Tempe, Arizona, blends soybeans with mint for a delicious and healthful topper for toasts. The soybean-mint spread can be made through step 3 up to 1 day ahead; cool, cover, and chill. You can assemble crostini up to 1 hour before serving; let stand at room temperature.

MAKES: About 32 appetizers; about 16 servings

- 1 **leek (about 8 oz. total)**
- ¼ **cup chopped shallots**
- 1 **clove garlic, peeled and minced**
- 2¼ **cups (12 oz.) frozen shelled soybeans, thawed**
- 5 **tablespoons olive oil**
  Salt and ground white pepper
- 2 **tablespoons finely chopped fresh mint leaves**
- 1 **slender (1½ to 2 in. wide) baguette (8 oz.)**
  Garlic-flavored cooking oil spray or 2 tablespoons olive oil
  About 8 ounces English cucumber
  About 32 fresh mint leaves, rinsed
  Chili powder
  Lime or lemon wedges

1. Trim and discard dark green tops and root ends from leek. Split white stalk lengthwise and rinse well to remove dirt between layers. Finely chop leek.

2. In a 10- to 12-inch frying pan over medium-high heat, stir leek, shallots, garlic, and soybeans in 2 tablespoons olive oil until leek is limp, 6 to 8 minutes.

Brie with Cranberry-Pecan Filling

PREP AND COOK TIME: 10 to 15 minutes

NOTES: You can assemble this layered brie (through step 3) up to 4 hours ahead; cover and chill. Let it come to room temperature before serving, or bake to serve warm (step 4).

MAKES: 8 servings

- 2 **tablespoons chopped pecans, plus 3 pecan halves**
- 2 **tablespoons chopped dried sweetened cranberries**
- ½ **teaspoon finely shredded orange peel**
- 1 **wedge or round (8 oz.) firm-ripe brie cheese, chilled**
- 1 **baguette (8 oz.), thinly sliced**

1. Place chopped pecans and pecan halves in a 9-inch pie pan. Bake in 325° regular or convection oven, shaking pan once, until chopped nuts are golden under skin, 6 to 8 minutes.

2. In a small bowl, mix toasted chopped pecans, cranberries, and orange peel.

3. Split cheese in half horizontally to make two layers. Set one layer, cut side up, on a plate or, if baking it, in a shallow, ovenproof ramekin or on an ovenproof rimmed plate. Spread cranberry mixture evenly over cheese. Set other layer, cut side down, on filling and press down gently. Arrange pecan halves on top. Serve at room temperature (see notes) or warm.

4. To serve warm, bake in a 325° regular or convection oven until cheese is warm and beginning to soften, 6 to 8 minutes. Serve baguette slices alongside.

Per serving: 189 cal., 47% (89 cal.) from fat; 8.5 g protein; 9.9 g fat (5.2 g sat.); 17 g carbo (1 g fiber); 351 mg sodium; 28 mg chol.

Radishes with Lemon Crème Fraîche and Tobiko

PREP TIME: About 15 minutes

NOTES: Jessica Gorin, chef at J Vineyards & Winery *(888/594-6326)* in California's Russian River Valley, serves these pretty bite-size appetizers with a 1998 J Vintage Brut. They can be made up to 2 hours ahead; cover and chill. Tobiko (flying fish roe) is available in Japanese or seafood markets and in specialty food stores.

MAKES: 24 appetizers; about 12 servings

> 12 radishes (about 1 in. wide)
> ¼ cup crème fraîche or sour cream
> ½ teaspoon grated lemon peel
> ½ teaspoon lemon juice
> Salt to taste

Mound neon-bright tobiko on radishes for easy, stylish finger food.

> About 3 tablespoons plain or wasabi-flavored tobiko (or some of each)

1. Trim stems and root ends off radishes; rinse well, and cut in half crosswise. If necessary, to make each half sit flat, trim a little off rounded end. If crème fraîche or sour cream is runny, use a small melon baller to scoop out centers of radishes, making depressions to hold filling; if crème fraîche is thick, leave radish halves flat.

2. In a small bowl, mix crème fraîche, lemon peel, and lemon juice. Add salt to taste.

3. Top or fill radish cups equally with crème fraîche mixture (about ½ teaspoon in each), then top equally with tobiko (a scant ¼ teaspoon on each). Arrange on a platter.

Per serving: 26 cal., 73% (19 cal.) from fat; 1.1 g protein; 2.1 g fat (1.2 g sat.); 0.6 g carbo (0.2 g fiber); 5.5 mg sodium; 19 mg chol.

Belgian Endive Shrimp Spears

PREP TIME: About 15 minutes

NOTES: Belgian endive leaves make great vessels for creamy fillings such as this lemony shrimp mixture with mustard. You can make the filling (step 1) up to 2 hours ahead; cover and chill. You can assemble the appetizers (step 2) up to 30 minutes before serving; cover and chill.

MAKES: 18 spears; about 9 servings

> ⅓ cup mayonnaise
> 1 teaspoon lemon juice
> 1 teaspoon Dijon mustard
> 8 ounces cooked tiny shrimp, rinsed, well drained, and gently patted dry
> 3 tablespoons thinly sliced fresh chives
> Salt and ground white pepper
> 18 red or white Belgian endive leaves (8 to 12 oz. total), rinsed and crisped

1. In a small bowl, mix mayonnaise, lemon juice, and mustard. Stir in shrimp and 2 tablespoons chives. Add salt and white pepper to taste.

2. Spoon equal portions shrimp mixture (about 1 tablespoon) on bottom end of each endive leaf; arrange on a platter. Sprinkle with remaining chives.

FOOD STYLING: KAREN SHINTO

Per serving: 87 cal., 69% (60 cal.) from fat; 5.6 g protein; 6.7 g fat (1 g sat.); 1.1 g carbo (0.6 g fiber); 118 mg sodium; 54 mg chol.

Potatoes with Smoked Trout and Apple

PREP AND COOK TIME: About 45 minutes

NOTES: This simplified version of an appetizer prepared by chef Keith Otter of Chandler's Restaurant *(208/726-1776)* in Ketchum, Idaho, shows off two of the state's culinary treasures. You can make the trout mixture (step 2) up to 1 hour ahead; cover and chill. The potatoes taste best when freshly baked, but you can mound the trout mixture on them up to 30 minutes before serving; let stand at room temperature.

MAKES: 32 appetizers; about 16 servings

> 16 red thin-skinned potatoes (each about 1½ in. wide; 1 lb. total), scrubbed
> About 1 tablespoon olive oil
> ½ cup sour cream
> 3 to 4 tablespoons prepared horseradish
> About 2 tablespoons minced green onion
> 1 tablespoon cider vinegar
> 1 cup finely chopped sweet apple
> 8 ounces smoked trout, skinned and finely chopped
> Salt and cayenne

1. Cut potatoes in half crosswise. If needed, to make each half sit flat, trim a little off the rounded end. Brush cut sides of potatoes with olive oil and set, cut side down, on a 12- by 15-inch baking sheet. Bake in a 400° regular or convection oven until browned and tender when pierced, 20 to 25 minutes.

2. Meanwhile, in a small bowl mix sour cream, 3 tablespoons horseradish, 2 tablespoons green onion, and the vinegar. Stir in apple and trout. Add salt, cayenne, and more horseradish to taste.

3. Mound a scant tablespoon of trout mixture on cut side of each potato half (hot or cool). If desired, sprinkle appetizers with a little more minced green onion.

Per serving: 76 cal., 46% (35 cal.) from fat; 4.3 g protein; 3.9 g fat (1.4 g sat.); 6.3 g carbo (0.7 g fiber); 162 mg sodium; 6.9 mg chol. ♦

Using wild rice

Cook it simply. Rinse and drain 1 cup **wild rice**; place in a 4-quart pan with 1 teaspoon **salt** and 1 quart **water.** Bring to a boil over high heat; lower heat to maintain a simmer, cover, and cook until rice is tender to bite, 45 to 60 minutes. Drain. Makes 2½ cups.

Enhance it with easy flavorings. After cooking and draining, stir in 1 to 2 tablespoons **butter** and chopped **parsley** to taste. If desired, add ¼ cup sliced toasted **almonds** or chopped toasted pecans, or ½ cup cooked **peas.**

Add it to baked goods. Substitute plain cooked wild rice for up to ⅓ of the white rice in rice pudding; add ½ cup wild rice to a favorite pancake, muffin, or scone recipe.

Pop it for a great snack. In a 4- to 5-quart pan over medium-high heat, heat 1 inch **vegetable oil** to 375°. Add ¼ cup uncooked **wild rice.** Rice should pop at once; working quickly, use a slotted spoon to transfer rice to paper towels to drain. Sprinkle with **salt** and **pepper** to taste. Makes 1¼ cups.

Wild rice adds earthy flavor to a Chinese-style rice porridge.

The call of the wild

Flavorful wild rice is perfect for the holiday table—or weeknight meals

By Molly Watson • Photographs by James Carrier

Growing up in Minnesota, I ate a lot of wild rice: as the backbone of nutty autumn side dishes; stuffed in poultry during the holidays; in rich soups and casseroles in the winter; or tossed with peas in spring or summer. My grandmother even added it to pancake batter. Now that I live in California, where wild rice is cultivated in abundance, I use it almost as often.

Wild rice—actually an aquatic grass—was once harvested by canoe in Minnesota, and it was correspondingly pricey. With cultivation on the rise, however, it is now moderately priced and widely available. Our recipes allow the full, earthy flavor of pure wild rice to shine through. Equally at home in a Thanksgiving feast or a weeknight dinner, and wonderful in everything from a tangy salad with cranberries to a homey Chinese-style congee, wild rice is as versatile as it is delicious.

Wild Rice Congee

PREP AND COOK TIME: About 1 hour

NOTES: This easy twist on traditional Chinese rice porridge makes a wonderful one-dish supper on a cold night. If desired, top with shredded leftover meat, such as roast chicken, duck, or pork. Baked tofu, found in the refrigerator case of natural-food stores and many supermarkets, is available in several flavors; any will work here.

MAKES: 2 or 3 servings

- ½ cup long-grain white rice
- ½ cup wild rice, rinsed and drained
- 1 quart fat-skimmed low-sodium chicken broth
- 1½ tablespoons Chinese rice wine or sake
- ¼ teaspoon salt
- ⅛ teaspoon hot chili flakes
- ½ teaspoon grated fresh ginger
- ¼ teaspoon minced garlic (optional)
- 1 cake (8 oz.) baked tofu, shredded or diced (see notes)
- 1 or 2 green onions, rinsed and thinly sliced
- ¼ cup chopped fresh cilantro
  Fried shallots (recipe follows)

1. In a 3- to 4-quart pan, combine white rice, wild rice, broth, rice wine, salt, chili flakes, ginger, garlic, and 1 cup water. Bring to a boil

Jewel-like cranberries and bright green onions make for a colorful wild rice salad.

FOOD STYLING: KAREN SHINTO

over medium-high heat. Cover and reduce heat to a bare simmer. Cook (without stirring) until the white rice has disintegrated into a thick, oatmeal-like porridge and the wild rice is split open and very tender, about 45 minutes.

2. Ladle into deep bowls and top with baked tofu, green onions, cilantro, and fried shallots to taste.

Per serving: 432 cal., 21% (90 cal.) from fat; 33 g protein; 10 g fat (1.1 g sat.); 53 g carbo (4.1 g fiber); 610 mg sodium; 0 mg chol.

Fried shallots. In a 6- to 8-inch frying pan over medium heat, stir ½ cup thinly sliced **shallots** in 1 tablespoon **vegetable oil** until crisp and golden, 6 to 10 minutes (shallots will absorb most of the oil).

Per tablespoon: 45 cal., 69% (31 cal.) from fat; 0.5 g protein; 3.4 g fat (0.4 g sat.); 3.4 g carbo (0.2 g fiber); 2.4 mg sodium; 0 mg chol.

Wild Rice and Cranberry Salad

PREP AND COOK TIME: About 1 hour, plus at least 4 hours to chill

NOTES: This holiday salad is best made several hours (or up to 1 day) in advance. Allow the salad to come to room temperature and garnish just before serving. Cutting the cranberries in half

(step 2) is time-consuming, but it makes a big difference in the texture of the finished salad. If desired, the cranberries may be steeped in sugar syrup (step 3) up to 1 day ahead; cover and chill in syrup (cranberries' color will deepen).

MAKES: 4 to 6 servings

- 1 **cup wild rice**
- 1 **tablespoon salt**
- ¾ **cup walnuts**
- 8 **ounces (2 cups) fresh or thawed frozen cranberries**
- ½ **cup sugar**
- 3 **tablespoons walnut or vegetable oil**
- 1 **tablespoon raspberry or rice vinegar**
- 3 **green onions, rinsed and chopped (including green tops)**
- ½ **cup dried cranberries, roughly chopped (optional)**

1. In a 4- to 6-quart pan, combine wild rice, salt, and 1 quart water. Bring to a boil over high heat; cover, reduce heat, and simmer until rice is tender to bite and most grains have just split open, 45 to 60 minutes. Drain in a colander and let cool.

2. Meanwhile, spread walnuts in a baking pan and toast in a 325° regular or convection oven until lightly golden under skins, about 10 minutes. Coarsely chop. Sort cranberries, discarding any stems and bruised or decayed fruit; cut each cranberry in half (see notes).

3. In a 2- to 3-quart pan over medium-high heat, stir the sugar and ½ cup water until the sugar is dissolved and mixture boils. Remove from heat; stir in the halved cranberries. Gently stir occasionally until insides of cranberries have turned red but are still firm, 8 to 12 minutes (see notes). Pour through a fine strainer into a bowl, reserving the cranberry-sugar syrup.

4. In a large bowl, gently mix wild rice, cranberry halves, oil, and vinegar. Stir in 2 tablespoons cranberry syrup; taste and add up to ¼ cup more syrup to sweeten and moisten salad as desired (reserve remaining syrup for other uses). Cover and chill for at least 4 hours or up to 1 day (see notes).

5. Stir in all but 2 tablespoons of the green onions, along with the walnuts

and dried cranberries (if using). Sprinkle with remaining green onions just before serving.

Per serving: 338 cal., 45% (153 cal.) from fat; 6.3 g protein; 17 g fat (1.5 g sat.); 45 g carbo (3.9 g fiber); 586 mg sodium; 0 mg chol.

Wild Rice Pilaf

PREP AND COOK TIME: 1½ hours

NOTES: This pilaf can be a side dish for rich meat dishes; with a salad, it makes a great midweek meal.

MAKES: 4 to 6 servings

- 2 **cups fat-skimmed low-sodium chicken broth**
- 1½ **cups wild rice**
- 8 **ounces bulk country-style pork sausage**
- 1 **onion (8 oz.), peeled and chopped**
- 4 **ounces mushrooms, rinsed, patted dry, and sliced**
- ½ **teaspoon salt**
- 3 **cloves garlic, peeled and minced**
- ¼ **cup dry white wine**
  Pepper

1. In a 3- to 4-quart pan over high heat, combine broth, 1½ cups water, and wild rice. Bring to a boil, then cover, reduce heat, and simmer until rice is tender to bite, 45 to 60 minutes. Remove from heat; do not drain.

2. In a 3- to 4-quart ovenproof pan or Dutch oven over medium-high heat, stir sausage until crumbly and browned, 5 to 7 minutes. Drain all but 1 tablespoon of the fat from pan.

3. Add onion to sausage and cook, stirring often, until limp, about 5 minutes. Add mushrooms and salt; stir until liquid has evaporated, about 5 minutes. Add garlic; stir until fragrant, about 2 minutes.

4. Pour in wine; stir, scraping bottom of pan to release any browned bits, until most of the liquid has evaporated, about 3 minutes. Add pepper to taste.

5. Add wild rice (with liquid) to sausage mixture; mix well. Cover pan and bake in a 350° regular or convection oven until most of the liquid has been absorbed, 35 to 40 minutes. Serve immediately.

Per serving: 256 cal., 27% (70 cal.) from fat; 13 g protein; 7.8 g fat (2.5 g sat.); 35 g carbo (3.3 g fiber); 464 mg sodium; 16 mg chol. ◆

Over easy

A simple festive brunch is both relaxed and special

By Charity Ferreira
Photographs by James Carrier

Brunch is an ideal meal for informal holiday-season entertaining. The centerpiece of this menu is inspired by the French salad *frisée aux lardons,* in which crisp greens, soft poached eggs, and bacon mingle deliciously with cracked black pepper. Turning this elegant dish into a thin flatbread pizza makes it a little more casual, substantial, and easy to serve—important considerations for morning entertaining.

Make the dough the night before, assemble the flatbreads before the guests arrive, and bake them just before you're ready to eat. Serve with ripe pears, fresh dates, and tangy vanilla-orange yogurt.

Top crisp flatbread with eggs, bacon, and frisée for a pretty brunch pizza.

FOOD STYLING: KAREN SHINTO

Brunch Flatbread with Eggs, Bacon, and Frisée

PREP AND COOK TIME: About $1\frac{1}{2}$ hours, plus about 45 minutes to rise

NOTES: The dough for these flatbreads can be made the night before serving; if you're not starting it ahead, just skip the chilling in step 2 and proceed to shape dough as directed in step 4. If you're short on time, you can use a 1-pound loaf of frozen bread dough. Thaw at room temperature, then divide and shape as directed in step 4. Purchased dough browns quickly; reduce baking time in step 6 by 5 minutes.

MAKES: 6 to 8 servings

1 **package ($2\frac{1}{4}$ teaspoons) active dry yeast**
About 1 teaspoon salt
About $\frac{1}{4}$ cup olive oil
$3\frac{1}{2}$ **to $3\frac{3}{4}$ cups all-purpose flour**

8 **ounces thick-cut bacon, chopped**
About $\frac{1}{4}$ cup yellow cornmeal
$1\frac{1}{3}$ **cups shredded parmesan or manchego cheese**
12 **large eggs**
Pepper
1 **tablespoon red wine vinegar**
3 **ounces baby spinach (about 2 cups), rinsed and crisped**
3 **ounces frisée lettuce leaves (about 2 cups), rinsed and crisped**

1. In a large bowl, sprinkle yeast over $1\frac{1}{2}$ cups warm (110°) water. Let stand until yeast is softened, about 5 minutes. Stir in 1 teaspoon salt and 1 tablespoon olive oil. Gradually stir or, with an electric mixer on low speed, beat in $3\frac{1}{2}$ cups flour until mixture forms a soft dough.

2. *If using a dough hook,* beat on high speed until dough no longer feels sticky and pulls cleanly from bowl, 5 to 7 min-

utes. If dough is still sticky, beat in more flour, 1 tablespoon at a time.

If kneading by hand, scrape dough onto a lightly floured board. Knead until smooth, springy, and no longer sticky, 15 to 20 minutes; add flour as required to prevent sticking. Place dough in an oiled bowl; turn dough over to coat top.

Cover dough with plastic wrap and let rise in a warm place until doubled, 35 to 45 minutes. Punch dough down, cover, and chill up to 8 hours (see notes).

3. Meanwhile, in a 10- to 12-inch frying pan over medium-high heat, stir bacon until browned and crisp, about 5 minutes. Transfer to paper towels to drain. Reserve 1 tablespoon bacon drippings to dress greens, if desired.

4. At least 2 hours before serving, remove dough from refrigerator and let

Sweet, juicy pears are delicious with dates and an orange-honey yogurt topping.

equally on top. Cut each oval in half lengthwise, then crosswise into eight slices. Add salt and pepper to taste.

Per serving: 547 cal., 44% (243 cal.) from fat; 25 g protein; 27 g fat (8.5 g sat.); 49 g carbo (2.7 g fiber); 849 mg sodium; 339 mg chol.

Pears and Dates with Vanilla-Orange Yogurt

PREP TIME: About 30 minutes

NOTES: You can make the vanilla-orange yogurt (step 1) up to 3 days ahead; cover and chill.

MAKES: 6 to 8 servings

- 1 pint regular or low-fat plain yogurt
- ½ vanilla bean, halved lengthwise, or 1 teaspoon vanilla extract
- 2 tablespoons frozen orange juice concentrate
- 1 tablespoon honey
- 5 ripe Bartlett pears (about 2½ lb. total), rinsed
- 8 ounces fresh Medjool dates (about 10), pitted and chopped

1. Spoon yogurt into a bowl. Scrape vanilla bean seeds into yogurt (reserve pod for other uses). Stir in orange juice concentrate and honey until blended.

2. Peel and core pears; cut lengthwise into 1-inch-thick slices. Arrange pears and dates in bowls and top each with about ¼ cup vanilla-orange yogurt.

Per serving: 205 cal., 11% (22 cal.) from fat; 3.2 g protein; 2.4 g fat (1.2 g sat.); 47 g carbo (5.2 g fiber); 26 mg sodium; 7.4 mg chol.

FOOD STYLING: KAREN SHINTO

Cranberry Mimosas

PREP TIME: About 5 minutes

NOTES: For a nonalcoholic version, substitute sparkling water for the sparkling wine.

MAKES: About 8 servings

- 3 cups cranberry juice, chilled
- 1 cup orange juice, chilled
- 1 bottle (750 ml.) sparkling wine, chilled (see notes)

In a large pitcher (at least 2½ qt.), combine cranberry juice, orange juice, and sparkling wine. Serve immediately, in champagne flutes.

Per serving: 133 cal., 0% (0.9 cal.) from fat; 0.4 g protein; 0.1 g fat (0 g sat.); 18 g carbo (0.1 g fiber); 9.7 mg sodium; 0 mg chol. ◆

stand at room temperature for 45 minutes (see notes). Scrape dough onto a lightly floured board and press gently to expel air from it. Divide dough into four pieces. Cover with plastic wrap and let rest 10 minutes. Roll or gently stretch one piece at a time into a 13- by 7-inch oval about ¹⁄₁₆ inch thick. Place each oval on a 12- by 15-inch rimless baking sheet oiled and dusted with cornmeal; if necessary, stretch dough to reshape.

5. Brush each oval with about ½ tablespoon olive oil and sprinkle with about ⅓ cup cheese. Arrange a quarter of the cooked bacon evenly over each.

6. Bake flatbreads two at a time in a 450° oven for 10 minutes. Remove from oven and crack 3 eggs onto each oval (for firm-cooked eggs, crack eggs onto flatbread 5 minutes into baking). Sprinkle lightly with salt and pepper.

7. Return flatbreads to oven, switching pan positions, and bake until crust is well browned, 5 to 8 minutes longer.

8. Meanwhile, in a large bowl, mix 1 tablespoon olive oil or reserved bacon drippings and the vinegar. Add spinach and frisée and mix to coat.

9. Slide each flatbread onto a cutting board or plate. Mound dressed greens

Steam heat

Cook shellfish in minutes in a versatile broth

By Linda Lau Anusasananan
Photograph by James Carrier

A simple dish like steamed clams or mussels doesn't take much more time than warming up a frozen dinner, but it provides a hands-on meal worth the minimal extra effort.

Throw a few ingredients into a pan for a flavorful broth to steam the shellfish in; our recipe offers three quick options. While it heats, scrub hard-shell clams or mussels, then add them to the bubbling liquid. Within five minutes, dinner's on. Add crusty bread and a favorite spinach salad, then sit down to a real dinner.

When the shells are empty and the last drop of broth has been drunk or sopped up with bread, move on to a leisurely cheese course. Since you spent so little time getting the meal on the table, there's plenty of time to linger over a ripe pear, a wedge of tangy blue cheese, and an indulgent glass of tawny port.

Steamed Clams or Mussels in Seasoned Broth

PREP AND COOK TIME: About 20 minutes

NOTES: As the shellfish cook, they release their natural briny juices into the broth. Clams tend to be naturally saltier than mussels; when cooking them, use water to make the broth.

MAKES: 2 servings

> **Seasoned broth (choices follow)**
>
> 3 **dozen clams in shells, suitable for steaming (about 2½ lb.), or mussels in shells (1¼ lb.)**
>
> **Chopped parsley, green onions, or fresh cilantro**
>
> **Lemon wedges**

Steam clams in tarragon-shallot broth for a hands-on dinner.

1. In a covered 5- to 6-quart pan over high heat, bring seasoned broth to a boil. Reduce heat to low and simmer until shellfish are cleaned.

2. Meanwhile, scrub clams or mussels well; pull beards off mussels if still attached. Discard any open shellfish that don't close when you tap them.

3. Return broth to a boil over high heat. Add shellfish, cover, and cook until shells pop open, 3 to 6 minutes. Spoon shellfish and broth into bowls. Sprinkle with parsley. Serve with lemon wedges to squeeze into broth.

Garlic-ginger broth. In pan, combine 1 cup **water** (for clams) or fat-skimmed reduced-sodium chicken broth (for mussels), 1 cup **sake** or dry white wine, 1 tablespoon chopped **garlic,** 1 tablespoon chopped **fresh ginger,** and ¼ teaspoon crushed **hot chili flakes.**

Per serving with clams: 154 cal., 5% (8.1 cal.) from fat; 12 g protein; 0.9 g fat (0.1 g sat.); 5.4 g carbo (0.2 g fiber); 56 mg sodium; 29 mg chol.

Creamy tarragon-shallot broth. In pan, combine 1 cup **water** (for clams) or clam juice (for mussels), 1 cup **dry white wine,** ½ cup chopped **shallots,** ¼ cup **whipping cream,** and 1 teaspoon **dried tarragon.**

Per serving with clams: 265 cal., 34% (90 cal.) from fat; 13 g protein; 10 g fat (5.8 g sat.); 11 g carbo (0.3 g fiber); 328 mg sodium; 62 mg chol.

Tomato-basil broth. In pan, combine 1 can (14½ oz.) **diced tomatoes** (including liquid), ½ cup **water** (for clams) or fat-skimmed reduced-sodium chicken broth (for mussels), ½ cup chopped **onion,** 1 tablespoon minced **garlic,** and 2 teaspoons **dried basil.**

Per serving with clams: 131 cal., 11% (14 cal.) from fat; 14 g protein; 1.5 g fat (0.2 g sat.); 17 g carbo (2.4 g fiber); 386 mg sodium; 29 mg chol. ◆

Broccoli rabe and
ricotta cheese
make a creamy,
low-fat sauce for
rice-shaped pasta.

Five fresh ways with ricotta

- Spread on toasted baguette slices and top with chopped tomatoes and chopped fresh herbs for quick crostini.

- Make calzones with purchased pizza dough; fill with ricotta and cooked spinach and mushrooms or your favorite pizza toppings.

- Blend with smoked salmon or trout and chopped herbs to make a spread for crackers.

- Fold into beaten eggs with cooked vegetables for a frittata.

- Mix with chopped chocolate, honey, vanilla, and grated orange peel; spoon it over fresh fruit.

It's the cheese

Pair low-fat ricotta with pasta

By Charity Ferreira
Photographs by James Carrier

Pasta and cheese are old friends, but the kind of cheese you use makes a big nutritional difference. When tossed with hot pasta along with a little cooking water, low-fat ricotta quickly creates a healthy but rich-tasting sauce. Its mild, fresh-milk flavor is a good foil for stronger accents like peppery broccoli rabe and olives, or chard with lemon and pistachios.

Orzo with Ricotta and Broccoli Rabe

PREP AND COOK TIME: About 25 minutes

MAKES: 4 to 6 servings

- 1 **pound dried orzo pasta**
- 2 **teaspoons olive oil**
- 2 **tablespoons minced garlic**
- 1 **teaspoon hot chili flakes**
- 1 **pound broccoli rabe or broccoli, rinsed, ends trimmed, and coarsely chopped**
- 1 **container (15 oz.) low-fat ricotta cheese**
- ¼ **cup chopped pitted kalamata olives**
  Salt and pepper

1. In a 5- to 6-quart pan over high heat, bring about 3 quarts water to a boil. Add orzo and cook, stirring occasionally, until tender to bite,

7 to 12 minutes. Drain, reserving 1½ cups pasta-cooking water. Return orzo to pan.

2. Meanwhile, heat oil in a 10- to 12-inch frying pan over medium heat. Add garlic; stir until fragrant but not brown, 1 to 2 minutes. Add chili flakes and broccoli rabe; stir 3 to 4 minutes. Add 1 cup of reserved water; simmer until greens are tender to bite, 6 to 8 minutes.

3. Add broccoli rabe mixture to orzo with ricotta, olives, and remaining ½ cup reserved water; mix, adding salt and pepper to taste.

Per serving: 410 cal., 17% (69 cal.) from fat; 19 g protein; 7.7 g fat (2.3 g sat.); 65 g carbo (2.1 g fiber); 172 mg sodium; 17 mg chol.

Whole-wheat spaghetti with chard and ricotta. Follow step 1 to cook 1 pound dried **whole-wheat spaghetti.** Follow step 2 to cook 1½ tablespoons minced **garlic** in 2 teaspoons **olive oil,** omitting the chili flakes and substituting 1 pound **green chard** (rinsed, ends trimmed, and coarsely chopped) for the broccoli rabe; cook until chard stems are tender to bite, 6 to 8 minutes. Mix chard mixture into hot spaghetti with 1 container (15 oz.) **low-fat ricotta,** ⅓ cup chopped **roasted, salted pistachios,** ¼ cup grated **pecorino** or parmesan **cheese,** 1½ tablespoons grated **lemon** peel, 1 tablespoon **lemon** juice, remaining ½ cup reserved pasta-cooking water, and **salt** and **pepper** to taste. Makes 4 to 6 servings.

Per serving: 430 cal., 23% (99 cal.) from fat; 22 g protein; 11 g fat (3.2 g sat.); 66 g carbo (11 g fiber); 260 mg sodium; 20 mg chol. ◆

The lightest cake of all

By Jerry Anne Di Vecchio
Photograph by James Carrier

Moist meringue can be topped with whipped cream flavored the way you like. We love it with Nutella.

FOOD STYLING: KAREN SHINTO

Soft meringue has earned its fan base in this country as a cloud on top of lemon pie. But in Mexico, it often becomes the main event as a tender torte. Removed from its pan and cooled, it relaxes into a soft cake shape, pale gold on the outside but dense and white throughout.

In Mexico, the topping is usually whipped cream, which smooths out and hides any dips and bumps in the torte. The combination is lovely with crushed berries. But for the holidays, I like to flavor the cream with a hazelnut-and-chocolate spread. For all of its fragility, the torte can be made in advance, cuts neatly, and holds its shape.

Meringue Cream Torte

PREP AND COOK TIME: About 45 minutes, plus 2 hours to cool and chill

NOTES: Chocolate-hazelnut spreads such as Nutella are available in the jam aisle of most supermarkets. Sprinkle the chilled torte with about ¾ cup semisweet chocolate curls if desired.

MAKES: 6 to 8 servings

- 5 large egg whites
- ½ teaspoon cream of tartar
- 1 cup sugar
- 1 teaspoon vanilla
- 2 tablespoons hazelnut-flavored liqueur or cold espresso
- ⅔ cup chocolate-hazelnut spread (see notes)
- 1 cup whipping cream

1. In a large bowl, with a mixer on high speed, beat egg whites and cream of tartar until frothy. Continuing to beat at high speed, add sugar in a slow, steady stream; continue to beat until mixture holds stiff peaks, 8 to 12 minutes. Beat in vanilla.

2. Scrape into a buttered and floured 8-inch cake pan with a removable rim at least 3 inches tall. With a flexible spatula, spread mixture out to edges of pan and smooth out top.

3. Bake in a 300° regular or convection oven until top is lightly browned and feels firm when gently pressed in the center, about 25 minutes.

4. Remove from oven and let stand for 20 minutes (meringue may shrink a little as it cools). Run a thin knife between meringue and pan rim, then remove rim. Carefully invert meringue onto a plate, then slide a long, thin spatula between pan bottom and meringue and gently lift the bottom off. Invert meringue again onto another plate so that it is right side up. Let cool completely.

5. In a bowl, whisk hazelnut liqueur into chocolate-hazelnut spread. In another bowl, whip cream until it holds soft peaks. Stir about ¼ cup of the whipped cream into the chocolate mixture until no white streaks remain. Fold chocolate mixture into remaining whipped cream, then whisk gently until mixture has a loose, spreadable consistency (take care not to overbeat or it will curdle).

6. With the spatula, spread chocolate-hazelnut cream around sides and over the top of the meringue. Chill torte uncovered for at least 1 hour, or cover with a large, inverted bowl (it shouldn't touch cream) and chill up to 24 hours.

7. Cut torte into wedges to serve.

Per serving: 322 cal., 45% (144 cal.) from fat; 4.3 g protein; 16 g fat (6.7 g sat.); 41 g carbo (0 g fiber); 70 mg sodium; 34 mg chol. ◆

Soy milk success

Nondairy milk adds nutty flavor

Ours is a two-carton household. Half of the family can drink only soy milk, while the other half can pour 2% over breakfast cereal until the stuff floats, with no apparent adverse digestive effects.

Cereal was the sole reason we stocked soy milk in our fridge until the other evening, when I was in the last stages of mashing potatoes for dinner and discovered we were out of milk. "No, we're not," my oldest son corrected. I looked suspiciously at the carton of soy milk in his hand. It'll never work, I thought darkly. But the two members of the family who weren't privy to my last-minute recipe change cleaned their plates more quickly than usual. The soy had given the potatoes a nutty flavor that we loved.

What other dishes, I wondered, might benefit from substituting soy for regular milk? This time of year, an obvious candidate is pumpkin pie, which can lure lactose-intolerant souls to their dairy doom. Turns out it's as simple as using a little less soy milk than the evaporated milk most recipes call for. And in our tests, the plates came back clean! —*Ben Marks*

Soy Milk Pumpkin Pie

PREP AND COOK TIME: About 1 hour and 10 minutes, plus at least 2 hours to cool

MAKES: 8 servings

- ¾ cup sugar
- 1¼ teaspoons ground cinnamon
- ½ teaspoon salt
- ¼ teaspoon ground ginger
- ⅛ teaspoon ground nutmeg
- ⅛ teaspoon ground cloves

Finally, a pumpkin pie for those who can't eat dairy products.

- 1 can (15 oz.) pumpkin
- 1¼ cups (10 oz.) soy milk
- 2 large eggs
  Pastry for a single-crust 9-inch pie, purchased (thawed if frozen) or homemade

1. In a large bowl, mix sugar, cinnamon, salt, ginger, nutmeg, and cloves. Add pumpkin, soy milk, and eggs; whisk until well blended. Pour mixture into unbaked pastry.

2. Set pie on bottom rack of a 425° regular or convection oven. Bake for 15 minutes, then reduce temperature to 350°; continue baking until center of pie is set and a knife inserted in the middle comes out clean, about 45 minutes longer.

3. Set pie on a rack until cool to touch, at least 2 hours. After serving, chill any remaining pie airtight.

Per serving: 247 cal., 32% (78 cal.) from fat; 3.6 g protein; 8.7 g fat (3.3 g sat.); 38 g carbo (1 g fiber); 277 mg sodium; 58 mg chol.

More ways to use soy

The slightly sweet, nutty flavor of soy milk is particularly well suited to dishes based on fruits or vegetables. To substitute soy, just reduce the amount of milk called for in your recipe by about 20 percent. Here are some of our favorite uses for soy milk:

Quiche. Soy seems to behave well in pies, both sweet and savory. Try it in a vegetable-laden quiche.

Cream of mushroom soup. Soy's flavor is a distinctive backdrop for earthy mushrooms. Make sure you don't boil the soup once the milk is added.

Muffins. Soy adds complexity to sweet blueberry or other fruit muffins. ◆

A soft spot for caramel

Surrender to sweet, gooey, dentist-be-darned dishes

By Elaine Johnson
Photographs by James Carrier

As far as meanings go, the word *caramel* is rich. It's a flavor, a color, and a process: to caramelize means to heat sugar until it melts and develops the bittersweet flavor and amber color we associate with the candy. Sugar can be caramelized alone, in which case it hardens to amber glass as it cools. Or it can be mixed with cream before or during the process to create thick sauces that scream for ice cream and candylike mixtures ideal for filling apple dumplings or cloaking sumptuous tortes.

Caramel-cloaked Chocolate-Hazelnut Torte

PREP AND COOK TIME: About 2¾ hours, plus 2½ hours for ganache to cool

NOTES: Make chocolate ganache first; let it cool while you bake the cake. Prepare cake through step 5 before starting caramel cloak. An accurate candy or instant-read thermometer that registers high temperatures is crucial to making the caramel; to coat cake evenly, it must cool just enough to be thick but still pourable, about 150°. Assemble torte through step 5 up to 1 day ahead and chill filled cake airtight; pour caramel over cold cake. Or complete entire recipe up to 1 day ahead and chill airtight; bring cake to room temperature to serve, about 1 hour, and warm sauce as directed in step 7.

MAKES: 8 to 10 servings

- 2 cups **hazelnuts** (about 10 oz.)
- 6 **large eggs,** separated
- ½ cup **sugar**
- 3 tablespoons **fine dried bread crumbs**
- 1 tablespoon **vanilla**

  Chocolate ganache (recipe follows; see notes)

  Caramel cloak (recipe follows; see notes)

1. Place nuts in a 10- by 15-inch baking pan. Roast in a 350° regular or convection oven, shaking pan occasionally, until the nuts are golden beneath skins, 10 to 12 minutes. Pour nuts into a towel and rub to remove loose skins. Let cool at least 15 minutes. Set aside eight completely skinned nuts. Whirl remaining nuts in a food processor until finely ground.

2. In a bowl, with a mixer on high speed, beat egg yolks and ¼ cup sugar, scraping bowl occasionally, until very thick and light-colored, about 4 minutes. Stir in ground nuts, bread crumbs, and vanilla.

3. In a large bowl, with clean beaters, beat egg whites on high speed until they hold soft peaks. Gradually add remaining ¼ cup sugar and continue to beat until egg whites hold short, distinct peaks, about 3 minutes total. Add half the whites to nut mixture and stir to blend well. Gently fold in remaining whites. Spread batter level in a buttered and floured 9-inch cheesecake pan with removable rim.

4. Bake in a 350° regular oven or 325° convection oven until cake is golden brown and springs back in the center when lightly pressed, 25 to 30 minutes. Let cool in pan for 10 minutes. Run a knife between cake and pan rim, then remove rim. Let cake cool on a rack about 45 minutes.

5. With a long, serrated knife, split cake in half horizontally. Gently slide a baking sheet under top cake layer and lift it off. Spread bottom cake layer evenly with chocolate ganache. Slide top layer, cut side down, back in place over ganache.

6. Set cake on rack in a 12- by 17-inch pan. Pour about 1½ cups warm (see notes) caramel cloak over cake—enough to coat it—starting at the center and spiraling to edges, letting caramel drip down sides to cover completely. Arrange reserved hazelnuts evenly around top edge of cake. Let stand until caramel stops dripping and is firm enough to cut, about 30 minutes.

7. Scrape caramel drips from pan back into the measuring cup containing remaining caramel cloak. Cook, uncovered, in a microwave oven at 30% power, stirring occasionally, until warm and fluid, about 2 minutes. Pour into a bowl.

8. Place cake on a plate. Cut into wedges with a sharp knife. Offer remaining caramel cloak to spoon over portions.

Per serving: 787 cal., 61% (477 cal.) from fat; 10 g protein; 53 g fat (22 g sat.); 77 g carbo (2.9 g fiber); 218 mg sodium; 206 mg chol.

Rich chocolate ganache fills a cake topped with a smooth caramel cloak.

Chocolate ganache. In a 2- to 3-quart pan over low heat, stir 8 ounces **bittersweet** or semisweet **chocolate,** chopped (about 1½ cups), and 1 cup **whipping cream** until melted and smoothly blended, 8 to 10 minutes. Let cool, stirring occasionally, until ganache no longer flows when pan is tilted, 2 to 2½ hours.

Caramel cloak. In a 3- to 4-quart pan, combine 1 cup *each* firmly packed **brown sugar, light corn syrup,** and **whipping cream;** ½ cup (¼ lb.) **butter;** and ¼ teaspoon **salt.** Bring to a boil over medium-high heat and stir occasionally until mixture reaches 240°, 12 to 14 minutes. Pour into a 1-quart glass measure and stir occasionally until mixture cools to 150°, about 25 minutes. Stir in 1 teaspoon **vanilla.** Pour over cake immediately.

Double-Caramel Apple Dumplings

PREP AND COOK TIME: About 1¼ hours
NOTES: Make the caramel sauce without the rum; if desired, stir rum into sauce after using ¼ cup in step 1. You can prepare dumplings through step 4 up to 1 day ahead; chill sauce, dumplings, and egg mixture separately airtight. Bake chilled dumplings as directed.
MAKES: 4 servings

- ⅔ cup **pecan halves**

  Caramel sauce (recipe follows; see notes)

- 4 **Golden Delicious apples** (4 to 6 oz. each)

1 tablespoon **lemon juice**

1 sheet **frozen puff pastry** (half of a 17.3-oz. package), thawed

1 **large egg**, beaten to blend with 1 tablespoon water

Vanilla ice cream (optional)

1. Set aside four pecan halves; chop remaining nuts. In a bowl, mix chopped nuts with ¼ cup caramel sauce.

2. Peel apples; core each, creating a 1-inch-wide hollow from top to bottom. Place apples in a bowl and coat with lemon juice.

3. On a lightly floured board, roll puff pastry into a 12-inch square. Cut into four equal squares and center an apple upright on each. Push nut mixture equally into apple hollows.

4. Brush egg mixture over a ½-inch-wide border around each pastry; reserve remaining egg. To wrap each dumpling, with floured fingers bring two opposite pastry corners up over apple and pinch tips together. Repeat with remaining two corners. Firmly pinch all tips together; pinch each seam, then fold over about ⅛ inch along the seam and pinch again, leaving no holes. Space dumplings evenly on a buttered 12- by 15-inch baking sheet.

5. Bake in a 375° regular or convection oven for 20 minutes. Dip reserved pecan halves in egg mixture (save remaining egg for other uses or discard); press a nut half on top of each dumpling. Bake until pastry is deep golden, 10 to 15 minutes longer in a regular oven, about 5 minutes in a convection oven.

Crisp, golden pastry wraps a caramel-filled apple.

6. With a wide spatula, transfer dumplings to plates. Accompany with remaining caramel sauce and ice cream, if desired.

Per serving: 868 cal., 59% (513 cal.) from fat; 9.4 g protein; 57 g fat (16 g sat.); 85 g carbo (4.1 g fiber); 196 mg sodium; 119 mg chol.

Caramel Sauce

PREP AND COOK TIME: About 20 minutes

NOTES: You can make this sauce up to 3 weeks ahead; chill airtight. Reheat, uncovered, in a microwave-safe bowl in a microwave oven at 30% power until warm and fluid, about 2 minutes.

MAKES: About 1 cup

1. In a 2- to 3-quart pan over medium heat, tilt and swirl ⅔ cup **sugar** often until melted and amber-colored, 5 to 7 minutes. Stir in 1 cup **whipping cream;** mixture will bubble and sugar will harden. Stir until sugar melts again and sauce boils, 6 to 8 minutes.

2. At once, pour sauce into a bowl. Stir in 1 teaspoon **vanilla.**

3. Let sauce cool for 10 minutes, then, if desired, stir in 3 tablespoons **rum.** Serve warm or cool.

Per tablespoon: 77 cal., 53% (41 cal.) from fat; 0.3 g protein; 4.6 g fat (2.9 g sat.); 8.8 g carbo (0 g fiber); 5.2 mg sodium; 17 mg chol.

Caramel Pudding

PREP AND COOK TIME: About 10 minutes

MAKES: 2 cups; 4 servings

2 cups **whole milk**

2 tablespoons **cornstarch**

1 **large egg**

⅔ cup **sugar**

2 teaspoons **vanilla**

1. In a bowl, whisk ½ cup milk, cornstarch, and egg until well blended.

2. In a 2- to 3-quart pan over medium-high heat, tilt and swirl sugar until melted and deep amber, about 4 minutes. Stir in remaining 1½ cups milk; mixture will bubble and sugar will harden. Stir until sugar melts again, about 2 minutes.

3. Whisk about ½ cup of the caramelized sugar mixture into cornstarch mixture, then return all to pan. Stir over medium-high heat until pudding thickens and begins to bubble, 3 to 5 minutes. Remove from heat and stir in vanilla. Pour into bowls and serve warm. Or let cool, chill airtight up to 2 days, and serve cold.

Per serving: 244 cal., 20% (48 cal.) from fat; 5.6 g protein; 5.3 g fat (2.9 g sat.); 43 g carbo (0 g fiber); 76 mg sodium; 70 mg chol. ◆

JOHN GRANEN

Jazzing up an American stand-by

"Mac and cheese—it's like an empty canvas," says chef Susan Jensen of Seattle's Blue Onion Bistro. "You can add practically anything to it."

Jensen encourages cheese experiments. "I haven't run across any that won't work. If you're trying a smoked cheese, though, go light-on it," she says.

—Lawrence Cheek

Blue Ribbon Mac and Cheese

PREP AND COOK TIME: About 25 minutes

NOTES: Blue Onion's standard version uses Tillamook medium cheddar for the cheese sauce, but this cranked-up iteration adds blue cheese. For a more toned-down version, omit the blue cheese.

MAKES: 5 or 6 servings

1. In a 5- to 6-quart pan over high heat, bring 2½ to 3 quarts **water** to a boil. Stir in 12 ounces **dried small elbow macaroni** or small pasta shells and cook until barely tender to bite, 8 to 9 minutes. Drain well and return to pan.

2. Meanwhile, in a 3- to 4-quart pan over high heat, bring 1 quart **whipping cream** to a boil, stirring occasionally. Remove from heat and add 3 cups **shredded cheddar cheese** (12 oz.); whisk until cheese is melted and sauce is smooth. Stir in 1 cup **crumbled blue cheese** (see notes). Pour sauce over hot pasta; mix to blend, adding **salt** to taste. Spoon into bowls. If desired, sprinkle servings with thinly sliced **green onion,** crumbled **crisp-cooked bacon, diced tomato,** and/or **chopped smoked salmon.**

Per serving: 971 cal., 69% (666 cal.) from fat; 29 g protein; 74 g fat (46 g sat.); 48 g carbo (1.4 g fiber); 673 mg sodium; 251 mg chol.

—Linda Lau Anusasanan

Savory holiday dishes

Readers' recipes tested in *Sunset's* kitchens

Photographs by James Carrier

Mexican Chicken and Dumplings

Katie McRae, Portland

Katie McRae adds some spicy touches to traditional, homey chicken stew with dumplings. She always makes a few of them without jalapeños for family members who don't enjoy spicy food.

PREP AND COOK TIME: About 1½ hours

MAKES: 4 to 6 servings

- 1 tablespoon olive oil
- 1 onion (8 oz.), peeled and diced
- 1 green bell pepper, rinsed, stemmed, seeded, and diced
- 1 clove garlic, peeled and minced
- 3 pounds skinned chicken thighs
- 1 can (15 oz.) fat-skimmed chicken broth
- 1 can (14½ oz.) Mexican-style stewed tomatoes
- 1 can (10 oz.) red enchilada sauce
- 1 cup all-purpose flour
- ½ cup yellow cornmeal
- 2 teaspoons baking powder
- ½ teaspoon salt
- 2 tablespoons chopped pickled jalapeño chilies
- 3 tablespoons butter, melted
- ¾ cup milk

1. Pour oil into a 5- to 6-quart pan over medium-high heat; when hot, add onion, bell pepper, and garlic and stir often until limp, 5 to 7 minutes.

Chili-flecked dumplings brighten stewed chicken and tomatoes.

2. Rinse chicken. Add broth, tomatoes, enchilada sauce, and chicken to pan; bring to a boil. Reduce heat, cover, and simmer, stirring occasionally, until chicken is no longer pink at the bone (cut to test), about 40 minutes.

3. Meanwhile, in a bowl, mix flour, cornmeal, baking powder, salt, and jalapeños. In a small bowl, whisk butter into milk; stir into flour mixture until well blended. Drop batter in tablespoon portions into simmering chicken mixture; cover and simmer gently until dumplings are cooked all the way through (cut to test), 10 to 12 minutes.

4. Ladle into wide, shallow bowls and serve immediately.

Per serving: 477 cal., 26% (126 cal.) from fat; 40 g protein; 14 g fat (5.7 g sat.); 47 g carbo (3 g fiber); 1,456 mg sodium; 121 mg chol.

Turkey Chowder

Betty Jean Nichols, Eugene, OR

Leftover turkey and mashed potatoes are the main ingredients in this quick, hearty chowder devised by Betty Jean Nichols. She prefers to use canned corn with red and green peppers, which adds flecks of color to the soup.

PREP AND COOK TIME: About 30 minutes

MAKES: About 3 quarts; 6 to 8 servings

- 2 slices bacon (about 2 oz. total), chopped
- 1 onion (8 oz.), peeled and chopped
- 1 quart low-fat (1%) milk
- 4 cups cooked mashed potatoes
- 3 cups ½-inch chunks cooked turkey
- 2 cans (11 oz. each) corn, drained (see note above)
- 2 tablespoons chopped fresh cilantro
- ½ teaspoon pepper
  Salt

1. In a 4- to 5-quart pan over medium-high heat, stir bacon often until browned around the edges, 3 to 4 minutes. Add onion and stir often until onion is limp, about 5 minutes.

2. Stir in milk, mashed potatoes, turkey, corn, cilantro, and pepper. Bring to a simmer and cook, stirring frequently, until soup is hot and slightly thickened, about 10 minutes. Add salt to taste. Ladle into bowls and serve immediately.

Per serving: 343 cal., 34% (117 cal.) from fat; 24 g protein; 13 g fat (4.3 g sat.); 36 g carbo (3.2 g fiber); 572 mg sodium; 52 mg chol.

Try cranberry salsa in a quesadilla with jack cheese and turkey.

Cranberry-Pepper Salsa

Tom Cooper, Kennewick, WA

Tom Cooper modified his grandmother's recipe to come up with this spicy salsa to serve at Thanksgiving.

PREP TIME: About 10 minutes, plus at least 4 hours to chill

MAKES: About 6 cups

- 8 ounces fresh cranberries, rinsed and sorted
- 2 apples (about 1 lb. total), rinsed, cored, and cut into chunks
- 1 orange (about 8 oz.), rinsed and cut into chunks (including peel)
- 1/3 cup sugar
- 1 red bell pepper (8 oz.), rinsed, stemmed, seeded, and diced
- 1 yellow bell pepper (8 oz.), rinsed, stemmed, seeded, and diced
- 1 onion (8 oz.), peeled and diced
- 2 fresh jalapeño chilies, rinsed, stemmed, seeded, and minced
- 2 cloves garlic, peeled and minced
- 1/4 cup chopped fresh cilantro
- 1/2 teaspoon salt

In a food processor, pulse cranberries, apples, and orange until coarsely puréed. Scrape into a bowl; stir in sugar, bell peppers, onion, jalapeños, garlic, cilantro, and salt. Cover and chill at least 4 hours or up to 2 days.

Per 1/4 cup: 38 cal., 3% (1 cal.) from fat; 0.4 g protein; 0.1 g fat (0 g sat.); 10 g carbo (1.3 g fiber); 49 mg sodium; 0 mg chol.

Southwest Stuffing

Naomi D'Abbracci, Cave Junction, OR

Naomi D'Abbracci collaborated with a friend on this recipe for a Southwest-themed Thanksgiving dinner. Bake an 8-inch pan of cornbread from your favorite recipe and cut into 1/2-inch cubes.

PREP AND COOK TIME: About 1 1/4 hours

MAKES: 8 to 10 servings

- 3/4 cup raw hulled pumpkin seeds (pepitas)
- 1 tablespoon cumin seeds
- 1 pound ground spicy pork sausage
- 1 onion (8 oz.), peeled and chopped
- 8 ounces celery (about 4 stalks), rinsed and chopped
- 2 tablespoons minced garlic
- 1/2 cup chopped canned peeled roasted red peppers
- 1 can (7 oz.) diced mild green chilies, drained
- 1/2 teaspoon salt
- 1/4 teaspoon hot chili flakes (optional)
- 9 cups cornbread cubes (see note above)
- 1 cup fat-skimmed chicken broth

1. In a 10- to 12-inch frying pan over medium heat, stir pumpkin seeds until lightly browned, 2 to 3 minutes; pour into a large bowl. Add cumin seeds to pan; stir until fragrant, 1 to 2 minutes. Add cumin seeds to pumpkin seeds.

2. In the same pan over medium-high heat, stir sausage until browned, about 8 minutes. Add onion, celery, and garlic; stir frequently until onion is limp, 5 to 8 minutes longer. Pour into bowl.

3. Stir in red peppers, chilies, salt, chili flakes, and cornbread cubes; mix well. Spread level in a buttered, shallow 3 1/2-quart baking dish. Drizzle broth evenly over mixture and cover with foil.

4. Bake in a 350° regular or convection oven for 25 minutes. Remove foil and continue baking until top is browned, 20 to 25 minutes longer. Let stand 10 minutes, then serve warm.

Per serving: 350 cal., 59% (207 cal.) from fat; 10 g protein; 23 g fat (7.8 g sat.); 25 g carbo (3 g fiber); 819 mg sodium; 53 mg chol.

Spinach Timbale

Nancy Nachman Silverman, Scottsdale, AZ

Nancy Nachman Silverman learned to make this custardy baked spinach dish from Marie-Blanche de Broglie, a Parisian cooking teacher. You can assemble it through step 2 up to a day ahead; cover and chill. Bake chilled mixture about 10 minutes longer.

PREP AND COOK TIME: About 1 1/2 hours

MAKES: 6 to 8 servings

- 1 1/2 pounds rinsed, stemmed spinach leaves
- 1 container (15 oz.) whole-milk ricotta cheese
- 3 large eggs
- 1/2 cup whipping cream
- 1/3 cup shredded Swiss cheese
- 3 canned anchovies, rinsed and patted dry
- 1/2 teaspoon salt
- 1/4 teaspoon pepper
- 1/4 teaspoon ground nutmeg

1. In a 5- to 6-quart pan over high heat, bring about 3 quarts water to a boil. Add half the spinach and cook until wilted, 1 to 2 minutes. Remove from water with a strainer and rinse under cold water until cool. Repeat to cook and cool remaining spinach. Squeeze or roll spinach tightly in a kitchen towel to remove as much water as possible.

2. In a food processor, whirl spinach, ricotta, eggs, cream, cheese, anchovies, salt, pepper, and nutmeg until well blended. Pour mixture into a buttered 2- to 2 1/2-quart soufflé or baking dish.

3. Bake on the middle rack of a 350° oven until top feels firm and looks solid when gently shaken, 45 to 50 minutes. Let cool 10 minutes.

Per serving: 204 cal., 66% (135 cal.) from fat; 13 g protein; 15 g fat (8.8 g sat.); 5.5 g carbo (2.2 g fiber); 353 mg sodium; 128 mg chol. ◆

A Kobe beef filet mignon, legendary for tenderness and flavor, is served with peppercorn-brandy sauce (see page 258).

December

Grand feast

An old-fashioned Christmas dinner comes with all the trimmings

By Sunset's Food Editorial Staff

Photographs by James Carrier

Food styling by Karen Shinto

As Ebenezer Scrooge finally learns in Charles Dickens's *A Christmas Carol,* the holiday is about generosity. Dinner reflects the spirit—for most people, a feast of particularly special, familiar foods, eaten with family and good friends.

This year, our entire food department collaborated on a Christmas menu, collecting and devising dishes that express the goodwill and happy times we'd like to share. Our first course and finale are traditional dishes revised with fresh flavors: crunchy salt crystals on little *gougères,* and poached cranberries, rich toffee sauce, and rum-flavored whipped cream in a festive trifle. The main course—a showy prime rib roast, creamed spinach, and parsley potatoes—echoes the spirit of Christmas past in the best way.

A thyme-rubbed rib roast is the centerpiece of our traditional holiday feast.

Start the festivities with savory, salt-topped cheese puffs and sparkling wine.

Salt-and-Pepper Cheese Puffs (Gougères)

PREP AND COOK TIME: About 1 hour

NOTES: These easy puffs are especially good made with strongly flavored, aged white English, Irish, or Canadian cheddar. We like to use imported sea salts with pretty, crunchy crystals, such as *fleur de sel,* Halen Môn, or Maldon, but any coarse sea salt will work. The puffs can be made up to 1 month ahead and frozen; cool, then freeze airtight. Reheat thawed puffs, uncovered, in a 375° oven until crisp and hot, about 5 minutes.

MAKES: 48 puffs; 12 to 14 servings

- ½ cup (¼ lb.) butter, cut into chunks
- 1½ cups all-purpose flour
- 6 large eggs, beaten to blend
- 1¼ cups shredded sharp cheddar cheese (see notes)
- 1½ teaspoons fresh-ground pepper
- Coarse sea salt (see notes)

1. In a 3- to 4-quart pan over high heat, bring 1½ cups water and the butter to a full rolling boil. Remove from heat, add flour all at once, and stir until mixture is a smooth, thick paste with no lumps. Add a quarter of the beaten eggs at a time, stirring vigorously after each addition until dough is no longer slippery. Stir in cheese and pepper.

2. Spoon dough into a large pastry bag fitted with a plain ½-inch round tip. Pipe in 48 equal mounds on two cooking parchment–lined or buttered 12- by 15-inch baking sheets. (Alternatively, drop dough mounds on sheets in slightly rounded tablespoon–size portions.) Sprinkle each mound with a few grains of coarse sea salt.

3. Bake in a 400° regular or convection oven until dry and well browned, about 30 minutes. Serve warm (see notes).

Per puff: 53 cal., 61% (32 cal.) from fat; 1.9 g protein; 3.6 g fat (2 g sat.); 3.1 g carbo (0.1 g fiber); 87 mg sodium; 35 mg chol.

Butter Lettuce Salad with Walnuts and Grapes

PREP AND COOK TIME: About 50 minutes

NOTES: You can toast the walnuts (step 1) up to 2 days ahead; when cool, wrap airtight and store at room temperature.

MAKES: 12 to 14 servings

- 3 cups walnut halves (9 oz.)
- ⅓ cup plus 1 tablespoon walnut oil
- 2 tablespoons sugar
  About 1 teaspoon salt
- ¼ cup Champagne vinegar
- ¼ cup minced shallots
- 2 tablespoons Dijon mustard
  About ¼ teaspoon fresh-ground pepper
- 1 pound butter lettuce, rinsed, crisped, and torn into bite-size pieces
- 3 cups rinsed and stemmed red seedless grapes, halved
- 1 cup finely slivered red onion, rinsed and drained
- ¼ cup chopped fresh tarragon

1. In a 10- by 15-inch baking pan, mix walnuts with 1 tablespoon oil, the sugar, and ½ teaspoon salt; spread level. Bake in a 350° oven, stirring occasionally, until nuts are golden brown, about 15 minutes. Let cool.

2. In a large bowl, mix vinegar, shallots, mustard, ½ teaspoon salt, and ¼ teaspoon pepper. Slowly whisk in ⅓ cup oil until vinaigrette is emulsified. Add lettuce, grapes, red onion, tarragon, and sugared walnuts; mix gently to coat, adding more salt and pepper to taste.

Per serving: 217 cal., 75% (162 cal.) from fat; 3.5 g protein; 18 g fat (1.6 g sat.); 14 g carbo (2 g fiber); 224 mg sodium; 0 mg chol.

Standing Rib Roast

PREP AND COOK TIME: About 2¾ hours, plus 30 minutes for meat to rest

NOTES: For easy carving, have the butcher cut the rib-eye muscle from the bones, then tie the meat and bones back together for roasting. After cooking, the roast should rest at least 10 minutes but may stand in a warm place up to 30 minutes. To serve, snip off the string, lift the roast off the bones, and slice the meat. Cut between the bones to

Butter lettuce salad

Prep plan

UP TO 1 MONTH AHEAD:
Make and freeze cheese
puffs.

UP TO 1 WEEK AHEAD:
Cook cranberries and toffee
sauce for trifle; cover separately and chill.

UP TO 2 DAYS AHEAD:
Toast walnuts for salad;
make cake for trifle and
wrap in plastic wrap to
store.

UP TO 1 DAY AHEAD: Make
creamed spinach; assemble
trifle.

**ABOUT 3¼ HOURS BEFORE
DINNER:** Prepare beef.

**ABOUT 3 HOURS BEFORE
DINNER:** Get roast into the
oven; garnish trifle with last
layer of cream and slivered
dates (chill, uncovered, until
ready to serve).

AS GUESTS ARRIVE: Re-
heat thawed cheese puffs.

**ABOUT 45 MINUTES
BEFORE DINNER:** Cook
potatoes.

**ABOUT 30 MINUTES
BEFORE DINNER:** Reheat
creamed spinach while beef
rests; finish pan juices for
roast.

**ABOUT 20 MINUTES
BEFORE DINNER:** Mix
salad.

serve them. Accompany the beef with prepared horseradish.

MAKES: 12 servings (without bone section; 14 with bones)

- 1 fat-trimmed, 4-bone beef rib-eye roast (about 8½ lb.; see notes)
- 1 tablespoon dried thyme
- 1½ teaspoons kosher or coarse sea salt
- 1½ teaspoons fresh-ground black pepper
- 1¼ cups fat-skimmed beef broth
- ¼ cup brandy or tawny port

1. Rinse meat and pat dry. In a small bowl, mix thyme, salt, and pepper. Rub mixture evenly all over roast. Set on a rack, bones down, in 10- by 15-inch roasting pan.

2. Roast beef in a 375° regular or convection oven until a thermometer inserted in the center of the narrow end reaches 135° for medium (the wide end should be about 125° for rare), about 2½ hours. As melting fat accumulates, to reduce spattering, ladle it from pan and discard.

3. Transfer roast to a platter and let stand in a warm place at least 10 minutes (see notes).

4. Meanwhile, skim off and discard remaining fat from pan drippings. Add beef broth to pan and stir to scrape up browned bits. Add brandy. Set pan over high heat and stir until mixture is boiling vigorously. Stir in juices accumulated from roast on platter. Pour sauce through a fine strainer into a small pitcher.

5. Carve roast (see notes) and serve with sauce.

Per serving: 332 cal., 46% (153 cal.) from fat; 41 g protein; 17 g fat (6.9 g sat.); 0.4 g carbo (0.1 g fiber); 359 mg sodium; 119 mg chol.

Creamed Spinach

PREP AND COOK TIME: About 30 minutes

NOTES: You can prepare through step 4 up to 1 day ahead; cool, cover airtight, and chill. Un-cover and bake in a 375° oven until spinach is hot in the center and bubbling at the edges, about 25 minutes. Add the cheese and bake until melted, about 5 minutes longer.

MAKES: 12 to 14 servings

- 4 pounds spinach leaves, rinsed and drained
- 1½ tablespoons butter or olive oil
- 1 onion (12 oz.), peeled and finely chopped
- 3 tablespoons all-purpose flour
- 1 teaspoon ground nutmeg
- ¾ teaspoon dried thyme
- 1½ cups fat-skimmed chicken broth

- 1½ cups whipping cream
- 1½ teaspoons salt
- 1 cup shredded Gruyère or Swiss cheese

1. Fill a 6- to 8-quart pan over high heat with spinach and turn frequently with a wide spatula; add more spinach as leaves wilt and shrink. When all the spinach is added and wilted, in 8 to 10 minutes, cook and stir leaves about 1 minute longer. Pour spinach into a colander to drain. Rinse and dry pan.

2. Melt butter in pan over medium-high heat. Add onion; stir often until limp, about 5 min-utes. Add flour, nutmeg, and thyme. Stir until flour is golden, 1 to 2 minutes. Remove from heat and whisk in broth, cream, and salt until mixture is smooth. Return to heat; stir until boiling, then reduce heat and simmer gently, stirring often, to blend flavors, 5 minutes.

3. Meanwhile, whirl spinach in a food proces-sor or use a knife to coarsely chop.

4. Add chopped spinach and its liquid to the cream sauce. Stir until bubbling. Pour into a shallow 3-quart casserole.

5. Bake in a 375° regular or convection oven until bubbling at edges, 6 to 8 minutes. Sprin-kle with cheese and bake until melted, about 5 minutes longer. Serve hot.

Per serving: 167 cal., 65% (108 cal.) from fat; 7.9 g protein; 12 g fat (7.4 g sat.); 8.6 g carbo (3.8 g fiber); 409 mg sodium; 41 mg chol.

Parsley Potatoes

PREP AND COOK TIME: About 45 minutes

NOTES: If potatoes are cooked before the rest of the main course, after step 1 return them to pan; cover and let stand up to 15 minutes.

MAKES: 12 to 14 servings

1. Scrub 4 pounds **red thin-skinned potatoes** (1½ in. wide; cut in half if larger). Place in a 6- to 8-quart pan and add enough water to cover by 1 inch. Set over high heat and bring to a simmer. Reduce heat so water barely simmers and cook, uncovered, just until potatoes are tender when pierced, about 30 minutes. Drain.

2. Pour potatoes into a bowl and add ⅓ cup chopped **parsley,** ¼ cup (⅛ lb.) melted **butter,** 1 teaspoon **salt,** and ½ teaspoon **coarse-ground pepper.** Mix gently to coat. Pour into a serving bowl.

Per serving: 123 cal., 26% (32 cal.) from fat; 2.5 g protein; 3.5 g fat (2.1 g sat.); 21 g carbo (2.3 g fiber); 208 mg sodium; 8.9 mg chol.

Sticky Toffee Trifle with Cranberries and Rum Whipped Cream

PREP AND COOK TIME: About 1½ hours, plus 1 hour to cool and 8 hours to chill

NOTES: We've designed this gorgeous, gooey dessert to serve more than the other dishes in the menu, for the sake of filling a large trifle dish and having leftovers. The trifle has several components, all of which can be made ahead of time (see "Prep Plan," page 248). The plump, moist Medjool dates are found in the produce section; if they're unavailable, use drier packaged dates.

MAKES: 16 to 20 servings

- 1½ cups orange juice
- 1 cup granulated sugar
- ½ teaspoon vanilla
- 12 ounces fresh or thawed frozen cranberries, rinsed and sorted
- ¾ cup chopped pitted Medjool dates plus ¼ cup slivered (11 oz. total; see notes)
- ¾ cup (⅜ lb.) butter, at room temperature
- 1 cup firmly packed brown sugar
- 4 large eggs
- 2 cups all-purpose flour
- 1½ teaspoons baking powder
- ½ teaspoon salt
- ¼ teaspoon baking soda
- 1 quart whipping cream
- ¼ cup dark rum
- 1 cup toffee sauce, at room temperature (recipe follows)

1. *To prepare cranberries:* In a 3- to 4-quart pan over medium-high heat, stir orange juice, ¾ cup granulated sugar, and the vanilla together until sugar is dissolved; bring mixture to a simmer. Add cranberries and simmer gently just until skins begin to split, about 5 minutes. Remove from heat and chill until cool, at least 30 minutes.

2. *To make cake:* In a blender or food processor, pour ½ cup boiling water over chopped dates and let stand 5 minutes. Whirl until smooth.

3. In a bowl, with a mixer on medium speed (use paddle attachment with standing mixer), beat butter, brown sugar, and date purée until well

No mere trifle—layers of date cake, cranberries, toffee sauce, and whipped cream make a lavish conclusion.

blended and smooth. Add eggs, one at a time, beating well after each addition.

4. In a bowl, stir together flour, baking powder, salt, and baking soda; stir into butter mixture until well blended. Scrape batter into a buttered and floured 9-inch square baking pan.

5. Bake in a 350° oven until a wood skewer inserted into the center comes out clean, 35 to 40 minutes. Let cake cool in pan on a rack for 10 minutes, then invert cake onto rack; remove pan and let cake cool completely.

6. Trim off brown edges of cake; reserve for another use or discard. Cut remaining cake into 1-inch cubes.

7. *To mix cream:* In a bowl, with a mixer on high speed, whip 2 cups cream with 2 tablespoons granulated sugar and 2 tablespoons rum until soft peaks form.

8. *To assemble trifle:* Layer a third of the cake cubes in the bottom of a 4- to 5-quart straight-sided glass bowl or trifle dish. Drizzle ⅓ cup toffee sauce evenly over cake. Spoon about 1 cup cranberries (including juices) over sauce. Spread about half of the whipped cream evenly over cranber-ries. Repeat with another layer of cake, sauce, cranberries, and whipped cream. Layer remaining third of the cake cubes over the whipped cream, drizzle with ⅓ cup toffee sauce, and spoon remaining cranberries over the top. Cover with plastic wrap and chill at least 8 hours.

9. *To serve:* In a bowl, with a mixer on high speed, whip remaining 2 cups cream with remaining 2 tablespoons granulated sugar and 2 tablespoons rum until soft peaks form. Spread whipped cream over trifle and garnish with sliv-ered dates. Scoop portions onto plates and pass remaining toffee sauce.

Per serving: 484 cal., 50% (241 cal.) from fat; 4.4 g protein; 27 g fat (16 g sat.); 58 g carbo (2.2 g fiber); 234 mg sodium; 127 mg chol.

Toffee sauce. In a 1- to 2-quart pan over medium heat, stir 1½ cups firmly packed **dark brown sugar,** ¼ cup (⅛ lb.) **butter,** 2 tablespoons **light corn syrup,** and 1 teaspoon **lemon juice** until sugar is dissolved and mixture is foamy, about 5 minutes. Whisk in 2 tablespoons **vanilla** and cook 1 minute longer. Whisk in 1½ cups **whipping cream** and remove from heat. Makes 2 cups. ◆

Colorful citrus salsa adds fresh flavor to delicate sole.

Sweet and sour

Mix and match citrus fruits for bright flavors in the dark of winter

By Kate Washington • Photographs by James Carrier

Citrus fruits, miraculously, peak just when almost everything else is decidedly out of season, bringing sweetness and light to a month that could use a little brightening up. The variety of citrus now widely available—from tiny kumquats to pummeloes as big as a person's head, and garnet-colored blood oranges to topazlike Ruby grapefruit—can add zest to any course.

Nut-Crusted Sole with Citrus Salsa

PREP AND COOK TIME: About 1 hour

MAKES: 4 to 6 servings

> Juice from citrus salsa (recipe follows)
>
> Orange juice (if needed)
>
> 1½ pounds petrale or other sole fillets (cut in half if very large), rinsed
>
> 1 cup cashews or pecans

> 1 cup panko (Japanese bread crumbs) or fresh bread crumbs
>
> ½ teaspoon salt
>
> ½ teaspoon fresh-ground pepper
>
> Vegetable oil
>
> 1 large egg, beaten with 1 tablespoon water
>
> Citrus salsa

1. Measure juice from citrus salsa. If needed, add orange juice to make ⅓ cup. Place fillets of sole in a heavy zip-lock plastic bag and pour in juice. Seal bag and chill for 15 minutes.

2. Meanwhile, in a blender or food processor, pulse cashews until finely ground. In a shallow bowl, mix nuts with panko, salt, and pepper.

3. Pour 2 tablespoons oil into a 10- to 12-inch nonstick frying pan over medium-high heat; when hot, lift sole fillets from juice. Dip each fillet in egg, then in cashew mixture to coat. Working in

batches, place fillets in a single layer in hot oil (do not crowd). Cook until browned on the bottom, about 2 minutes; turn with a wide spatula and cook until other side is browned and fish is opaque but still moist-looking in center (cut to test), about 2 minutes longer. Drain briefly on paper towels; keep warm in a 200° oven. Repeat to fry remaining fish, wiping out pan with paper towels and adding 2 tablespoons oil between batches.

4. Transfer fillets to plates and top with citrus salsa; serve at once with remaining salsa alongside.

Per serving: 362 cal., 52% (189 cal.) from fat; 28 g protein; 21 g fat (4 g sat.); 15 g carbo (0.4 g fiber); 438 mg sodium; 90 mg chol.

Citrus Salsa

PREP TIME: About 30 minutes

MAKES: About 3 cups

> 1 Ruby grapefruit (12 oz.)
>
> 1 Honey tangerine (6 oz.)
>
> 1 Valencia or navel orange (6 oz.)
>
> 1 blood orange (4 oz.)
>
> 1 Meyer lemon (4 oz.)
>
> 1 lime (3 oz.)
>
> 1 avocado (8 oz.)
>
> 6 kumquats (about 2 oz.), minced
>
> 1 fresh hot red chili, rinsed, seeded, and minced
>
> 2 tablespoons chopped fresh mint
>
> ½ teaspoon salt

1. Working on a cutting board with a juice well, cut off and discard ends from grapefruit, tangerine, orange, blood orange, lemon, and lime. With a small, sharp knife, cut peels and outer membranes from fruit and discard. Squeeze any juice from membranes into a 1-cup measure and reserve.

2. Cut fruit crosswise into ½-inch-thick slices, then cut slices into cubes, discarding seeds. Pour juice from well of cutting board into glass measure; reserve for nut-crusted sole.

3. Pit, peel, and dice avocado. In a bowl, gently mix citrus cubes, avocado, kumquats, chili, mint, and salt.

Per ¼ cup: 47 cal., 43% (20 cal.) from fat; 0.8 g protein; 2.2 g fat (0.3 g sat.); 7.9 g carbo (1.5 g fiber); 99 mg sodium; 0 mg chol.

Peel deal

When using citrus fruit, you often have a pile of peels left over; use them in simple candied peel.

Candied citrus peel. Put 12 ounces rinsed, quartered **citrus peels** (including white pith; if using peels reserved from another use, scrape off any clinging fruit) in a 2- to 3-quart pan and add water to cover. Boil over high heat for 1 minute, then reduce heat and simmer for 30 minutes. Drain; repeat process twice. When peels are cool, scrape away any white pith thicker than ¼ inch. Cut peels lengthwise into strips (¼ in. wide). In pan, combine 1½ cups **granulated sugar,** ¼ cup **light corn syrup,** and 1½ cups water. Set over medium-high heat and cook, swirling occasionally, until sugar is dissolved. Add peels, reduce heat, and simmer, stirring occasionally, until translucent, about 1 hour. Transfer peels to a wire rack set over waxed paper. Let stand until barely moist to touch, about 2 hours. Roll peels in **superfine sugar** and set on a clean wire rack; let dry completely, 8 hours or overnight. Store airtight, covering peels completely with sugar, up to 2 months. Makes 1 pound.

Per ounce: 213 cal., 0.4% (0.9 cal.) from fat; 0.3 g protein; 0.1 g fat (0 g sat.); 55 g carbo (1.1 g fiber); 7.6 mg sodium; 0 mg chol.

Thai Pummelo Salad

PREP TIME: 30 minutes

NOTES: This refreshing Thai salad is a delicious relish for pork satay (recipe follows).

MAKES: 4 to 6 servings

- 3 **pummeloes (1½ lb. each)**
- 2 **cups diced (¼ in.) English cucumbers**
- ¼ **cup minced fresh cilantro**
- 1 **fresh serrano or jalapeño chili, rinsed, stemmed, seeded, and minced**
  About 2 tablespoons Asian fish sauce *(nuoc mam or nam pla)*
- ½ **cup chopped unsalted roasted peanuts**

1. Cut off and discard thick pummelo skins. With your fingers, divide pummeloes into segments. Pull off and discard membranes; pull fruit into ½-inch chunks. Place in a bowl.

2. Gently stir in cucumbers, cilantro, chili, and 2 tablespoons fish sauce. Taste and add more fish sauce if desired; if making up to 1 day ahead, cover and chill (salad will become juicier). Sprinkle with peanuts just before serving.

Per serving: 171 cal., 35% (59 cal.) from fat; 6.2 g protein; 6.6 g fat (0.9 g sat.); 25 g carbo (1.6 g fiber); 202 mg sodium; 0 mg chol.

Pork Satay

1. In a zip-lock plastic bag, mix 2 tablespoons minced **shallots,** 2 tablespoons **Asian fish sauce** *(nuoc mam* or *nam pla),* 1 tablespoon firmly

Chill citrus segments in spiced syrup for a light, elegant winter dessert.

packed **dark brown sugar,** and 1½ teaspoons fresh-ground **pepper.** Rinse 12 ounces boned fat-trimmed **pork butt** (shoulder). Slice into thin strips (⅛ in. thick; if pork is difficult to slice thinly, freeze just until firm, 20 to 30 minutes) and add to bag. Seal bag, turn to coat meat, and chill for 1 hour. Thread pork strips flat onto wooden skewers (cut blunt ends off skewers if necessary to fit in pan). Discard marinade.

2. Set a 10- to 12-inch ridged grill pan over high heat. When hot, lightly coat with **vegetable oil.** Working in batches, lay pork skewers flat in pan (do not crowd). Cook, turning once, until browned on both sides and no longer pink in the center (cut to test), 6 to 8 minutes total. Transfer skewers to a platter or small plates and serve with **Thai pummelo salad** (recipe precedes) on the side. Makes 4 to 6 appetizer servings.

Per serving: 120 cal., 49% (59 cal.) from fat; 12 g protein; 6.5 g fat (1.8 g sat.); 3.1 g carbo (0.1 g fiber); 190 mg sodium; 39 mg chol.

Blood Orange and Grapefruit Compote

PREP TIME: 30 minutes, plus 1 hour to chill

MAKES: 4 to 6 servings

- ¼ **cup sugar**
- 2 **tablespoons grenadine**
- 1 **tablespoon thin slices fresh ginger**
- 4 **cardamom pods, crushed**
- 1 **piece (2 in. long) vanilla bean**
- 6 **blood oranges (4 oz. each)**
- 3 **Ruby grapefruit (12 oz. each)**

1. In a 1½- to 2-quart pan over medium-low heat, stir sugar, grenadine, ginger, cardamom pods, vanilla bean, and ¾ cup water until sugar is dissolved. Simmer, stirring occasionally, for 15 minutes. Remove from heat; let stand 30 minutes.

2. Meanwhile, using a sharp knife, cut off and discard ends from oranges and grapefruit. Carefully slice off peel and outer membrane, following the curve of the fruit. With your fingers or the knife, gently pry sections of fruit from inner membranes and place in a shallow bowl; discard membranes.

3. Pour syrup through a fine strainer into bowl with citrus segments; discard spices. Cover and chill for at least 1 hour or up to 1 day. Spoon fruit and syrup into compote glasses.

Per serving: 114 cal., 0.8% (0.9 cal.) from fat; 1.1 g protein; 0.1 g fat (0 g sat.); 27 g carbo (2.3 g fiber); 0.3 mg sodium; 0 mg chol. ◆

Make it sweet

Bring back the tradition of homemade candy for the holidays

By Charity Ferreira and Kate Washington
Photographs by James Carrier
Food styling by Karen Shinto

Is there anything more delicious, more purely self-indulgent, than a square of dark, creamy fudge or a piece of crunchy, buttery toffee? And when it's homemade, the treat is sweet indeed.

At its elemental best, most candy is nothing more than sugar and a few flavorings, transformed through a sweet alchemy from a syrup base into favorites like brittle, toffee, fudge, or marshmallows. Some simpler confections—buttermints and barks, like our white chocolate studded with cranberries and pistachios—require no sugar syrup or cooking at all. All of our recipes and tips have been tested by novice and experienced candymakers alike, to give you all the information you need for great results.

Homemade candy is a delicacy to have on hand for nibbling or offering to drop-in guests. Beautifully packaged, it also makes a personal gift for the holidays: Five-spice cashew brittle or charmingly decorated marshmallows will inspire visions of sugarplums for everyone on your list.

Almond Toffee

PREP AND COOK TIME: About 45 minutes, plus at least 1 1/2 hours to cool

NOTES: A candy thermometer is useful in making this toffee, but you can also go by the color; look for a rich caramel shade in step 2.

MAKES: About 3 pounds

Buttery almond toffee and crunchy five-spice cashew brittle are perfect Christmas treats.

1 1/2 cups whole raw almonds
3 1/3 cups sugar
1 1/2 cups (3/4 lb.) butter
1/4 cup light corn syrup
1/2 teaspoon salt
1 tablespoon vanilla
12 ounces bittersweet or semisweet chocolate, finely chopped

1. Place almonds in a baking pan. Bake in a 350° regular or convection oven, shaking pan occasionally, until golden beneath skins, 10 to 12 minutes. When cool enough to handle, chop finely.

2. In a 5- to 6-quart pan over medium-low heat, stir sugar, butter, corn syrup, salt, and 3/4 cup water until butter is melted and sugar is dissolved. Increase heat to medium-high and cook, stirring occasionally with a wooden spoon or heatproof spatula, until mixture is deep golden brown (300° on a candy thermometer; see notes), 10 to 15 minutes. Remove from heat and stir in vanilla

and half the chopped almonds. Immediately pour mixture into a 10- by 15-inch baking pan with 1-inch-tall sides. Let toffee cool at room temperature until set, at least 30 minutes.

3. Meanwhile, place chocolate in the top of a double boiler or in a heatproof bowl. Bring a few inches of water to a simmer in bottom of double boiler or a pan that the bowl can nest in; remove pan from heat. Place chocolate over water and let stand, stirring occasionally, until melted and smooth, about 10 minutes.

4. Pour chocolate over cooled toffee; with a knife or an offset spatula, spread level. Sprinkle remaining almonds evenly over chocolate. Let stand at room temperature until chocolate is set, at least 1 hour (or chill about 30 minutes).

5. To remove, gently twist pan to release toffee, then chop or break into chunks. Store airtight at room temperature for up to 2 days, or chill airtight up to 1 month.

Per ounce: 158 cal., 54% (85 cal.) from fat; 1 g protein; 9.4 g fat (5 g sat.); 20 g carbo (0.4 g fiber); 85 mg sodium; 16 mg chol.

Cashew Brittle

PREP AND COOK TIME: About 30 minutes, plus at least 1 hour to cool

NOTES: This basic cooking method and ratio of sugar to nuts can be used to make other types of brittle as well. A candy thermometer is useful for making this brittle, but you can also go by color; look for a shade between pale gold and deep amber in step 2. The darker the color, the deeper the toasty, caramel flavor of the finished candy.

If you can't find Chinese five spice, substitute ¼ teaspoon *each* ground cinnamon, ground cloves, ground ginger, and ground anise seeds.

MAKES: About 2 pounds

- 12 ounces raw cashews
- 3 cups sugar
- 2 tablespoons light corn syrup
- 1½ teaspoons Chinese five spice (see notes)
- ½ teaspoon salt

1. Line a 10- by 15-inch baking pan with cooking parchment; generously butter parchment (or generously butter a nonstick pan). Spread cashews in another baking pan. In a 350° regular or convection oven, bake until golden brown, 8 to 10 minutes. Keep cashews warm.

2. Meanwhile, combine sugar, corn syrup, and 1 cup water in a 2- to 3-quart pan. Set over medium heat and stir just until sugar has dissolved, 4 to 5 minutes. Increase heat to high and boil without stirring until syrup is amber-colored (330° to 335° on a candy thermometer; see notes), 12 to 20 minutes. When sugar begins to brown around edges of pan, swirl mixture in pan gently to ensure that mixture caramelizes evenly.

3. Remove from heat and, working quickly, stir in warm cashews, five spice, and salt. Mixture will foam; when foaming subsides slightly, pour mixture into prepared baking pan and use a flexible spatula to spread into a thin, even layer. Let stand in a cool, dry place until cool and hard to touch, at least 1 hour.

4. Break brittle into irregular pieces. Store airtight up to 2 weeks.

Per ounce: 139 cal., 34% (47 cal.) from fat; 1.9 g protein; 5.2 g fat (1 g sat.); 23 g carbo (0.4 g fiber); 42 mg sodium; 0.6 mg chol.

Creamy Chocolate Fudge

PREP AND COOK TIME: About 1 hour, plus at least 3½ hours to cool and set

NOTES: You will need a candy thermometer to make this fudge. Be sure to read "Candy Basics" at right and "Fudge Pointers" on page 254 before beginning.

MAKES: 3 pounds

- 4 cups sugar
- 1½ cups whipping cream
- ¼ cup light corn syrup
- 6 ounces unsweetened chocolate, finely chopped
- 6 ounces bittersweet or semisweet chocolate, finely chopped
- ¼ cup (⅛ lb.) butter, cut into chunks
- 2 teaspoons vanilla

1. In a 3- to 4-quart heavy-bottomed pan over medium-low heat, stir sugar, cream, and corn syrup, continually scraping the bottom of the pan with a heatproof flexible spatula, until sugar is completely dissolved, about 15 minutes. Stir in unsweetened and bittersweet chocolate until melted. Increase heat to medium and bring mixture to a simmer.

2. Cook, occasionally stirring mixture and brushing down sides of pan with a wet pastry brush, until mixture reaches 235° on a candy thermometer. Remove from heat and pour into a large bowl or the bowl of a standing mixer. Add butter and vanilla but do not stir; insert candy thermometer and let mixture stand undisturbed until cooled to 110°, 1½ to 2 hours.

3. Line a 9-inch square pan with foil; lightly butter foil. With a sturdy wooden spoon or the paddle attachment of standing mixer, beat the chocolate mixture vigorously (on high speed if using mixer; reduce speed if motor starts to labor) until mixture thickens and loses its glossy sheen, about 5 minutes with a mixer, about 10 minutes by hand. Scrape into pan, smooth top, and chill until firm to the touch, at least 2 hours, or up to 1 day.

4. Lift foil to remove fudge from pan; cut fudge into 1-inch squares. Store cut fudge

Judge caramelization by color or temperature.

Candy basics

Before you begin, read the recipe all the way through and assemble all the tools and ingredients you will need. Many candy recipes require that you act quickly once the sugar syrup reaches the desired temperature.

Choose the right pans. Heavy-bottomed stainless steel pans are best for cooking sugar mixtures. Thin, lightweight pans conduct heat unevenly, which makes cooking times unpredictable.

Use a candy thermometer when called for. They measure temperatures up to 400°. You'll find them in the kitchen-gadget section of many supermarkets, priced between $5 and $15.

Submerge the bottom of the thermometer completely in the sugar syrup to get an accurate reading. Using a narrow pan with tall sides makes the mixture deeper, but, if necessary, you can gently tilt a shallower pan to get an accurate reading.

Melt chocolate gently for best texture and appearance. If chocolate gets too hot while melting, it may not set up properly and will develop "bloom" (white streaks) on the surface when stored. Stirring chopped chocolate in a pan or bowl over hot, not simmering, water maintains an even, low temperature, resulting in firmly set chocolate with a glossy surface.

Pour fudge after beating.

Fudge pointers

More than any other candy, fudge requires precision in temperature and technique. Following these pointers will ensure creamy, melt-in-your-mouth fudge every time.

Dissolve the sugar *completely over low heat* (step 1) before bringing the mixture to a simmer. Using superfine sugar, also sold as "baker's sugar," makes this easier. To check whether the sugar has dissolved, scrape the pan bottom with a heatproof spatula, pull the spatula up, let the syrup on it cool for a few seconds, then rub a drop between your fingers. If you can feel grains of sugar, it hasn't dissolved yet.

Prevent sugar crystals from forming on the side of the pan as the mixture cooks (step 2) by brushing down the sides of the pan with a wet pastry brush a few times.

Let the mixture cool to lukewarm (exactly 110°) before beating it (step 3); otherwise, the fudge may stiffen and become grainy. Pouring it into a large, shallow bowl helps it cool faster, but don't stir it too early.

Beat the fudge well once it has cooled to 110° to make sure it sets up properly. Chocolate fudge thickens more than maple fudge at this stage, but both dull slightly and take on a lighter color after beating; that's when they're ready to pour into the pan.

airtight in the refrigerator up to 1 week. For longer storage (up to 1 month), wrap uncut fudge airtight, chill, and cut into squares as desired. Serve at room temperature.

Per ounce: 137 cal., 43% (59 cal.) from fat; 0.8 g protein; 6.5 g fat (3.9 g sat.); 21 g carbo (0.6 g fiber); 16 mg sodium; 11 mg chol.

Maple Walnut Fudge

PREP AND COOK TIME: About 1 hour, plus at least 3 hours to cool and set

NOTES: You will need a candy thermometer to make this fudge. Make sure you buy pure maple syrup rather than artificially flavored syrup. Read "Candy Basics" on page 253 and "Fudge Pointers" at left before beginning.

MAKES: 3 pounds

> 2   cups firmly packed light brown sugar
> 2   cups granulated sugar
> 1½ cups whipping cream
> ¾   cup pure maple syrup (see notes)
> ¼   cup light corn syrup
> ¼   cup (⅛ lb.) butter, cut into chunks
> 2   teaspoons vanilla
> 1   cup chopped toasted walnuts

1. In a 5- to 6-quart heavy-bottomed pan over low heat, stir brown sugar, granulated sugar, cream, maple syrup, and corn syrup, continually scraping the bottom of the pan with a heatproof flexible spatula, until sugar is completely dissolved, about 15 minutes. Increase heat to medium and bring mixture to a simmer.

2. Cook, occasionally stirring mixture and brushing down sides of pan with a wet pastry brush, and watching carefully to make sure mixture doesn't bubble over (reduce heat if it threatens to), until mixture reaches 240° on a candy thermometer, 10 to 15 minutes. Remove from heat and pour into a large bowl or the bowl of a standing mixer. Add butter and vanilla but do not stir; insert candy thermometer and let mixture stand undisturbed until cooled to 110°, about 1 hour.

3. Line a 9-inch square pan with foil; lightly butter foil. With a sturdy wooden spoon or the paddle attachment of standing mixer, beat maple mixture vigorously (on high speed if using mixer; reduce speed if motor starts to labor) until mixture thickens and turns from a shiny caramel color to pale beige, about 10 minutes with a mixer, about

15 minutes by hand. Stir in walnuts. Scrape into pan and chill until firm to the touch, at least 2 hours, or up to 1 day.

4. Lift foil to remove fudge from pan; cut fudge into 1-inch squares. Store cut fudge airtight in the refrigerator up to 1 week. For longer storage (up to 1 month), wrap uncut fudge airtight, chill, and cut into squares as desired. Serve at room temperature.

Per ounce: 132 cal., 33% (44 cal.) from fat; 0.5 g protein; 4.9 g fat (2.2 g sat.); 23 g carbo (0.1 g fiber); 20 mg sodium; 11 mg chol.

Buttermints

PREP TIME: About 1 hour, plus about 12 hours to dry

NOTES: If you want to tint the mints with pale, muted colors, use a toothpick in step 2 to add a drop or two of gel food coloring, which comes in much subtler shades than regular food coloring; it's available at stores that sell cake-decorating and candymaking supplies. Peppermint oil is also available at candymaking supply stores. You can substitute ¼ teaspoon peppermint extract for the oil, although the flavor will not be as intense.

MAKES: 1¼ pounds

> About 4¼ cups powdered sugar
> ¼   cup (⅛ lb.) butter, at room temperature
> ¼   cup whipping cream
> ⅛   teaspoon peppermint oil (see notes)
> Food coloring, optional (see notes)

1. In a bowl, with a mixer on low speed (use the paddle attachment if using a standing mixer), mix 4¼ cups powdered sugar, the butter, cream, and peppermint oil until well blended. The mixture will be stiff; if it becomes too stiff to mix with the mixer, turn it out onto a surface lightly sprinkled with powdered sugar and knead by hand, working in more powdered sugar as necessary, until mixture is soft and smooth but not sticky.

2. Divide mixture into eighths. If desired, add a drop of food coloring to each piece (see notes) and knead with your hands until the color is evenly distributed. Working with one piece at a time on a powdered sugar–dusted surface (cover remaining portions with plastic wrap to prevent them from drying out), roll each piece into a rope about 28 inches long and ¼ inch thick (cut the ropes in half if necessary to roll out easily).

3. With a small, sharp knife, cut rope into ¼-inch squares. Place mints on a waxed paper–lined baking sheet. Cover with a second sheet of waxed paper.

4. Let mints stand at room temperature until dry, about 12 hours. Store in an airtight container at room temperature for up to 2 days, or in the refrigerator for up to 1 month.

Per ounce: 129 cal., 24% (31 cal.) from fat; 0.1 g protein; 3.4 g fat (2.1 g sat.); 25 g carbo (0 g fiber); 26 mg sodium; 9.8 mg chol.

Honey Marshmallows

PREP AND COOK TIME: 1 hour, plus at least 6 hours to set

NOTES: Using pasteurized egg whites, available in supermarkets, removes any concern about bacteria in the eggs. If you cut the marshmallows into shapes, choose a cookie cutter with a simple shape; trees and stars worked well in our tests. Very small or intricate cutter shapes did not produce good results. Roll the odd-shaped scraps in more cornstarch and powdered sugar and save them for floating on top of hot cocoa.

MAKES: About 1½ pounds

- ½ **cup cornstarch**
- ¾ **cup powdered sugar**
- ¼ **cup pasteurized egg whites (see notes) or 2 large egg whites, at room temperature**
- ¼ **teaspoon salt**
- ¼ **cup unflavored gelatin**
- 2 **cups granulated sugar**
- 3 **tablespoons honey**
- 2 **tablespoons light corn syrup**
- 2 **teaspoons vanilla**
    Colored sugar, turbinado sugar, and/or decorative sprinkles (optional)

1. In a small bowl, mix cornstarch and powdered sugar. Oil bottom and sides of a 12- by 18-inch baking pan with 1-inch-tall sides. Dust with about ¼ cup of the cornstarch mixture, coating thoroughly and shaking off excess (reserve remaining mixture).

2. In a small bowl, with an electric mixer on high speed, beat egg whites and salt just until stiff peaks form (no need to wash beaters if using in step 5).

3. In the large bowl of a standing mixer or another large, deep bowl, combine gelatin and ¾ cup cold water. Let stand until gelatin granules are swollen and soft, 10 to 15 minutes.

4. Meanwhile, in a heavy, straight-sided 2- to 3-quart pan over medium-high heat, stir granulated sugar, honey, corn syrup, and ¾ cup water until sugar is completely dissolved, 2 to 4 minutes. Raise heat to high and boil without stirring until mixture reaches 260° on a candy thermometer, about 10 minutes. Immediately remove pan from heat.

5. Beating with standing mixer (fitted with wire whisk) or handheld mixer on low speed, pour hot sugar syrup into gelatin mixture in a slow, steady stream (mixture may foam), stopping to scrape sides of bowl with a heatproof flexible spatula as needed. When all the syrup is incorporated and gelatin has dissolved, beat at high speed until foamy, about 2 minutes. Add beaten egg whites and vanilla and beat at high speed, scraping down sides of bowl as needed, until mixture is thick, very billowy, and glossy and just begins to pull away from sides of bowl, 8 to 10 minutes. (If you're using a handheld mixer, marshmallow may begin to creep up beater; stop motor, scrape down beaters, and reduce mixer speed.)

6. Scrape mixture into prepared pan. Using a narrow, flat-bladed spatula, smooth top so it's level with sides of

Dip cookie cutters in cornstarch to cut marshmallows.

pan. Let stand, uncovered, at room temperature until firmly set but still tacky to touch, at least 6 hours, or overnight.

7. Dust a work surface generously with some of the remaining cornstarch mixture. Loosen edges of marshmallow from pan; lift out in a sheet and transfer to surface, cornstarch side down. To make shaped marshmallows, dip a cookie cutter (see notes) in remaining cornstarch mixture and cut marshmallow sheet into shapes, dipping cutter in between each cut. Roll sides of marshmallow shapes in remaining cornstarch mixture, then sprinkle tops with colored sugar, turbinado sugar, or other decorations as desired. Alternatively, to make squares, use a sharp knife dipped in cornstarch mixture to cut marshmallow sheet into cubes; coat with cornstarch mixture, then transfer marshmallows to a colander and shake off excess (discard any remaining cornstarch mixture). Store airtight at room temperature up to 1 month.

Per ounce: 100 cal., 2% (1.8 cal.) from fat; 1.7 g protein; 0.2 g fat (0 g sat.); 23 g carbo (0 g fiber); 39 mg sodium; 0 mg chol.

Cranberry-Pistachio Bark

PREP TIME: About 20 minutes, plus at least 4 hours to set

NOTES: Read the information about melting chocolate in "Candy Basics" (page 253) before making this bark. The time it takes for the bark to set firmly varies greatly according to the temperature of your home; if you are making bark on a day when you are doing other holiday cooking, let it stand in a room that is cooler than the kitchen. Do not set bark by chilling it in the refrigerator, as it may collect condensation.

MAKES: About 3¾ pounds

1. Line a 12- by 15-inch baking sheet with cooking parchment; butter parchment. Chop 2 pounds **white chocolate** and place with 1 tablespoon **solid vegetable shortening** in a large, heatproof bowl that will nest in a 3- to 4-quart pan. Heat 1 inch of water in the pan just until steaming. Remove from heat and place bowl with white chocolate over water (bowl shouldn't touch water). Stir occasionally just until melted and smooth.

2. Remove bowl from pan and stir in 2 cups *each* **shelled unsalted raw pistachios** and **dried cranberries.** Using a flexible spatula, scrape mixture onto buttered parchment and spread ³/₈ to ¹/₂ inch thick (mixture should cover almost all of sheet). Sprinkle with an additional 1 cup *each* pistachios and dried cranberries and gently press into white-chocolate mixture.

3. Let stand at cool room temperature (see notes) until completely firm, 4 to 6 hours, or overnight. Break bark into irregular pieces. Store airtight in a cool place up to 1 month.

Per ounce: 141 cal., 48% (68 cal.) from fat; 1.3 g protein; 7.5 g fat (4.2 g sat.); 16 g carbo (1 g fiber); 22 mg sodium; 0.2 mg chol.

Rocky Road Bark

PREP TIME: About 20 minutes, plus at least 4 hours to set

NOTES: See notes for cranberry-pistachio bark, on page 255.

MAKES: About 3 pounds

1. Line a 12- by 15-inch baking sheet with cooking parchment; butter parchment. Chop 2 pounds **milk chocolate** and place with 1 tablespoon **solid vegetable shortening** in a large, heatproof bowl that will nest in a 3- to 4-quart pan. Heat 1 inch of water in the pan just until steaming. Remove from heat and place bowl with chocolate over water (bowl shouldn't touch water). Stir occasionally just until melted and smooth.

2. Remove bowl from pan and stir in 2 cups *each* **mini marshmallows** and coarsely chopped **walnuts.** Using a flexible spatula, scrape mixture onto buttered parchment and spread about ³/₈ to ¹/₂ inch thick (mixture should cover almost all of sheet). Sprinkle with an additional 1 cup *each* marshmallows and walnuts and gently press into chocolate mixture.

3. Let stand at cool room temperature until completely firm, 4 to 6 hours, or overnight. Break bark into irregular

Rocky road bark and a mug of hot chocolate satisfy the kid in anyone.

pieces. Store airtight in a cool place up to 2 weeks.

Per ounce: 158 cal., 63% (99 cal.) from fat; 2.4 g protein; 11 g fat (4 g sat.); 15 g carbo (0.9 g fiber); 18 mg sodium; 4.2 mg chol.

Peppermint Bark

PREP TIME: About 20 minutes, plus at least 4 hours to set

NOTES: See notes for cranberry-pistachio bark, on page 255.

MAKES: About 4 pounds

1. Line a 12- by 15-inch baking sheet with cooking parchment; butter parchment. Chop 2 pounds **bittersweet chocolate** and place with 1 tablespoon **solid vegetable shortening** in a large, heatproof bowl that will nest in a 3- to 4-quart pan. Heat 1 inch of water in the pan just until steaming. Remove from heat and place bowl with chocolate over water (bowl shouldn't touch water). Stir occasionally just until melted and smooth.

2. Meanwhile, place 2 pounds **pepper-mint candy** in a heavy zip-lock plastic bag; pound with a mallet or rolling pin to crush. Transfer 1¹/₄ cups of the crushed peppermint candy to a fine strainer and sharply knock side of strainer to sift the fine dust into the melted chocolate. Reserve candy in strainer.

3. Remove bowl from pan and stir remaining crushed, unsifted peppermint into melted chocolate mixture. Using a flexible spatula, scrape onto buttered parchment and spread ¹/₄ to ¹/₂ inch thick (mixture should cover almost all of sheet). Sprinkle with reserved crushed peppermint from strainer and gently press into chocolate mixture.

4. Let stand at cool room temperature until completely firm, 4 to 6 hours, or overnight. Break bark into irregular pieces. Store airtight in a cool place up to 1 month.

Per ounce: 128 cal., 37% (47 cal.) from fat; 1 g protein; 5.2 g fat (2.7 g sat.); 22 g carbo (0.3 g fiber); 10 mg sodium; 0.2 mg chol. ◆

Put the rub on chicken

Spa cooking inspires light, zesty weeknight fare

By Linda Lau Anusasananan
Photograph by James Carrier

An unusual apple-chipotle salsa adds fresh crunch to spice-rubbed chicken.

FOOD STYLING: KAREN SHINTO

Weeknight dinners in December can be a dilemma. Winter's cold nights make you long for something warm and spicy, while the rich fare of the holiday season leaves you yearning for a simple, healthy meal. For an easy solution, we look to spa chefs, the masters of light, flavorful cooking. We've used a chili-spiked spice rub, adapted from *Canyon Ranch Cooks* (Rodale, Emmaus, PA, 2003; $30; www.rodalestore.com), by Barry Correia and Scott Uehlein. The rub lends a rich warm color and lively flavor to lean chicken breasts, and Canyon Ranch's piquant apple-chipotle salsa makes a delicious topping. Start this quick meal with our refreshing orange and onion salad, and round out the main course with purchased black beans, simple sautéed greens, and warm flour tortillas. Mango sorbet, topped with crunchy crushed meringues, is a sweet ending.

Chicken with Green Apple–Chipotle Salsa

PREP AND COOK TIME: About 35 minutes

MAKES: 4 servings

- 1 cup diced (¼ in.) Granny Smith apple (unpeeled, rinsed)
- ½ cup diced (¼ in.) red onion
- ½ cup diced (¼ in.) red bell pepper
- ¼ cup chopped fresh cilantro
- ¼ cup apple juice
- ¼ cup red wine vinegar
- ¼ teaspoon ground dried chipotle chili or cayenne
- 4 boned, skinned chicken breast halves (5 to 6 oz. each)

Chili spice mix (recipe follows)
1 tablespoon olive oil

1. To make salsa, in a bowl, mix apple, onion, bell pepper, cilantro, apple juice, vinegar, and chili. Cover and chill.

2. Rinse chicken and pat dry. Rub chili spice mix over all sides of chicken breasts.

To grill, coat both sides of chicken breasts lightly with olive oil and lay on a grill over medium-high coals or medium-high heat on a gas grill (you can hold your hand at grill level only 3 to 4 seconds); close lid if using gas. Cook, turning once, until chicken is no longer pink in center of thickest part (cut to test), 6 to 8 minutes total.

To sauté, set a 10- to 12-inch nonstick frying pan over medium heat. When pan is hot, add oil and tilt to coat bottom. Lay chicken breasts, slightly apart, in pan (if using a 10-inch pan, cook chicken in two batches, using half the oil at a time; keep cooked breasts warm, lightly covered, in 200° oven). Cook, turning once, until chicken is no longer pink in center of thickest part (cut to test), 10 to 12 minutes total; reduce heat slightly if chicken begins to brown excessively.

3. Transfer chicken to plates. Serve with green apple–chipotle salsa.

Per serving: 233 cal., 21% (50 cal.) from fat; 34 g protein; 5.6 g fat (1 g sat.); 11 g carbo (1.4 g fiber); 682 mg sodium; 82 mg chol.

Chili spice mix. In a small bowl, mix 1 tablespoon **paprika**, 1 teaspoon *each* **salt** and **pepper**, ½ teaspoon **chili powder**, ½ teaspoon firmly packed **brown sugar**, and ⅛ teaspoon **cayenne**.

Orange and onion salad. With a small, sharp knife, cut top and bottom off 3 **oranges** (10 oz. each), cutting deeply enough to reveal flesh. Set orange, with one cut end down, on board. Slice down sides of oranges to remove white pith and deep enough to reveal flesh; discard peels. Thinly slice orange flesh crosswise into rounds. Arrange orange slices on a platter. Peel 1 **white onion** (5 oz.); cut half into thin rounds. Separate rounds into rings and rinse and drain; distribute evenly over oranges. (Reserve remaining onion half for another use.) Mix 2 tablespoons **white wine vinegar** and 1 tablespoon **extra-virgin olive oil**. Drizzle evenly over onions; sprinkle with **salt** and fresh-ground **pepper** to taste. Makes 4 servings.

Per serving: 115 cal., 30% (35 cal.) from fat; 1.6 g protein; 3.9 g fat (0.5 g sat.); 21 g carbo (4.3 g fiber); 3.2 mg sodium; 0 mg chol. ◆

Best beef

Kobe-style beef is tender, flavorful, and now available in the West

Until recently, Japan boasted the best beef in the world but harbored a secret. Kobe cattle are legendary for their tender meat—and for the massages and beer- and sake-laced diet they're given. But since the early 1970s, many of those Kobe cows have actually been raised in the United States, where both land and feed are cheaper. Here, as in the Kobe region of Japan, they come from the ancient Wagyu breed, which yields meat finely marbled with fat and therefore both tender and flavorful. You wouldn't expect this to be good health news, but the fat is less saturated than that in other beef, and the meat is lower in cholesterol.

Even better news: Western producers of Kobe-style Wagyu—who are doing it sans sake and massages but with traditional feed routines and without growth hormones—are beginning to market their meat here. And while it's not cheap, it doesn't command $100 a portion, as it can in Japan. Bala Kironde, owner of Preferred Meats in San Francisco *(www.preferredmeats.com or 510/632-4065),* explains, though, that not all Wagyu is created equal: Breeding counts, among other things, and there are various grades. He stands by Kobe from Idaho's Snake River Farms (in high-end supermarkets or from Snake River Farms, *www.snakeriverfarms.com or 800/657-6305).*

James Ormsby, executive chef of

Two kinds of pepper give extra flair to tender Kobe beef.

PlumpJack Cafe in San Francisco *(415/563-4755),* serves several cuts of Snake River Kobe. He offers this simple tenderloin—quickly sautéed to sear the outside but not melt the marbling inside—for a special holiday meal.

Kobe Pepper Filet Mignon

PREP AND COOK TIME: About 25 minutes

NOTES: Rounds cut from the small end of the beef tenderloin are sold as filet mignon; substitute USDA prime or choice beef for the Kobe if desired. Start the potatoes first, then make the green peppercorn sauce; keep it warm over low heat while you cook the beef. Demiglace and stock bases are sold in some supermarkets, specialty food stores, and some cookware stores (such as Williams-Sonoma); reconstitute a stock base to the demiglace level to use in the sauce.

MAKES: 4 servings

4 pieces Kobe-style beef tenderloin (cut from small end, each about 1½ in. thick and 8 oz.; see notes), fat trimmed

Kosher salt

3 tablespoons cracked black pepper

2 tablespoons olive oil

2 tablespoons butter

Rosemary roasted potato wedges (recipe follows)

Green peppercorn–brandy sauce (recipe follows)

1. Rinse beef and pat dry. Season all over with salt. Put cracked black pepper on a small, rimmed plate.

2. Heat olive oil and butter in a 10- to 12-inch frying pan over medium-high heat. When butter just begins to brown, press a flat side of each piece of beef into pepper to form an even crust (discard any leftover pepper); set beef, pepper side down, in pan and cook until browned on the bottom, 4 to 5 minutes. Turn pieces and cook until other sides are browned and a thermometer inserted into the center reaches 125° for rare, about 8 minutes longer, or 135° for medium-rare, 12 to 13 minutes.

3. Transfer beef to warm plates and let rest for 5 minutes. Mound rosemary roasted potato wedges alongside beef. Pass green peppercorn–brandy sauce to add to taste.

Per serving of beef: 506 cal., 59% (297 cal.) from fat; 48 g protein; 33 g fat (13 g sat.); 3.1 g carbo (1.3 g fiber); 183 mg sodium; 156 mg chol.

Rosemary roasted potato wedges. Scrub 4 **russet potatoes** (8 oz. each) and cut lengthwise into 3/4-inch-thick wedges; pat dry. In a large bowl, mix potatoes with 1 tablespoon **olive oil,** 1 tablespoon chopped **fresh rosemary** leaves, 1/2 teaspoon **salt,** and 1/4 teaspoon **pepper.** Spread level in a 10- by 15-inch nonstick baking pan. Bake in a 450° regular or convection oven, turning occasionally with a wide spatula, until potatoes are golden brown and tender when pierced, 35 to 40 minutes. Makes 4 servings.

Per serving: 210 cal., 15% (32 cal.) from fat; 4.9 g protein; 3.6 g fat (0.5 g sat.); 41 g carbo (3 g fiber); 301 mg sodium; 0 mg chol.

Green peppercorn–brandy sauce. In a 1 1/2- to 2-quart pan over medium heat, melt 1 tablespoon **butter;** add 2 tablespoons minced **shallots** and stir often until limp but not brown, 2 to 3 minutes. Add 1/2 cup **brandy** and 1 tablespoon **sherry vinegar;** increase heat to medium-high and boil, stirring often, until liquid is almost evaporated, 5 to 6 minutes. Add 2 cups **veal** or beef **demiglace** (see preceding notes); reduce heat and simmer, stirring occasionally and skimming off any residue that comes to the surface, for 10 minutes. Stir in 2 tablespoons drained **green peppercorns in brine** and **salt** to taste. Just before serving, over low heat, whisk in 2 more tablespoons butter; pour into a gravy boat. Makes about 2 cups.

Per 1/4 cup: 42 cal., 55% (23 cal.) from fat; 0.7 g protein; 2.5 g fat (0.9 g sat.); 4.4 g carbo (0 g fiber); 398 mg sodium; 3.9 mg chol.

—*Sara Schneider*

Sweet spiced madeleines will inspire fond memories.

JAMES CARRIER; FOOD STYLING: KAREN SHINTO

Mad about madeleines

Petite, buttery madeleines are nothing more than moist little cakes baked in a pan with shell-shaped indentations. Traditionally made with sponge-cake batter flavored with a little lemon peel, madeleines can be made from other kinds of cake batter as well. Almond paste, cinnamon, cloves, and orange peel give this rich version holiday appeal. Combine some with a pretty package of tea for a gift, or curl up with a good book and enjoy them yourself.

Orange-Spice Madeleines

PREP AND COOK TIME: About 45 minutes

NOTES: If you like, while they're still warm, dust the cookies with 2 tablespoons of powdered sugar mixed with 1/2 teaspoon cinnamon. Although best fresh, they can be stored airtight at room temperature for up to 1 week.

MAKES: About 14 madeleines

- 2 **ounces almond paste,** cut into chunks
- 1/2 **cup sugar**
- 6 **tablespoons butter,** at room temperature
- 1 **large egg**
- 1 **teaspoon grated orange peel**
- 1/2 **teaspoon vanilla**
- 1/3 **cup milk**
- 3/4 **cup all-purpose flour**
- 1/2 **teaspoon baking powder**
- 1/4 **teaspoon ground cinnamon**
- 1/8 **teaspoon ground cloves**
- 1/8 **teaspoon salt**

1. In a large bowl, with your fingers or a pastry blender, rub or cut almond paste into sugar until well blended. With a mixer on medium speed, beat in butter until smooth. Beat in egg, orange peel, and vanilla, scraping down sides of bowl as necessary. Stir in milk.

2. In another bowl, mix flour with baking powder, cinnamon, cloves, and salt. Stir into butter mixture until well blended. Spoon batter into buttered and floured 2-inch-long madeleine molds (fill each hollow about 3/4 full).

3. Bake in a 350° oven until tops of madeleines are lightly browned and spring back when gently pressed, 12 to 15 minutes. Invert pan over a rack to release madeleines. Serve warm, or cool completely and store airtight.

Per madeleine: 132 cal., 49% (65 cal.) from fat; 1.9 g protein; 7.2 g fat (3.7 g sat.); 15 g carbo (0.2 g fiber); 102 mg sodium; 31 mg chol.

—*Charity Ferreira*

Warm winter favorites

Readers' recipes tested in *Sunset's* kitchens

Quick Chicken Cassoulet

Russell Ito, San Mateo, CA

Russell Ito combined leftover roast chicken with a few pantry ingredients to create an easily assembled chicken and white bean stew. If you don't have leftover chicken, buy roasted chicken at a supermarket or deli, or bake an 8-ounce boned, skinned chicken breast in a 350° oven until no longer pink in the center, about 20 minutes.

PREP AND COOK TIME: About 1 hour and 10 minutes

MAKES: 4 to 6 servings

- 1 **cup fresh or dried bread crumbs**
- 2½ **tablespoons olive oil**
- ⅓ **cup minced shallots**
- 4 **cloves garlic, peeled and minced**
- 1 **carrot (about 4 oz.), peeled and diced (¼ in.)**
- 2 **cans (15 oz. each) small white beans, drained and rinsed**
- 1 **cup 1-inch chunks cooked chicken (see note above)**
- 8 **ounces cooked chicken or duck sausages, sliced crosswise ¼ inch thick**
- 1 **can (14 oz.) diced tomatoes**
- 1 **teaspoon herbes de Provence**
- 1 **dried whole bay leaf**
- ½ **cup fat-skimmed chicken broth**
- ½ **teaspoon salt**
- ¼ **teaspoon pepper**

1. In a bowl, mix bread crumbs and 2 tablespoons oil until well combined.

2. Pour remaining ½ tablespoon oil into a 3-quart ovenproof pan over

Shortcut cassoulet starts with canned beans and cooked chicken.

medium heat. When hot, add shallots, garlic, and carrot and stir occasionally until carrot is tender, about 7 minutes. Add beans, chicken, sausages, tomatoes, herbes de Provence, bay leaf, chicken broth, salt, and pepper; stir until well combined.

3. Cover cassoulet and bake in a 350° regular or convection oven until beans are hot, about 30 minutes; uncover and sprinkle top evenly with bread-crumb mixture. Bake until top is browned and edges are bubbling, about 20 minutes longer.

Per serving: 294 cal., 37% (108 cal.) from fat; 24 g protein; 12 g fat (2.1 g sat.); 24 g carbo (5.2 g fiber); 866 mg sodium; 51 mg chol.

Spicy Braised Pork Shoulder

Mickey Strang, McKinleyville, CA

Mickey Strang likes bone-in pork shoulder because she can combine it

with a few other ingredients in a Dutch oven and then forget about it until dinnertime. She serves this spicy pork with rice and beans, and notes that leftovers make a great taco or enchilada filling. To peel the pearl onions, drop them in boiling water for 1 to 2 minutes, then drain. When onions are cool enough to handle, trim off root ends and squeeze onions to slip out of peels.

PREP AND COOK TIME: About 4¼ hours

MAKES: 4 to 6 servings

- 3½ **pounds bone-in pork shoulder**
  Salt and pepper
- 1 **can (14½ oz.) diced tomatoes**
- 8 **ounces pearl onions, peeled (see note above), or 1 onion (8 oz.), peeled and chopped**
- 2 **drained canned chipotle or jalapeño chilies**
- 2 **cloves garlic, peeled and minced**

1. Rinse pork and pat dry. Sprinkle all over with salt and pepper. Place in a

JAMES CARRIER; FOOD STYLING: KAREN SHINTO (2)

4- to 6-quart Dutch oven or other heavy pan with a lid. Add tomatoes, onions, chilies, and garlic.

2. Cover and bake in a 250° regular or convection oven, checking every half hour after the first 2½ hours, until meat is very tender when pierced with a fork, 3½ to 4 hours. (If pan gets dry, add ½ cup water to pan.)

3. With two large forks, pull meat from bone and pull apart into large chunks. Transfer pork to a serving platter. Pour pan juices into a bowl to spoon over pork.

Per serving: 365 cal., 64% (234 cal.) from fat; 25 g protein; 26 g fat (8.8 g sat.); 7.2 g carbo (0.7 g fiber); 249 mg sodium; 100 mg chol.

Dolmas Pilaf

Leilani McCoy, Seattle

Leilani McCoy loves Greek food, and stuffed grape leaves in particular. Her reluctance to spend the time it takes to roll and fill dolmas led her to a creative solution: this moist and flavorful rice, lamb, and grape-leaf pilaf.

PREP AND COOK TIME: About 45 minutes

MAKES: 4 to 6 servings

- 3 tablespoons olive oil
- 1 pound ground lamb
- 1 onion (8 oz.), peeled and chopped
- 2 cups long-grain white rice
- 1 cup rinsed, chopped preserved grape leaves (reserve 2 tablespoons brine from jar)
- 2 tablespoons chopped parsley
- 2 tablespoons chopped fresh dill
- ½ cup pine nuts
- ½ cup dried currants

1. Heat oil in a 4- to 6-quart pan over medium-high heat. Add lamb and onion and stir frequently until lamb is crumbly and browned and onion is limp, 5 to 7 minutes.

2. Add rice, grape leaves, parsley, dill, pine nuts, currants, reserved grape leaf brine, and 4 cups water. Bring to a boil. Reduce heat to maintain a simmer, cover, and cook until rice is tender to bite, 20 to 25 minutes.

Per serving: 615 cal., 45% (279 cal.) from fat; 21 g protein; 31 g fat (9.6 g sat.); 63 g carbo (2.5 g fiber); 279 mg sodium; 55 mg chol.

Maple Nut-Filled Dates

Leslie Freeman, Boise

After a day of skiing, Leslie Freeman wanted a bite of something quick, rich, and sweet. She came up with these cheese-filled dates, which make a great appetizer or après-ski snack. She uses Bellwether Farms' flavorful, creamy crescenza cheese, made in Sonoma County, California. You can substitute another soft cheese, such as teleme or brie.

PREP AND COOK TIME: About 15 minutes

MAKES: 20 date halves; 8 to 10 servings

- 10 Medjool dates
- ¼ cup soft cheese (see note above)
- 1 tablespoon butter
- ¼ cup chopped walnuts
- ¼ cup maple syrup

1. Cut dates in half lengthwise and remove pits. Spoon about ½ teaspoon cheese into the cavity of each date half. Arrange dates on a serving plate.

2. Melt butter in a 1- to 2-quart pan over low heat. Raise heat to medium and cook until butter is foamy and starting to brown. Add nuts; stir constantly for 1 minute. Add syrup and lower heat to maintain a simmer. Cook 1 minute, stirring frequently. Remove from heat.

3. Lift nuts from syrup with a slotted spoon and press a few pieces into the cheese in each date. Drizzle syrup over dates and serve warm.

Per serving: 114 cal., 35% (40 cal.) from fat; 1.8 g protein; 4.4 g fat (1.5 g sat.); 18 g carbo (1.3 g fiber); 41 mg sodium; 5.1 mg chol.

Warm maple syrup and toasted walnuts top cheese-filled dates.

Caramel-Banana Bread Pudding

Roxanne Chan, Albany, CA

Roxanne Chan created this rich, creamy bread pudding to mimic the flavors of a favorite bar cookie.

PREP AND COOK TIME: About 1½ hours

MAKES: 8 servings

- 4 cups 1-inch cubes of sturdy white bread
- 2 bananas (8 oz. total), peeled and sliced crosswise
- 1 cup (6 oz.) semisweet chocolate chips
- ½ cup pecan halves
- ½ cup prepared caramel sauce, at room temperature
- 3 cups milk (whole or 2%)
- 3 large eggs
- 3 ounces cream cheese, at room temperature
- ½ teaspoon ground cinnamon

1. Arrange bread cubes evenly in a buttered 9-inch square baking pan. Arrange banana slices over bread cubes, then sprinkle with chocolate and nuts. Drizzle caramel sauce evenly over the top.

2. In a blender, whirl milk, eggs, cream cheese, and cinnamon until smooth. Pour over bread cubes. Let stand at room temperature 15 minutes.

3. Bake in a 325° regular or convection oven until top is set, 50 minutes to 1 hour. Let stand at least 10 minutes after removing from oven, then serve warm.

Per serving: 388 cal., 49% (189 cal.) from fat; 9.5 g protein; 21 g fat (9.4 g sat.); 46 g carbo (2.4 g fiber); 273 mg sodium; 106 mg chol. ◆

Global sparklers

It's happened twice this year: I've been sitting in a restaurant in a foreign country, and all around me the discreet hiss and pop of Champagne corks punctuated the clamor of conversation. But it wasn't Champagne—sparkling wine from that eponymous region in France—people were drinking. The first time, it was New Zealand sparklers, sipped with abandon during Sunday brunch. The second time, at 11 P.M. in a seafood restaurant in Barcelona, Spain, the waiters didn't even ask if anyone wanted sparkling wine; they just brought bottle after bottle to every table.

You see, something has changed in much of the world. People are no longer under the impression that Champagne is the only sparkling wine worth drinking, or that bubbles are only for celebrations. From the trattorias of Italy to the cafes of Argentina, people are drinking sparklers because bubbles are refreshing, and the wines are extraordinary matches for a wide range of foods.

In my favorite wine shop recently, I found sparklers from Spain, Germany, Italy, Argentina, New Zealand, and Australia as well as Champagne; and from closer to home, New Mexico, Oregon, and Washington as well as California. Most were made by the painstaking, labor-intensive traditional method (*méthode champenoise*), meaning that the bubbles formed naturally inside each bottle. And in almost every case the wines were a deal, if not an outright steal. So this month, think globally—and beyond New Year's Eve. In addition to Champagne and California sparkling wine, try these.

Chandon Fresco Extra Dry *(Argentina), $12.* Full of vanilla, with slightly exotic notes and persistent bubbles,

this is the Argentinean sister of Moët & Chandon in France and Domaine Chandon in California.

Gruet Brut NV *(New Mexico), $14.* Made from grapes grown near the town of Truth or Consequences, New Mexico, Gruet may be the biggest testament there is to the fact that delicious sparklers can and are being made in unexpected places. Lemony and crisp, with a nice touch of yeastiness.

Rivetti La Spinetta Moscato d'Asti 2001 *(Piedmont, Italy), $16.* One of Italy's most irresistible delicacies (it's not the same as Asti Spumante), with notes of peach and ginger. Low in alcohol and just lightly fizzy rather than fully sparkling, Moscato d'Asti is traditionally served on Christmas morning.

Sumarroca Cava Extra Brut Reserva NV *(Penedes, Spain), $8.* Many terrific cavas (top Spanish sparklers) are available in the United States. Most are fresh, frothy, and satisfying, with an equally satisfying price. This one from Sumarroca is a great crowd-pleaser, with delicious tropical notes.

Yalumba "D Black" 1998 *(Barossa Valley, Australia), $25.* In Australia, sparkling reds—and I mean deep lipstick red—have a cult following. Most are made from Shiraz (Syrah), though some (like this one) are Cabernet-Shiraz blends. Fascinating chocolate, earth, and black raspberry flavors. If you like red wine and texture, this is for you. —*Karen MacNeil-Fife*

Sage advice

Crisp, delicious fried sage leaves are the kind of smart touch chefs love to use to dress up winter dishes. Why let them claim all the kitchen wisdom? It's almost shamefully easy to fry the leaves: it just takes 15 seconds in a tiny bit of hot oil—and sage is sturdy, so no worries about it crumbling. You can use the common variety, which darkens to a deep gray-green, or search out variegated sage for a more dramatic look. A few fried leaves are wonderful floated on a savory squash soup, garnishing an hors d'oeuvres tray, or planted on a comforting bowl of polenta with parmesan cheese; for extra impact, fry up a big batch and arrange the sage around a lavish Christmas pork roast.

Fried sage leaves. Rinse about 20 large fresh **sage leaves** and lay flat on a

Add a bright touch to winter dishes with fried sage.

double layer of paper towels; cover with more towels and press gently to flatten and dry leaves. Pour **olive** or canola **oil** into a narrow 1- to 1½-quart pan over medium-high heat to a depth of ¼ inch. When hot (oil will ripple), lower heat to medium and add sage leaves, a few at a time, in a single layer. Fry just until oil stops bubbling around leaves, 10 to 15 seconds (do not let brown), then remove carefully with tongs and drain on more paper towels. Sprinkle with **salt** to taste. Use at once, or store between layers of paper towels in an airtight container at room temperature for up to 1 day.

—*Kate Washington*

Articles Index

Index of Recipe Titles

Low-Fat Recipes

General Index